CLYMER®

HONDA

TRX500 RUBICON • 2001-2004

The world's finest publisher of mechanical how-to manuals

PRIMEDIA
Information Data Products

P.O. Box 12901, Overland Park, Kansas 66282-2901

Copyright ©2005 PRIMEDIA Business Magazines & Media Inc.

FIRST EDITION
First Printing March, 2005

Printed in U.S.A.

CLYMER and colophon are registered trademarks of PRIMEDIA Business Magazines & Media Inc.

ISBN: 0-89287-920-3

Library of Congress: 2005921837

AUTHOR: Mike Morlan.

TECHNICAL PHOTOGRAPHY: Mike Morlan.

TECHNICAL ILLUSTRATIONS: Errol McCarthy.

WIRING DIAGRAMS: Bob Meyer and Lee Buell.

EDITOR: Lee Buell.

PRODUCTION: Julie Jantzer-Ward.

TOOLS AND EQUIPMENT: K & L Supply Co. at www.klsupply.com.

COVER: Mark Clifford Photography at www.markclifford.com. 2004 Rubicon courtesy of Cal Coast Motorsports, Ventura, CA.

CLYMER®

Publisher Shawn Etheridge

PRIMEDIA
Business Magazines & Media
P.O. Box 12901, Overland Park, KS 66282-2901 • 800-262-1954 • 913-967-1719

The following books and guides are published by PRIMEDIA Business Directories & Books.

More information available at *primediabooks.com*

CONTENTS

QUICK REFERENCE DATA

ATV INFORMATION

MODEL:_____ YEAR:_____

VIN NUMBER:_____

ENGINE SERIAL NUMBER:_____

CARBURETOR SERIAL NUMBER OR I.D. MARK:_____

COLOR CODE:_____

TIRE INFLATION PRESSURE

	Front and rear tires psi (kPa)
Normal pressure	3.6 (25)
Minimum pressure	3.2 (22)
Maximum pressure	4.1 (28)

RECOMMENDED LUBRICANTS, FLUIDS AND FUEL

Engine coolant type	Honda HP or ethylene-glycol*
Engine oil	
Grade	API SF or SG
Viscosity	SAE10W-40*
Differential oil	
Front and rear gearcase	Hypoid gear oil SAE 80
Air filter	Foam air filter oil
Brake fluid	DOT 3 or 4
Steering and suspension lubricant	Multipurpose grease
Fuel	Octane rating of 86 or higher

*Refer to the text for additional information.

ENGINE OIL CAPACITY

	Liters	U.S. qt.
Oil change only	4.7	5.0
Oil and filter change	4.9	5.2
After engine disassembly	5.5	5.8

FRONT AND REAR DIFFERENTIAL OIL CAPACITY

	ml	U.S. oz.
Front differential		
Oil change	241	8.2
After disassembly	275	9.3
Rear differential		
Oil change	90	3.0
After disassembly	100	3.4

TUNE-UP SPECIFICATIONS

Engine compression	608-902 kPa (88-131 psi) @ 450 rpm
Engine idle speed	1300-1500 rpm
Ignition timing (F mark)	15°@ 1400 rpm
Spark plug gap	0.8-0.9 mm (0.032-0.036 in.)
Spark plug type	
Standard	NGK IJR7A9 or Denso VX22BC
Cold weather operation*	NGK IJR6A9 or Denso VX20BC
Valve clearance	
Intake	0.15 mm (0.006 in.)
Exhaust	0.23 mm (0.009 in.)

*Below 4° C (41° F).

MAINTENANCE TORQUE SPECIFICATIONS

	N•m	in.-lb.	ft.-lb.
Engine oil drain bolt	25	–	18
Engine oil filter center bolt	18	159	–
Front differential gearcase			
Oil fill cap	12	106	–
Drain plug	12	106	–
Oil tank drain bolt	25	–	18
Rear differential gearcase			
Drain plug	12	106	–
Oil check plug	12	106	–
Oil fill cap	12	106	–
Spark plug	18	159	–
Tie rod locknut	54	–	40
Timing hole cap	10	88	–
Valve adjuster locknut	17	150	–
Wheel nuts (front and rear)	64	–	47

CHAPTER ONE

GENERAL INFORMATION

This detailed and comprehensive manual covers the 2001-2004 Honda TRX500 Rubicon models.

The text provides complete information on maintenance, tune-up, repair and overhaul. Hundreds of photographs and illustrations, created during the complete disassembly of the ATV, guide the reader through every job. All procedures are in step-by-step format and designed for the reader who may be working on the ATV for the first time.

MANUAL ORGANIZATION

A shop manual is a tool and, as in all Clymer manuals, the chapters are thumb tabbed for easy reference. Main headings are listed in the table of contents and the index. Frequently used specifications and capacities from the tables at the end of each individual chapter are listed in the *Quick Reference Data* section at the front of the manual. Specifications and capacities are provided in U.S. Standard and metric units of measure.

During some of the procedures there are references to headings in other chapters or sections of the manual. When a specific heading is called out in a step it is *italicized* as it appears in the manual. If a sub-heading is indicated as being "in this section," it is located within the same main heading. For ex-

ample, the sub-heading *Handling Gasoline Safely* is located within the main heading *SAFETY.*

This chapter provides general information on shop safety, tools and their usage, service fundamentals and shop supplies. **Tables 1-8**, located at the end of the chapter, list the following:

Table 1 lists engine and frame serial numbers.

Table 2 lists ATV dimensions.

Table 3 lists ATV weight.

Table 4 lists metric, inch and fractional equivalents.

Table 5 lists conversion formulas.

Table 6 lists general torque specifications.

Table 7 lists technical abbreviations.

Table 8 lists metric tap and drill sizes.

Chapter Two provides methods for quick and accurate diagnosis of problems. Troubleshooting procedures present typical symptoms and logical methods to pinpoint and repair the problem.

Chapter Three explains all routine maintenance necessary to keep the ATV running well. Chapter Three also includes recommended tune-up procedures, eliminating the need to constantly consult the chapters on the various assemblies.

Subsequent chapters describe specific systems such as the engine, transmission, clutch, drive, fuel, suspension, brakes and body. Each disassembly, repair and assembly procedure is discussed in step-by-step form.

WARNINGS, CAUTIONS AND NOTES

The terms WARNING, CAUTION and NOTE have specific meanings in this manual.

A WARNING emphasizes areas where injury or even death could result from negligence. Mechanical damage may also occur. WARNINGS *are to be taken seriously.*

A CAUTION emphasizes areas where equipment damage could result. Disregarding a CAUTION could cause permanent mechanical damage, though injury is unlikely.

A NOTE provides additional information to make a step or procedure easier or clearer. Disregarding a NOTE could cause inconvenience, but would not cause equipment damage or injury.

SAFETY

Professional mechanics can work for years and never sustain a serious injury or mishap. Follow these guidelines and practice common sense to safely service the ATV.

1. Do not operate the ATV in an enclosed area. The exhaust gasses contain carbon monoxide, an odorless, colorless and tasteless poisonous gas. Carbon monoxide levels build quickly in small, enclosed areas and can cause unconsciousness and death in a short time. Make sure to properly ventilate the work area, or operate the ATV outside.

2. *Never* use gasoline or any extremely flammable liquid to clean parts. Refer to *Cleaning Parts* and *Handling Gasoline Safely* in this section.

3. *Never* smoke or use a torch in the vicinity of flammable liquids, such as gasoline or cleaning solvent.

4. If welding or brazing on the ATV, remove the fuel tank to a safe distance at least 15 m (50 ft.) away.

5. Use the correct type and size of tools to avoid damaging fasteners.

6. Keep tools clean and in good condition. Replace or repair worn or damaged equipment.

7. When loosening a tight fastener, be guided by what would happen if the tool slipped.

8. When replacing fasteners, make sure the new fasteners are the same size and strength as the original ones.

9. Keep the work area clean and organized.

10. Wear eye protection *any time* the safety of the eyes is in question. This includes procedures that in-volve drilling, grinding, hammering, compressed air and chemicals.

11. Wear the correct clothing for the job. Tie up or cover long hair so it does not get caught in moving equipment.

12. Do not carry sharp tools in clothing pockets.

13. Always have an approved fire extinguisher available. Make sure it is rated for gasoline (Class B) and electrical (Class C) fires.

14. Do not use compressed air to clean clothes, the ATV or the work area. Debris may blow into the eyes or skin. *Never* direct compressed air at anyone. Do not allow children to use or play with compressed air equipment.

15. When using compressed air to dry rotating parts, hold the part so it does not rotate. The air jet is capable of rotating parts at extreme speed. The part may disintegrate or become damaged, causing serious injury.

16. Do not inhale the dust created by brake pad and clutch wear. These particles may contain asbestos. In addition, some types of insulating materials and gaskets may contain asbestos. Inhaling asbestos particles is hazardous to health.

17. Never work on the ATV while someone is working under it.

18. When placing the ATV on a stand, make sure it is secure before walking away.

Handling Gasoline Safely

Gasoline is a volatile, flammable liquid and is one of the most dangerous items in the shop. Because gasoline is used so often, many people forget it is hazardous. Only use gasoline as fuel for gasoline internal combustion engines. Keep in mind when working on the machine that gasoline is always present in the fuel tank, fuel line and throttle body. To avoid a disastrous accident when working around the fuel system, carefully observe the following precautions:

1. *Never* use gasoline to clean parts. Refer to *Cleaning Parts* in this section.

2. When working on the fuel system, work outside or in a well-ventilated area.

3. Do not add fuel to the fuel tank or service the fuel system while the ATV is near open flames, sparks or where someone is smoking. Gasoline vapor is heavier than air; it collects in low areas and is more easily ignited than liquid gasoline.

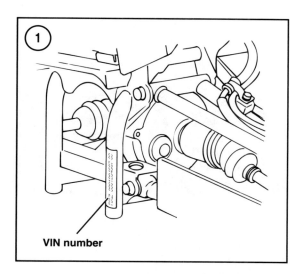

VIN number

sure the proper amounts according to the manufacturer.

3. Work in a well-ventilated area.

4. Wear chemical-resistant gloves.

5. Wear safety glasses.

6. Wear a vapor respirator if the instructions call for it.

7. Wash hands and arms thoroughly after cleaning parts.

8. Keep chemical products away from children and pets.

9. Thoroughly clean all oil, grease and cleaner residue from any part that must be heated.

10. Use a nylon brush when cleaning parts. Metal brushes may cause a spark.

11. When using a parts washer, only use the solvent recommended by the manufacturer. Make sure the parts washer is equipped with a metal lid that lowers in case of fire.

4. Allow the engine to cool completely before working on any fuel system component.

5. Do not store gasoline in glass containers. If the glass breaks, a serious explosion or fire may occur.

6. Immediately wipe up spilled gasoline with rags. Store the rags in a metal container with a lid until they can be properly disposed of, or place them outside in a safe place for the fuel to evaporate.

7. Do not pour water onto a gasoline fire. Water spreads the fire and makes it more difficult to put out. Use a class B, BC or ABC fire extinguisher to extinguish the fire.

8. Always turn off the engine before refueling. Do not spill fuel onto the engine or exhaust system. Do not overfill the fuel tank. Leave an air space at the top of the tank to allow room for the fuel to expand due to temperature fluctuations.

Warning Labels

Most manufacturers attach information and warning labels to the ATV. These labels contain instructions that are important to personal safety when operating, servicing, transporting and storing the ATV. Refer to the owner's manual for the description and location of labels. Order replacement labels from the manufacturer if they are missing or damaged.

Cleaning Parts

Cleaning parts is one of the more tedious and difficult service jobs performed in the home garage. Many types of chemical cleaners and solvents are available for shop use. Most are poisonous and extremely flammable. To prevent chemical exposure, vapor buildup, fire and serious injury, observe each product warning label and note the following:

1. Read and observe the entire product label before using any chemical. Always know what type of chemical is being used and whether it is poisonous and/or flammable.

2. Do not use more than one type of cleaning solvent at a time. If mixing chemicals is required, mea-

SERIAL NUMBERS

Serial numbers are stamped on various locations on the frame, engine, transmission and throttle body. Record these numbers in the *Quick Reference Data* section in the front of the manual. Have these numbers available when ordering parts.

The VIN number label is located on the left, front frame down tube (**Figure 1**).

The frame serial number is stamped on the front bracket attached to the front frame down tubes (**Figure 2**).

The engine serial number is stamped on a raised pad on the right side of the rear crankcase (**Figure 3**).

The carburetor serial number is located on the left side of the carburetor body (**Figure 4**).

The color identification label is located on the upper frame tube (**Figure 5**).

FASTENERS

Proper fastener selection and installation is important to ensure the ATV operates as designed and can be serviced efficiently. The choice of original equipment fasteners is not arrived at by chance. Make sure replacement fasteners meet all the same requirements as the originals.

Threaded Fasteners

Threaded fasteners secure most of the components on the ATV. Most are tightened by turning them clockwise (right-hand threads). If the normal rotation of the component being tightened would loosen the fastener, it may have left-hand threads. If a left-hand threaded fastener is used, it is noted in the text.

Two dimensions are required to match the thread size of the fastener: the number of threads in a given distance and the outside diameter of the threads.

The two systems currently used to specify threaded fastener dimensions are the U.S. Standard system and the metric system (**Figure 6**). Pay particular attention when working with unidentified fasteners; mismatching thread types can damage threads.

> *NOTE*
> *To ensure the fastener threads are not mismatched or cross-threaded, start all fasteners by hand. If a fastener is difficult to start or turn, determine the cause before tightening with a wrench.*

The length (L, **Figure 7**), diameter (D) and distance between thread crests (pitch) (T) classify metric screws and bolts. A typical bolt may be identified by the numbers, 8—1.25 × 130. This indicates the bolt has a diameter of 8 mm, the distance between thread crests is 1.25 mm and the length is 130 mm. Always measure bolt length as shown in L, **Figure 7** to avoid purchasing replacements of the wrong length.

The numbers on the top of the fastener (**Figure 7**) indicate the strength of metric screws and bolts. The higher the number, the stronger the fastener. Typically, unnumbered fasteners are the weakest.

Many screws, bolts and studs are combined with nuts to secure particular components. To indicate

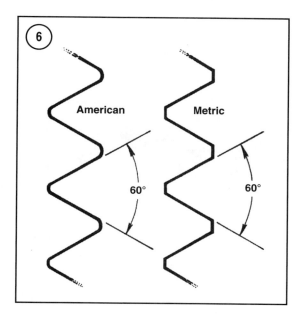

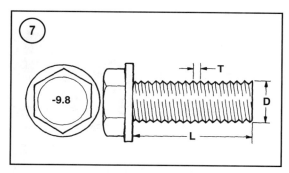

sive damage. It is essential to use an accurate torque wrench as described in this chapter.

Specifications for torque are provided in Newton-meters (N•m), foot-pounds (ft.-lb.) and inch-pounds (in.-lb.). Refer to **Table 6** for general torque specifications. To determine the torque requirement, first determine the size of the fastener as described in *Threaded Fasteners* in this section. Torque specifications for specific components are at the end of the appropriate chapters. Torque wrenches are covered in *Basic Tools* in this chapter.

Self-Locking Fasteners

Several types of bolts, screws and nuts incorporate a system that creates interference between the two fasteners. Interference is achieved in various ways. The most common types are the nylon insert nut and a dry adhesive coating on the threads of a bolt.

Self-locking fasteners offer greater holding strength than standard fasteners, which improves their resistance to vibration. All self-locking fasteners cannot be reused. The materials used to form the lock become distorted after the initial installation and removal. Discard and replace self-locking fasteners after removing them. Do not replace self-locking fasteners with standard fasteners.

Washers

The two basic types of washers are flat washers and lockwashers. Flat washers are simple discs with a hole to fit a screw or bolt. Lockwashers are used to prevent a fastener from working loose. Washers can be used as spacers and seals or can help distribute fastener load and prevent the fastener from damaging the component.

As with fasteners, when replacing washers make sure the replacement washers are of the same design and quality.

the size of a nut, manufacturers specify the internal diameter and the thread pitch.

The measurement across two flats on a nut or bolt indicates the wrench size.

> *WARNING*
> *Do not install fasteners with a strength classification lower than what was originally installed by the manufacturer. Doing so may cause equipment failure and/or damage.*

Torque Specifications

The materials used in the manufacturing of the ATV may be subjected to uneven stresses if the fasteners of the various subassemblies are not installed and tightened correctly. Improperly installed fasteners or fasteneres that work loose can cause exten-

Cotter Pins

A cotter pin is a split metal pin inserted into a hole or slot to prevent a fastener from loosening. In certain applications, such as the rear axle, the fastener must be secured in this way. For these applications, a cotter pin and castellated (slotted) nut is used.

To use a cotter pin, first make sure the diameter is correct for the hole in the fastener. After correctly tightening the fastener and aligning the holes, insert the cotter pin through the hole and bend the ends over the fastener (**Figure 8**). Unless instructed, never loosen a tightened fastener to align the holes. If the holes do not align, tighten the fastener enough to achieve alignment.

Cotter pins are available in various diameters and lengths. Measure the length from the bottom of the head to the tip of the shortest pin.

Snap Rings and E-clips

Snap rings (**Figure 9**) are circular-shaped metal retaining clips required to secure parts and gears in place on parts such as shafts, pins or rods. External type snap rings are used to retain items on shafts. Internal type snap rings secure parts within housing bores. In some applications, in addition to securing the component(s), snap rings of varying thicknesses also determine endplay. These are usually called selective snap rings.

The two basic types of snap rings are machined and stamped snap rings. Machined snap rings (**Figure 10**) can be installed in either direction because both faces have sharp edges. Stamped snap rings (**Figure 11**) are manufactured with a sharp and a round edge. When installing a stamped snap ring in a thrust application, install the sharp edge facing away from the part producing the thrust.

E-clips are used when it is not practical to use a snap ring. Remove E-clips with a flat blade screwdriver by prying between the shaft and E-clip. To install an E-clip, center it over the shaft groove and push or tap it into place.

Observe the following when installing snap rings:

1. Remove and install snap rings with snap ring pliers. Refer to *Basic Tools* in this chapter.

2. In some applications, it may be necessary to replace snap rings after removing them.

3. Compress or expand snap rings only enough to install them. If overly expanded, they lose their retaining ability.

4. After installing a snap ring, make sure it seats completely.

5. Wear eye protection when removing and installing snap rings.

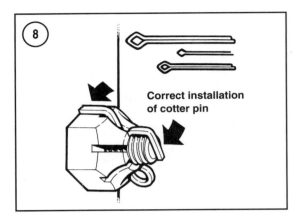

Correct installation of cotter pin

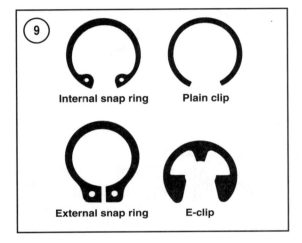

Internal snap ring   Plain clip

External snap ring   E-clip

SHOP SUPPLIES

Lubricants and Fluids

Periodic lubrication helps ensure a long service life for any type of equipment. Using the correct type of lubricant is as important as performing the lubrication service, although in an emergency the wrong type is better than not using one. The following section describes the types of lubricants most often required. Make sure to follow the manufacturer's recommendations for lubricant types.

Engine oils

Engine oil for four-stroke ATV engine use is classified by three standards: the American Petroleum Institute (API) service classification, the Society of Automotive Engineers (SAE) viscosity rating and the Japanese Automobile Standards Organization (JASO) T 903 Standard rating.

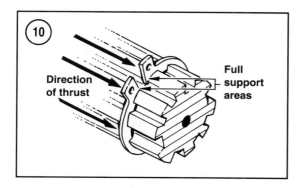

Direction of thrust

Full support areas

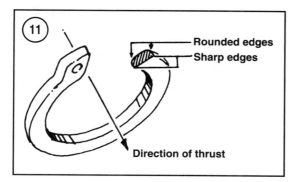

Rounded edges

Sharp edges

Direction of thrust

The API and SAE information is on all oil container labels. The JASO information is found on oil containers sold by the oil manufacturer specifically for ATV use. Two letters indicate the API service classification. The number or sequence of numbers and letter (10W-40 for example) is the oil's viscosity rating. The API service classification and the SAE viscosity index are not indications of oil quality.

The API service classification indicates the oil meets specific lubrication standards. The first letter in the classification *S* indicates the oil is for gasoline engines. The second letter indicates the standard the oil satisfies.

The JASO certification label identifies two separate oil classifications and a registration number to ensure the oil has passed all JASO certification standards for use in four-stroke ATV engines. The classifications are: MA (high friction applications) and MB (low friction applications). Only oil that has passed JASO standards can carry the JASO certification label.

NOTE
*Refer to **Engine Oil and Filter** in Chapter Three for further information on API, SAE and JASO ratings.*

Always use an oil with a classification recommended by the manufacturer. Using an oil with a different classification can cause engine damage.

Viscosity is an indication of the oil's thickness. Thin oils have a lower number while thick oils have a higher number. Engine oils fall into the 5- to 50-weight range for single-grade oils.

Most manufacturers recommend multi-grade oil. These oils perform efficiently across a wide range of operating conditions. Multi-grade oils are identified by a *W* after the first number, which indicates the low-temperature viscosity.

Engine oils are most commonly mineral (petroleum) based, but synthetic and semi-synthetic types are used more frequently. When selecting engine oil, follow the manufacturer's recommendation for type, classification and viscosity.

Greases

Grease is lubricating oil with added thickening agents. The National Lubricating Grease Institute (NLGI) grades grease. Grades range from No. 000 to No. 6, with No. 6 being the thickest. Typical multipurpose grease is NLGI No. 2. For specific applications, manufacturers may recommend water-resistant type grease or one with an additive such as molybdenum disulfide (MoS_2).

Brake fluid

Brake fluid is the hydraulic fluid used to transmit hydraulic pressure (force) to the wheel brakes. Brake fluid is classified by the Department of Transportation (DOT). Current designations for brake fluid are DOT 3, DOT 4 and DOT 5. This classification appears on the fluid container.

Each type of brake fluid has its own definite characteristics. Do not intermix different types of brake fluid because this may cause brake system failure. DOT 5 brake fluid is silicone based. DOT 5 is not compatible with other brake fluids or in systems for which it was not designed. Mixing DOT 5 fluid with other fluids may cause brake system failure. When adding brake fluid, *only* use the fluid recommended by the manufacturer.

Brake fluid damages any plastic, painted or plated surface it contacts. Use extreme care when working with brake fluid and remove any spills immediately with soap and water.

Hydraulic brake systems require clean and moisture-free brake fluid. Never reuse brake fluid. Keep containers and reservoirs properly sealed.

> *WARNING*
> *Never put a mineral-based (petroleum) oil into the brake system. Mineral oil causes rubber parts in the system to swell and break apart, causing complete brake failure.*

Coolant

Coolant is a mixture of water and antifreeze used to dissipate engine heat. Ethylene glycol is the most common form of antifreeze. Check the ATV manufacturer's recommendations when selecting antifreeze. Most require one specifically designed for use in aluminum engines. These types of antifreeze have additives that inhibit corrosion.

Only mix antifreeze with distilled water. Impurities in tap water may damage internal cooling system passages.

Cleaners, Degreasers and Solvents

Many chemicals are available to remove oil, grease and other residue from the ATV. Before using cleaning solvents, consider how they are used and disposed of, particularly if they are not water-soluble. Local ordinances may require special procedures for the disposal of many types of cleaning chemicals. Refer to *Safety* in this chapter.

Use brake parts cleaner to clean brake system components because it leaves no residue. Use electrical contact cleaner to clean electrical connections and components without leaving any residue. Carburetor cleaner is a powerful solvent used to remove fuel deposits and varnish from fuel system components. Use this cleaner carefully because it may damage finishes.

Generally, degreasers are strong cleaners used to remove heavy accumulations of grease from engine and frame components.

Most solvents are designed to be used with a parts washing cabinet for individual component cleaning. For safety, use only nonflammable or high flash point solvents.

Gasket Sealant

Sealant is used in combination with a gasket or seal. In other applications, such as between crankcase halves, only a sealant is used. Follow the manufacturer's recommendation when using a sealant. Use extreme care when choosing a sealant different from the type originally recommended. Choose sealant based on its resistance to heat, various fluids and its sealing capabilities.

A common sealant is room temperature vulcanization sealant (RTV). This sealant cures at room temperature over a specific time period. This allows the repositioning of components without damaging gaskets.

Moisture in the air causes the RTV sealant to cure. Always install the tube cap as soon as possible after applying RTV sealant. RTV sealant has a limited shelf life and does not cure properly if the shelf life has expired. Keep partial tubes sealed and discard them if they have surpassed the expiration date.

Applying RTV sealant

Clean all old gasket residue from the mating surfaces. Remove all gasket material from blind threaded holes to avoid inaccurate bolt torque. Spray the mating surfaces with aerosol parts cleaner and then wipe with a lint-free cloth. The area must be clean for the sealant to adhere.

Apply RTV sealant in a continuous bead 2-3 mm (0.08-0.12 in.) thick. Circle all the fastener holes unless otherwise specified. Do not allow any sealant to enter these holes. Assemble and tighten the fasteners to the specified torque within the time frame recommended by the sealant manufacturer.

Gasket Remover

Aerosol gasket remover can help remove stubborn gaskets. This product can speed up the removal process and prevent damage to the mating surface that may be caused by using a scraping tool. Most of these types of products are very caustic. Follow the gasket remover manufacturer's instructions for use.

Threadlocking Compound

A threadlocking compound is a fluid applied to the threads of fasteners. After tightening the fas-

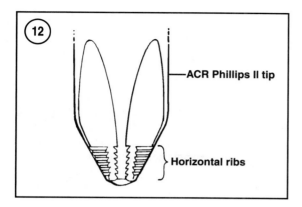

tener, the fluid dries and becomes a solid filler between the threads. This makes it difficult for the fastener to work loose from vibration or heat expansion and contraction. Some threadlocking compounds also provide a seal against fluid leaks.

Before applying a threadlocking compound, remove any old compound from both thread areas and clean them with aerosol parts cleaner. Use the compound sparingly. Excess fluid can run into adjoining parts.

> *CAUTION*
> *Threadlocking compounds are anaerobic and stress, crack and attack most plastics. Use caution when using these products in areas where there are plastic components.*

Threadlocking compounds are available in a wide range of compounds for various strength, temperature and repair applications. Follow the manufacturer's recommendations regarding compound selection.

BASIC TOOLS

Most of the procedures in this manual can be carried out with simple hand tools and test equipment familiar to the home mechanic. Always use the correct tools for the job at hand. Keep tools organized and clean. Store them in a tool chest with related tools organized together.

Quality tools are essential. The best are constructed of high-strength alloy steel. These tools are light, easy to use and resistant to wear. Their working surface is devoid of sharp edges and carefully polished. They have an easy-to-clean finish and are comfortable to use. Quality tools are a good investment.

Some of the procedures in this manual specify special tools. In many cases the tool is illustrated in use. Those with a large tool kit may be able to use a suitable substitute or fabricate a suitable replacement. However, in some cases, the specialized equipment or expertise may make it impractical for the home mechanic to perform the procedure. When necessary, such operations come with the recommendation to have a dealership or specialist perform the task. It may be less expensive to have a professional perform these jobs, especially when considering the cost of equipment.

When purchasing tools to perform the procedures covered in this manual, consider the tool's potential frequency of use. If a tool kit is just now being started, consider purchasing a basic tool set from a quality tool supplier. These sets are available in many tool combinations and offer substantial savings when compared to individually purchased tools. As work experience grows and tasks become more complicated, specialized tools can be added.

Screwdrivers

Screwdrivers of various lengths and types are mandatory for the simplest tool kit. The two basic types are the slotted tip (flat blade) and the Phillips tip. These are available in sets that often include an assortment of tip sizes and shaft lengths.

As with all tools, use a screwdriver designed for the job. Make sure the size of the tip conforms to the size and shape of the fastener. Use them only for driving screws. Never use a screwdriver for prying or chiseling metal. Repair or replace worn or damaged screwdrivers. A worn tip may damage the fastener, making it difficult to remove.

Phillips-head screws are often damaged by incorrectly fitting screwdrivers. Quality Phillips screwdrivers are manufactured with their crosshead tip machined to Phillips Screw Company specifications. Poor quality or damaged Phillips screwdrivers can back out (camout) and round over the screw head. In addition, weak or soft screw materials can make removal difficult.

The best type of screwdriver to use on Phillips screws is the ACR Phillips II screwdriver, patented by the Phillips Screw Company. ACR stands for the horizontal anti-camout ribs found on the driving faces or flutes of the screwdriver's tip (**Figure 12**). ACR Phillips II screwdrivers were designed as part of a manufacturing drive system to be used with ACR Phillips II screws, but they work well on all common Phillips screws. A number of tool companies offer ACR Phillips II screwdrivers in different tip sizes and interchangeable bits to fit screwdriver bit holders.

NOTE
Another way to prevent camout and to increase the grip of a Phillips screwdriver is to apply valve grinding compound or Permatex Screw & Socket Gripper onto the screwdriver tip. After loosening or tightening the screw, clean the screw recess to prevent engine oil contamination.

Wrenches

Open-end, box-end and combination wrenches (**Figure 13**) are available in a variety of types and sizes.

The number stamped on the wrench refers to the distance between the work areas. This size must match the size of the fastener head.

The box-end wrench is an excellent tool because it grips the fastener on all sides. This reduces the chance of the tool slipping. The box-end wrench is designed with either a 6- or 12-point opening. For stubborn or damaged fasteners, the 6-point provides superior holding because it contacts the fastener across a wider area at all six edges. For general use, the 12-point works well. It allows the wrench to be removed and reinstalled without moving the handle over such a wide arc.

An open-end wrench is fast and works best in areas with limited overhead access. It contacts the fastener at only two points and is subject to slipping if under heavy force or if the tool or fastener is worn. A box-end wrench is preferred in most instances, especially when breaking loose and applying the final tightness to a fastener.

The combination wrench has a box-end on one end and an open-end on the other. This combination makes it a convenient tool.

Adjustable Wrenches

An adjustable wrench, or Crescent wrench (**Figure 14**), can fit nearly any nut or bolt head that has clear access around its entire perimeter. An adjust-

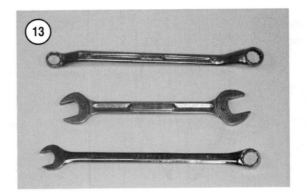

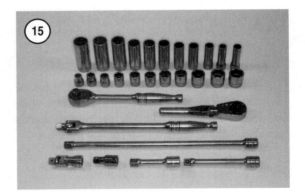

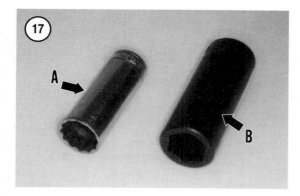

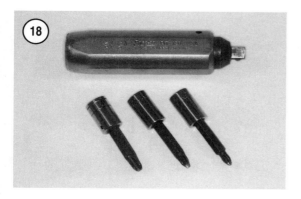

able wrench is best used as a backup wrench to keep a large nut or bolt from turning while the other end is being loosened or tightened with a box-end or socket wrench.

Adjustable wrenches contact the fastener at only two points, which makes them more subject to slipping off the fastener. Because one jaw is adjustable and may become loose, this shortcoming is aggravated. Make certain the solid jaw is the one transmitting the force.

Socket Wrenches, Ratchets and Handles

Sockets that attach to a ratchet handle (**Figure 15**) are available with 6-point or 12-point openings (**Figure 16**) and different drive sizes. The drive size indicates the size of the square hole that accepts the ratchet handle. The number stamped on the socket is the size of the work area and must match the fastener head.

As with wrenches, a 6-point socket provides superior-holding ability, while a 12-point socket needs to be moved only half as far to reposition it on the fastener.

Sockets are designated for either hand or impact use. Impact sockets are made of thicker material for more durability. Compare the size and wall thickness of a 19-mm hand socket (A, **Figure 17**) and the 19-mm impact socket (B). Use impact sockets when using an impact driver or air tools. Use hand sockets with hand-driven attachments.

> *WARNING*
> *Do not use hand sockets with air or impact tools because they may shatter and cause injury. Always wear eye protection when using impact or air tools.*

Various handles are available for sockets. Use the speed handle for fast operation. Flexible ratchet heads in varying lengths allow the socket to be turned with varying force and at odd angles. Extension bars allow the socket setup to reach difficult areas. The ratchet is the most versatile. It allows the user to install or remove the nut without removing the socket.

Sockets combined with any number of drivers make them undoubtedly the fastest, safest and most convenient tool for fastener removal and installation.

Impact Drivers

An impact driver provides extra force for removing fasteners by converting the impact of a hammer into a turning motion. This makes it possible to remove stubborn fasteners without damaging them. Impact drivers and interchangeable bits (**Figure 18**) are available from most tool suppliers. When using a socket with an impact driver, make sure the socket is designed for impact use. Refer to *Socket Wrenches, Ratchets and Handles* in this section.

> *WARNING*
> *Do not use hand sockets with air or impact tools because they may shatter and cause injury. Always wear eye protection when using impact or air tools.*

Allen Wrenches

Use Allen or setscrew wrenches (**Figure 19**) on fasteners with hexagonal recesses in the fastener head. These wrenches are available in L-shaped bar, socket and T-handle types. A metric set is required when working on most ATVs. Allen bolts are sometimes called socket bolts.

Torque Wrenches

Use a torque wrench with a socket, torque adapter or similar extension to tighten a fastener to a measured torque. Torque wrenches come in several drive sizes (1/4, 3/8, 1/2 and 3/4) and have various methods of reading the torque value. The drive size indicates the size of the square drive that accepts the socket, adapter or extension. Common methods of reading the torque value are the deflecting beam, the dial indicator and the audible click (**Figure 20**).

When choosing a torque wrench, consider the torque range, drive size and accuracy. The torque specifications in this manual provide an indication of the range required.

A torque wrench is a precision tool that must be properly cared for to maintain accuracy. Store torque wrenches in cases or separate padded drawers within a toolbox. Follow the manufacturer's instructions for their care and calibration.

Torque Adapters

Torque adapters or extensions extend or reduce the reach of a torque wrench. The torque adapter shown in **Figure 21** is used to tighten a fastener that cannot be reached because of the size of the torque wrench head, drive and socket. If a torque adapter changes the effective lever length (**Figure 22**), the torque reading on the wrench does not equal the actual torque applied to the fastener. It is necessary to recalibrate the torque setting on the wrench to compensate for the change of lever length. When using a torque adapter at a right angle to the drive head, calibration is not required because the effective length has not changed.

To recalculate a torque reading when using a torque adapter, use the following formula and refer to **Figure 22**:

$$TW = \frac{TA \times L}{L + A}$$

TW is the torque setting or dial reading on the wrench.

TA is the torque specification and the actual amount of torque is applied to the fastener.

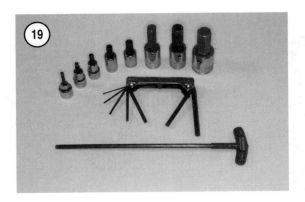

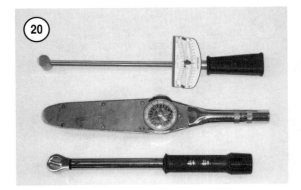

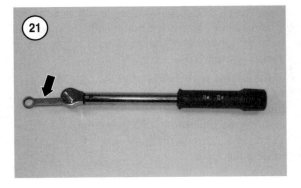

A is the amount the adapter increases (or in some cases reduces) the effective lever length as measured along the centerline of the torque wrench.

L is the lever length of the wrench as measured from the center of the drive to the center of the grip.

The effective length is the sum of *L* and *A*.

Example:

TA = 20 ft.-lb.
A = 3 in.
L = 14 in.
TW = $\frac{20 \times 14}{14 + 3} = \frac{280}{17}$ = 16.5 ft. lb.

TORQUE WRENCH EFFECTIVE LEVER LENGTH

L + A = Effective length (E)

L = Effective length

No calculation needed

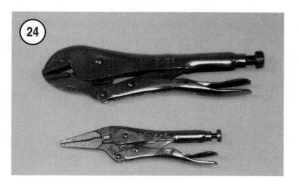

In this example, the torque wrench would be set to the recalculated torque value (TW = 16.5 ft.-lb.). When using a beam-type wrench, tighten the fastener until the pointer aligns with 16.5 ft.-lb. In this example, although the torque wrench is pre-set to 16.5 ft.-lb., the actual torque is 20 ft.-lb.

Pliers

Pliers come in a wide range of types and sizes. Pliers are useful for holding, cutting, bending, and crimping. Do not use them to turn fasteners. **Figure 23** and **Figure 24** show several types of useful pliers. Each design has a specialized function. Slip-joint pliers are general-purpose pliers used for gripping and bending. Diagonal cutting pliers are needed to cut wire and can be used to remove cotter pins. Use needlenose pliers to hold or bend small objects. Locking pliers (**Figure 24**), sometimes called Vise-Grips, are used to hold objects very tightly. They have many uses ranging from holding two parts together to gripping the end of a broken stud. Use caution when using locking pliers because the sharp jaws damage the objects they hold.

Snap Ring Pliers

Snap ring pliers are specialized pliers with tips that fit into the ends of snap rings to remove and install them.

Snap ring pliers (**Figure 25**) are available with a fixed action (either internal or external) or convertible (one tool works on both internal and external snap rings). They may have fixed tips or interchangeable ones of various sizes and angles. For general use, select a convertible type pliers with interchangeable tips (**Figure 25**).

> *WARNING*
> *Snap rings can slip and fly off when removing and installing them. Also, the snap ring pliers' tips may break. Always wear eye protection when using snap ring pliers.*

Hammers

Various types of hammers are available to fit a number of applications. Use a ball-peen hammer to strike another tool, such as a punch or chisel. Use soft-faced hammers when a metal object must be struck without damaging it. *Never* use a metal-faced hammer on engine and suspension components because damage occurs in most cases.

Always wear eye protection when using hammers. Make sure the hammer face is in good condition and the handle is not cracked. Select the correct hammer for the job and make sure to strike the object squarely. Do not use the handle or the side of the hammer to strike an object.

PRECISION MEASURING TOOLS

The ability to accurately measure components is essential to perform many of the procedures described in this manual. Equipment is manufactured to close tolerances, and obtaining consistently accurate measurements is essential to determine which components require replacement or further service.

Each type of measuring instrument (**Figure 26**) is designed to measure a dimension with a certain degree of accuracy and within a certain range. When

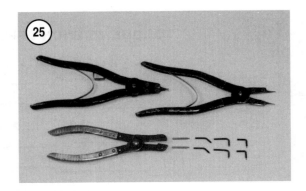

selecting the measuring tool, make sure it is applicable to the task.

As with all tools, measuring tools provide the best results if cared for properly. Improper use can damage the tool and cause inaccurate results. If any measurement is questionable, verify the measurement using another tool. A standard gauge is usually provided with micrometers to check accuracy and to calibrate the tool if necessary.

Precision measurements can vary according to the experience of the person performing the procedure. Accurate results are only possible if the mechanic possesses a feel for using the tool. Heavy-handed use of measuring tools produces less accurate results. Hold the tool gently by the fingertips to easily feel the point at which the tool contacts the object. This feel for the equipment produces more accurate measurements and reduces the risk of damaging the tool or component. Refer to the following sections for specific measuring tools.

Feeler Gauge

Use feeler or thickness gauges (**Figure 27**) for measuring the distance between two surfaces.

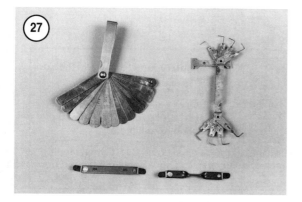

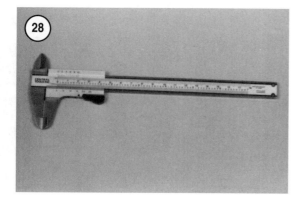

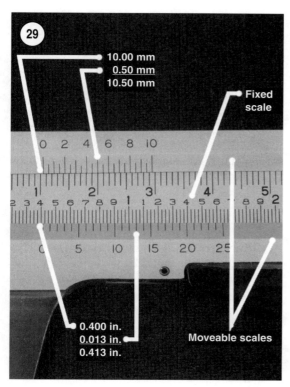

10.00 mm
0.50 mm
10.50 mm

Fixed scale

0 2 4 6 8 10

0 5 10 15 20 25

0.400 in.
0.013 in.
0.413 in.

Moveable scales

A feeler gauge set consists of an assortment of steel strips of graduated thickness. Each blade is marked with its thickness. Blades can be of various lengths and angles for different procedures.

A common use for a feeler gauge is to measure valve clearance. Use wire (round) type gauges to measure spark plug gap.

Calipers

Calipers (**Figure 28**) are excellent tools for obtaining inside, outside and depth measurements. Although not as precise as a micrometer, they allow reasonable precision, typically to within 0.05 mm (0.001 in.). Most calipers have a range up to 150 mm (6 in.).

Calipers are available in dial, vernier or digital versions. Dial calipers have a dial readout that provides convenient reading. Vernier calipers have marked scales that must be compared to determine the measurement. The digital caliper uses a liquid-crystal display (LCD) to show the measurement.

Properly maintain the measuring surfaces of the caliper. There must not be any dirt or burrs between the tool and the object being measured. Never force the caliper to close around an object. Close the caliper around the highest point so it can be removed with a slight drag. Some calipers require calibration. Always refer to the manufacturer's instructions when using a new or unfamiliar caliper.

To read a vernier caliper refer to **Figure 29**. The fixed scale is marked in 1-mm increments. Ten individual lines on the fixed scale equal 1 cm. The movable scale is marked in 0.05 mm (hundredth) increments. To obtain a reading, establish the first number by the location of the 0 line on the movable scale in relation to the first line to the left on the fixed scale. In this example, the number is 10 mm. To determine the next number, note which of the lines on the movable scale align with a mark on the fixed scale. A number of lines may seem close, but only one aligns exactly. In this case, 0.50 mm is the reading to add to the first number. Adding 10 mm and 0.50 mm equals a measurement of 10.50 mm.

Micrometers

A micrometer is an instrument designed for linear measurement using the decimal divisions of the inch or meter (**Figure 30**). Many types and styles of

30 **DECIMAL PLACE VALUES***

0.1	Indicates 1/10 (one tenth of an inch or millimeter)
0.010	Indicates 1/100 (one one-hundreth of an inch or millimeter)
0.001	Indicates 1/1000 (one one-thousandth of an inch or millimeter)

*This chart represents the values of figures placed to the right of the decimal point. Use it when reading decimals from one-tenth to one one-thousandth of an inch or millimeter. It is not a conversion chart (for example: 0.001 in. is not equal to 0.001 mm).

micrometers are available, but most of the procedures in this manual call for an outside micrometer. Use the outside micrometer to measure the outside diameter of cylindrical forms and the thickness of materials.

A micrometer's size indicates the minimum and maximum size of a part it can measure. The usual sizes (**Figure 31**) are 0-25 mm (0-1 in.), 25-50 mm (1-2 in.), 50-75 mm (2-3 in.) and 75-100 mm (3-4 in.).

Micrometers that cover a wider range of measurements are available. These use a large frame with interchangeable anvils of various lengths. This type of micrometer offers a cost savings, but its overall size may make it less convenient.

Adjustment

Before using a micrometer, check its adjustment as follows:
1. Clean the anvil and spindle faces.
2A. To check a 0-25 mm or 0-1 in. micrometer:
   a. Turn the thimble until the spindle contacts the anvil. If the micrometer has a ratchet stop, use it to ensure the proper amount of pressure is applied.
   b. If the adjustment is correct, the 0 mark on the thimble aligns exactly with the 0 mark on the sleeve line. If the marks do not align, the micrometer is out of adjustment.
   c. Follow the manufacturer's instructions to adjust the micrometer.
2B. To check a micrometer larger than 25 mm or 1 in use the standard gauge supplied by the manufacturer. A standard gauge is a steel block, disc or rod machined to an exact size.

31

   a. Place the standard gauge between the spindle and anvil, and measure its outside diameter or length. If the micrometer has a ratchet stop, use it to ensure the proper amount of pressure is applied.
   b. If the adjustment is correct, the 0 mark on the thimble aligns exactly with the 0 mark on the sleeve line. If the marks do not align, the micrometer is out of adjustment.
   c. Follow the manufacturer's instructions to adjust the micrometer.

Care

Micrometers are precision instruments. They must be used and maintained with great care. Note the following:
1. Store micrometers in protective cases or separate padded drawers in a toolbox.
2. When in storage, make sure the spindle and anvil faces do not contact each other or another object. If they do, temperature changes and corrosion may damage the contact faces.

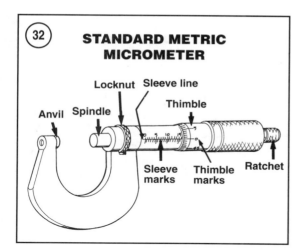

(32) **STANDARD METRIC MICROMETER**

Locknut — Sleeve line
Anvil — Spindle — Thimble
Sleeve marks — Thimble marks — Ratchet

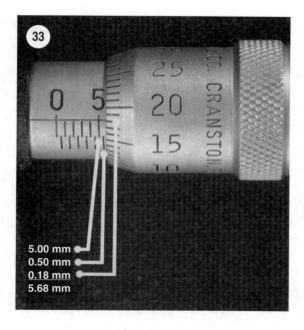

(33)

5.00 mm
0.50 mm
0.18 mm
5.68 mm

3. Do not clean a micrometer with compressed air. Dirt forced into the tool causes wear.

4. Lubricate micrometers with WD-40 to prevent corrosion.

Reading

When reading a micrometer, numbers are taken from different scales and added together. The following sections describe how to read the measurements of various types of outside micrometers.

For accurate results, properly maintain the measuring surfaces of the micrometer. There cannot be any dirt or burrs between the tool and the measured object. Never force the micrometer to close around an object. Close the micrometer around the highest point so it can be removed with a slight drag.

Metric micrometer

The standard metric micrometer (**Figure 32**) is accurate to one one-hundredth of a millimeter (0.01 mm). The sleeve line is graduated in millimeter and half millimeter increments. The marks on the upper half of the sleeve line equal 1.00 mm. Each fifth mark above the sleeve line is identified with a number. The number sequence depends on the size of the micrometer. A 0-25 mm micrometer, for example, has sleeve marks numbered 0 through 25 in 5 mm increments. This numbering sequence continues with larger micrometers. On all metric micrometers, each mark on the lower half of the sleeve equals 0.50 mm.

The tapered end of the thimble has 50 lines marked around it. Each mark equals 0.01 mm. One complete turn of the thimble aligns its 0 mark with the first line on the lower half of the sleeve line, or 0.50 mm.

When reading a metric micrometer, add the number of millimeters and half-millimeters on the sleeve line to the number of one one-hundredth millimeters on the thimble. Perform the following steps while referring to **Figure 33**:

1. Read the upper half of the sleeve line and count the number of lines visible. Each upper line equals 1 mm.

2. See if the half-millimeter line is visible on the lower sleeve line. If so, add 0.50 mm to the reading in Step 1.

3. Read the thimble mark that aligns with the sleeve line. Each thimble mark equals 0.01 mm.

> *NOTE*
> *If a thimble mark does not align exactly with the sleeve line, estimate the amount between the lines. For accurate readings in two-thousandths of a millimeter (0.002 mm), use a metric vernier micrometer.*

4. Add the readings from Steps 1-3.

Standard inch micrometer

The standard inch micrometer (**Figure 34**) is accurate to one-thousandth of an inch or 0.001. The sleeve is marked in 0.025 in. increments. Every fourth sleeve mark is numbered 1, 2, 3, 4, 5, 6, 7, 8, 9. These numbers indicate 0.100, 0.200, 0.300 and so on.

The tapered end of the thimble has 25 lines marked around it. Each mark equals 0.001 in. One complete turn of the thimble aligns its zero mark with the first mark on the sleeve, or 0.025 in.

To read a standard inch micrometer, perform the following steps and refer to **Figure 35**:

1. Read the sleeve and find the largest number visible. Each sleeve number equals 0.100 in.

2. Count the number of lines between the numbered sleeve mark and the edge of the thimble. Each sleeve mark equals 0.025 in.

3. Read the thimble mark that aligns with the sleeve line. Each thimble mark equals 0.001 in.

NOTE
If a thimble mark does not align exactly with the sleeve line, estimate the amount between the lines. For accurate readings in ten-thousandths of an inch (0.0001 in.), use a vernier inch micrometer.

4. Add the readings from Steps 1-3.

Telescoping and Small Bore Gauges

Use telescoping gauges (**Figure 36**) and small bore gauges (**Figure 37**) to measure bores. Neither gauge has a scale for direct readings. Use an outside micrometer to determine the reading.

To use a telescoping gauge, select the correct size gauge for the bore. Compress the movable post and carefully insert the gauge into the bore. Carefully move the gauge in the bore to make sure it is centered. Tighten the knurled end of the gauge to hold the movable post in position. Remove the gauge and measure the length of the posts. Telescoping gauges are typically used to measure cylinder bores.

Small bore gauges are typically used to measure valve guides. To use a small bore gauge, select the correct size gauge for the bore. Carefully insert the gauge into the bore. Tighten the knurled end of the gauge to carefully expand the gauge fingers to the limit within the bore. Do not overtighten the gauge

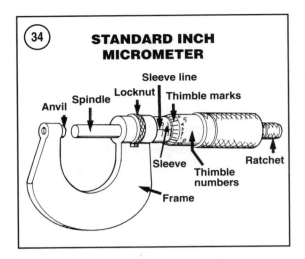

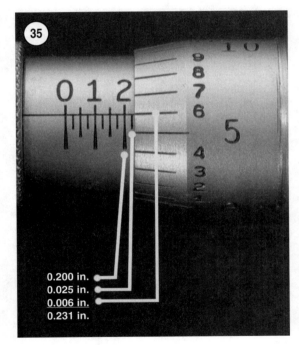

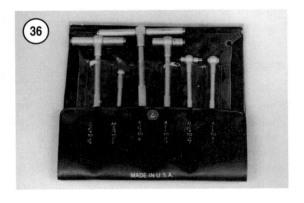

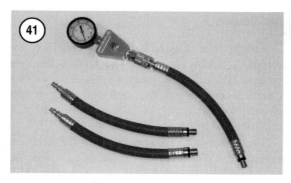

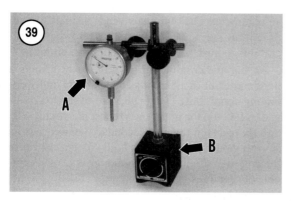

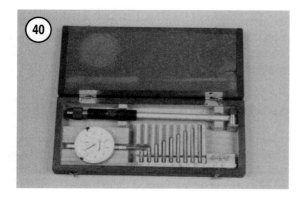

because there is no built-in release. Excessive tightening can damage the bore surface and damage the tool. Remove the gauge and measure the outside dimension (**Figure 38**).

Dial Indicator

A dial indicator (A, **Figure 39**) is a gauge with a dial face and needle used to measure variations in dimensions and movements. Measuring brake rotor runout is a typical use for a dial indicator.

Dial indicators are available in various ranges and graduations and with three basic types of mounting bases: magnetic (B, **Figure 39**), clamp or screw-in stud. When purchasing a dial indicator, select one with a continuous dial (A, **Figure 39**).

Cylinder Bore Gauge

A cylinder bore gauge is similar to a dial indicator. The gauge set shown in **Figure 40** consists of a dial indicator, handle and different length adapters (anvils) to fit the gauge to various bore sizes. The bore gauge is used to measure bore size, taper and out-of-round. When using a bore gauge, follow the manufacturer's instructions.

Compression Gauge

A compression gauge (**Figure 41**) measures combustion chamber (cylinder) pressure, usually in psi or kg/cm^2. The gauge adapter is either inserted or screwed into the spark plug hole to obtain the reading. Disable the engine so it does not start, and hold the throttle in the wide-open position when performing a compression test. An engine that does not have adequate compression cannot be properly tuned. Refer to Chapter Three.

Multimeter

A multimeter (**Figure 42**) is an essential tool for electrical system diagnosis. The voltage function indicates the voltage applied or available to various electrical components. The ohmmeter function tests circuits for continuity, or lack of continuity, and measures the resistance of a circuit.

Some manufacturers' specifications for electrical components are based on results using a specific test meter. Results may vary if using a meter not recommended by the manufacturer. Such requirements are noted when applicable.

Ohmmeter (analog) calibration

Each time an analog ohmmeter is used or if the scale is changed, the ohmmeter must be calibrated.

Digital ohmmeters do not require calibration.
1. Make sure the meter battery is in good condition.
2. Make sure the meter probes are in good condition.
3. Touch the two probes together and observe the needle location on the ohms scale. The needle must align with the 0 mark to obtain accurate measurements.
4. If necessary, rotate the meter ohms adjust knob until the needle and 0 mark align.

ELECTRICAL SYSTEM FUNDAMENTALS

A thorough study of the many types of electrical systems used in today's ATVs is beyond the scope of this manual. However, a general understanding of electrical basics is necessary to perform simple diagnostic tests.

Refer to *Electrical Testing* in Chapter Two for typical test procedures and equipment. Refer to Chapter Nine for specific system test procedures.

Voltage

Voltage is the electrical potential or pressure in an electrical circuit and is expressed in volts. The more pressure (voltage) in a circuit, the more work can be performed.

Direct current (DC) voltage means the electricity flows in one direction. All circuits powered by a battery are DC circuits.

Alternating current (AC) means the electricity flows in one direction momentarily and then switches to the opposite direction. Alternator output is an example of AC voltage. This voltage must be changed or rectified to direct current to operate in a battery powered system.

Resistance

Resistance is the opposition to the flow of electricity within a circuit or component and is measured in ohms. Resistance causes a reduction in available current and voltage.

Resistance is measured in an inactive circuit with an ohmmeter. The ohmmeter sends a small amount of current into the circuit and measures how difficult it is to push the current through the circuit.

An ohmmeter, although useful, is not always a good indicator of a circuit's actual ability under operating conditions. This is because of the low voltage (6-9 volts) the meter uses to test the circuit. The voltage in an ignition coil secondary winding can be several thousand volts. Such high voltage can cause the coil to malfunction, even though it tests acceptable during a resistance test.

Resistance generally increases with temperature. Perform all testing with the component or circuit at room temperature. Resistance tests performed at high temperatures may indicate high resistance readings and cause unnecessary replacement of a component.

Amperage

Amperage is the unit of measurement for the amount of current within a circuit. Current is the actual flow of electricity. The higher the current, the more work can be performed up to a given point. If the current flow exceeds the circuit or component capacity, it damages the system.

BASIC SERVICE METHODS

Most of the procedures in this manual are straightforward and can be performed by anyone reasonably competent with tools. However, consider personal capabilities carefully before performing any operation involving major disassembly.

1. *Front*, in this manual, refers to the front of the ATV. The front of any component is the end closest to the front of the ATV. The left and right sides refer to the position of the parts as viewed by the rider sitting on the seat facing forward.

2. Whenever servicing an engine or suspension component, secure the ATV in a safe manner.

3. Tag all similar parts for location and mark all mating parts for position. Record the number and thickness of any shims when removing them. Identify parts by placing them in sealed and labeled plastic sandwich bags.

4. Tag disconnected wires and connectors with masking tape and a marking pen. Do not rely on memory alone.

5. Protect finished surfaces from physical damage or corrosion. Keep gasoline and other chemicals off painted surfaces.

6. Use penetrating oil on frozen or tight bolts. Avoid using heat where possible. Heat can warp, melt or affect the temper of parts. Heat also damages the finish of paint and plastics.

7. When a part is a press fit or requires a special tool to remove, the information or type of tool is identified in the text. Otherwise, if a part is difficult to remove or install, determine the cause before proceeding.

8. To prevent objects or debris from falling into the engine, cover all openings.

9. Read each procedure thoroughly and compare the illustrations to the actual components before starting the procedure. Perform the procedure in sequence.

10. Recommendations are occasionally made to refer service to a dealership or specialist. In these cases, the work can be performed more economically by the specialist than by the home mechanic.

11. The term *replace* means to discard a defective part and replace it with a new part. *Overhaul* means to remove, disassemble, inspect, measure, repair and/or replace parts as required to recondition an assembly.

12. Some operations require using a hydraulic press. If a press is not available, have these operations performed by a shop equipped with the necessary equipment. Do not use makeshift equipment that may damage the ATV.

13. Repairs are much faster and easier if the ATV is clean. Degrease the ATV with a commercial degreaser; follow the directions on the container for the best results. Clean all parts with cleaning solvent when removing them.

CAUTION
Do not direct high-pressure water at steering bearings, fuel hoses, wheel bearings, suspension and electrical components. Water may force grease out of the bearings and possibly damage the seals.

14. If special tools are required, have them available before starting the procedure. When special tools are required, they are described at the beginning of the procedure.

15. Make diagrams of similar-appearing parts. For instance, crankcase bolts are often not the same lengths. Do not rely on memory alone. Carefully laid out parts can become disturbed, making it difficult to reassemble the components correctly.

16. Make sure all shims and washers are reinstalled in the same location and position.

17. Whenever rotating parts contact a stationary part, look for a shim or washer.

18. Use new gaskets if there is any doubt about the condition of old ones.

19. If using self-locking fasteners, replace them with new ones. Do not install standard fasteners in place of self-locking ones.

20. Use grease to hold small parts in place if they tend to fall out during assembly. Do not apply grease to electrical or brake components.

Removing Frozen Fasteners

If a fastener cannot be removed, several methods may be used to loosen it. First, apply penetrating oil such as Liquid Wrench or WD-40. Apply it liberally and let it penetrate for 10-15 minutes. Rap the fastener several times with a small hammer. Do not hit it hard enough to cause damage. Reapply the penetrating oil if necessary.

For frozen screws, apply penetrating oil as described, then insert a screwdriver in the slot and rap the top of the screwdriver with a hammer. This loosens the rust so the screw can be removed in the normal way. If the screw head is too damaged to use this method, grip the head with locking pliers and twist the screw out.

Avoid applying heat unless specifically instructed. Heat may melt, warp or remove the temper from parts.

Removing Broken Fasteners

If the head breaks off a screw or bolt, several methods are available for removing the remaining portion. If a large portion of the remainder projects out, try gripping it with locking pliers. If the projecting portion is too small, file it to fit a wrench or cut a slot in it to fit a screwdriver (**Figure 43**).

If the head breaks off flush, use a screw extractor. To do this, centerpunch the exact center of the remaining portion of the screw or bolt. Drill a small hole in the screw and tap the extractor into the hole. Back the screw out with a wrench on the extractor (**Figure 44**).

Repairing Damaged Threads

Occasionally threads are stripped through carelessness or impact damage. Often the threads can be repaired by running a tap (for internal threads on nuts) or die (for external threads on bolts) through the threads (**Figure 45**). To clean or repair spark plug threads, use a spark plug tap.

If an internal thread is damaged, it may be necessary to install a Helicoil or some other type of thread insert. Follow the manufacturer's instructions when installing the insert.

If it is necessary to drill and tap a hole, refer to **Table 8** for metric tap and drill sizes.

Stud Removal/Installation

A stud removal tool (**Figure 46**) is available from most tool suppliers. This tool makes the removal and installation of studs easier. If one is not available, thread two nuts onto the stud and tighten them

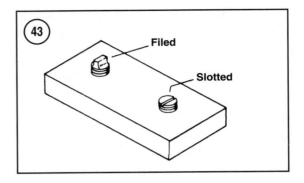

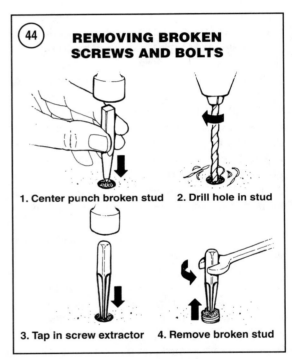

REMOVING BROKEN SCREWS AND BOLTS

1. Center punch broken stud
2. Drill hole in stud
3. Tap in screw extractor
4. Remove broken stud

against each other. Remove the stud by turning the lower nut (**Figure 47**).

1. Measure the height of the stud above the surface.

2. Thread the stud removal tool onto the stud and tighten it, or thread two nuts onto the stud.

3. Remove the stud by turning the stud remover or the lower nut.

4. Remove any threadlocking compound from the threaded hole. Clean the threads with an aerosol parts cleaner.

5. Install the stud removal tool onto the new stud or thread two nuts onto the stud.

6. Apply threadlocking compound to the threads of the stud.

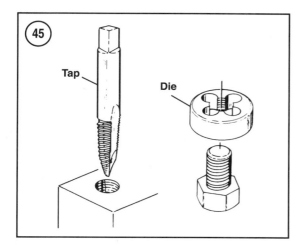

Tap

Die

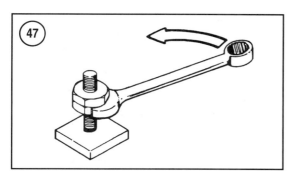

7. Install the stud and tighten with the stud removal tool or the top nut.

8. Install the stud to the height noted in Step 1 or its torque specification.

9. Remove the stud removal tool or the two nuts.

Removing Hoses

When removing stubborn hoses, do not exert excessive force on the hose or fitting. Remove the hose clamp and carefully insert a small screwdriver or pick tool between the fitting and hose. Apply a spray lubricant under the hose and carefully twist the hose off the fitting. Clean the fitting of any corrosion or rubber hose material with a wire brush. Clean the inside of the hose thoroughly. Do not use any lubricant when installing the hose (new or old). The lubricant may allow the hose to come off the fitting, even with the clamp secure.

Bearings

Bearings are used in the engine and transmission assembly to reduce power loss, heat and noise resulting from friction. Because bearings are precision parts, they must be maintained with proper lubrication and maintenance. If a bearing is damaged, replace it immediately. When installing a new bearing, prevent damaging it. Bearing replacement procedures are included in the individual chapters where applicable; however, use the following sections as a guideline.

NOTE
Unless otherwise specified, install bearings with the manufacturer's mark or number facing outward.

Removal

While bearings are normally removed only when damaged, there may be times when it is necessary to remove a bearing in good condition. However, improper bearing removal damages the bearing and possibly the shaft or case. Note the following when removing bearings:

1. When using a puller to remove a bearing from a shaft, do not damage the shaft. Always place a piece of metal between the end of the shaft and the puller screw. In addition, place the puller arms next to the inner bearing race. Refer to **Figure 48**.

2. When using a hammer to remove a bearing from a shaft, do not strike the hammer directly against the shaft. Instead, use a brass or aluminum rod between the hammer and shaft (**Figure 49**) and make sure to support both bearing races with wooden blocks as shown.

3. The ideal method of bearing removal is with a hydraulic press. Note the following when using a press:

   a. Always support the inner and outer bearing races with a suitable size wooden or aluminum spacer (**Figure 50**). If only the outer race is supported, pressure applied against the balls and/or the inner race damages them.

b. Always make sure the press arm (**Figure 50**) aligns with the center of the shaft. If the arm is not centered, it may damage the bearing and/or shaft.

c. The moment the shaft is free of the bearing, it drops to the floor. Secure or hold the shaft to prevent it from falling.

Installation

1. When installing a bearing in a housing, apply pressure to the *outer* bearing race (**Figure 51**). When installing a bearing on a shaft, apply pressure to the *inner* bearing race (**Figure 52**).

2. When installing a bearing as described in Step 1, some type of driver is required. Never strike the bearing directly with a hammer or it damages the bearing. When installing a bearing, use a piece of pipe or a driver with a diameter that matches the bearing inner race. **Figure 53** shows the correct way to use a driver and hammer to install a bearing.

3. Step 1 describes how to install a bearing in a case half or over a shaft. However, when installing a bearing over a shaft and into the housing at the same time, a tight fit is required for both outer and inner bearing races. In this situation, install a spacer under the driver tool so pressure is applied evenly across both races. Refer to **Figure 54**. If the outer race is not supported as shown, the balls push against the outer bearing race and damage it.

Interference fit

1. Follow this procedure when installing a bearing over a shaft. When a tight fit is required, the bearing inside diameter is smaller than the shaft. In this case, driving the bearing on the shaft using normal methods may cause bearing damage. Instead, heat the bearing before installation. Note the following:

a. Secure the shaft so it is ready for bearing installation.

b. Clean all residues from the bearing surface of the shaft. Remove burrs with a file or sandpaper.

c. Fill a suitable pot or beaker with clean mineral oil. Place a thermometer rated above 120° C (248° F) in the oil. Support the ther-

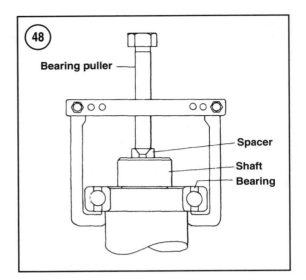

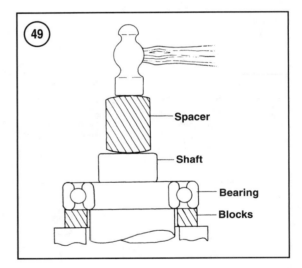

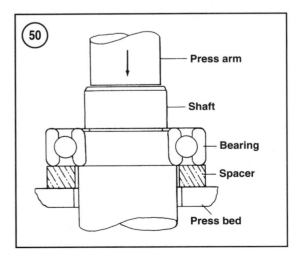

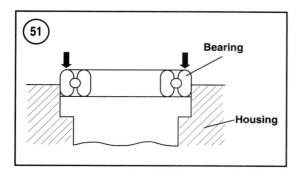

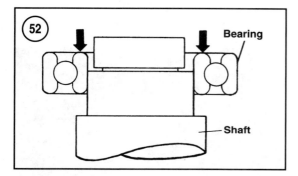

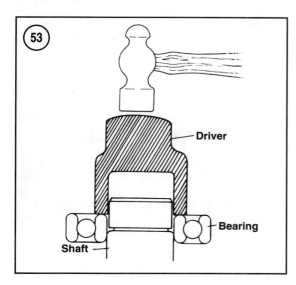

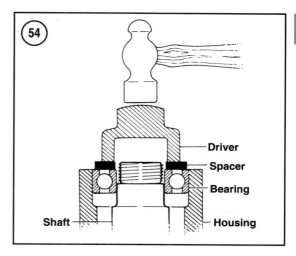

from the pot and quickly install it. If necessary, place a socket on the inner bearing race and tap the bearing into place. As the bearing chills, it tightens on the shaft, so installation must be done quickly. Make sure the bearing is installed completely.

2. Follow this step when installing a bearing in a housing. Bearings are generally installed in a housing with a slight interference fit. Driving the bearing into the housing using normal methods may damage the housing or cause bearing damage. Instead, heat the housing before the bearing is installed. Note the following:

CAUTION
Before heating the housing in this procedure, wash the housing thoroughly with detergent and water. Rinse and rewash the cases as required to remove all traces of oil and other chemical deposits.

a. Heat the housing to approximately 100° C (212° F) in an oven or on a hot plate. Place tiny drops of water on the housing to check it is the proper temperature; if they sizzle and evaporate immediately, the temperature is correct. Heat only one housing at a time.

CAUTION
Do not heat the housing with a propane or acetylene torch. Never bring a flame into contact with the bearing or housing. The direct heat destroys the case hardening of the bearing and likely warps the housing.

mometer so it does not rest on the bottom or side of the pot.

d. Remove the bearing from its wrapper and secure it with a piece of heavy wire bent to hold it in the pot. Hang the bearing in the pot so it does not touch the bottom or sides of the pot.

e. Turn the heat on and monitor the thermometer. When the oil temperature rises to approximately 120° C (248° F), remove the bearing

b. Remove the housing from the oven or hot plate, and hold onto the housing with welding gloves. It is hot!

NOTE
Remove and install the bearings with a suitable size socket and extension.

c. Hold the housing with the bearing side down and tap the bearing out. Repeat for all bearings in the housing.

d. Before heating the bearing housing, place the new bearing in a freezer, if possible. Chilling a bearing slightly reduces its outside diameter while the heated bearing housing assembly is slightly larger due to heat expansion. This makes bearing installation easier.

NOTE
Always install bearings with the manufacturer's mark or number facing outward.

e. While the housing is still hot, install the new bearing(s) into the housing. Install the bearings by hand, if possible. If necessary, lightly tap the bearing(s) into the housing with a driver placed on the outerbearing race (**Figure 51**). Do not install new bearings by driving on the inner-bearing race. Install the bearing(s) until it seats completely.

Seal Replacement

Seals (**Figure 55**) contain oil, water, grease or combustion gasses in a housing or shaft. Improperly removing a seal can damage the housing or shaft. Improperly installing the seal can damage the seal. Note the following:

1. Prying is generally the easiest and most effective method of removing a seal from the housing. However, always place a rag underneath the pry tool (**Figure 56**) to prevent damage to the housing. Note the seal's installed depth or if it is installed flush.

2. Pack waterproof grease in the seal lips before the seal is installed.

3. In most cases, install seals with the manufacturer's numbers or marks facing out.

4. Install seals with a socket or driver placed on the outside of the seal as shown in **Figure 57**. Drive the seal squarely into the housing until it is to the correct depth or flush (**Figure 58**) as noted during re-

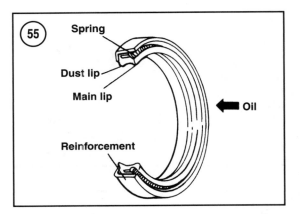

moval. Never install a seal by hitting against the top of it with a hammer.

STORAGE

Several months of non-use can cause a general deterioration of the ATV. This is especially true in areas of extreme temperature variations. This deterioration can be minimized with careful preparation for storage. A properly stored ATV is much easier to return to service.

Storage Area Selection

When selecting a storage area, consider the following:
1. The storage area must be dry. A heated area is best, but not necessary. It should be insulated to minimize extreme temperature variations.
2. If the building has large window areas, mask them to keep sunlight off the ATV.
3. Avoid buildings in industrial areas where corrosive emissions may be present. Avoid areas close to saltwater.
4. Consider the area's risk of fire, theft or vandalism. Check with an insurer regarding ATV coverage while in storage.

Preparing the ATV for Storage

The amount of preparation an ATV should undergo before storage depends on the expected length of non-use, storage area conditions and personal preference. Consider the following list the minimum requirement:
1. Wash the ATV thoroughly. Make sure all dirt, mud and debris are removed.

2. Start the engine and allow it to reach operating temperature. Drain the engine oil regardless of the riding time since the last service. Fill the engine with the recommended type of oil.
3. Drain all gasoline from the fuel tank, fuel hose and carburetor. Make sure the fuel tank filler cap is tightened securely and the vent hose is connected properly.
4. Remove the spark plug and pour a teaspoon (15-20 ml) of engine oil into the cylinders. Place a rag over the opening and slowly turn the engine over to distribute the oil. Reinstall the spark plug.
5. Remove the battery. Store the battery in a cool, dry location. Charge the battery once a month.
6. Cover the exhaust opening.
7. Apply a protective substance to the plastic and rubber components. Make sure to follow the manufacturer's instructions for each type of product being used.
8. Place the ATV on jackstands. Rotate the tires periodically to prevent a flat spot from developing and damaging the tire.
9. Cover the ATV with old bed sheets or something similar. Do not cover it with any plastic material that traps moisture.

Returning the ATV to Service

The amount of service required when returning an ATV to service after storage depends on the length of non-use and storage conditions. In addition to performing the reverse of the above procedure, make sure the brakes, throttle and engine stop switch work properly before operating the ATV. Refer to Chapter Three and evaluate the service intervals to determine which areas require service.

Table 1 ENGINE AND FRAME SERIAL NUMBERS

Model	Engine starting serial number	Frame starting serial number
2001		
TRX500FA	TE26E-8000001~	478TE260*14000001~
2002		
TRX500FA	TE26E-8000001~	478TE260*24100001~
2003		
TRX500FA	TE26E-8100001~	478TE260*34200001~
2004		
TRX500FA	TE26E-8200001~	478TE260*44300001~
TRX500FGA	TE26E-8200001~	478TE264*44300001~
*Unspecified digit.		

Table 2 GENERAL DIMENSIONS

	mm	in.
Overall width	1184	46.6
Overall length	2072	81.6
Overall height		
2001-2003	1194	47.0
2004	1198	47.2
Wheelbase	1287	50.7
Front tread	914	36.0
Rear tread	925	36.4
Seat height	862	33.9
Footpeg height	337	13.3
Ground clearance	198	7.8

Table 3 WEIGHT SPECIFICATIONS

	kg	lb.
Dry weight		
2001-2003	273	602
2004	271	597
Curb weight		
2001-2003	285	628
2004	283	624

Table 4 DECIMAL AND METRIC EQUIVALENTS

Fractions	Decimal in.	Metric mm	Fractions	Decimal in.	Metric mm
1/64	0.015625	0.39688	33/64	0.515625	13.09687
1/32	0.03125	0.79375	17/32	0.53125	13.49375
3/64	0.046875	1.19062	35/64	0.546875	13.89062
1/16	0.0625	1.58750	9/16	0.5625	14.28750
5/64	0.078125	1.98437	37/64	0.578125	14.68437
3/32	0.09375	2.38125	19/32	0.59375	15.08125
7/64	0.109375	2.77812	39/64	0.609375	15.47812
1/8	0.125	3.1750	5/8	0.625	15.87500
9/64	0.140625	3.57187	41/64	0.640625	16.27187
5/32	0.15625	3.96875	21/32	0.65625	16.66875
11/64	0.171875	4.36562	43/64	0.671875	17.06562
3/16	0.1875	4.76250	11/16	0.6875	17.46250
13/64	0.203125	5.15937	45/64	0.703125	17.85937
7/32	0.21875	5.55625	23/32	0.71875	18.25625
15/64	0.234375	5.95312	47/64	0.734375	18.65312
1/4	0.250	6.35000	3/4	0.750	19.05000
17/64	0.265625	6.74687	49/64	0.765625	19.44687
9/32	0.28125	7.14375	25/32	0.78125	19.84375
19/64	0.296875	7.54062	51/64	0.796875	20.24062
5/16	0.3125	7.93750	13/16	0.8125	20.63750
21/64	0.328125	8.33437	53/64	0.828125	21.03437
11/32	0.34375	8.73125	27/32	0.84375	21.43125
23/64	0.359375	9.12812	55/64	0.859375	22.82812
3/8	0.375	9.52500	7/8	0.875	22.22500
25/64	0.390625	9.92187	57/64	0.890625	22.62187
13/32	0.40625	10.31875	29/32	0.90625	23.01875
27/64	0.421875	10.71562	59/64	0.921875	23.41562
7/16	0.4375	11.11250	15/16	0.9375	23.81250
29/64	0.453125	11.50937	61/64	0.953125	24.20937
15/32	0.46875	11.90625	31/32	0.96875	24.60625
31/64	0.484375	12.30312	63/64	0.984375	25.00312
1/2	0.500	12.70000	1	1.00	25.40000

Table 5 CONVERSION FORMULAS

Multiply:	By:	To get the equivalent of:
Length		
Inches	25.4	Millimeter
Inches	2.54	Centimeter
Miles	1.609	Kilometer
Feet	0.3048	Meter
Millimeter	0.03937	Inches
Centimeter	0.3937	Inches
Kilometer	0.6214	Mile
Meter	0.0006214	Mile
Fluid volume		
U.S. quarts	0.9463	Liters
U.S. gallons	3.785	Liters
U.S. ounces	29.573529	Milliliters
Imperial gallons	4.54609	Liters
Imperial quarts	1.1365	Liters
Liters	0.2641721	U.S. gallons
Liters	1.0566882	U.S. quarts
Liters	33.814023	U.S. ounces
Liters	0.22	Imperial gallons
Liters	0.8799	Imperial quarts
Milliliters	0.033814	U.S. ounces
Milliliters	1.0	Cubic centimeters
Milliliters	0.001	Liters
Torque		
Foot-pounds	1.3558	Newton-meters
Foot-pounds	0.138255	Meters-kilograms
Inch-pounds	0.11299	Newton-meters
Newton-meters	0.7375622	Foot-pounds
Newton-meters	8.8507	Inch-pounds
Meters-kilograms	7.2330139	Foot-pounds
Volume		
Cubic inches	16.387064	Cubic centimeters
Cubic centimeters	0.0610237	Cubic inches
Temperature		
Fahrenheit	$(F - 32°) \times 0.556$	Centigrade
Centigrade	$(C \times 1.8) + 32°$	Fahrenheit
Weight		
Ounces	28.3495	Grams
Pounds	0.4535924	Kilograms
Grams	0.035274	Ounces
Kilograms	2.2046224	Pounds
Pressure		
Pounds per square inch	0.070307	Kilograms per square centimeter
Kilograms per square centimeter	14.223343	Pounds per square inch
Kilopascals	0.1450	Pounds per square inch
Pounds per square inch	6.895	Kilopascals
Speed		
Miles per hour	1.609344	Kilometers per hour
Kilometers per hour	0.6213712	Miles per hour

Table 6 GENERAL TORQUE SPECIFICATIONS

Fastener	N•m	in.-lb.	ft.-lb.
5 mm			
Bolt and nut	5.0	44	–
Screw	4.0	35	–
6 mm			
Bolt and nut	10	88	–
	(continued)		

Table 6 GENERAL TORQUE SPECIFICATIONS (continued)

Fastener	N•m	in.-lb.	ft.-lb.
6 mm (continued)			
Small flange bolt (8-mm head)	10	88	–
Large flange bolt (8-mm head)	12	106	–
Large flange bolt (10-mm head)	12	106	–
Screw	9	80	–
8 mm			
Bolt and nut	22	–	16
Screw	26	–	19
10 mm			
Bolt and nut	34	–	25
Flange bolt	39	–	29
12 mm			
Bolt and nut	54	–	40

Table 7 TECHNICAL ABBREVIATIONS

ABDC	After bottom dead center
ATDC	After top dead center
BBDC	Before bottom dead center
BDC	Bottom dead center
BTDC	Before top dead center
C	Celsius (centigrade)
cc	Cubic centimeters
cid	Cubic inch displacement
CDI	Capacitor discharge ignition
cu. in.	Cubic inches
F	Fahrenheit
ft.	Feet
ft.-lb.	Foot-pounds
gal.	Gallons
H/A	High altitude
hp	Horsepower
in.	Inches
in.-lb.	Inch-pounds
I.D.	Inside diameter
kg	Kilograms
kgm	Kilogram meters
km	Kilometer
kPa	Kilopascals
L	Liter
m	Meter
MAG	Magneto
ml	Milliliter
mm	Millimeter
N•m	Newton-meters
O.D.	Outside diameter
oz.	Ounces
psi	Pounds per square inch
pt.	Pint
qt.	Quart
rpm	Revolutions per minute
TPS	Throttle position sensor

Table 8 METRIC TAP AND DRILL SIZES

Metric size	Drill equivalent	Decimal fraction	Nearest fraction
3 × 0.50	No. 39	0.0995	3/32
3 × 0.60	3/32	0.0937	3/32
4 × 0.70	No. 30	0.1285	1/8
4 × 0.75	1/8	0.125	1/8
5 × 0.80	No. 19	0.166	11/64
5 × 0.90	No. 20	0.161	5/32
6 × 1.00	No. 9	0.196	13/64
7 × 1.00	16/64	0.234	15/64
8 × 1.00	J	0.277	9/32
8 × 1.25	17/64	0.265	17/64
9 × 1.00	5/16	0.3125	5/16
9 × 1.25	5/16	0.3125	5/16
10 × 1.25	11/32	0.3437	11/32
10 × 1.50	R	0.339	11/32
11 × 1.50	3/8	0.375	3/8
12 × 1.50	13/32	0.406	13/32
12 × 1.75	13/32	0.406	13/32

1

CHAPTER TWO

TROUBLESHOOTING

The troubleshooting procedures described in this chapter provide typical symptoms and logical methods for isolating the cause(s). There may be several ways to solve a problem, but only a systematic approach is successful in avoiding wasted time and possibly unnecessary parts replacement.

Gather as much information as possible to aid in diagnosis. Never assume anything and do not overlook the obvious. Make sure there is fuel in the tank. Make sure the fuel shutoff valve is on. If the ATV has been sitting for any length of time, fuel deposits may have gummed up the carburetor jets. Gasoline loses its volatility after standing for long periods and water condensation may have diluted the gas. Drain the old gas and fill the tank with fresh gas. Make sure the engine stop switch is in the run position. Make sure the spark plug wire is connected securely to the spark plug.

If a quick check does not reveal the problem, proceed with one of the troubleshooting procedures described in this chapter. After defining the symptoms, follow the procedure that most closely relates to the condition(s).

In most cases, expensive and complicated test equipment is not needed to determine whether repairs can be performed at home. A few simple checks could prevent an unnecessary repair charge and lost time while the ATV is at a dealership's service department. On the other hand, be realistic and do not attempt repairs beyond personal capabilities. Many service departments do not accept work that involves the reassembly of damaged or abused equipment; if they do, expect the cost to be high.

If the ATV does require the attention of a professional, describe symptoms and conditions accurately and fully. The more information a technician has available, the easier it is to diagnose the problem.

By following the lubrication and maintenance schedule described in Chapter Three, the need for troubleshooting can be reduced by eliminating possible problems before they occur. However, even with the best care the ATV may require troubleshooting.

ENGINE OPERATING REQUIREMENTS

Figure 1 explains basic four-stroke engine operation. Refer to this information when troubleshooting or repairing the engine.

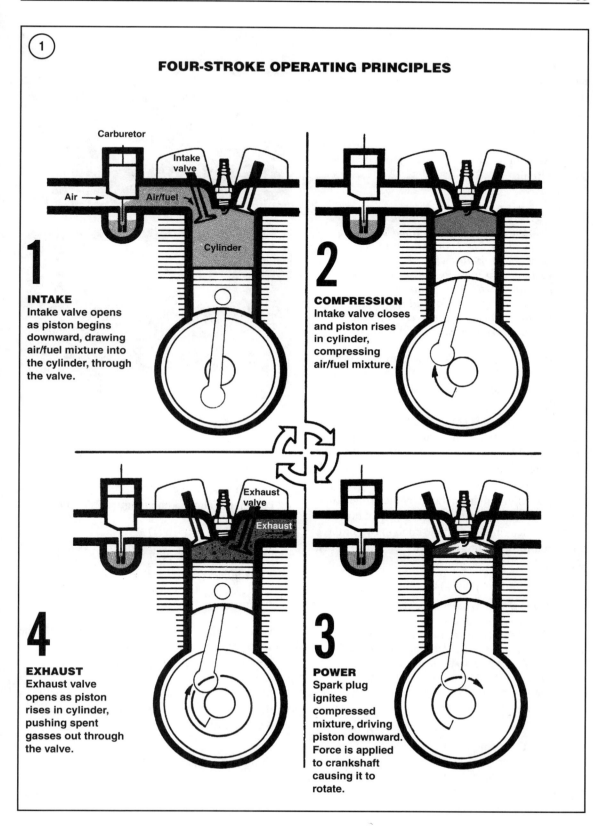

① FOUR-STROKE OPERATING PRINCIPLES

Carburetor

Intake valve

Air →   Air/fuel

Cylinder

1

INTAKE
Intake valve opens
as piston begins
downward, drawing
air/fuel mixture into
the cylinder, through
the valve.

2

COMPRESSION
Intake valve closes
and piston rises
in cylinder,
compressing
air/fuel mixture.

Exhaust valve

Exhaust

4

EXHAUST
Exhaust valve
opens as piston
rises in cylinder,
pushing spent
gasses out through
the valve.

3

POWER
Spark plug
ignites
compressed
mixture, driving
piston downward.
Force is applied
to crankshaft
causing it to
rotate.

STARTING THE ENGINE

If the engine refuses to start, the following outline serves as a guide for the basic starting procedure. In all cases, make sure there is an adequate supply of fuel in the tank.

A rich air/fuel mixture is required when starting a cold engine. To accomplish this, the carburetor is equipped with a choke (starter jet) circuit and primer circuit.

> *NOTE*
> *The knob that actuates the starter jet is often incorrectly identified as the choke knob. The knob does not operate a choke plate, which is found in some carburetors to richen the mixture for starting. The knob operates the starter jet, which allows additional fuel into the carburetor bore to produce a rich mixture for starting.*

Use the choke circuit when the ambient temperature is -15° to 35° C (5° to 95° F). Use the primer circuit when the ambient temperature is below -15° C (5° F).

The choke circuit is controlled by the cable knob (**Figure 2**) mounted on the handlebar. To open the choke circuit for starting a cold engine, pull up the knob. After the engine starts and warms up, push down the knob all the way.

The primer circuit is operated by the primer knob (**Figure 3**) mounted on the carburetor float bowl. To use the primer circuit, push the knob in two or three times before operating the starter button or recoil starter.

> *CAUTION*
> *When trying to start the engine in the following procedure, do not operate the starter for more than 5 seconds at a time because starter damage due to overheating may result. Wait approximately 10 seconds before operating the starter button again. If necessary, use the recoil starter.*

Starting a Cold Engine

1. Shift the transmission into neutral so the neutral indicator light glows. Set the parking brake.
2. Turn the ignition switch on.

> *NOTE*
> *The on position of the ignition switch is indicated by a vertical line.*

3. Turn the fuel valve on.
4. Pull up the choke knob (**Figure 2**) to on.

> *NOTE*
> *If the ambient temperature is below -15° C (5° F), push the primer knob (**Figure 3**) two or three times before operating the starter button or recoil starter.*

5. With the throttle completely closed, push the starter button or operate the recoil starter.
6. When the engine starts, push the throttle slightly to keep it running.
7. Idle the engine for approximately one minute or until the throttle responds cleanly, then push the choke knob off.

Starting a Warm or Hot Engine

1. Shift the transmission into neutral so the neutral indicator light glows. Set the parking brake.

2. Turn the ignition switch on.

NOTE
The on position of the ignition switch
is indicated by a vertical line.

3. Turn the fuel valve on.

4. Make sure the choke knob (**Figure 2**) is pushed down off.

5. Open the throttle slightly and push the starter button or operate the recoil starter.

Starting a Flooded Engine

If the engine is difficult to start and there is a strong gasoline smell, the engine is probably flooded. If so, push down the choke knob (**Figure 2**) to off. Open the throttle all the way and push the starter button, or operate the recoil starter until the engine starts. If the engine is flooded badly, it may be necessary to remove the spark plug and dry its insulator or install a new plug. When a flooded engine first starts to run, it initially coughs and runs slowly as it burns the excess fuel. As the excess fuel is burned, the engine accelerates quickly. Release the throttle at this point. Because a flooded engine smokes badly when it first begins to run, start the engine outside and in a well-ventilated area with its muffler pointing away from all objects. Do not start a flooded engine in a garage or other closed area.

NOTE
*If the engine refuses to start, check the carburetor overflow hose attached to the fitting at the bottom of the float bowl (**Figure 4**). If fuel is running out of the hose, the float valve is stuck open or leaking, allowing the carburetor to overfill. If this problem exists, remove the carburetor and correct the problem as described in Chapter Eight.*

STARTING DIFFICULTY

If the engine cranks but is difficult to start or does not start at all, do not discharge the battery. Check for obvious problems first. Go down the following list step by step. Perform each step while remembering the three engine operating requirements described in this chapter.

If the engine still does not start, refer to the appropriate troubleshooting procedure in this chapter.

1. Make sure the choke lever is in the correct position. Refer to *Starting the Engine* in this chapter.

2. Make sure the tank has fuel. Fill the tank if necessary. If the fuel is old, drain and fill with a fresh tank. Check for a clogged fuel tank vent tube (**Figure 5**). Remove the tube from the filler cap, then wipe off one end and blow through it. Remove the filler cap and check for a plugged hose nozzle.

3. Disconnect the fuel line (**Figure 6**) from the carburetor and insert the end of the hose into a clear

container. Turn the fuel valve on and see if fuel flows freely. If fuel does not flow and there is a fuel filter installed in the fuel line, remove the filter and turn the fuel valve on again. If fuel flows, the filter is clogged and must be replaced. If no fuel comes out, the fuel valve may be shut off, blocked by foreign matter or the fuel cap vent may be plugged. Reconnect the fuel line to the carburetor fitting.

4. If a flooded cylinder is suspected or there is a strong smell of gasoline, open the throttle all the way and push the starter button or operate the recoil starter. If the cylinder is severely flooded (fouled or wet spark plug), remove the spark plug and dry the base and electrode thoroughly with a soft cloth. Reinstall the plug and start the engine. Refer to *Starting the Engine* in this chapter.

5. Check the carburetor overflow hose on the bottom of the float bowl (**Figure 4**). If fuel is running from the hose, the float valve is stuck open or leaking. Turn the fuel valve off and tap the carburetor a few times. Then turn on the fuel valve. If fuel continues to run out of the hose, remove and repair the carburetor as described in Chapter Eight. Check the carburetor vent hoses to make sure they are clear. Check the end of the hoses for contamination.

> *NOTE*
> *If fuel is reaching the carburetor, the fuel system could still be the problem. The jets (pilot and main) could be plugged or the air filter could be severely restricted. However, before removing the carburetor, continue with Step 6 to make sure the ignition provides an adequate spark.*

6. Make sure the engine stop switch (**Figure 7**) is operating correctly. If necessary, test the engine stop switch as described in Chapter Nine.

> *NOTE*
> *If an aftermarket kill switch has been installed, check the switch for proper operation. This switch may be faulty.*

7. If the spark plug high-tension wire and cap is not (**Figure 8**) on tight, push it on and slightly rotate it to clean the electrical connection between the spark plug and the wire connector. Hold the high-tension wire and screw the plug cap on tightly.

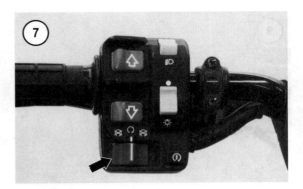

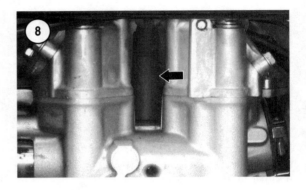

> *NOTE*
> *If the engine still does not start, continue with the following.*

8. Perform a spark test as described in the *Engine Fails to Start (Spark Test)* section in this section. If there is a strong spark, perform Step 9. If there is no spark or if the spark is very weak, test the ignition system as described in the *Ignition System* section in this chapter.

9. Check cylinder compression as follows:
   a. Move the engine stop switch (**Figure 7**) off.
   b. Turn the fuel valve off.
   c. Remove the spark plug and ground the spark plug shell against the cylinder head.
   d. Place your finger tightly over the spark plug hole.
   e. Operate the starter, or have an assistant operate the recoil starter. When the piston comes up on the compression stroke, pressure in the cylinder should force your finger from the spark plug hole. If so, the cylinder likely has sufficient compression to start the engine.

> *NOTE*
> *A compression problem may exist even though it seems good with the*

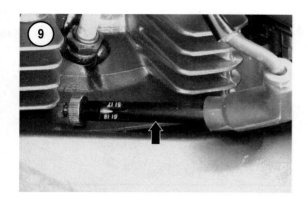

*previous test. Check engine compression using a compression gauge as described in the **Tune-up** section in Chapter Three.*

Engine Fails to Start (Spark Test)

An engine that refuses to start or is difficult to start is frustrating. More often than not, the problem is minor and can be found with a simple and logical troubleshooting approach.

Perform the following spark test to determine if the ignition system is producing adequate spark. When checking spark, turn the engine stop switch to RUN and the ignition switch on.

> *CAUTION*
> *Before removing the spark plug in Step 1, clean all dirt and debris away from the plug base. Dirt that falls into the cylinder causes rapid engine wear.*

1. Disconnect the plug wire and remove the spark plug.

> *NOTE*
> *A spark tester (**Figure 9**, typical) is a useful tool for checking the ignition system. Insert this tool in the spark plug cap and ground its base against the cylinder head. A number of different spark testers are available through motorcycle and automotive parts stores. The spark tester shown in **Figure 9** is manufactured by Motion Pro.*

2. If using an adjustable spark tester, set its air gap to 6 mm (0.24 in.).

3. Insert the spark plug (or spark tester) into the plug cap and touch its base against the cylinder head to ground it (**Figure 9**, typical). Position the plug so the electrodes are visible.

> *CAUTION*
> *Mount the spark plug or spark tester away from the plug hole in the cylinder head so the spark from the plug or tester cannot ignite the gasoline vapor in the cylinder.*

4. Turn the engine over with the starter button or operate the recoil starter. A fat blue spark should be evident across the spark plug electrodes or spark tester terminals.

> *WARNING*
> *Do not hold or touch the spark plug (or spark checker), wire or connector when making a spark check. A serious electrical shock may result.*

5. If the spark is good, check for one or more of the following possible malfunctions:
   a. Obstructed fuel line or fuel filter (if used).
   b. Low compression or engine damage.
   c. Flooded engine.

6. If the spark is weak (white or yellow in color) or if there is no spark, check for one or more of the following conditions:
   a. Fouled or wet spark plug. If a spark jumps across a spark tester but not across the original spark plug, the plug is fouled. Repeat the spark test with a new spark plug.
   b. Loose or damaged spark plug cap connection. Hold the spark plug wire and turn the spark plug cap to tighten it. Then install the spark plug into the cap and repeat the spark test. If there is still no spark, bypass the plug cap as described in the next step.
   c. Check for a damaged spark plug cap. Hold the spark plug wire and unscrew the spark plug cap (**Figure 8**). Hold the end of the spark plug wire 6 mm (0.24 in.) from the cylinder head as shown in **Figure 10**. Have an assistant turn the engine over and repeat the spark test. If there is a strong spark, the spark plug cap is faulty. Replace the plug cap and repeat the spark test.
   d. Loose or damaged spark plug wire connections (at coil and plug cap).

e. Faulty ignition coil or faulty ignition coil ground wire connection.
f. Faulty ECM unit or stator coil(s).
g. Sheared flywheel key.
h. Loose flywheel nut.
i. Loose electrical connections.
j. Dirty electrical connections.

NOTE
If the engine backfires during starting, the ignition timing may be incorrect. Because the ignition timing is not adjustable, incorrect ignition timing may be caused by a loose flywheel, sheared flywheel key, loose ignition pulse generator mounting screws or connector or a damaged or defective ignition system component. Refer to **Ignition System** *in this chapter.*

Engine is Difficult to Start

The following section groups the three main engine operating systems with probable causes.

Electrical System

If an ignition problem occurs, it can usually be traced to a point in the wiring harness, at the connectors or in one of the switches.

1. Spark plug:
   a. Fouled spark plug.
   b. Incorrect spark plug gap.
   c. Incorrect spark plug heat range (too cold). Refer to Chapter Three.
   d. Worn or damaged spark plug electrodes.
   e. Damaged spark plug.
   f. Damaged spark plug cap or spark plug wire.

NOTE
Refer to **Reading Spark Plugs** *in Chapter Three for additional information.*

2. Ignition coil:
   a. Loose or damaged ignition coil leads.
   b. Cracked ignition coil body—look for carbon tracks on the ignition coil.
   c. Loose or corroded ground wire.
3. Switches and wiring:
   a. Dirty or loose fitting terminals.
   b. Damaged wires or connectors (**Figure 11**).

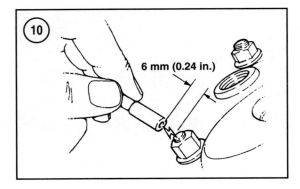

c. Damaged ignition switch.
d. Damaged engine stop switch.
4. Electrical components:
   a. Damaged ignition pulse generator.
   b. Damaged ECM unit.
   c. Sheared flywheel Woodruff key.

Fuel System

A contaminated fuel system causes engine starting and performance related problems. It only takes a small amount of dirt in the fuel valve, fuel line or carburetor to cause a problem.

1. Air filter:
   a. Plugged air filter element.
   b. Plugged air filter housing.
   c. Leaking or damaged air filter housing-to-carburetor air boot.
2. Fuel valve:
   a. Plugged fuel hose.
   b. Plugged fuel valve filter.
3. Fuel tank:
   a. No fuel.
   b. Plugged fuel filter.
   c. Plugged fuel tank breather hose (**Figure 5**).
   d. Contaminated fuel.
4. Carburetor:
   a. Plugged or damaged choke system.
   b. Plugged main jet.
   c. Plugged pilot jet.
   d. Loose pilot jet or main jet.
   e. Plugged pilot jet air passage.
   f. Incorrect float level.
   g. Leaking or damaged float.
   h. Worn or damaged needle valve.

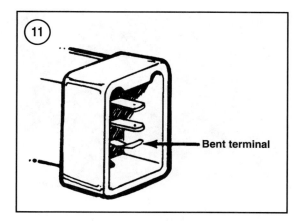

Bent terminal

Engine Compression

Check engine compression as described in Chapter Three. To obtain a more accurate gauge of engine wear, perform an engine leak down test. Refer to *Cylinder Leakdown Test* in this chapter.

1. Cylinder and cylinder head:
   a. Loose spark plug.
   b. Missing spark plug gasket.
   c. Leaking cylinder head gasket.
   d. Leaking cylinder base gasket.
   e. Worn or seized piston, piston rings and/or cylinder.
   f. Loose cylinder and/or cylinder head fasteners.
   g. Cylinder head incorrectly installed and/or torqued.
   h. Warped cylinder head.
   i. Valve(s) adjusted too tight.
   j. Bent valve.
   k. Worn valve and/or seat.
   l. Worn or damaged valve guide(s).
   m. Damaged compression release cam (mounted on camshaft).
   n. Bent pushrod(s).
   o. Damaged cam follower.
2. Piston and piston rings:
   a. Worn piston rings.
   b. Damaged piston rings.
   c. Piston seizure or piston damage.
3. Crankcase and crankshaft:
   a. Seized connecting rod.
   b. Damaged crankcases.

POOR IDLE SPEED PERFORMANCE

If the engine starts but off-idle performance is poor (engine hesitates or misfires), check the following:
1. Clogged or damaged air filter element.
2. Carburetor:
   a. Plugged pilot jet.
   b. Loose pilot jet.
   c. Damaged choke system.
   d. Incorrect throttle cable adjustment.
   e. Incorrect pilot screw adjustment.
   f. Flooded carburetor (visually check carburetor overflow hose for fuel).
   g. Vacuum piston does not slide smoothly in carburetor bore.
   h. Loose carburetor.
   i. Damaged intake tube O-ring.
3. Fuel:
   a. Water and/or alcohol in fuel.
   b. Old fuel.
4. Electrical system:
   a. Damaged spark plug.
   b. Damaged ignition coil.
   c. Damaged ignition pulse generator.
   d. Damaged ECM unit.
5. Engine damage. Refer to *Engine Compression* in this chapter.

POOR MEDIUM AND HIGH SPEED PERFORMANCE

Refer to *Engine is Difficult to Start*, then check the following:
1. Carburetor:
   a. Incorrect fuel level.
   b. Incorrect jet needle clip position.
   c. Plugged or loose main jet.
   d. Plugged fuel line.
   e. Plugged fuel valve.
   f. Plugged fuel tank vent tube.
2. Plugged air filter element.
3. Engine:
   a. Incorrect valve timing.
   b. Weak valve springs.
4. Other considerations:
   a. Overheating.
   b. Clutch slippage.
   c. Brake drag.
   d. Engine oil level too high.

ELECTRIC STARTING SYSTEM

This section describes troubleshooting procedures for the electric starting system. A fully charged battery, ohmmeter and jumper cables are required to perform many of these troubleshooting procedures. Before troubleshooting the starting circuit, make sure:

1. The battery is fully charged.
2. Battery cables are the proper size and length. Replace cables that are undersized or damaged.
3. All electrical connections are clean and tight.
4. The wiring harness is in good condition, with no worn or frayed insulation or loose harness sockets.
5. The fuel system is filled with an adequate supply of fresh gasoline.

Description

An electric starter is used on all models. The starter is mounted horizontally at the rear of the engine and located behind the right engine cover (**Figure 12**).

The electric starting system requires a fully charged battery to provide the large amount of current required to operate the starter. A charge coil (mounted on the stator plate) and a voltage regulator, connected in circuit with the battery, keep the battery charged while the engine is running. The battery can also be charged externally.

The starting circuit consists of the battery, starter, gear position switch, neutral indicator, starter relay, ignition switch and engine stop switch.

The starter relay (**Figure 13**) carries the heavy electrical current to the starter. Depressing the starter switch allows current to flow through the starter relay coil. The starter relay contacts close and allow current to flow from the battery through the starter relay to the starter.

When the ignition switch is turned on and the engine stop switch is in the RUN position, the starter motor can be operated only if the transmission is in neutral or the front brake lever is applied.

CAUTION
Do not operate the starter continuously for more than 5 seconds. Allow the starter to cool for at least 10 seconds between attempts to start the engine.

Starter Troubleshooting

NOTE
The following procedure isolates a starter problem when attempting to start in neutral. If the starter operates in neutral but not when the transmission is in gear and the front brake lever is applied, check the front brake switch circuit.

When operating the starter switch, turn the engine stop switch to RUN and the ignition switch on. Make sure the transmission is in neutral.

If the starter does not operate, perform the following tests:

1. Remove the seat as described in Chapter Fifteen.
2. Remove the lid above the battery.
3. First check the 30-amp main fuse. Open the fuse holder, pull out the fuse and visually inspect it. If the fuse is blown, replace it as described in the *Fuses* section in Chapter Nine. If the main fuse is good, reinstall it, then continue with Step 4.
4. Test the battery as described in the *Battery* section in Chapter Three. Note the following:
   a. If the battery is fully charged, perform Step 5.
   b. If necessary, clean and recharge the battery. If the battery is damaged, replace it.
5. Check for loose, corroded or damaged battery cables. Check at the battery, starter motor, starter relay and all cable-to-frame connections.
6. Turn the ignition switch on, then push the starter button and listen for a click sound at the starter relay switch (**Figure 13**). Note the following:
   a. If the relay clicked, perform Step 7.
   b. If the relay did not click, go to Step 8.
7. Test the battery as follows:

a. Park the ATV on level ground and set the parking brake. Shift the transmission into neutral.

b. Disconnect the cable from the starter motor terminal (**Figure 14**).

WARNING
Because a spark is produced in the following steps, perform this procedure away from gasoline or other volatile liquids. Make sure there is no spilled gasoline or gasoline fumes in the work area.

c. Momentarily connect a jumper cable (thick gauge wire) from the positive battery terminal to the starter terminal (**Figure 14**). If the starter is working properly, it turns when making the jumper cable connection.

d. If the starter did not turn, remove the starter and service it as described in Chapter Nine.

e. If the starter turned, check for a loose or damaged starter motor cable. If the cable is good, the starter relay (**Figure 13**) is faulty. Replace the starter relay and retest.

8. Test the following items as described in Chapter Nine:

a. Gear position switch.

b. Ignition switch.

c. Diode.

9. Perform the starter relay voltage test as described in the *Starter Relay* section in Chapter Nine. Note the following:

a. If the voltmeter shows battery voltage, continue with Step 10.

b. If there was no voltage reading, check the ignition switch and starter switch as described in Chapter Nine. If both switches are good, check continuity of the yellow/red wire between the starter switch and the starter relay.

10. Perform the starter relay continuity test as described in the *Starter Relay* section in Chapter Nine. Note the following:

a. If the meter reading is correct, continue with Step 10.

b. If the meter reading is incorrect, check for an open circuit in the yellow/red and light green/red wires. Check the wire ends for loose or damaged connectors.

11. If the starting system problem was not found after performing these steps in order, recheck the wiring system for dirty or loose-fitting terminals or damaged wires; clean and repair as required.

12. Make sure all connectors disconnected during this procedure are free of corrosion and reconnected properly.

Starter Turns Slowly

If the starter motor turns slowly and all engine components and systems are normal, perform the following:

1. Test the battery as described in Chapter Three.

2. Check for the following:

a. Loose or corroded battery terminals.

b. Loose or corroded battery ground cable.

c. Loose starter cable.

3. Remove, disassemble and bench test the starter as described in the *Starter* in Chapter Nine.

4. Check the starter for binding during operation. Disassemble the starter and check the armature shaft for bending or damage. Also check the starter clutch as described in Chapter Five.

Starter Turns but the Engine Does Not

If the starter turns but the engine does not, perform the following:

1. Check for a damaged starter clutch (Chapter Five).
2. Check for damaged starter reduction gears (Chapter Five).

CHARGING SYSTEM

The charging system consists of the battery, alternator and a voltage regulator/rectifier. A 30-amp main fuse protects the circuit.

A malfunction in the charging system generally causes the battery to remain undercharged.

Battery Discharging

1. Check all the connections. Make sure they are tight and free of corrosion.
2. Perform the *Charging System Current Draw Test* as described in Chapter Nine. If the current leakage exceeds 1.0 mA, perform Step 3. If the current leakage is 1.0 mA or less, perform Step 4.
3. Disconnect the black regulator/rectifier connector, then repeat the *Charging System Current Draw Test*. Note the following:
   a. If the test results are incorrect, the ignition switch may be faulty or the wiring harness is shorted; test the ignition switch as described in Chapter Nine.
   b. If the test readings are correct, replace the regulator/rectifier unit and retest.
4. Perform the *Charging Voltage Test* in Chapter Nine. Note the following:
   a. If the test readings are correct, perform Step 5.
   b. If the test readings are incorrect, go to Step 6.
5. Test the battery with a battery tester and note the following:

NOTE
If a battery tester is not accessible, remove the battery and take it to a dealership for testing.

   a. If the test readings are correct, check for an open circuit in the wiring harness and for dirty or loose-fitting terminals; clean and repair as required.

   b. If the test readings are incorrect, the battery is faulty or electrical components are overloading the charging system.
6. Perform the battery charging line and ground line tests as described in the *Regulator/Rectifier Wiring Harness Test* in Chapter Nine. Note the following:
   a. If the test readings are correct, perform Step 7.
   b. If the test readings are incorrect, check for an open circuit in the wiring harness and for dirty or loose-fitting terminals; clean and repair as required.
7. Perform the charging coil line tests at the regulator/rectifier connector as described in the *Regulator/Rectifier Wiring Harness Test* in Chapter Nine. Note the following:
   a. If the test readings are incorrect, replace the alternator and retest.
   b. If the test readings are correct, replace the regulator/rectifier unit and retest.

Battery Overcharging

If the battery is overcharging, the regulator/rectifier unit is faulty. Replace the regulator/rectifier unit as described in Chapter Nine.

IGNITION SYSTEM

All models are equipped with a capacitor discharge ignition (CDI) system. This solid state system uses no contact breaker point or other moving parts.

Because of the solid state design, problems with the capacitor discharge system are rare. If a problem occurs, it generally causes a weak spark or no spark at all. An ignition system with a weak spark or no spark is relatively easy to troubleshoot. It is difficult, however, to troubleshoot an ignition system that only malfunctions when the engine is hot or under load.

Test Notes

Honda recommends the use of the Honda peak voltage adapter (part no. 07HGJ-0020100) with a commercially available digital multimeter with an impedance of 10M ohms/DCVminimum to troubleshoot the ignition system. Because these are not practical tools for the home mechanic, the following troubleshooting section isolates and tests the different ignition system components and wiring that can be performed by the home mechanic. If the problem cannot be located after performing the troubleshooting procedure, refer further testing to a Honda dealership.

Troubleshooting

> *NOTE*
> *If the problem is intermittent, perform the tests with the engine cold, then hot. Then compare the test results.*

1. Perform the following ignition spark gap test as follows:

> *NOTE*
> *If an adjustable spark tester is not available, perform the spark test as described in the **Engine Fails to Start (Spark Test)** in this chapter.*

a. Disconnect the plug wire.

> *NOTE*
> *A spark tester is a useful tool to check the ignition system. **Figure 9** shows the Motion Pro Ignition System Tester. This tool is inserted in the spark plug cap and its base is ground against the cylinder head. The tool's air gap is adjustable, which allows seeing and hearing the spark while testing the intensity of the spark.*

b. Adjust the spark tester so the air gap distance is 6 mm (0.24 in.).

c. Insert the spark tester into the plug cap and touch its base against the cylinder head to ground it (**Figure 9**, typical). Position the tester so the terminals are visible.

> *CAUTION*
> *If the spark plug was removed from the engine, position the spark tester away from the plug hole in the cylinder head so the spark from the tester cannot ignite the gasoline vapors in the cylinder.*

d. Turn the engine over with the starter button or operate the recoil starter. A fat blue spark should jump between the spark tester terminals.

> *WARNING*
> *Do not hold the spark tester or connector or a serious electrical shock may result.*

e. If the spark jumps the gap and is dark blue, the ignition system is good. If the spark does not jump the gap, hold the spark plug cable and twist the plug cap a few times to tighten it. Then recheck the spark gap. If there is still no spark or if it jumps the gap but is yellow or white, continue with Step 2.

f. Remove the spark tester from the spark plug cap.

2. Unscrew the spark plug cap (**Figure 8**) from the ignition coil plug wire and hold the end of the wire 6 mm (0.24 in.) from the cylinder head and away from the spark plug hole as shown in **Figure 10**. Have an assistant turn over the engine. A fat blue spark should be evident passing from the end of the wire to the cylinder head. If there is no spark, perform Step 3.

3. Test the ignition coil as described in Chapter Nine. Note the following:

a. If the ignition coil is good, perform Step 4.

b. If the ignition coil fails to pass the tests described in Chapter Nine, the ignition coil is probably faulty. However, before replacing the ignition coil, take it to a dealership and have them test the spark with an ignition coil tester. Replace the ignition coil if faulty and retest the ignition system.

4. Test the engine stop switch as described under *Switches* in left handlebar housing in Chapter Nine. Note the following:

a. If the switch is good, perform Step 5.

b. If the switch fails to pass the test as described in Chapter Nine, the switch is faulty and must be replaced. Replace the switch and retest the ignition system.

5. Test the ignition switch as described in the *Switches* in Chapter Nine. Note the following:

a. If the switch is good, perform Step 6.

b. If the switch fails to pass the test as described in Chapter Nine, the switch is faulty and must be replaced. Replace the switch and retest the ignition system.

6. Perform the pulse generator *Peak Voltage Test* in Chapter Nine. Note the following:

a. If the test reading is correct, perform Step 7.

b. If the test reading is incorrect, replace the pulse generator as described in Chapter Nine.

7. If a damaged component was not identified, check the ignition system wiring harness and connectors. Check for damaged wires or loose, dirty or damaged connectors. If the wiring and connectors are good, proceed to Step 8.

8. If all preceeding steps do not identify a faulty component, the ECM unit (**Figure 15**) is faulty and must be replaced.

> *NOTE*
> *The ECM unit cannot be tested effectively using conventional equipment. Because ignition system problems are most often caused by an open or short circuit or poor wiring connections, replace the ECM only after determining all other ignition system components are functioning properly. The ECM is expensive and once purchased, generally cannot be returned. Therefore, repeat the preceding tests to verify the condition of the ignition system before replacing the ECM.*

9. Install all parts previously removed. Make sure all of the connections are free of corrosion and are reconnected properly.

LIGHTING SYSTEM

Faulty Bulbs

If the headlight or taillight bulb(s) continually burn out, check for one or more of the following conditions:

1. Incorrect bulb type. Refer to Chapter Nine for the correct replacement bulb types.
2. Damaged battery.
3. Damaged rectifier/regulator.
4. Damaged ignition switch and/or light switch.

Headlight Operates Darker than Normal

Check for one or more of the following conditions:

1. Incorrect bulb type. Refer to Chapter Nine for the correct replacement bulbs.
2. Charging system problem.
3. Too many electric accessories added to the wiring harness. If one or more aftermarket electrical accessories have been connected to the wiring system, disconnect them one at a time and then start the

engine and check the headlight operation. If this is the cause of the problem, contact the aftermarket manufacturer for more information.

4. Incorrect ground connection.
5. Poor main and/or light switch electrical contacts.

Lighting System Troubleshooting

If the headlight and/or taillight do not work, perform the following test procedures:

1. Check for a blown bulb as described in Step 1 in the following section.
2. Check all of the lighting system connectors and wires for loose or damaged connections.
3. Check the main fuse as described in Chapter Nine. Replace a blown or damaged fuse.
4. Test the battery as described in Chapter Three. Note the following:
   a. If the battery is fully charged, perform Step 5.
   b. If necessary, clean and recharge the battery. If the battery is damaged or does not hold a charge, replace it. If the ATV was bought used, check the battery to make sure it is the correct size and type recommended by Honda. Refer to the *Battery* section in Chapter Three.
5. Test the ignition switch as described in Chapter Nine. If the ignition switch is good, continue with Step 6.
6. If the problem is not located, perform the *Lighting System Check* in the following section.

Headlight

If the headlights do not come on, perform the following test:

1. Remove the headlight bulb (Chapter Nine).

a. The headlight bulb has three terminals. Connect an ohmmeter between any two terminals. The reading should be 0 ohms. Repeat the test between the remaining terminal and another terminal. The reading should be 0 ohms. Replace the bulb if the ohmmeter indicates an open circuit between any two terminals.

b. Connect an ohmmeter to one of the headlight socket terminals and to its mating electrical connector, then check for continuity. Repeat for the other wires and their terminals. Each reading should indicate continuity. If any reading does not meet specifications, replace the headlight socket if it cannot be repaired.

c. If both sets of readings were correct, proceed to Step 2.

2. In Step 3 and Step 4, connect voltmeter leads to the wiring harness electrical connectors.

3. Connect the voltmeter positive lead to the headlight connector white lead and the voltmeter negative lead to the headlight connector green lead. Turn the ignition switch on and the dimmer switch to its LO position. Note the voltmeter reading:

a. If the voltmeter reads battery voltage, continue with Step 4.

b. If the voltmeter does not read battery voltage check the wiring harness from the ignition switch to the headlight socket for damage.

4. Turn the ignition switch off. Connect the voltmeter positive lead to the headlight connector blue/black lead and the voltmeter negative lead to the headlight connector green lead. Turn the ignition switch on and the dimmer switch to its HI position. Note the voltmeter reading:

a. If the voltmeter reads battery voltage, continue with Step 5.

b. If the voltmeter does not read battery voltage, check the wiring harness from the ignition switch to the headlight socket for damage.

5. Turn the ignition switch off and disconnect the voltmeter leads.

Assist headlight

If the assist headlight does not come on, perform the following test:

NOTE
The assist headlight uses a quartz-halogen bulb. Because traces of oil on this type of bulb reduces the life of the bulb, do not touch the bulb glass. Clean any traces of oil or other chemicals from the bulb with a cloth moistened in isopropyl alcohol or lacquer thinner.

1. Remove the assist headlight bulb (Chapter Nine) and disconnect the bulb socket 2-pin connector from the main wiring harness.

a. Connect an ohmmeter to the bulb terminals. The reading should be 0 ohms. Replace the bulb if the ohmmeter reads infinity.

b. Connect an ohmmeter to one assist headlight socket terminal and its mating electrical connector. Repeat for the other wire. Each reading should be 0 ohms. If not, replace the assist headlight socket if it cannot be repaired.

c. If both sets of readings are correct, continue with Step 2.

2. Connect the voltmeter positive lead to the assist headlight connector brown lead and the voltmeter negative lead to the assist headlight connector green lead. Turn the ignition switch on and the dimmer switch to HI or LO. If the voltmeter does not read battery voltage, check the switches and wiring harness.

Taillight

If the taillight does not light, perform the following test:

1. Remove the taillight bulb (Chapter Nine) and disconnect the taillight socket connectors (**Figure 16**) from the wiring harness.

a. Connect an ohmmeter to the bulb terminals. The reading should be 0 ohms. Replace the bulb if the ohmmeter reads infinity.

b. Connect an ohmmeter to a taillight socket terminal and to its mating electrical connector to check continuity. Repeat for the other wire. Each reading should be 0 ohms. If any reading indicates an open circuit, replace the taillight socket if it cannot be repaired.

2. In Step 3, connect voltmeter leads to the taillight socket electrical connectors of the main wiring harness (**Figure 16**).

3. Connect the voltmeter positive lead to the taillight connector brown lead and the voltmeter negative lead to the taillight connector green lead. Turn the light switch on and note the voltmeter reading:

a. If the voltmeter reads battery voltage, continue with Step 4.

b. If the voltmeter does not read battery voltage, check the wiring harness for damage.

4. Turn the light switch off and disconnect the voltmeter leads. If the voltmeter reads battery voltage in Step 4, the taillight wiring circuit is good.

COOLING SYSTEM

Air passing through the radiator and the oil cooler cools the engine. At a preset temperature determined by the coolant thermosensor, the cooling fan operates, thereby drawing air through the radiator. The coolant and oil thermosensors trigger the temperature warning light.

Refer to the *Engine Overheating* section for cooling system components if a problem occurs. Refer to **Figure 17** for a troubleshooting chart that addresses the electrical components of the cooling system.

COMBINATION METER

All models are equipped with a combination meter (**Figure 18**). The combination meter includes a multifunction digital display that provides a speedometer, odometer, tripmeter, hourmeter and clock. A central processing unit (CPU) computer chip is contained within the combination meter. On TRX500FGA models, GPS information is also displayed on the combination meter.

A speed sensor (**Figure 19**) mounted on the engine provides driveshaft speed to the CPU in the combination meter.

Troubleshooting

Use the troubleshooting procedure in **Figure 20** to isolate a combination meter malfunction. Also refer to the wiring diagrams at the end of this manual for the specific model and year.

FUEL SYSTEM

Many riders automatically assume the carburetor is at fault if the engine does not run properly. While fuel system problems are not uncommon, carburetor adjustment is seldom the answer. In many cases, adjusting the carburetor only compounds the problem by making the engine run worse.

When troubleshooting the fuel system, start at the fuel tank and work through the system, reserving the carburetor as the final point. Most fuel system problems result from an empty fuel tank, a plugged fuel filter or fuel valve or sour fuel. Fuel system troubleshooting is covered thoroughly in the *Engine Is Difficult To Start, Poor Idle Speed Performance* and *Poor Medium and High Speed Performance* sections in this chapter.

The carburetor choke can also present problems. A choke stuck open causes a hard starting problem; one that sticks closed causes a flooding condition. Check choke operation by moving the choke knob (**Figure 2**) by hand. The choke should move freely without binding or sticking in one position. If necessary, remove the choke as described in the *Carburetor Disassembly* in Chapter Eight and inspect the plunger and spring for excessive wear or damage.

ENGINE OVERHEATING

Engine overheating is a serious problem because it can quickly cause engine seizure and damage. The following section groups five main systems with probable causes that can lead to engine overheating.

1. Ignition system:
   a. Incorrect spark plug gap.
   b. Incorrect spark plug heat range. Refer to Chapter Three.
   c. Faulty ECM unit/incorrect ignition timing.

2

COOLING SYSTEM TROUBLESHOOTING CHART

NOTE:
Most dealerships do not accept returned electrical components. If necessary, have the dealership test the suspected component before ordering a replacement.

NOTE:
Refer to Chapter Nine and wiring diagram for location of components and connectors.

NOTE:
Be sure the neutral and reverse indicators operate properly before using the following chart.

TEMPERATURE INDICATOR DOES NOT LIGHT

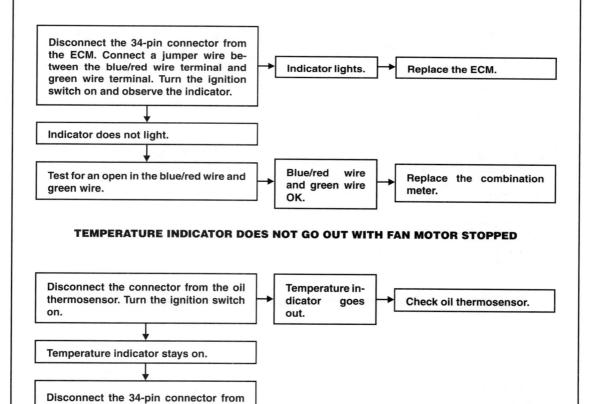

Disconnect the 34-pin connector from the ECM. Connect a jumper wire between the blue/red wire terminal and green wire terminal. Turn the ignition switch on and observe the indicator.	Indicator lights.	Replace the ECM.

Indicator does not light.

Test for an open in the blue/red wire and green wire.	Blue/red wire and green wire OK.	Replace the combination meter.

TEMPERATURE INDICATOR DOES NOT GO OUT WITH FAN MOTOR STOPPED

Disconnect the connector from the oil thermosensor. Turn the ignition switch on.	Temperature indicator goes out.	Check oil thermosensor.

Temperature indicator stays on.

Disconnect the 34-pin connector from the ECM. Disconnect the connector from the combination meter. Check for continuity between the blue/red wire terminals of both connectors.	No continuity.	Repair wiring.

Continuity.

(continued)

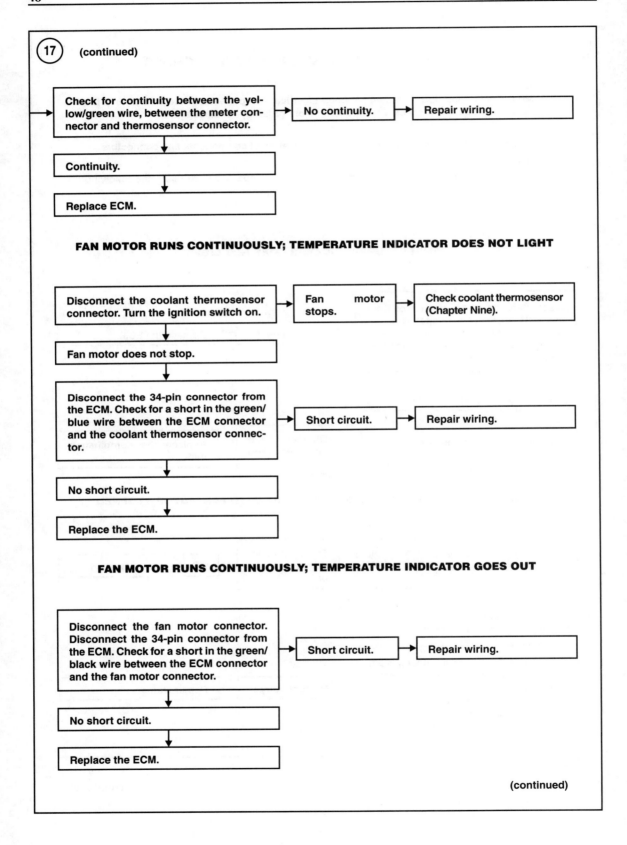

(17) (continued)

Check for continuity between the yellow/green wire, between the meter connector and thermosensor connector. → No continuity. → Repair wiring.

Continuity.

Replace ECM.

FAN MOTOR RUNS CONTINUOUSLY; TEMPERATURE INDICATOR DOES NOT LIGHT

Disconnect the coolant thermosensor connector. Turn the ignition switch on. → Fan motor stops. → Check coolant thermosensor (Chapter Nine).

Fan motor does not stop.

Disconnect the 34-pin connector from the ECM. Check for a short in the green/blue wire between the ECM connector and the coolant thermosensor connector. → Short circuit. → Repair wiring.

No short circuit.

Replace the ECM.

FAN MOTOR RUNS CONTINUOUSLY; TEMPERATURE INDICATOR GOES OUT

Disconnect the fan motor connector. Disconnect the 34-pin connector from the ECM. Check for a short in the green/black wire between the ECM connector and the fan motor connector. → Short circuit. → Repair wiring.

No short circuit.

Replace the ECM.

(continued)

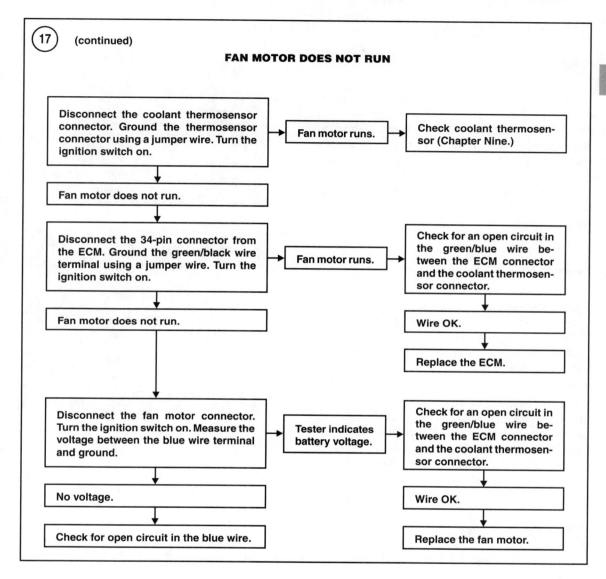

(17) (continued)

FAN MOTOR DOES NOT RUN

Disconnect the coolant thermosensor connector. Ground the thermosensor connector using a jumper wire. Turn the ignition switch on. → Fan motor runs. → Check coolant thermosensor (Chapter Nine.)

Fan motor does not run.

Disconnect the 34-pin connector from the ECM. Ground the green/black wire terminal using a jumper wire. Turn the ignition switch on. → Fan motor runs. → Check for an open circuit in the green/blue wire between the ECM connector and the coolant thermosensor connector.

Wire OK.

Replace the ECM.

Fan motor does not run.

Disconnect the fan motor connector. Turn the ignition switch on. Measure the voltage between the blue wire terminal and ground. → Tester indicates battery voltage. → Check for an open circuit in the green/blue wire between the ECM connector and the coolant thermosensor connector.

Wire OK.

Replace the fan motor.

No voltage.

Check for open circuit in the blue wire.

2. Engine compression system:
   a. Cylinder head gasket leakage.
   b. Heavy carbon buildup in combustion chamber.
3. Fuel system:
   a. Carburetor fuel level too low.
   b. Incorrect carburetor adjustment or jetting.
   c. Loose carburetor boot clamps.
   d. Leaking or damaged carburetor-to-air filter housing air boot.
   e. Incorrect air/fuel mixture.
4. Engine load:
   a. Dragging brake(s).
   b. Damaged drivetrain components.

   c. Slipping clutch.
   d. Engine oil level too high.
5. Cooling system malfunction:
   a. Low coolant level.
   b. Air in cooling system.
   c. Clogged radiator, hose or engine coolant passages.
   d. Thermostat stuck closed.
   e. Clogged or damaged oil cooler.
   f. Worn or damaged radiator cap.
   g. Damaged water pump.
   h. Damaged fan motor switch.
   i. Damaged fan motor.
   j. Damaged coolant temperature sensor.

ENGINE

Preignition

Preignition is the premature burning of fuel and is caused by hot spots in the combustion chamber. The fuel ignites before spark ignition occurs. Glowing deposits in the combustion chamber, inadequate cooling or an overheated spark plug can all cause preignition. This is first noticed as a power loss but eventually causes damage to internal parts of the engine because of the higher combustion chamber temperature.

Detonation

Commonly called spark knock or fuel knock, detonation is the violent explosion of fuel in the combustion chamber instead of the controlled burn that occurs during normal combustion. Damage can result. Use of low octane gasoline is a common cause of detonation.

Even when using a high octane gasoline, detonation can still occur. Other causes are over-advanced ignition timing, lean fuel mixture at or near full throttle, inadequate engine cooling or the excessive accumulation of carbon deposits in the combustion chamber and on the piston crown.

Power Loss

Several factors can cause a lack of power and speed. Look for a clogged air filter or a fouled or damaged spark plug. A galled piston or cylinder, incorrect piston clearance or worn or sticking piston rings may be responsible. Look for loose bolts, defective gaskets or leaking machined mating surfaces on the cylinder head, cylinder or crankcase.

Piston Seizure

This may be caused by incorrect bore clearance, piston rings with an improper end gap, compression leak, incorrect air/fuel mixture, spark plug of the wrong heat range or incorrect ignition timing. Overheating from any cause may result in piston seizure.

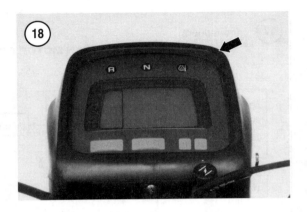

Piston Slap

Piston slap is an audible slapping or rattling noise caused by excessive piston-to-cylinder clearance. If allowed to continue, piston slap eventually causes the piston skirt to crack and shatter.

To prevent piston slap, clean the air filter element on a regular schedule. If piston slap is heard, disassemble the engine top end and measure the cylinder bore and piston diameter and check for excessive clearance. Replace parts that exceed service limits or show damage.

ENGINE NOISES

1. A knocking or pinging during acceleration can be caused by using a lower octane fuel than recommended or a poor quality fuel. Incorrect carburetor jetting or a spark plug that is too hot can also cause pinging. Refer to *Correct Spark Plug Heat Range* in Chapter Three. Check also for excessive carbon buildup in the combustion chamber or a faulty ECM unit.

(20)

COMBINATION METER/SPEED SENSOR TROUBLESHOOTING CHART

2

NOTE:
Most dealerships do not accept returned electrical components. If necessary, have the dealership test the suspected component before ordering a replacement.

NOTE:
Refer to Chapter Nine and wiring diagram for location of components and connectors.

Disconnect the 14-pin combination meter connector and perform the following tests.

↓

At the wiring harness connector half of the 14-pin connector, connect the positive lead of a voltmeter to the black/brown wire terminal. Connect the negative test lead to ground. Turn the ignition switch on. The tester should indicate battery voltage. → No battery voltage. → Check the black/brown wire for an open circuit. Repair if necessary.

↓

Tester indicates battery voltage.

↓

Connect the positive lead of a voltmeter to the red/black wire terminal. Connect the negative test lead to ground. The tester should indicate battery voltage all the time. → No battery voltage. → Check the red/black wire for an open circuit. Repair if necessary.

↓

Tester indicates battery voltage.

↓

Connect an ohmmeter to the green wire terminal and to ground. The ohmmeter should indicate continuity all the time. → No continuity. → Check the green wire for an open circuit. Repair if necessary.

↓

Continuity.

↓

Disconnect the three-pin, black speed sensor connector on right side of the frame. At the wiring harness connector half of the three-pin connector, connect the positive lead of a voltmeter to the black/blue wire terminal. Connect the negative test lead to the green wire terminal. Turn the ignition switch on. The tester should indicate battery voltage. → No battery voltage. → Check the black/blue and green wires for open circuits. Repair if necessary.

(continued)

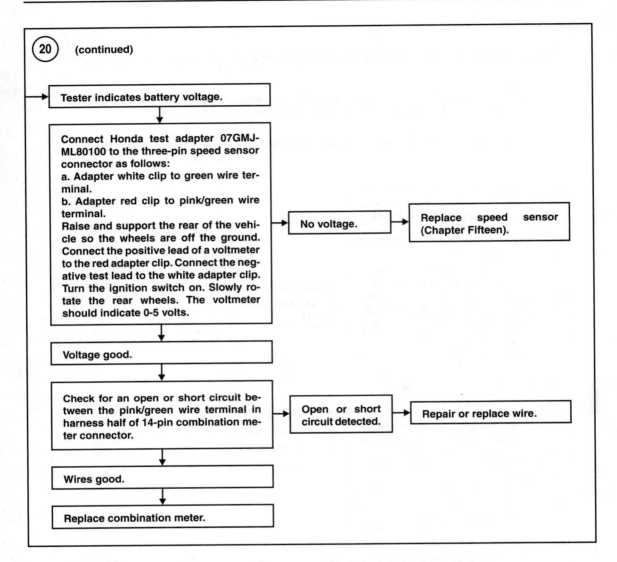

20 (continued)

Tester indicates battery voltage.

Connect Honda test adapter 07GMJ-ML80100 to the three-pin speed sensor connector as follows:
a. Adapter white clip to green wire terminal.
b. Adapter red clip to pink/green wire terminal.
Raise and support the rear of the vehicle so the wheels are off the ground. Connect the positive lead of a voltmeter to the red adapter clip. Connect the negative test lead to the white adapter clip. Turn the ignition switch on. Slowly rotate the rear wheels. The voltmeter should indicate 0-5 volts.

→ No voltage. → Replace speed sensor (Chapter Fifteen).

Voltage good.

Check for an open or short circuit between the pink/green wire terminal in harness half of 14-pin combination meter connector.

→ Open or short circuit detected. → Repair or replace wire.

Wires good.

Replace combination meter.

2. Slapping or rattling noises at low speed or during acceleration can be caused by excessive piston-to-cylinder wall clearance. Check also for a bent connecting rod or worn piston pin and/or piston pin holes in the piston.

3. A knocking or rapping while decelerating is usually caused by excessive rod bearing clearance.

4. A persistent knocking and vibration or other noise is usually caused by worn main bearings. If the main bearings are good, consider the following:

   a. Loose engine mounts.

   b. Cracked frame.

   c. Balancer gear improperly installed.

   d. Worn or damaged balancer gear bearings.

   e. Leaking cylinder head gasket.

   f. Exhaust pipe leakage at cylinder head.

   g. Stuck piston ring.

   h. Broken piston ring.

   i. Partial engine seizure.

   j. Excessive connecting rod small end bearing clearance.

   k. Excessive connecting rod big end side clearance.

   l. Excessive crankshaft runout.

   m. Worn or damaged primary drive gear.

5. A rapid on-off squeal is caused by compression leak around cylinder head gasket or spark plug.

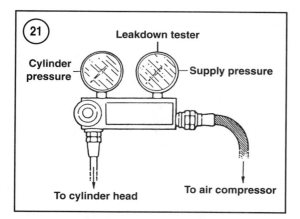

1. Start and run the engine until it reaches normal operating temperature. Turn the engine off.

2. Remove the air filter assembly as described in Chapter Three. Open and secure the throttle in the wide-open position.

3. Remove the spark plug.

4. Position the piston at TDC on the compression stroke. Refer to *Valve Clearance Check and Adjustment* in Chapter Three.

CAUTION
The engine may turn when air pressure is applied to the cylinder. Be sure nothing, such as a wrench, is attached to the crankshaft or related assemblies when performing the leakdown test.

5. Connect the cylinder leakdown tester into the spark plug hole (**Figure 22**).

6. Make a cylinder leakdown test following the tester manufacturer's instructions. Listen for air leaking while noting the following:

    a. Air leaking through the exhaust pipe indicates a leaking exhaust valve.

    b. Air leaking through the carburetor indicates a leaking intake valve.

    c. Air leaking through the crankcase breather tube indicates worn piston rings.

7. A cylinder with 10 percent or more cylinder leakage requires further service.

8. Remove the tester and reinstall the spark plug.

ENGINE OIL PRESSURE TEST

Check the engine oil pressure after installing a new oil pump, reassembling the engine or when troubleshooting the lubrication system.

An oil pressure gauge (Honda part No. 07ZMJ-HN2A100 or an equivalent) and an oil pressure gauge attachment (07KPJ-VD6010A or an equivalent) are required to test the oil pressure.

1. Park the ATV on level ground.

2. Start the engine and run it until it is at normal operating temperature, then turn it off.

NOTE
Be sure to clean the area around the oil gallery plug before removal.

3. Remove the oil gallery plug (**Figure 23**) and sealing washer. Do not allow any debris to enter the engine during this test.

CYLINDER LEAKDOWN TEST

A cylinder leakdown test can determine if an engine problem is caused by leaking valves, a blown head gasket or broken, worn or stuck piston rings. A cylinder leakdown test is performed by applying compressed air to the cylinder and then measuring the percent of leakage. A cylinder leakdown tester and an air compressor are required to perform this test (**Figure 21**). Follow the tester manufacturer's directions along with the following information when performing a cylinder leakdown test:

4. Connect the oil pressure gauge to the engine. Make sure the fitting is tight to prevent oil leakage.

5. Recheck the engine oil level.

6. Start the engine and allow it to reach normal operating temperature.

7. Increase engine speed to 1400 rpm and read the oil pressure on the gauge. The correct reading is 150 kPa (22 psi).

8. Increase engine speed to 5000 rpm and read the oil pressure on the gauge. The correct reading is 800 kPa (116 psi).

9. Allow the engine to return to idle, then shut it off.

10. Remove the test equipment from the engine.

11. If the oil pressure readings are lower or higher than specified, inspect the check valve as follows:

   a. Extract the spring and check valve (**Figure 24**) from the oil passage.
   b. Inspect the spring and check valve for contamination and damage.
   c. Install the check valve so the pin end is up, then install the spring onto the check valve.

12. If the check valve and spring are OK, check the lubrication system.

13. Install the oil gallery plug (**Figure 23**) and a new sealing washer. Tighten the plug to 34 N•m (26 ft.-lb.).

14. Start the engine and check for leaks.

CLUTCH

All clutch service, except adjustment, requires partial engine disassembly to identify and cure the problem. Refer to Chapter Six.

The TRX500 is equipped with a centrifugal clutch (**Figure 25**).

Clutch Slipping

1. Worn clutch shoe.
2. Loose, weak or damaged clutch spring.
3. Incorrectly assembled clutch.
4. Oil additives.

Clutch Dragging

1. Weak clutch weight springs.
2. Warped clutch plates.

SUB-TRANSMISSION

All models are equipped with a sub-transmission that provides low, drive and reverse gears. The desired gear is selected using the gearshift selector lever (**Figure 26**).

Difficult Shifting

If the shift shaft does not move smoothly from one gear to the next, check the following:

1. Shift linkage:
   a. Misadjusted gearshift linkage.
   b. Bent or damaged gearshift linkage.
2. Stopper arm:
   a. Seized or damaged stopper arm roller.
   b. Weak or damaged stopper arm spring.
   c. Loose stopper arm mounting bolt.
   d. Incorrectly assembled stopper arm assembly.
3. Shift drum and shift forks:
   a. Bent shift fork(s).
   b. Damaged shift fork guide pin(s).
   c. Seized shift fork (on shaft).
   d. Broken shift fork or shift fork shaft.

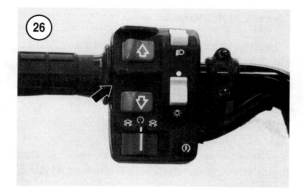

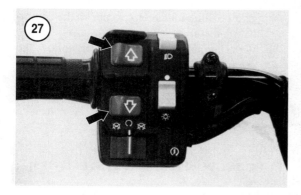

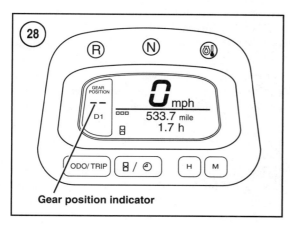

Gear position indicator

e. Damaged shift drum groove(s).
f. Damaged shift drum bearing surfaces.

Gears Pop Out Of Mesh

If the transmission shifts into gear but then slips or pops out, check the following:

1. Stopper arm:
   a. Damaged stopper arm.
   b. Weak or damaged stopper arm spring.

2. Shift drum:
   a. Incorrect thrust play.
   b. Worn or damaged shift drum groove(s).
3. Bent shift fork(s).
4. Transmission:
   a. Worn or damaged gear dogs.
   b. Excessive gear thrust play.
   c. Worn or damaged transmission shaft circlips or thrust washers.

MAIN (AUTOMATIC) TRANSMISSION

The main transmission is a hydraulically powered unit that may be automatically shifted by the Engine Control Module (ECM) or the rider using the electric shift switches (**Figure 27**). The transmission is shifted using an electric motor that rotates the shift shaft through a set of reduction gears. Refer to Chapter Nine.

The ECM controls the shift mechanism. Refer to Chapter Nine. The ECM can detect faults and enters a *failure mode* if a problem exists. In the failure mode the electric system is disabled and does not function. The ECM provides a trouble code if it detects a problem. The ECM leaves the failure mode and resets automatically when the ignition switch is turned off, but returns to the failure mode if the problem persists when the ignition switch is turned back on.

Trouble Codes

If the ECM detects an existing problem, it displays a trouble code by blinking a dash (–) on the combination meter (**Figure 28**) where the selected gear normally appears. The number of dashes (–) displayed correspond to the trouble code number.

NOTE
The combination meter must function properly for the ECU to display a trouble code. Troubleshoot the combination meter if it does not function properly.

Trouble Code Retrieval

Proceed as follows to obtain the ECM trouble code:

1. Be sure the transmission is in neutral and the *N* appears on the combination meter display.

2. Turn the ignition switch off.

3. Set the parking brake.

4. Simultaneously push the UP and DOWN shift buttons (**Figure 27**). Continue to hold the buttons while performing Step 5.

5. Turn the ignition switch on and quickly release the shift buttons.

6. Push in both shift buttons again for more than 2 seconds, then release. The trouble code symbol (–) should appear.

> *NOTE*
> *If the N appears instead of trouble code symbol (–), the retrieval attempt failed and must be repeated.*

7. Count the number of dashes and refer to **Table 1**. Note that more than one trouble code may be displayed. The most recent trouble code is displayed first.

8. The code sequence appears as follows:

    a. Dash (–) initially visible for 3 seconds.

    b. Off for 2 seconds.

    c. Displays latest trouble code.

    d. Off for 2 seconds.

    e. Displays earlier trouble code (if set).

    f. Off for 2 seconds.

    g. Repeat trouble code sequence.

> *NOTE*
> *If the dashes (–) are rapid and a trouble code is unobtainable, there is a system failure. Troubleshoot trouble code 3 or 7.*

9. After obtaining the trouble code, refer to **Figure 29** for troubleshooting information.

Trouble Code Deletion

To delete a trouble code, perform the steps to display the code. While the code is blinking, push in both shift buttons. To confirm erasure, the indicator flashes in a repeating sequence of 2 seconds on, 3 seconds off. Turn the ignition switch off.

No-code Malfunctions

In some situations, the trouble indicator flashes, but a trouble code may not be set. Note the following occurrences:

1. The automatic transmission does not shift with the mode select switch in the D1 or D2 position. Follow the troubleshooting procedure for trouble code 3 in **Figure 29**.

2. The automatic transmission does not shift with the mode select switch in the ESP position. Perform the following:

    a. Turn the ignition switch on and note if the gear position indicator appears on the combination meter.

    b. If the indicator does not appear, follow the troubleshooting procedure for trouble code 3 in **Figure 29**.

    c. If the indicator shows L, D, N or R, follow the troubleshooting procedure for trouble code 7 in **Figure 29**.

GLOBAL POSITIONING SYSTEM (GPS)

Model TRX500FGA is equipped with a global positioning system (GPS). The system consists of two components, one inside the combination meter and a receiver mounted inside the assist headlight housing. The GPS determines the ATV position only when the ignition switch is on. The time for the GPS to display the ATV position varies according to the time lapsed since the ignition was on, and how far the ATV traveled from the position the GPS was last active. Note the following starting situations:

1. Hot start—If less than 2 hours lapsed between turning the ignition off and back on, GPS should display position within 25 seconds.

2. Warm start—If more than 2 hours lapsed between turning the ignition off and back on, GPS should display position within approximately 2 minutes.

3. Cold start—The GPS may require approximately 8 minutes to display the ATV position if the following occurs:

    a. One month elapsed between turning the ignition off and back on.

    b. The ATV moved over 60 miles (100 km) during the time the ignition was turned off.

    c. The battery was disconnected.

TROUBLE CODE TROUBLESHOOTING CHART

NOTE:
Before replacing the ECM, take the vehicle to a Honda dealership or other qualified repair shop for further testing. Most parts suppliers do not accept the return of electrical components. Confirm the ECM is faulty before purchasing a replacement.

NOTE:
After installing an ECM, throttle position sensor or angle sensor, perform the initialization procedure described in Chapter Nine.

TROUBLE CODE 1: IGNITION PULSE GENERATOR SYSTEM

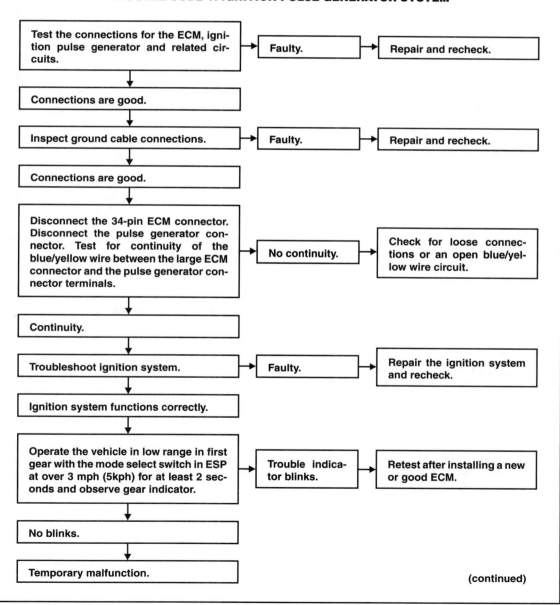

Test the connections for the ECM, ignition pulse generator and related circuits. → Faulty. → Repair and recheck.

Connections are good.

Inspect ground cable connections. → Faulty. → Repair and recheck.

Connections are good.

Disconnect the 34-pin ECM connector. Disconnect the pulse generator connector. Test for continuity of the blue/yellow wire between the large ECM connector and the pulse generator connector terminals. → No continuity. → Check for loose connections or an open blue/yellow wire circuit.

Continuity.

Troubleshoot ignition system. → Faulty. → Repair the ignition system and recheck.

Ignition system functions correctly.

Operate the vehicle in low range in first gear with the mode select switch in ESP at over 3 mph (5kph) for at least 2 seconds and observe gear indicator. → Trouble indicator blinks. → Retest after installing a new or good ECM.

No blinks.

Temporary malfunction.

(continued)

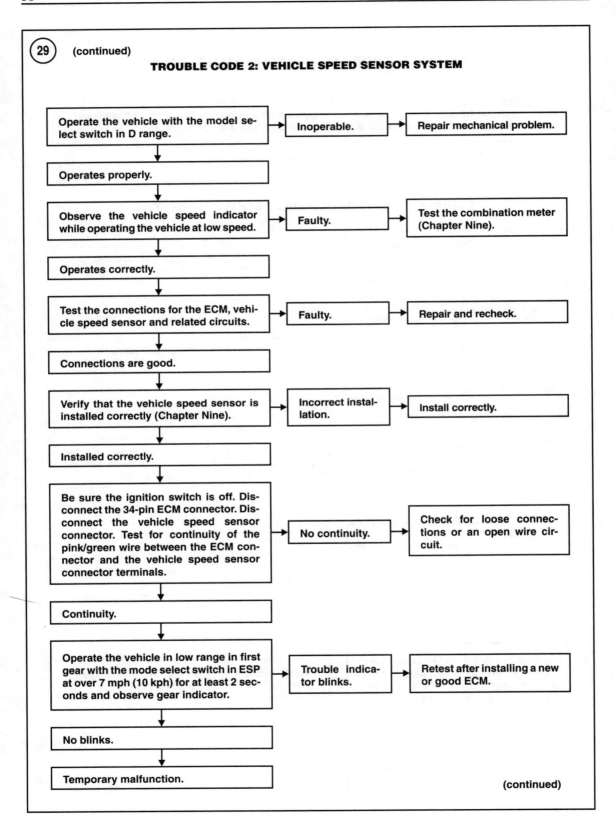

(29) (continued)

TROUBLE CODE 2: VEHICLE SPEED SENSOR SYSTEM

Operate the vehicle with the model select switch in D range. → Inoperable. → Repair mechanical problem.

Operates properly.

Observe the vehicle speed indicator while operating the vehicle at low speed. → Faulty. → Test the combination meter (Chapter Nine).

Operates correctly.

Test the connections for the ECM, vehicle speed sensor and related circuits. → Faulty. → Repair and recheck.

Connections are good.

Verify that the vehicle speed sensor is installed correctly (Chapter Nine). → Incorrect installation. → Install correctly.

Installed correctly.

Be sure the ignition switch is off. Disconnect the 34-pin ECM connector. Disconnect the vehicle speed sensor connector. Test for continuity of the pink/green wire between the ECM connector and the vehicle speed sensor connector terminals. → No continuity. → Check for loose connections or an open wire circuit.

Continuity.

Operate the vehicle in low range in first gear with the mode select switch in ESP at over 7 mph (10 kph) for at least 2 seconds and observe gear indicator. → Trouble indicator blinks. → Retest after installing a new or good ECM.

No blinks.

Temporary malfunction.

(continued)

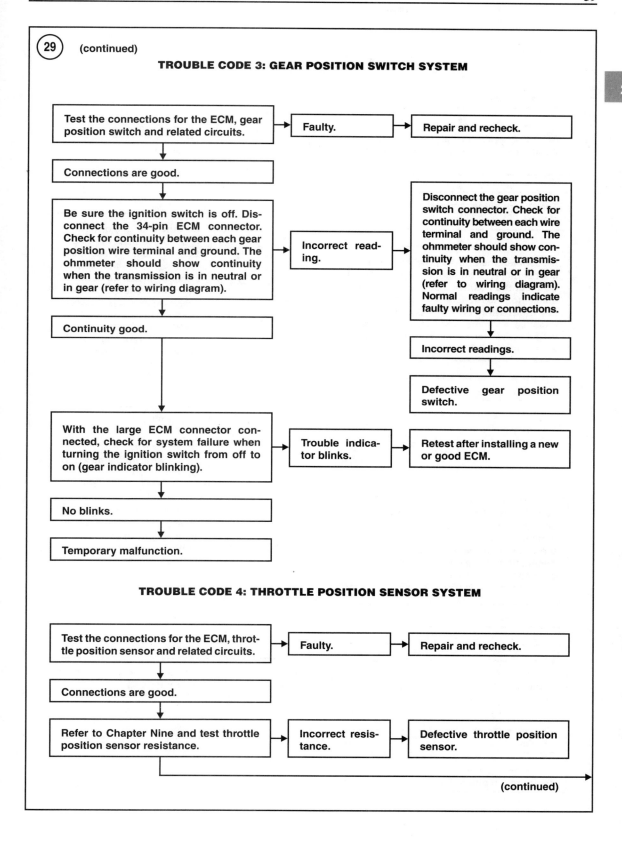

(29) (continued)

TROUBLE CODE 3: GEAR POSITION SWITCH SYSTEM

Test the connections for the ECM, gear position switch and related circuits. → Faulty. → Repair and recheck.

↓

Connections are good.

↓

Be sure the ignition switch is off. Disconnect the 34-pin ECM connector. Check for continuity between each gear position wire terminal and ground. The ohmmeter should show continuity when the transmission is in neutral or in gear (refer to wiring diagram). → Incorrect reading. → Disconnect the gear position switch connector. Check for continuity between each wire terminal and ground. The ohmmeter should show continuity when the transmission is in neutral or in gear (refer to wiring diagram). Normal readings indicate faulty wiring or connections.

↓

Continuity good.

↓ (Incorrect readings.)

↓

Defective gear position switch.

With the large ECM connector connected, check for system failure when turning the ignition switch from off to on (gear indicator blinking). → Trouble indicator blinks. → Retest after installing a new or good ECM.

↓

No blinks.

↓

Temporary malfunction.

TROUBLE CODE 4: THROTTLE POSITION SENSOR SYSTEM

Test the connections for the ECM, throttle position sensor and related circuits. → Faulty. → Repair and recheck.

↓

Connections are good.

↓

Refer to Chapter Nine and test throttle position sensor resistance. → Incorrect resistance. → Defective throttle position sensor.

(continued)

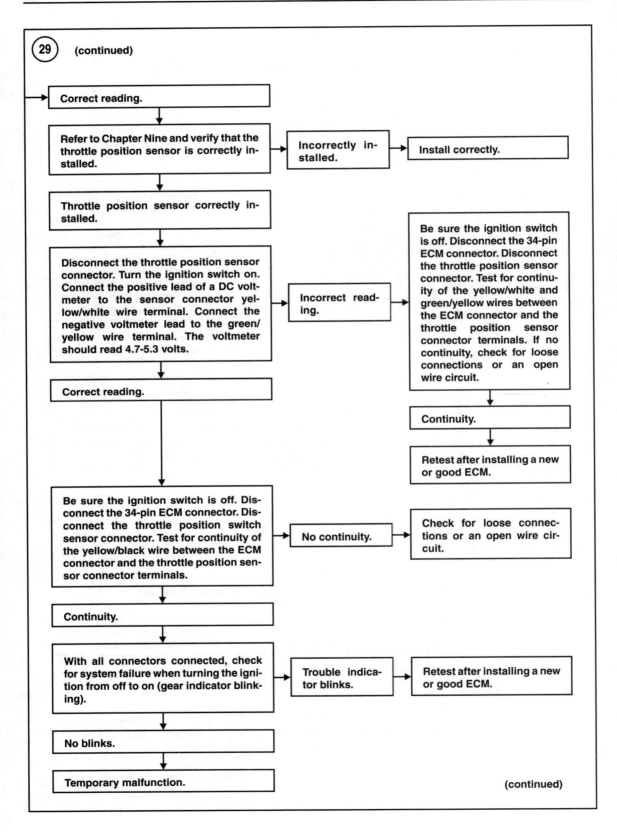

29 (continued)

Correct reading.

Refer to Chapter Nine and verify that the throttle position sensor is correctly installed. → Incorrectly installed. → Install correctly.

Throttle position sensor correctly installed.

Disconnect the throttle position sensor connector. Turn the ignition switch on. Connect the positive lead of a DC voltmeter to the sensor connector yellow/white wire terminal. Connect the negative voltmeter lead to the green/yellow wire terminal. The voltmeter should read 4.7-5.3 volts. → Incorrect reading. → Be sure the ignition switch is off. Disconnect the 34-pin ECM connector. Disconnect the throttle position sensor connector. Test for continuity of the yellow/white and green/yellow wires between the ECM connector and the throttle position sensor connector terminals. If no continuity, check for loose connections or an open wire circuit.

Correct reading.

Continuity.

Retest after installing a new or good ECM.

Be sure the ignition switch is off. Disconnect the 34-pin ECM connector. Disconnect the throttle position switch sensor connector. Test for continuity of the yellow/black wire between the ECM connector and the throttle position sensor connector terminals. → No continuity. → Check for loose connections or an open wire circuit.

Continuity.

With all connectors connected, check for system failure when turning the ignition from off to on (gear indicator blinking). → Trouble indicator blinks. → Retest after installing a new or good ECM.

No blinks.

Temporary malfunction.

(continued)

(29) (continued)

TROUBLE CODE 5: ANGLE SENSOR SYSTEM (MOTOR LOCK)

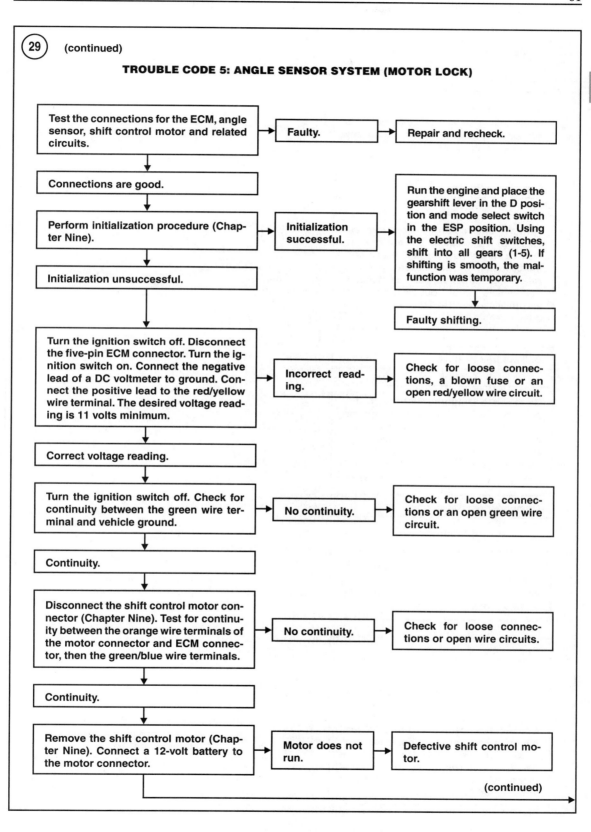

Test the connections for the ECM, angle sensor, shift control motor and related circuits. → Faulty. → Repair and recheck.

Connections are good.

Perform initialization procedure (Chapter Nine). → Initialization successful. → Run the engine and place the gearshift lever in the D position and mode select switch in the ESP position. Using the electric shift switches, shift into all gears (1-5). If shifting is smooth, the malfunction was temporary. → Faulty shifting.

Initialization unsuccessful.

Turn the ignition switch off. Disconnect the five-pin ECM connector. Turn the ignition switch on. Connect the negative lead of a DC voltmeter to ground. Connect the positive lead to the red/yellow wire terminal. The desired voltage reading is 11 volts minimum. → Incorrect reading. → Check for loose connections, a blown fuse or an open red/yellow wire circuit.

Correct voltage reading.

Turn the ignition switch off. Check for continuity between the green wire terminal and vehicle ground. → No continuity. → Check for loose connections or an open green wire circuit.

Continuity.

Disconnect the shift control motor connector (Chapter Nine). Test for continuity between the orange wire terminals of the motor connector and ECM connector, then the green/blue wire terminals. → No continuity. → Check for loose connections or open wire circuits.

Continuity.

Remove the shift control motor (Chapter Nine). Connect a 12-volt battery to the motor connector. → Motor does not run. → Defective shift control motor.

(continued)

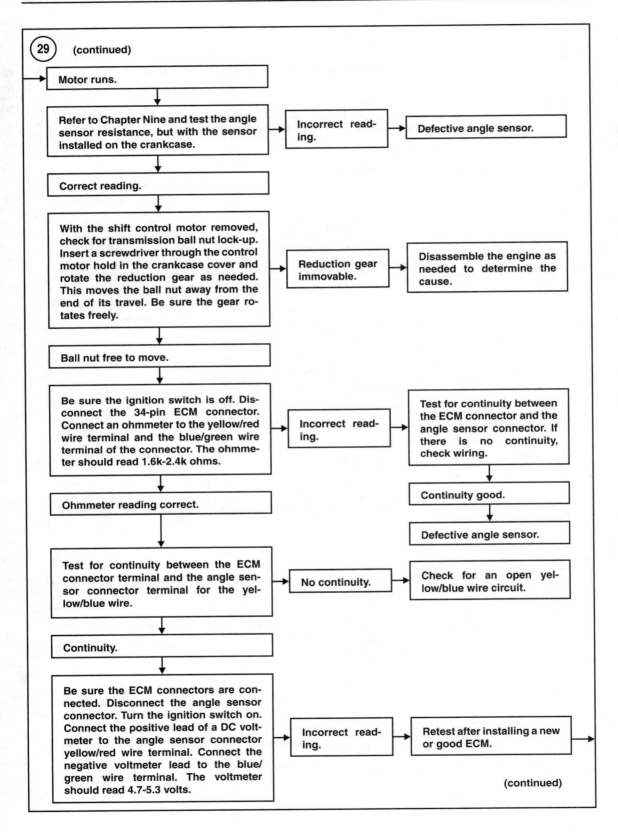

(29)   (continued)

Motor runs.

Refer to Chapter Nine and test the angle sensor resistance, but with the sensor installed on the crankcase. → Incorrect reading. → Defective angle sensor.

Correct reading.

With the shift control motor removed, check for transmission ball nut lock-up. Insert a screwdriver through the control motor hold in the crankcase cover and rotate the reduction gear as needed. This moves the ball nut away from the end of its travel. Be sure the gear rotates freely. → Reduction gear immovable. → Disassemble the engine as needed to determine the cause.

Ball nut free to move.

Be sure the ignition switch is off. Disconnect the 34-pin ECM connector. Connect an ohmmeter to the yellow/red wire terminal and the blue/green wire terminal of the connector. The ohmmeter should read 1.6k-2.4k ohms. → Incorrect reading. → Test for continuity between the ECM connector and the angle sensor connector. If there is no continuity, check wiring.

→ Continuity good.

→ Defective angle sensor.

Ohmmeter reading correct.

Test for continuity between the ECM connector terminal and the angle sensor connector terminal for the yellow/blue wire. → No continuity. → Check for an open yellow/blue wire circuit.

Continuity.

Be sure the ECM connectors are connected. Disconnect the angle sensor connector. Turn the ignition switch on. Connect the positive lead of a DC voltmeter to the angle sensor connector yellow/red wire terminal. Connect the negative voltmeter lead to the blue/green wire terminal. The voltmeter should read 4.7-5.3 volts. → Incorrect reading. → Retest after installing a new or good ECM.

(continued)

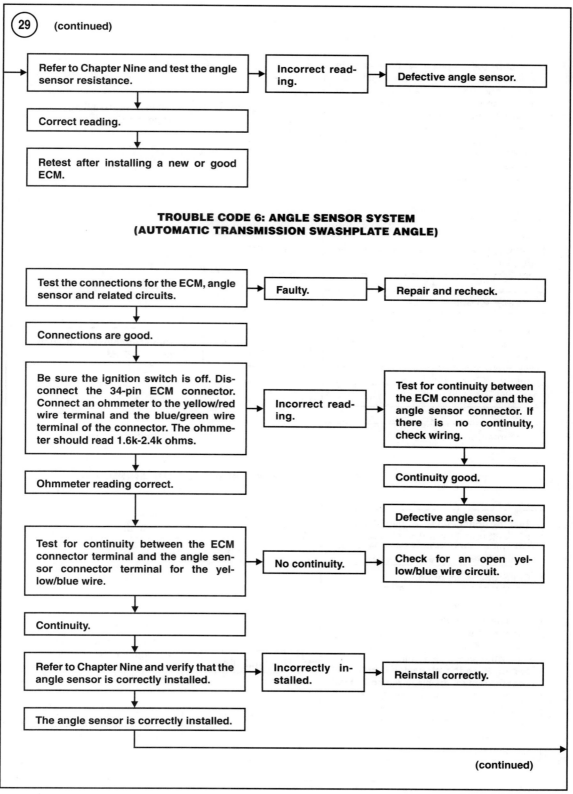

(29) (continued)

Refer to Chapter Nine and test the angle sensor resistance. → Incorrect reading. → Defective angle sensor.

Correct reading.

Retest after installing a new or good ECM.

TROUBLE CODE 6: ANGLE SENSOR SYSTEM
(AUTOMATIC TRANSMISSION SWASHPLATE ANGLE)

Test the connections for the ECM, angle sensor and related circuits. → Faulty. → Repair and recheck.

Connections are good.

Be sure the ignition switch is off. Disconnect the 34-pin ECM connector. Connect an ohmmeter to the yellow/red wire terminal and the blue/green wire terminal of the connector. The ohmmeter should read 1.6k-2.4k ohms. → Incorrect reading. → Test for continuity between the ECM connector and the angle sensor connector. If there is no continuity, check wiring.

Ohmmeter reading correct. | Continuity good.

| Defective angle sensor.

Test for continuity between the ECM connector terminal and the angle sensor connector terminal for the yellow/blue wire. → No continuity. → Check for an open yellow/blue wire circuit.

Continuity.

Refer to Chapter Nine and verify that the angle sensor is correctly installed. → Incorrectly installed. → Reinstall correctly.

The angle sensor is correctly installed.

(continued)

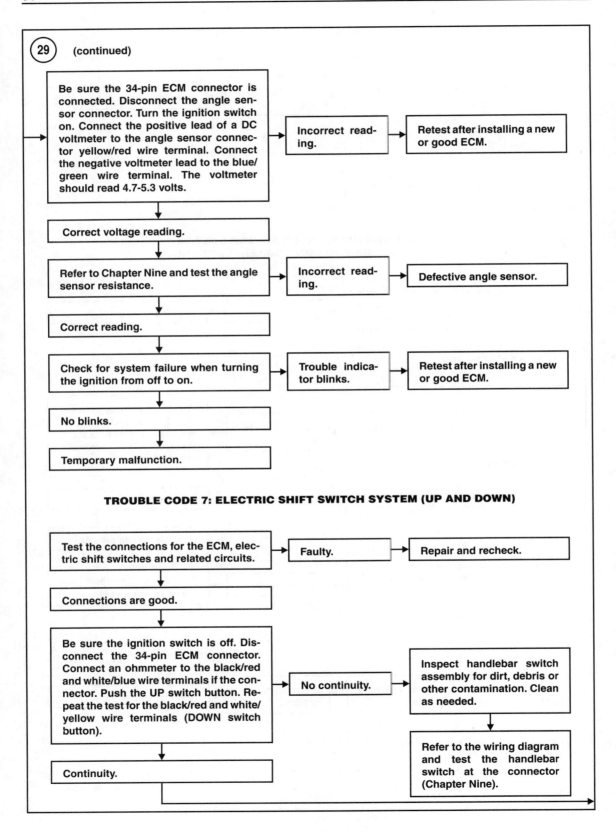

(29) (continued)

Be sure the 34-pin ECM connector is connected. Disconnect the angle sensor connector. Turn the ignition switch on. Connect the positive lead of a DC voltmeter to the angle sensor connector yellow/red wire terminal. Connect the negative voltmeter lead to the blue/green wire terminal. The voltmeter should read 4.7-5.3 volts. → Incorrect reading. → Retest after installing a new or good ECM.

Correct voltage reading.

Refer to Chapter Nine and test the angle sensor resistance. → Incorrect reading. → Defective angle sensor.

Correct reading.

Check for system failure when turning the ignition from off to on. → Trouble indicator blinks. → Retest after installing a new or good ECM.

No blinks.

Temporary malfunction.

TROUBLE CODE 7: ELECTRIC SHIFT SWITCH SYSTEM (UP AND DOWN)

Test the connections for the ECM, electric shift switches and related circuits. → Faulty. → Repair and recheck.

Connections are good.

Be sure the ignition switch is off. Disconnect the 34-pin ECM connector. Connect an ohmmeter to the black/red and white/blue wire terminals if the connector. Push the UP switch button. Repeat the test for the black/red and white/yellow wire terminals (DOWN switch button). → No continuity. → Inspect handlebar switch assembly for dirt, debris or other contamination. Clean as needed.

↓

Refer to the wiring diagram and test the handlebar switch at the connector (Chapter Nine).

Continuity.

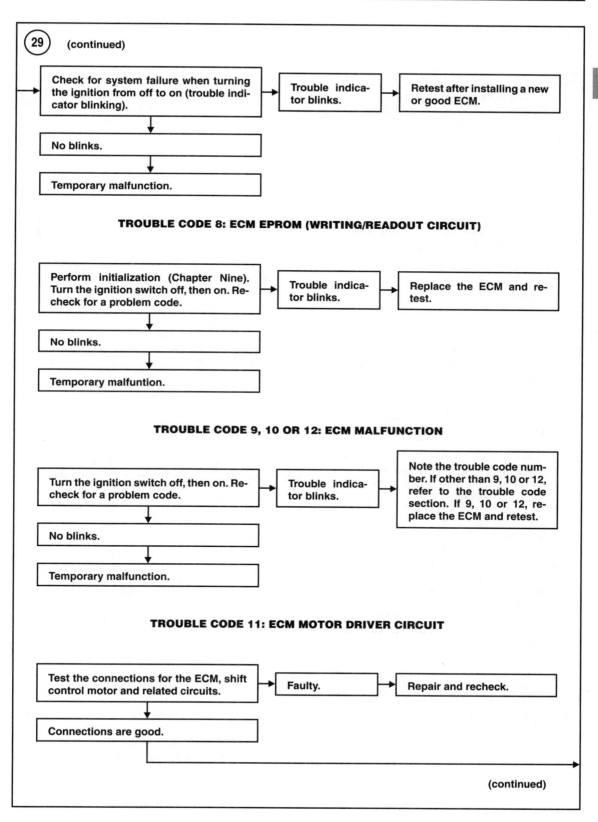

(29) (continued)

Check for system failure when turning the ignition from off to on (trouble indicator blinking). → Trouble indicator blinks. → Retest after installing a new or good ECM.

No blinks.

Temporary malfunction.

TROUBLE CODE 8: ECM EPROM (WRITING/READOUT CIRCUIT)

Perform initialization (Chapter Nine). Turn the ignition switch off, then on. Recheck for a problem code. → Trouble indicator blinks. → Replace the ECM and retest.

No blinks.

Temporary malfuntion.

TROUBLE CODE 9, 10 OR 12: ECM MALFUNCTION

Turn the ignition switch off, then on. Recheck for a problem code. → Trouble indicator blinks. → Note the trouble code number. If other than 9, 10 or 12, refer to the trouble code section. If 9, 10 or 12, replace the ECM and retest.

No blinks.

Temporary malfunction.

TROUBLE CODE 11: ECM MOTOR DRIVER CIRCUIT

Test the connections for the ECM, shift control motor and related circuits. → Faulty. → Repair and recheck.

Connections are good.

(continued)

2

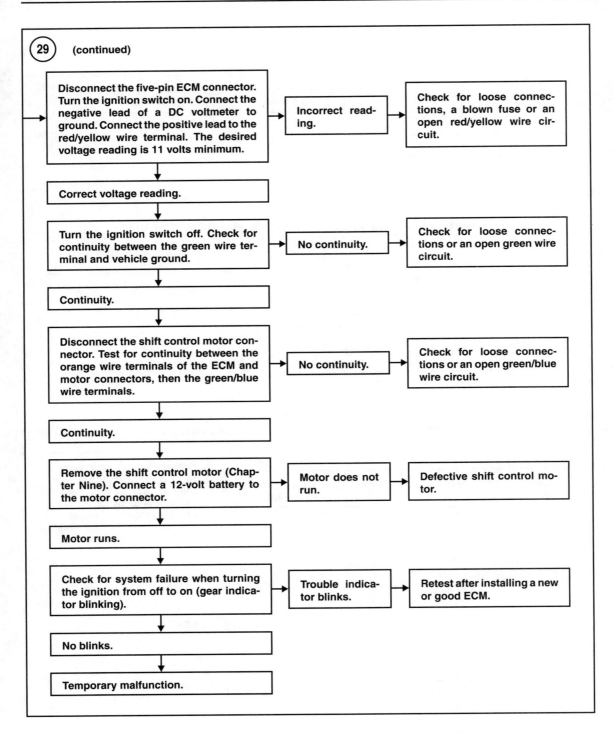

㉙ (continued)

Disconnect the five-pin ECM connector. Turn the ignition switch on. Connect the negative lead of a DC voltmeter to ground. Connect the positive lead to the red/yellow wire terminal. The desired voltage reading is 11 volts minimum. → Incorrect reading. → Check for loose connections, a blown fuse or an open red/yellow wire circuit.

Correct voltage reading.

Turn the ignition switch off. Check for continuity between the green wire terminal and vehicle ground. → No continuity. → Check for loose connections or an open green wire circuit.

Continuity.

Disconnect the shift control motor connector. Test for continuity between the orange wire terminals of the ECM and motor connectors, then the green/blue wire terminals. → No continuity. → Check for loose connections or an open green/blue wire circuit.

Continuity.

Remove the shift control motor (Chapter Nine). Connect a 12-volt battery to the motor connector. → Motor does not run. → Defective shift control motor.

Motor runs.

Check for system failure when turning the ignition from off to on (gear indicator blinking). → Trouble indicator blinks. → Retest after installing a new or good ECM.

No blinks.

Temporary malfunction.

Troubleshooting

The GPS indicator on the combination meter blinks if an error occurs. However, other problems may not cause the indicator to blink. If the GPS in- dicator blinks, but the antenna and segment indicators are not visible (**Figure 30**), follow the trouble- shooting procedure under *GPS Indicator Blinks* in **Figure 31**. If the GPS exceeds the normal startup time as described in the previous paragraph, follow

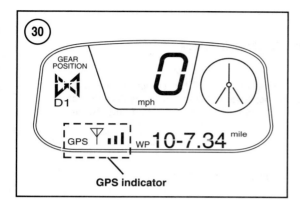

GPS indicator

the troubleshooting procedure under *GPS Startup Time Excessive* in **Figure 31**.

DRIVETRAIN TROUBLESHOOTING

Noise is usually the first indication of a drivetrain problem. It is not always easy to diagnose the trouble by determining the source of the noise and the operating conditions that produce it.

To help determine the cause of the trouble, first note whether the noise is a hum, growl or knock; whether it is produced when the ATV is accelerating under load or coasting; and whether it is heard when the ATV is going straight or making a turn.

Drivetrain service procedures are covered in Chapter Twelve (front) and Chapter Thirteen (rear).

CAUTION
Improperly diagnosed noises can lead to rapid and excessive drivetrain wear and damage. If not familiar with the operation and repair of the front and rear final drive assemblies, refer troubleshooting to a qualified Honda dealership.

Oil Inspection

Drain the gearcase oil (Chapter Three) into a clean container. Rub the drained oil between two fingers and check for the presence of metallic particles. Also check the drain bolt for metal particles. While a small amount of particles in the oil is normal, an abnormal amount of debris is an indication of bearing or gear damage.

Front Differential Troubleshooting

Consistent noise while cruising

1. Low oil level.
2. Gear oil contamination.
3. Chipped or damaged gear teeth.
4. Worn or damaged ring gear bearing.
5. Worn or damaged ring gear.
6. Worn pinion gear or shaft side washers.
7. Worn or damaged ring gear and drive pinion.
8. Incorrect ring gear and drive pinion tooth contact.

Consistent gear noises during coasting

1. Damaged or chipped gears.
2. Gear oil contamination.
3. Incorrect ring gear and drive pinion tooth contact.

Gear noise during normal operation

1. Low oil level.
2. Gear oil contamination.
3. Chipped or damaged gear teeth.
4. Incorrect ring gear and drive pinion tooth contact.

Overheating

1. Low oil level.
2. Insufficient ring gear and drive pinion gear backlash.

Oil leak

1. Oil level too high.
2. Plugged breathe hole or tube.
3. Damaged oil seal(s).
4. Loose cover mounting bolts.
5. Housing damage.

Abnormal noises during starting or acceleration

1. Worn or damaged cone spring or shim.
2. Excessive pinion gear backlash.
3. Worn differential splines.
4. Excessive ring gear and drive pinion backlash.
5. Loose fasteners.

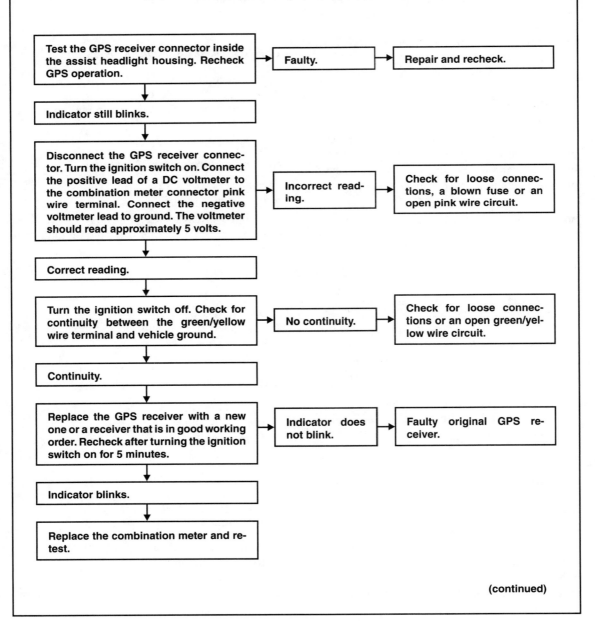

③① **GPS TROUBLESHOOTING CHART**

NOTE:
Before replacing the GPS receiver or combination meter, take the vehicle to a Honda dealership or other qualified repair shop for further testing. Most parts suppliers do not accept the return of electrical components. Confirm that the GPS is faulty before purchasing a replacement.

GPS INDICATOR BLINKS (COMMUNICATION ERROR)

Test the GPS receiver connector inside the assist headlight housing. Recheck GPS operation. → Faulty. → Repair and recheck.

Indicator still blinks.

Disconnect the GPS receiver connector. Turn the ignition switch on. Connect the positive lead of a DC voltmeter to the combination meter connector pink wire terminal. Connect the negative voltmeter lead to ground. The voltmeter should read approximately 5 volts. → Incorrect reading. → Check for loose connections, a blown fuse or an open pink wire circuit.

Correct reading.

Turn the ignition switch off. Check for continuity between the green/yellow wire terminal and vehicle ground. → No continuity. → Check for loose connections or an open green/yellow wire circuit.

Continuity.

Replace the GPS receiver with a new one or a receiver that is in good working order. Recheck after turning the ignition switch on for 5 minutes. → Indicator does not blink. → Faulty original GPS receiver.

Indicator blinks.

Replace the combination meter and re-test.

(continued)

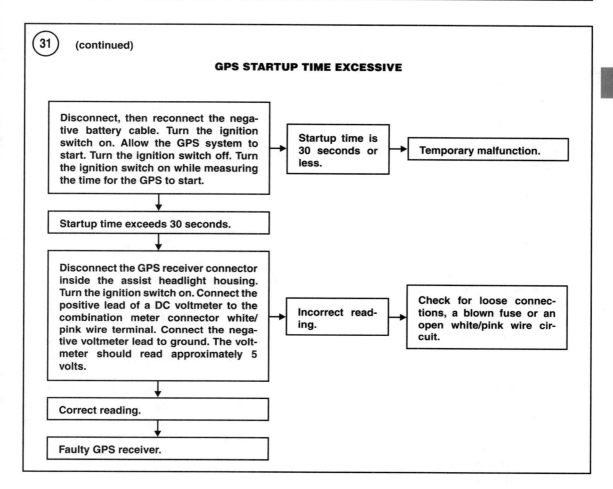

Abnormal noises when turning

1. Worn or damaged cone spring or shim.
2. Damaged driveshaft splines.
3. Worn or damaged cams or face cams.
4. Worn or damaged ring gear bearing.

Rear Differential Troubleshooting

Excessive noise

1. Low oil level.
2. Excessive ring gear and pinion gear backlash.
3. Worn or damaged drive pinion and splines.
4. Damaged driven flange and wheel hub.
5. Worn or damaged driven flange and ring gear shaft.

HANDLING

Poor handling reduces overall performance and may cause loss of control and a crash. If poor handling occurs, check the following items:

1. If the handlebars are difficult to turn, check for the following:
   a. Low tire pressure.
   b. Incorrect throttle cable routing.
   c. Damaged steering shaft bushing and/or bearing.
   d. Bent steering shaft or frame.
   e. Steering shaft nut too tight.

2. If there is excessive handlebar shake or vibration, check for the following:
   a. Loose or damaged handlebar clamps.
   b. Incorrect handlebar clamp installation.
   c. Bent or cracked handlebar.
   d. Worn wheel bearing(s).
   e. Excessively worn or damaged tire(s).

f. Damaged rim(s).

g. Loose, missing or broken engine mount bolts and mounts.

h. Cracked frame, especially at the steering head.

i. Incorrect tire pressure.

j. Damaged shock absorber damper rod.

k. Leaking shock absorber damper housing.

l. Sagged shock spring(s).

m. Loose or damaged shock mount bolts.

3. If the rear suspension is too soft, check for the following:

a. Rear tire pressure too low.

b. Damaged shock absorber damper rod.

c. Leaking shock absorber damper housing.

d. Sagged shock spring.

e. Loose or damaged shock mount bolts.

4. If the rear suspension is too hard, check for the following:

a. Rear tire pressure too high.

b. Incorrect shock absorber adjustment.

c. Damaged shock absorber damper rod.

d. Leaking shock absorber damper housing.

e. Sagged shock spring.

f. Loose or damaged shock mount bolts.

5. Frame—check the following:

a. Damaged frame.

b. Cracked or broken engine mount brackets.

6. Wobbling wheel:

a. Loose wheel nuts.

b. Loose or incorrectly installed wheel hub.

c. Excessive wheel bearing play.

d. Loose wheel bearing.

e. Bent wheel rim.

f. Bent frame or other suspension component.

7. If ATV pulls to one side:

a. Incorrect tire pressure.

b. Incorrect tie rod adjustment.

c. Bent or loose tie rod.

d. Incorrect wheel alignment.

e. Bent frame or other suspension component.

FRAME NOISE

Noises traced to the frame or suspension are usually caused by loose, worn or damaged parts. Various noises are related to the frame are listed below:

1. Drum brake noise—A screeching sound during braking is the most common drum brake noise.

Some other drum brake associated noises can be caused by:

a. Glazed brake lining or drum surface.

b. Excessively worn brake linings or drums.

c. Warped brake drum.

2. Front or rear shock absorber noise—Check for the following:

a. Loose shock absorber mounting bolts.

b. Cracked or broken shock spring.

c. Damaged shock absorber.

3. Some other frame associated noises can be caused by:

a. Cracked or broken frame.

b. Broken swing arm or shock linkage.

c. Loose engine mounting bolts.

d. Damaged steering shaft bearings.

e. Loose mounting bracket.

BRAKES

The front and rear brakes are critical to riding performance and safety. Inspect the brakes frequently and repair any problem immediately. When replacing or refilling the front brake fluid, use only DOT 3 or DOT 4 brake fluid from a sealed container. Refer to Chapter Thirteen for additional information on brake fluid selection and drum brake service.

Front Drum Brake Troubleshooting

If the front drum brakes are not working properly, check for one or more of the following conditions:

1. Incorrect front brake adjustment.

2. Air in brake line.

3. Brake fluid level too low.

4. Loose brake hose banjo bolts. Brake fluid is leaking out.

5. Loose or damaged brake hose or line.

6. Worn or damaged brake drum.

7. Worn or damaged brake linings.

8. Oil on brake drum or brake lining surfaces.

9. Worn or damaged wheel cylinder(s).

10. Weak or damaged brake return springs.

Rear Drum Brake Troubleshooting

If the rear drum brake is not working properly, check for one or more of the following conditions:

1. Incorrect rear brake adjustment.

2. Incorrect brake cam lever position.

3. Worn or damaged brake drum.
4. Worn or damaged brake linings.
5. Oil on the brake drum or brake lining surfaces.
6. Worn or damaged wheel cylinder(s).
7. Weak or damaged brake return springs.

Water Entering the Front Brake Drum(s)

1. Damaged waterproof seal.
2. Incorrectly installed waterproof seal.

3. Loose or unsealed wheel cylinder assembly.
4. Damaged hub O-ring.
5. Loose front axle nut.
6. Damaged brake panel O-ring.
7. Damaged wheel hub dust seal.
8. Damaged brake drum dust seal.
9. Damaged brake drum.
10. Damaged steering knuckle axle seal.
11. Loose brake panel mounting bolt(s).
12. Incorrect breather tube routing.

Table 1 TRANSMISSION TROUBLE CODES

No. of Trouble Indicator Blinks	Faulty System	Probable Faulty Component
1	Ignition pulse generator system	Ignition pulse generator, related wiring or ECM
2	Vehicle speed sensor system	Vehicle speed sensor, related wiring or ECM
3	Gear position switch system	Gear position switch, related wiring or ECM
4	Throttle position switch system	Throttle position switch, related wiring or ECM
5	Angle sensor system (Motor lock)	Angle sensor or related wiring, ECM, shift control motor, motor transmission section, automatic transmission
6	Angle sensor system (Automatic Transmission Swashplate Angle)	Angle sensor, related wiring or ECM
7	Electric shift switch system (up and down)	Shift switch or related wire harness or ECM
8	ECM EPROM (writing/readout circuit)	ECM
9	ECM malfunction voltage convert circuit	ECM
10	ECM malfunction fail-safe circuit	ECM
11	ECM motor driver circuit	ECM
12	ECM malfunction CPU	ECM

CHAPTER THREE

LUBRICATION, MAINTENANCE AND TUNE-UP

This chapter explains lubrication, maintenance and tune-up procedures.

Table 1 lists the recommended maintenance and lubrication schedule for all models.

Table 2 lists tire inflation specifications.

Table 3 lists tune-up specifications.

Table 4 lists battery capacity.

Table 5 lists recommended lubricants, fluids and fuel.

Table 6 lists engine oil capacity.

Table 7 lists front and rear differential oil capacity.

Table 8 lists toe-out specifications.

Table 9 lists maintenance and tune-up torque specifications.

Tables 1-9 are located at the end of this chapter.

PRE-RIDE CHECK LIST

Perform the following checks before the first ride of the day. All of these checks are described in this chapter. If a component requires service, refer to the appropriate section.

1. Inspect all fuel lines and fittings for leakage.
2. Make sure the fuel tank is full of fresh gasoline.
3. Make sure the engine oil level is correct.
4. Make sure the coolant level is correct in the coolant reservoir.
5. Check the throttle operation for proper operation in all steering positions. Open the throttle all the way and release it. The throttle should close quickly with no binding or roughness.
6. Check that the brake levers operate properly with no binding. Replace any broken lever. Check the lever housings for damage.
7. Check the brake fluid level in the front master cylinder reservoir. Add DOT 3 or DOT 4 brake fluid if necessary.
8. Check the parking brake operation and adjust if necessary.
9. Inspect the front and rear suspension. Make sure they have a good solid feel. Turn the handlebar from side to side to check steering play. Service the steering assembly if excessive play is noted. Make sure the handlebar cables do not bind.
10. Check the driveshaft boots for damage.
11. Check the front and rear differential oil level. Top off if necessary.
12. Check tire pressure (**Table 2**).
13. Check the exhaust system for looseness or damage.
14. Check for missing or damaged skid plates.

4 mm
(0.16 in.)

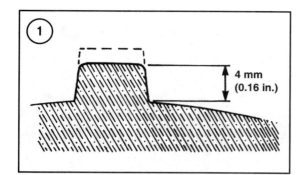

15. Check the tightness of all fasteners, especially engine, steering and suspension mounting hardware.

16. Make sure the headlights and taillight work.

17. Check that all switches work properly.

18. Check the air filter drain tube for contamination.

19. If carrying cargo, check that it is properly secured.

20. Start the engine, then stop it with the engine stop switch. If the engine stop switch does not work properly, test the switch as described in the *Switches* section in Chapter Nine.

MAINTENANCE SCHEDULE

Table 1 provides the maintenance schedule for all models. Strict adherence to these recommendations helps ensure long ATV service. Perform the services more often when operating the ATV commercially and in dusty or other harsh conditions.

Most of the services shown in **Table 1** are described in this chapter. However, some procedures that require more than minor disassembly or adjustment are covered in the appropriate chapter and are so indicated.

TIRES AND WHEELS

Tire Pressure

Check and adjust tire pressure (**Table 2**) to maintain the smoothness of the tire, good traction and handling and to get the maximum life from the tire. Check tire pressure when the tires are cold.

> *WARNING*
> *Always inflate both tire sets (front and rear) to the correct air pressure. If the ATV is run with unequal air pressures, the ATV may run toward one side, causing poor handling.*

> *CAUTION*
> *Do not overinflate the tires because they can be permanently distorted and damaged.*

Tire Inspection

The tires take a lot of punishment due to the variety of terrain they are subjected to. Inspect them daily for excessive wear, cuts, abrasions or punctures. If a nail or other object is found in the tire, mark its location with a light crayon before removing it. Service the tire as described in Chapter Ten.

To gauge tire wear, inspect the height of the tread knobs. If the average tread knob height measures 4 mm (0.16 in.) or less (**Figure 1**), replace the tire as described in Chapter Ten.

> *WARNING*
> *Do not ride the ATV with damaged or excessively worn tires. Tires in these conditions can cause loss of control. Replace damaged or excessively worn tires immediately.*

Rim Inspection

Inspect the wheel rims for damage. Rim damage may cause an air leak or knock it out of alignment. Improper wheel alignment can cause vibration and an unsafe riding condition.

Make sure the wheel nuts (**Figure 2**) are tightened securely on each wheel. Tighten the wheel nuts in a crossing pattern to 64 N•m (47 ft.-lb.).

BATTERY

Many electrical system troubles can be traced to battery neglect. Inspect and clean the battery at periodic intervals.

Battery Application

A maintenance-free battery is used on all models. This battery is sealed at the time of service and does not require additional water. Do not remove the sealing caps to add electrolyte or water or the battery may be damaged.

NOTE
*Because a maintenance-free battery requires a higher voltage charging system, do not replace a maintenance-free battery with a standard battery. Always replace the battery with its correct type and designated capacity. Refer to the battery capacity specifications in **Table 4** when purchasing a new battery.*

Safety Precautions

When working with batteries, use extreme care to avoid spilling or splashing the electrolyte. This solution contains sulfuric acid, which can ruin clothing and cause serious chemical burns. If the electrolyte is spilled or splashed on clothing or skin, immediately neutralize the affected area with a solution of baking soda and water. Then flush the area with an abundance of clean water. While the TRX500 uses a sealed battery, it vents gasses and electrolyte can leak through cracks in the battery case.

WARNING
Battery electrolyte is extremely harmful when splashed into eyes or onto an open sore. Always wear safety glasses and appropriate work clothes when working with batteries. If the electrolyte gets into someone's eyes, flush them thoroughly with clean water and get prompt medical attention.

When charging a battery, highly explosive hydrogen gas forms in each cell. Some of this gas escapes through filler cap openings and can form an explosive atmosphere in and around the battery. This con-

dition can persist for several hours. Sparks, an open flame or a lighted cigarette can ignite the gas, causing an internal battery explosion and possible serious injury.

When servicing the battery, note the following precautions to prevent an explosion or injury:
1. Do not smoke or permit any open flame near any battery being charged or near a recently charged battery.
2. Do not disconnect live circuits at battery terminals because a spark usually occurs when a live circuit is broken.
3. Use caution when connecting or disconnecting any battery charger. Make sure its power switch is off before making or breaking connections. Poor connections are a common cause of electrical arcs that cause explosions.
4. Keep all children and pets away from charging equipment and batteries.
5. Do not try to open the maintenance-free battery.

Battery Removal/Installation

On all models covered in this manual, the negative terminal of the battery is grounded. When removing

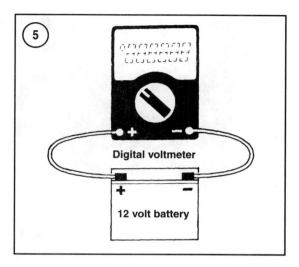

Digital voltmeter

12 volt battery

3

the battery, disconnect the negative cable first, then the positive cable. This sequence reduces the chance of a tool shorting to ground when disconnecting the *hot* positive cable.

WARNING
When performing the following procedures, protect eyes, skin and clothing. If electrolyte gets into someone's eyes, flush the eyes thoroughly with clean water and get prompt medical attention.

1. Read the information listed in the *Service Precautions* in this section, then continue with Step 2.
2. Make sure the ignition switch is turned off.
3. Remove the seat (Chapter Fifteen).
4. Remove the lid over the electrical compartment cover (**Figure 3**).
5. Disconnect the negative battery cable (A, **Figure 4**) from the battery.
6. Push back the red terminal cover (B, **Figure 4**), then disconnect the positive battery cable from the battery.
7. Detach the rubber battery strap (C, **Figure 4**), then remove the battery (D).
8. Service the battery as described in this section.

NOTE
If detached, connect the lower end of the battery retaining strap before installing the battery.

9. Install the battery into the battery box with the terminals facing in the direction shown in **Figure 4**.

10. Attach the battery retaining strap.
11. Coat the battery terminals with a thin layer of dielectric grease. This helps retard corrosion and decomposition of the terminals.
12. Attach the positive battery cable to the battery, then place the red terminal cover over the positive terminal (B, **Figure 4**).
13. Attach the negative battery cable (A, **Figure 4**) to the battery.
14. Install the lid (**Figure 3**).
15. Install the seat (Chapter Fifteen).

Inspection

For a preliminary test, connect a digital voltmeter to the battery negative and positive terminals and measure battery voltage (**Figure 5**). A fully charged battery reads between 13.0-13.2 volts. If the voltmeter reads 12.3 volts or less, the battery is under charged. If necessary, charge the battery as described in this chapter.

Battery Testing

A bench type battery tester can be used to accurately test the maintenance-free battery. When using a battery tester, follow the manufacturer's instructions and test results. For best results, make sure the tester's cables are in working order and clamp tightly onto the battery terminals.

NOTE
A battery tester suitable for testing motorcycle batteries can be ordered through a dealership from K&L Supply Co. in Santa Clara, California.

Charging

Always follow the manufacturer's instructions when using a battery charger.

CAUTION
Never connect a battery charger to the battery with the battery leads still connected. Always remove the battery from the ATV before charging it.

1. Remove the battery as described in this section.

2. Connect the positive charger lead to the positive battery terminal and the negative charger lead to the negative battery terminal.

> *CAUTION*
> *Do not exceed the recommended charging amperage rate or charging time on the label attached to the battery (**Figure 6**). The high current forced into the battery overheats the battery and damages the battery plates.*

3. Set the charger to 12 volts. If the charger output is variable, select a low setting. Use the following suggested charging amperage and length of charging time:

   a. Standard charge: 1.4 amps at 5 to 10 hours.

   b. Quick charge: 6.0 amps at 1 hour.

4. Turn the charger on.

5. After charging the battery at the rate specified on the battery, turn off the charger and disconnect the charger leads.

6. Connect a digital voltmeter to the battery terminals (**Figure 5**) and measure battery voltage. A fully charged battery reads 13.0-13.2 volts.

7. If the battery voltage remains stable for 1 hour, the battery is charged.

8. Clean the battery cable connectors, battery terminals and case. Coat the terminals with a thin layer of dielectric grease. This helps to retard corrosion and decomposition of the battery terminals.

9. Reinstall the battery as described in this chapter.

Battery Cables

To ensure good electrical contact between the battery and the electrical cables, keep the cables clean and free of corrosion.

1. If the electrical cable terminals are badly corroded, disconnect them from the battery as described in *Battery Removal/Installation* in this section.

2. Thoroughly clean each connector with a wire brush and then with a water and baking soda solution. Wipe dry with a clean cloth.

3. After cleaning, apply a thin layer of dielectric grease to the battery terminals before reattaching the cables.

4. If disconnected, reconnect the battery cables as described in *Battery Removal/Installation* in this chapter.

5. Coat the terminals with a thin layer of dielectric grease. This helps retard corrosion and decomposition of the battery terminals.

Replacement

Always replace the sealed battery with another sealed-type battery. The ATV charging system is designed to operate with this type of battery in the system.

Before installing a new battery, make sure it is fully charged. Failure to do so prevents the battery from ever obtaining a complete charge.

> *NOTE*
> *Recycle the old battery. The lead plates and the plastic case can be recycled. Most motorcycle dealers accept an old battery in trade after the purchase of a new one. Never place an old battery in household trash because it is illegal in most states to place any acid or lead (heavy metal) contents in landfills.*

PERIODIC LUBRICATION

Refer to **Table 1** for lubrication service intervals.

Engine Oil and Filter

Recommended engine oil

Honda recommends the use of Honda GN4 4-stroke oil or an equivalent 10W-40 engine oil with an API service classification of SG or higher. Try to use the same brand of oil at each oil change. Do not use oils with graphite or molybdenum additives because these can cause clutch slippage and other

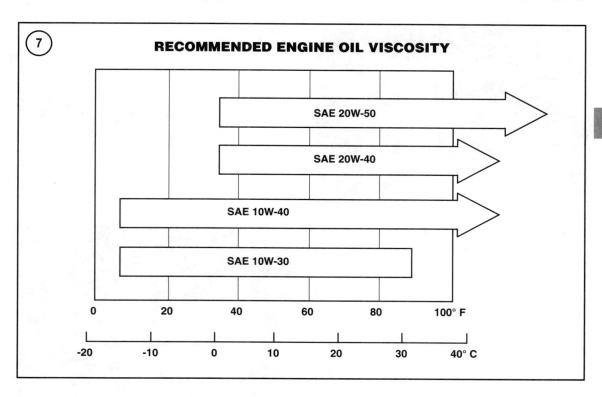

RECOMMENDED ENGINE OIL VISCOSITY

⑦

SAE 20W-50

SAE 20W-40

SAE 10W-40

SAE 10W-30

| 0 | 20 | 40 | 60 | 80 | 100° F |

| -20 | -10 | 0 | 10 | 20 | 30 | 40° C |

3

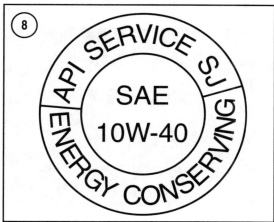

⑧ API SERVICE SJ
SAE 10W-40
ENERGY CONSERVING

clutch related problems. Refer to **Figure 7** for the correct oil weight recommended to use in anticipated ambient temperatures (not engine oil temperature).

NOTE
*Do not use oils labeled **Energy Conserving** in the service designation circles on the oil container (**Figure 8**). Energy conserving oils contain additives which may harm motorcycle clutch components.*

Engine oil level check

Check the engine oil level with the dipstick cap mounted on the right side of the engine.

1. Park the ATV on level ground and set the parking brake.

NOTE
Due to the large quantity of oil contained in the engine and oil tank and the dry sump design, the engine must be run for the period specified to be sure the oil in the oil tank reaches its normal operating level.

2. Start the engine. If the engine is at normal operating temperature, let it run 5 minutes. If the engine is cold, run the engine for 10 minutes.

3. Shut off the engine and let the oil drain into the crankcase for a few minutes.

4. Unscrew and remove the dipstick cap (A, **Figure 9**) and wipe the dipstick clean. Reinsert it onto the threads in the hole; do not screw it in. Remove the dipstick and check the oil level.

5. The level is correct when it is between the two dipstick lines (**Figure 10**).

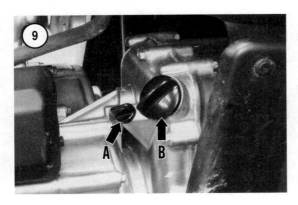

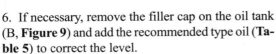

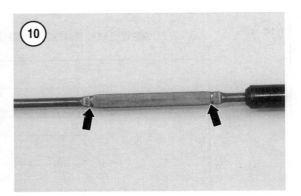

6. If necessary, remove the filler cap on the oil tank
(B, **Figure 9**) and add the recommended type oil (**Table 5**) to correct the level.

7. Replace the dipstick O-ring if damaged.

8. Install the dipstick and/or oil fill cap (**Figure 9**)
and tighten it securely.

Engine oil and filter change

Table 1 lists the recommended oil and filter
change intervals. This assumes the ATV operates in
moderate climates. If it operates in dusty conditions,
the oil gets dirty more quickly and requires more frequent oil changes.

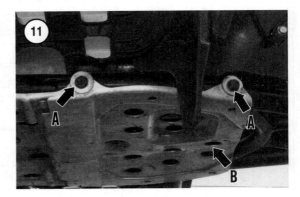

NOTE
*The TRX500 contains significantly
more oil than the usual ATV or motorcycle. Make sure the drain pan holds
the drained oil.*

NOTE
*Some service stations and oil retailers
accept used oil for recycling. Do not
discard oil in household trash or pour
it onto the ground. Never add brake
fluid or any other type of petro-
leum-based fluid to any engine oil to
be recycled. Most oil retailers may not
accept the oil if it is combined with
other fluids.*

NOTE
*Running the engine heats the oil,
which enables the oil to flow more
freely and carry contaminates and
sludge out with it when drained.*

1. Park the ATV on level ground and apply the parking brake.

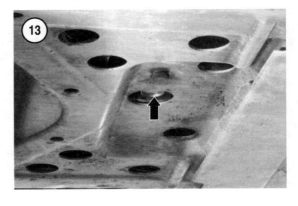

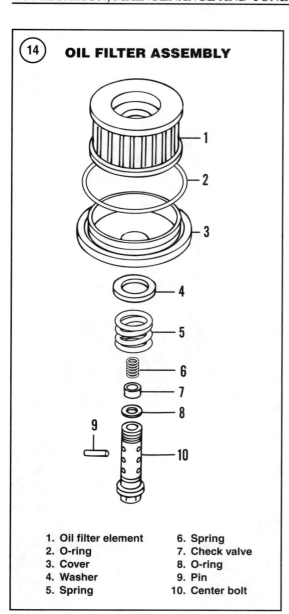

OIL FILTER ASSEMBLY
(14)

1. Oil filter element
2. O-ring
3. Cover
4. Washer
5. Spring
6. Spring
7. Check valve
8. O-ring
9. Pin
10. Center bolt

(15)

(16)

2. Start the engine and let it warm to normal operating temperature. Shut the engine off.

3. Remove the front skid plate bolts on each side (A, **Figure 11**), then remove the skid plate (B).

4. Place a clean drain pan underneath the engine.

> *NOTE*
> *Both the engine and oil tank must be drained, otherwise dirty oil remains in undrained oil compartments.*

5. Remove the drain plug (A, **Figure 12**) located in the bottom of the oil tank and allow the oil to drain.

6. Remove the drain plug (**Figure 13**) located in the bottom of the engine and allow the oil to drain.

7. Allow the oil to drain completely.

8. To replace the oil filter, perform the following:

   a. Remove the engine oil filter cover center bolt (B, **Figure 12**), then remove the filter assembly (**Figure 14**).

   b. Remove and discard the oil filter.

> *NOTE*
> *A pressure relief valve resides inside the center bolt (**Figure 15**). Service is not required except to replace damaged components. Refer to **Figure 14**.*

   c. Clean the spring, filter cover and center bolt in solvent and dry thoroughly.

   d. Replace any cracked or damaged O-rings.

   e. Lubricate each O-ring with engine oil.

   f. Install the center bolt into the filter cover (**Figure 16**).

   g. Install the spring (A, **Figure 17**) and washer (B).

   h. Install the new oil filter (C, **Figure 17**).

   i. Install the oil filter assembly and tighten the center bolt to 18 N•m (159 in.-lb.).

3

9. Replace the drain plug washer if damaged or if it was leaking.

10. Install the drain plugs and tighten to 25 N•m (18 ft.-lb.).

11. Fill the engine with the correct weight and quantity oil; refer to *Recommended Engine Oil* in this section. Refer to **Table 7** for engine oil capacity.

NOTE
*Honda lists three different engine oil capacities (**Table 7**), each specified for the type of service being performed. Make sure to install the correct oil capacity.*

12. Start the engine and run at idle speed.

13. Turn the engine off and check the drain bolts and oil filter cover for leaks.

14. Install the front skid plate.

15. Check the oil level and adjust if necessary.

WARNING
Prolonged contact with used oil may cause skin cancer. Wash your hands with soap and water after handling or coming in contact with motor oil.

Oil screen

Two oil screens are used. One is located inside the engine (**Figure 18**) and one is located inside the oil tank. Disassembly is required to service the oil screens; servicing them is not part of the engine periodic maintenance schedule. However, service the oil screens when troubleshooting a lubrication system problem or when internal engine damage occurs.

Front Differential Gearcase

Recommended gearcase oil

Honda recommends Honda shaft drive oil or an equivalent SAE 80 hypoid gear oil (**Table 5**).

Oil level check

1. Park the ATV on a level surface and set the parking brake.

2. Wipe clean the area around the oil fill cap and unscrew the oil fill plug (**Figure 19**).

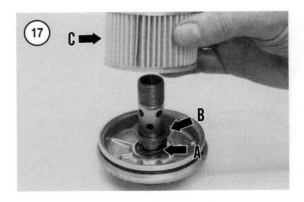

3. The oil level should be level with the bottom thread of the fill plug hole. If the oil level is low, add hypoid gear oil (**Table 5**) until the level is correct.

4. Inspect the oil fill plug O-ring and replace if damaged.

5. Install the oil fill cap and tighten as specified in **Table 9**.

Oil change

The recommended oil change interval is listed in **Table 1**.

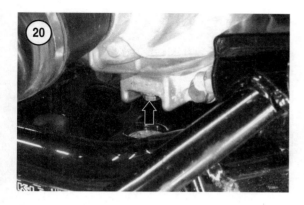

NOTE
A short ride heats the front differential gearcase oil, which enables the oil to flow more freely and carry more contaminates and sludge when drained.

1. Ride the ATV until normal operating temperature is reached, then park the ATV on a level surface and set the parking brake. Turn the engine off.

NOTE
Skid plate removal is not necessary for access to drain plug.

2. Place a drain pan underneath the drain plug (**Figure 20**).

3. Remove the oil fill plug (**Figure 19**).

4. Remove the drain plug (**Figure 20**) and allow the oil to drain.

5. Replace the drain plug gasket if leaking or damaged.

6. Install the drain plug and gasket and tighten to 12 N•m (106 in.-lb.).

7. Insert a funnel into the oil fill plug hole and pour in the recommended type (**Table 5**) and quantity (**Table 7**) of gear oil.

8. Remove the funnel and check the oil level. It should come up to the bottom thread of the fill plug hole. Add additional oil if necessary.

9. Inspect the oil fill plug O-ring and replace if damaged.

10. Install the oil fill plug (**Figure 19**) and tighten to 12 N•m (106 in.-lb.).

11. Test ride the ATV and check for leaks. After the test ride recheck the oil level and adjust if necessary.

12. Discard old oil in the same manner as outlined in *Engine Oil and Filter Change* in this chapter.

Rear Differential Gearcase

Recommended gearcase oil

Honda recommends Honda shaft drive oil or an equivalent SAE 80 hypoid gear oil (**Table 5**).

Oil level check

1. Park the ATV on a level surface and set the parking brake.

2. Wipe the area around the oil check plug (**Figure 21**) and remove it. Oil should immediately start to flow out of the check hole. If oil flows out of the hole, the oil level is correct. Reinstall the oil check plug and tighten to 12 N•m (106 in.-lb.). If oil did not flow out of the hole, continue with Step 3.

3. Remove the oil fill cap (**Figure 22**) and slowly add hypoid gear oil (**Table 5**) until oil starts to flow out of the check hole. Reinstall the oil check plug and tighten to 12 N•m (106 ft.-lb.).

4. Install the oil fill cap (**Figure 22**) and tighten to 12 N•m (106 in.-lb.).

Oil change

The recommended oil change interval is listed in **Table 1**.

> *NOTE*
> *A short ride heats the rear gearcase oil, which enables the oil to flow more freely and carry more contaminates and sludge out when drained.*

1. Ride the ATV until normal operating temperature is reached, then park the ATV on a level surface and set the parking brake. Turn the engine off.

2. Place a drain pan underneath the drain plug (**Figure 23**). Unscrew the drain plug and remove it. Allow the oil to drain out.

3. Wipe clean the area around the oil fill cap and unscrew the oil fill cap (**Figure 22**).

4. Inspect the drain plug washer and replace if leaking or damaged.

5. When the oil stops draining, install the drain plug and gasket and tighten to 12 N•m (106 in.-lb.).

6. Insert a funnel into the oil fill cap hole and add the recommended type (**Table 5**) and quantity (**Table 7**) gear oil.

7. Inspect the oil fill cap O-ring and replace if damaged.

8. Install the oil fill cap (**Figure 22**) and tighten to 12 N•m (106 in.-lb.).

9. Test ride the ATV and check for leaks.

10. Discard old oil in the same manner as outlined in *Engine Oil and Filter Change* in this chapter.

Control Cable Lubrication

Clean and lubricate the throttle, brake, choke and reverse cables at the intervals indicated in **Table 1**. In addition, check the cables for kinks, excessive wear, damage or fraying that could cause the cables to fail or stick. Cables are expendable items even under the best conditions.

1. Disconnect the cable to be lubricated. Note the following:
   a. To service the throttle cable, refer to *Throttle Housing and Cable* in Chapter Eight.
   b. To service the brake cables, refer to *Rear Brake Pedal and Cable* and *Rear Brake Lever/Parking Brake Cable* in Chapter Fourteen.
   c. To service the choke cable, refer to *Choke Cable Replacement* in Chapter Eight.

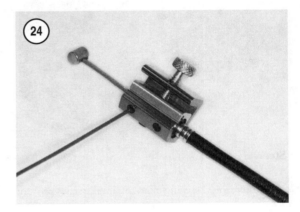

2. Attach a cable lubricator to the end of the cable following the manufacturer's instructions (**Figure 24**).

3. Inject cable lubricant into the cable until it begins to flow out of the other end of the cable. Do not use chain lube as a cable lubricant.

> *NOTE*
> *Place a shop cloth at the end of the cable to catch the oil as it runs out.*

4. Disconnect the lubricator.

5. Apply a light coat of grease to the cable ends before reconnecting them. Reconnect the cable and adjust as described in this chapter.

6. Reverse Step 1 to reconnect the cables.

7. After lubricating the throttle cable, operate the throttle lever at the handlebar. It should open and close smoothly with no binding.

8. After lubricating the brake cable(s), check brake operation.

UNSCHEDULED LUBRICATION

The services listed in this section are not included in **Table 1** (maintenance and lubrication schedule). However, lubricate these items throughout the service year. Lubrication and service intervals depend on ATV use. Use a water-resistant grease when grease is specified in the following sections.

Steering Shaft Lubrication

Remove the steering shaft (Chapter Eleven) and lubricate the bushing with grease. At the same time, check the lower bearing and seals for damage.

Front Upper and Lower Arm Lubrication

Remove the upper and lower arm pivot bolts and lubricate the bolts and bushings with grease. Refer to Chapter Eleven for service.

Front Wheel Bearing Seals

Lubricate the front wheel bearing seals with grease. If the front wheel bearings are not sealed, lubricate them. Refer to Chapter Eleven for service.

Rear Shock Absorber Mounting Bolt Lubrication

Remove the front (Chapter Eleven) and rear (Chapter Thirteen) shock absorbers and lubricate the mounting bolts with grease.

PERIODIC MAINTENANCE

Periodic maintenance intervals are listed in **Table 1**.

Air Box Drain Tube

Inspect the drain tube (**Figure 25**) mounted on the bottom of the air box. If the hose is filled with water, dirt and other debris, clean and reoil the air filter. Clean the air box and drain the drain tube at the same time.

Air Filter

A clogged air filter decreases the efficiency and life of the engine. Never run the engine without an air filter properly installed. Dust that enters the engine can cause engine wear and clog carburetor jets and passages.

Refer to **Figure 26**.

Removal and installation

1. Remove the seat (Chapter Fifteen).
2. Release the air box cover retaining clips and remove the cover (**Figure 27**).
3. Loosen the air filter hose clamp (A, **Figure 28**) and remove the air filter assembly (B).
4. Disassemble, clean and oil the air filter as described in the following procedure.
5. Check the air box and carburetor boot for dirt or other contamination.
6. Wipe the inside of the air box with a clean rag. If more extensive cleaning is required, remove and clean the air box (Chapter Eight).
7. Cover the air box opening with a clean shop rag.
8. Inspect all fittings, hoses and connections from the air box to the carburetor.
9. Inspect the crankcase breather foam filter (A, **Figure 29**). If dirty, clean the filter using soapy water and let it dry. When installing the filter, do not push it too far into the opening.
10. Inspect the carburetor vent foam filter (B, **Figure 29**). If dirty, clean the filter using soapy water and let it dry.
11. Assemble the air filter as described under *Air Filter Cleaning and Reoiling* in this section.
12. Install the air filter into the air box (**Figure 28**). Tighten the air filter hose clamp (A, **Figure 28**) securely.

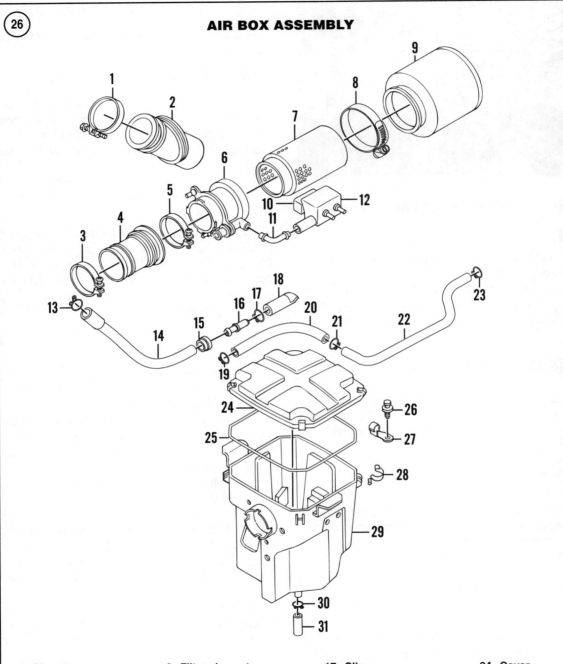

AIR BOX ASSEMBLY

1. Clamp
2. Air intake duct tube
3. Clamp
4. Intake hose
5. Clamp
6. Tube
7. Element core
8. Clamp
9. Filter element
10. Breather filter element
11. Tube
12. Breather joint
13. Clip
14. Vent tube
15. Grommet
16. Fitting
17. Clip
18. Vent air filter element
19. Clip
20. Crankcase breather hose
21. Clip
22. Tube
23. Clip
24. Cover
25. Gasket
26. Trim clip
27. Bracket
28. Clamp
29. Air box
30. Clip
31. Drain tube

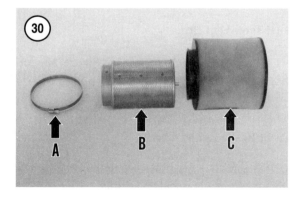

13. Install the air box cover (**Figure 27**) and secure with the retaining clips.

14. Install the seat (Chapter Fifteen).

Air filter cleaning and reoiling

Service the air filter element in a well-ventilated area, away from all sparks and flames.

1. Remove the hose clamp (A, **Figure 30**), then remove the element core (B) from the filter element (C).

> *WARNING*
> *Do not clean the filter element with gasoline.*

2. Clean the filter element with a filter solvent to remove oil and dirt.

3. Inspect the filter element. Replace if it is torn or broken in any area.

4. Fill a clean pan with liquid detergent and warm water.

5. Submerge the filter element in the cleaning solution and gently work the cleaner into the filter pores. Soak and squeeze (gently) the filter element to clean it.

> *CAUTION*
> *Do not wring or twist the filter element when cleaning it. This could damage the filter pores or tear the filter loose at a seam. This would allow unfiltered air to enter the engine and cause rapid wear.*

6. Rinse the filter element under warm water while soaking and gently squeezing it.

7. Repeat Step 6 and Step 7 until there is no dirt being rinsed from the filter element.

8. After cleaning the element, inspect it again carefully. If it is torn or broken in any area, replace it. Do not run the engine with a damaged filter element.

9. Set the filter element aside and allow to dry thoroughly.

10. Clean and dry the element core. Check the element core for damage and replace if necessary.

> *CAUTION*
> *Make sure the filter element is completely dry before oiling it.*

11. Properly oiling an air filter element is a messy but important job. Wear a pair of disposable rubber

gloves when performing this procedure. Oil the filter as follows:

    a. Purchase a box of gallon size storage bags. The bags can be used when cleaning the filter as well as for storing engine and carburetor parts during disassembly service procedures.

    b. Place the filter element into a storage bag.

    c. Pour foam filter oil onto the filter to soak it.

    d. Gently squeeze and release the filter to soak filter oil into the filter's pores. Repeat until all the filter's pores are saturated with oil.

    e. Remove the filter element from the bag and check the pores for uneven oiling. This is indicated by light or dark areas on the filter element. If necessary, soak the filter element and squeeze it again.

    f. When the filter oiling is even, squeeze the filter element a final time.

    g. Pour the leftover filter oil from the bag back into the bottle for reuse.

    h. Dispose of the plastic bag.

12. Install the filter element onto the element core. Install the clamp (A, **Figure 30**).

13. Install the filter assembly as described in this chapter.

Fuel Line Inspection

> *WARNING*
> *Some fuel may spill when performing the procedure in this section. Because gasoline is extremely flammable, perform the following procedure away from all open flames (including appliance pilot lights) and sparks. Do not smoke or allow someone who is smoking in the work area. Always work in a well-ventilated area. Wipe up any spills immediately.*

Inspect the fuel line (**Figure 31**) for leaks, cracks, hardness, age deterioration or other damage. Make sure each end of the hose is secured with a hose clamp. Check the carburetor overflow and vent hose ends for contamination.

> *WARNING*
> *A damaged or deteriorated fuel line presents a dangerous fire hazard to both the rider and machine.*

Fuel Tank Vent Hose

Check the fuel tank vent hose (**Figure 32**) for proper routing and make sure it is not kinked. Check the end of the hose for contamination.

Front Brake Lining Check

1. Remove the rubber inspection cap (**Figure 33**) from the front wheel and brake drum.

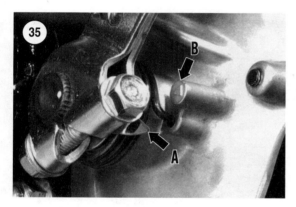

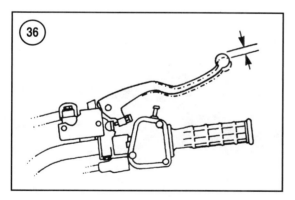

2. Move the ATV in either direction until the inspection hole aligns with one of the brake linings.

NOTE
Figure 34 shows a brake shoe with the brake drum removed for clarity. It is not necessary to remove the brake drum for this procedure.

3. Measure the lining thickness (**Figure 34**). The standard lining thickness is 4.0 mm (0.16 in.). The service limit is 1.0 mm (0.04 in.). If the lining thick-

ness appears thin or excessively worn, remove the brake drum (Chapter Fourteen) to inspect and measure the lining thickness.
4. Repeat Step 3 for the other three front brake linings.
5. Install the rubber inspection cap (**Figure 33**).

Rear Brake Lining Check

Apply the rear brake fully. If the indicator plate (A, **Figure 35**) aligns with the fixed index mark on the brake panel (B), replace both rear brake shoes (Chapter Fourteen).

Front Brake Adjustment

1. Perform the *Front Brake Lining Check* in this section. If the brake lining thickness is within specifications, continue with Step 2.
2. Apply the front brake lever and measure the amount of free play travel until the front brakes start to engage (**Figure 36**). The correct front brake lever free play measurement is 25-30 mm (1-1 1/4 in.). If the brake linings contact the brake drum too early or too late, continue with Step 3 to adjust the front brakes.

NOTE
Contamination inside the brake drum can cause the brakes to engage too soon. If inspection reveals dirt or other debris inside the drum, remove the brake drum and inspect the drum surface and brake linings as described in Chapter Fourteen.

3. Support the ATV with the front wheels off the ground.
4. Remove the rubber plug (**Figure 33**) from one of the brake drums.
5. Turn the wheel to align the hole with one of the brake adjusters (**Figure 37**).

NOTE
Each wheel is equipped with two brake adjusters. It does not matter which adjuster is adjusted first.

6. Insert a slotted screwdriver into the hole (**Figure 38**) and rotate the adjuster in the direction of the arrow cast on the wheel cylinder (**Figure 37**) until the drum is locked and can no longer move. From this position, rotate the adjuster in the opposite direction

three clicks. Apply the front brake lever several times.

7. Rotate the wheel and check that the brake is not dragging on the drum.

> *NOTE*
> *A buildup of rust and dirt in the brake drum can cause the brake linings to drag.*

8. Turn the wheel to align the hole with the other brake adjuster and repeat Step 6 and Step 7.

9. Repeat Steps 4-8 for the opposite front wheel.

10. After adjusting the brakes on both front wheels, recheck the brake lever free play (Step 2). It should be within specification.

> *NOTE*
> *If the free play is excessive after adjusting the brakes, there is probably air in the brake line. Bleed the front brakes, (Chapter Fourteen) then recheck the brake lever free play.*

11. Install the rubber plug (**Figure 33**) into each brake drum.

12. Install the front wheels (Chapter Eleven).

13. Lower the ATV so all four wheels are on the ground.

> *WARNING*
> *Do not ride the ATV until the brakes are working properly.*

Rear Brake Adjustment

1. Before adjusting the rear brake, check the brake pedal, brake cables and adjusters for loose or damaged connections. Replace or repair any damage before continuing with Step 2.

2. Lubricate the rear brake cables as described in this chapter.

3. Release the parking brake if it is set.

4. Perform the *Rear Brake Lining Check* in this chapter. If the brake lining thickness is within specifications, continue with Step 5.

5. Apply the rear brake lever and measure the amount of free play travel until the rear brake starts to engage (**Figure 39**). The correct rear brake lever free play is 15-20 mm (5/8-3/4 in.). Note the following:

    a. If the brake linings contact the brake drum too early or too late, perform Step 6.

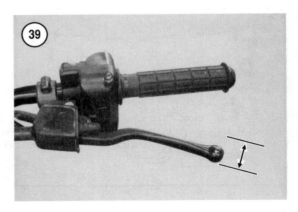

    b. If the free play travel is within specification, go to Step 7.

> *NOTE*
> *Contamination inside the brake drum can cause the brakes to apply too soon. If inspection reveals dirt or other debris inside the drum, remove the brake drum and inspect the drum surface and brake linings as described in Chapter Fourteen.*

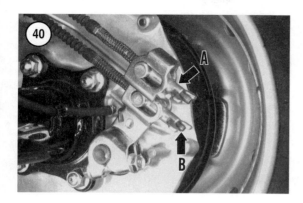

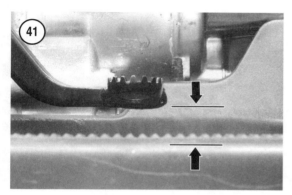

6. Turn the *upper* adjusting nut (A, **Figure 40**) in or out to achieve the correct amount of free play.

> *NOTE*
> *Make sure the cutout relief in the adjust nut is properly seated on the collar.*

7. At the brake pedal, apply the rear brake and check the pedal free play. With the pedal in the rest position, apply the brake pedal and check the distance it travels until the rear brake is applied (**Figure 41**). The correct brake pedal free play is 15-20 mm

(5/8-3/4 in.). If out of adjustment, turn the lower adjusting nut (B, **Figure 40**) in or out to achieve the correct amount of free play.

> *NOTE*
> *Make sure the cutout relief in the adjusting nut is properly seated on the collar.*

8. Support the ATV with the rear wheels off the ground.

9. Rotate the rear wheels and make sure the brake is not dragging. If the brake is dragging, repeat this procedure until there is no drag.

> *NOTE*
> *Brake drag can also be caused by dirt and other contamination in the brake drum and on the brake linings. If necessary, remove the brake drum (Chapter Fourteen) and check the brake drum and linings.*

10. Lower the ATV so all four wheels are on the ground.

Brake Fluid Level Check

1. Turn the handlebar so the master cylinder is level.
2. Check the brake fluid level through the master cylinder inspection window (A, **Figure 42**). The level should be above the *lower* level line. If necessary, add brake fluid as follows:

> *NOTE*
> *If the brake fluid is low, check the front brake lining wear as described in this chapter.*

a. Clean any dirt from the cover and master cylinder.
b. Remove the two cover screws, cover (B, **Figure 42**) and diaphragm.
c. Add new DOT 3 or DOT 4 brake fluid to raise the brake fluid level.

> *WARNING*
> *Use brake fluid clearly marked DOT 3 or 4. Others may cause brake failure. Do not intermix different brands or types of brake fluid because they may not be compatible. Do not intermix a silicone based (DOT 5) brake fluid because it can cause brake component*

damage leading to brake system fail-ure.

CAUTION
Be careful when handling brake fluid. Do not spill it on painted or plastic surfaces because it destroys the surface. Immediately wash the area with soap and water and thoroughly rinse off.

   d. Reinstall the diaphragm and cover (B, **Figure 42**). Install the screws and tighten securely.

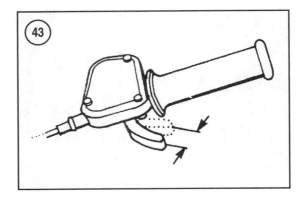

Brake Hoses

Inspect the brake hoses for cracks, cuts, bulges, deterioration and leaks. Check the metal brake lines for cracks and leaks. Refer to Chapter Fourteen for service procedures.

Throttle Cable Check and Adjustment

1. Before adjusting the throttle cable, operate the throttle lever and make sure it opens and closes properly with the handlebar turned in different positions. If not, check the throttle cable for damage or improper routing. Check the throttle lever for damage. Replace or repair any damage before continuing with Step 2.

2. Lubricate the throttle cable as described in this chapter.

3. Operate the throttle lever and measure the amount of free play travel (**Figure 43**) until the cable play is taken up and the carburetor lever starts to move. The correct throttle lever free play measurement is 3-8 mm (1/8-5/16 in.). If the free play is out of specification, continue with Step 4.

4. At the upper throttle cable adjuster on the handlebar, slide the rubber boot (A, **Figure 44**) off the adjuster and loosen the cable adjuster locknut (B). Turn the adjuster in or out until the free play is correct. Hold the adjuster and tighten the locknut securely. Recheck the throttle lever free play while noting the following:

   a. If the proper amount of free play cannot be achieved at the throttle end of the cable, continue with Step 5.

   b. If the free play measurement is correct, slide the rubber boot (A, **Figure 44**) over the adjuster, then go to Step 11.

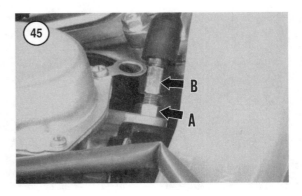

5. Loosen the upper cable adjuster locknut and loosen the adjuster (B, **Figure 44**) to obtain as much throttle cable free play as possible.

6. Remove the seat (Chapter Fifteen).

7. Slide the rubber boot off the lower cable adjuster and loosen the cable adjuster locknut (A, **Figure 45**). Turn the adjuster (B, **Figure 45**) to remove some of the cable free play, then tighten the locknut (A).

8. Repeat Step 4 to adjust the throttle lever free play. If necessary, readjust the lower (B, **Figure 45**) and upper (B, **Figure 44**) cable adjusters until the free play is correct. Then tighten both cable adjuster

10. Make sure the throttle lever moves freely from its fully closed to fully open positions and has 3-8 mm (0.12-0.32 in.) of free play.

11. Apply the parking brake.

12. Start the engine and allow it to idle in neutral. Turn the handlebar from side to side. If the engine speed increases as the handlebar is being turned, the throttle cable is routed incorrectly or there is not enough cable free play. Readjust the throttle cable, or if necessary, replace the throttle cable as described in Chapter Eight.

> *NOTE*
> *A damaged throttle cable prevents the engine from idling properly.*

Choke Cable Inspection

There is no choke cable adjustment. Inspect the choke cable as described in this procedure:

1. Operate the choke knob (**Figure 46**), checking that the lever moves smoothly and the cable is working properly.

2. If necessary, lubricate the choke cable as described in this chapter.

3. Visually inspect the choke cable for cracks or other damage. If necessary, replace the choke cable as described in Chapter Eight.

Spark Arrestor

Clean the spark arrestor at the interval indicated in **Table 1** or sooner if a considerable amount of slow riding is done.

> *WARNING*
> *Clean the muffler only when the engine is cold.*

1. Remove the bolts (**Figure 47**) securing the spark arrestor and remove the spark arrestor.

2. If necessary, lightly tap the edge of the arrestor so it can be removed from the canister.

3. Clean the screen mesh on the spark arrestor (**Figure 48**) with a soft bristle brush.

4. Install a new gasket on the spark arrestor, then bolt it back into the muffler canister.

locknuts securely. Slide the rubber boots over the cable adjusters.

> *WARNING*
> *Do not turn either adjuster so far out that the adjuster cannot be tightened securely with the locknut. This could allow the throttle to stick open and cause loss of ATV control.*

9. If the throttle cable cannot be adjusted properly, the cable has stretched excessively and must be replaced as described in Chapter Eight.

Steering Shaft and Front Suspension Inspection

Inspect the steering system and front suspension at the interval indicated in **Table 1**. If any of the following mentioned front suspension and steering fasteners are loose, refer to Chapter Eleven for the correct service procedures and tightening torques.

1. Park the ATV on level ground and set the parking brake.

2. Visually inspect all components of the steering system. Repair or replace damaged components as described in Chapter Eleven.

3. Check the shock absorbers as described in the next section.

4. Remove the handlebar cover (Chapter Fifteen). Check that the handlebar holder bolts are tight. Reinstall the combination meter cover or handlebar cover.

5. Make sure the front axle nuts are tight and that all cotter pins are in place.

6. Check that the cotter pins are in place on all steering components. If any cotter pin is missing, check the nut for looseness. Tighten the nut to the specified torque and install a new cotter pin as described in Chapter Eleven.

7. Check the steering shaft play as follows:

    a. Support the ATV with the front wheels off the ground.

    b. To check steering shaft radial play, move the handlebar from side to side (without attempting to move the wheels). If radial play is excessive, the upper steering bushing is probably worn or the bushing holder mounting bolts (**Figure 49**) are loose. Replace the upper bushing or tighten the bushing holder bolts as necessary.

    c. To check steering shaft thrust play, lift up and then push down on the handlebar. If there is excessive thrust play, check the lower steering shaft nut (**Figure 50**) for looseness. If the nut is tightened properly, check the lower steering shaft bearing for excessive wear or damage.

    d. If necessary, service the steering shaft as described in Chapter Eleven.

    e. Lower the ATV so all four tires are on the ground.

8. Check the steering knuckle and tie rod ends as follows:

    a. Turn the handlebar quickly from side to side. If there is appreciable looseness between the handlebar and tires, check the tie rod ends for excessive wear or damage.

    b. Service the steering knuckle and tie rods as described in Chapter Eleven.

NOTE
If any cotter pins were removed in this section, install new cotter pins during reassembly.

Shock Absorber Inspection

1. Check the front and rear shock absorbers for oil leaks, a bent damper rod or other damage.

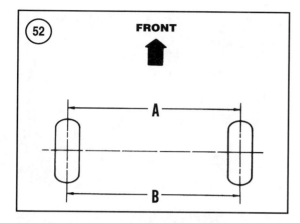

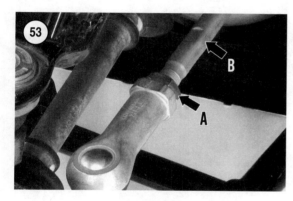

Adjust toe-out by changing the length of the tie rods.

1. Inflate all four tires to the recommended pressure specified in **Table 2**.

2. Park the ATV on level ground and set the parking brake. Then raise and support the front of the ATV so both front tires just clear the ground.

3. Turn the handlebar so the wheels are facing in the straight-ahead position.

4. Using a tape measure, carefully measure the distance between the center of both front tires as shown in A, **Figure 52**. Mark the tires with a piece of chalk at these points. Record the measurement.

5. Rotate each tire exactly 180° and measure the distance between the center of both front tires at B, **Figure 52**. Record the measurement.

6. Subtract the measurement in Step 5 from Step 4. Refer to the specification in **Table 8**. If the toe-out measurement is incorrect, continue with Step 7. If the measurement is correct, go to Step 10.

7. Loosen the locknut (A, **Figure 53**) at each end of both tie rods.

8. Use a wrench on the flat portion (B, **Figure 53**) of the tie rods and slowly turn both tie rods the same amount until the toe-out measurement is correct.

NOTE
*Turn both tie rods the same number of turns. This ensures the tie rod length remains the same on each side. To check the lengths of the tie rods, refer to **Tie Rods** in Chapter Eleven.*

WARNING
If the tie rods are not adjusted equally, the handlebar is not centered while traveling straight ahead. This condition may cause loss of ATV control. If necessary, refer adjustment to a Honda dealership or qualified shop.

9. When the toe-out adjustment is correct, hold each tie rod in place and tighten the locknuts to 54 N•m (40 ft.-lb.).

10. Lower the ATV so both front wheels are on the ground.

11. Start the engine and make a slow test ride on level ground. Ride in a straight-ahead position while checking that the handlebar does not turn toward the left- or right-side.

2. If necessary, replace the shock absorbers as described in Chapter Eleven (front) or Chapter Thirteen (rear).

Front Axle Joint Boot Inspection

At the interval specified in **Table 1**, inspect the front axle joint boots (**Figure 51**) for tearing or other damage. Replace damaged boots as described in Chapter Eleven.

Toe Adjustment

Toe-in is a condition where the front of the tires are closer together than the back (**Figure 52**). If the wheels are toed-out, the front of the tires are farther apart than the rear of the tires. On model TRX500, the wheels should be toed out. Check the toe adjustment at the interval specified in **Table 1**, after servicing the front suspension or when replacing the tie rods.

Rear Suspension Check

1. Support the ATV so the rear wheels are off the ground.
2. Try to move the rear axle (**Figure 54**) sideways while checking for excessive play at the swing arm bearings.
3. If there is any play, check the swing arm pivot bolts for looseness (Chapter Thirteen). If they are tightened properly, the swing arm bearings may require replacement. Refer to Chapter Thirteen.
4. Lower the ATV so all tires are on the ground.

Skid Plates

Check the front, middle and rear skid plates for damage and loose mounting bolts. Repair or replace damaged skid plates. Replace missing or damaged mounting bolts. Tighten the mounting bolts securely.

Fasteners

Constant vibration can loosen many of the fasteners on the ATV. Check the tightness of all fasteners, especially those on:
1. Engine mounting hardware.
2. Cylinder head bracket bolts.
3. Engine crankcase covers.
4. Handlebar.
5. Gearshift lever.
6. Brake pedal and lever.
7. Exhaust system.
8. Steering and suspension components.

COOLING SYSTEM

Check, inspect and service the cooling system at the intervals specified in **Table 1**.

> *WARNING*
> *When performing any service work on the engine or cooling system, never remove the radiator cap, coolant drain bolt or disconnect any coolant hose while the engine and radiator are hot. Scalding fluid and steam may be blown out under pressure and cause serious injury.*

Coolant Type

If adding coolant to the cooling system, use Pro Honda HP coolant or a high-quality ethylene-glycol coolant containing silicate-free corrosion inhibitors for aluminum engines. If mixing antifreeze and water, use a 50:50 mixture of distilled water. Use only soft or distilled water. Never use tap water because this damages engine parts. Distilled, or purified, water can be purchased at supermarkets or drug stores in gallon containers. Never use an alcohol-based antifreeze.

Refer also to Chapter Ten for coolant service information.

Coolant Level

1. Park the ATV on level ground.
2. Start the engine and allow it to idle until it reaches normal operating temperature.
3. Check the coolant level in the reservoir (**Figure 55**). It should be between the UPPER and LOWER level marks.
4. If necessary, remove the coolant reservoir cap and add coolant into the reservoir (not the radiator)

to bring the level to the UPPER mark. Refer to *Coolant Type* in this section.
5. Reinstall the reservoir cap.

Cooling System Inspection

1. Check all cooling system hoses for damage or deterioration. Replace any questionable hose. Make sure all hose clamps are tight.

> *NOTE*
> *There are dual cooling systems, one for coolant cooling and one for oil cooling. Be sure to inspect and clean both radiators in Step 2.*

2. Carefully clean any dirt and debris from the radiator core (A, **Figure 56**) and the oil cooler radiator (B). Use a whiskbroom, compressed air or low-pressure water. If an object has hit the radiator, carefully straighten the fins with a screwdriver.

ENGINE TUNE-UP

The following paragraphs discuss each phase of a tune-up. Perform the steps in the order given. Unless otherwise specified, the engine should be cold before starting any tune-up procedure.

Camshaft Chain Adjustment

The engine is equipped with an automatic camshaft chain tensioner. No adjustment is required.

Valve Clearance Check and Adjustment

Check and adjust the valve clearance while the engine is cold (below 35° C [95° F]).
1. Park the ATV on level ground and set the parking brake.
2. Remove the recoil starter cover (**Figure 57**).
3. Remove the fuel tank and the engine heat guard (Chapter Eight).
4. Remove the bolts and the intake and exhaust valve covers (**Figure 58**).
5. Remove the spark plug. This makes it easier to turn the engine with the recoil starter and align the timing marks.
6. Remove the timing hole cap (**Figure 59**).

7. The engine must be set to top dead center (TDC) on its compression stroke when checking and adjusting the valve clearance. Perform the following:

   a. Pull the recoil starter handle slowly and align the *T* mark on the flywheel with the index mark on the rear crankcase cover (**Figure 60**).

   b. Move both rocker arms by hand. When the engine is set at TDC on its compression stroke, both rocker arms have some side clearance, indicating the intake and exhaust valves are closed. If the rocker arms are tight (indicating the valves are open), turn the crankshaft 360° and realign the *T* mark as described in substep a. The engine should now be set at TDC on its compression stroke.

8. Check the clearance of both the intake valve and exhaust valve by inserting a flat feeler gauge between the rocker arm pad and the valve stem (A, **Figure 61**). Refer to **Table 9** for the intake and exhaust valve clearances. When the clearance is correct, there is a slight resistance on the feeler gauge when it is inserted and withdrawn.

9. To correct the valve clearance, perform the following:

   a. Loosen the locknut (B, **Figure 61**) and turn the adjuster (C) in or out until the clearance is correct. There should be a slight resistance felt when the feeler gauge is drawn from between the adjuster and valve tip.

   b. Hold the adjuster to prevent it from turning and tighten the locknut securely as shown in **Figure 61**.

   c. Recheck the clearance to make sure the adjuster did not move when the locknut was tightened. If necessary, readjust the valve clearance.

10. Install the spark plug and spark plug cap. Tighten the spark plug to 18 N•m (159 in.-lb.).

11. Inspect the O-ring in each valve cover (**Figure 62**) for cracks or other damage and replace if necessary.

12. Install the valve covers (**Figure 58**) and tighten the mounting bolts securely.

13. Install the timing hole cap and O-ring and tighten to 10 N•m (88 in.-lb.).

14. Install the engine heat guard and fuel tank (Chapter Eight).

15. Install the recoil starter cover (**Figure 57**).

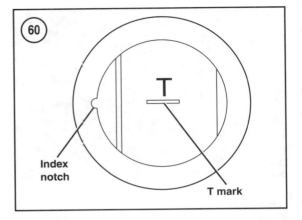

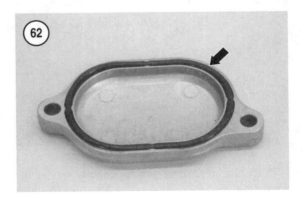

Cylinder Compression

A cylinder compression test is one of the quickest ways to check the condition of the rings, head gasket, piston and cylinder. It is a good idea to check compression during each tune-up, and compare it with the reading obtained at the next tune-up. This helps spot any developing problems.

1. Warm the engine to normal operating temperature.

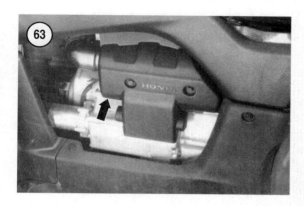

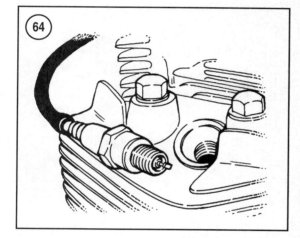

NOTE
The battery must be fully charged when cranking the engine over with the starter or a false compression reading may be obtained. Because the engine must be turning at least 450 rpm when making the compression test, do not use the recoil starter to turn the engine over.

6. Hold the throttle wide open and crank the engine with the starter for several revolutions until the gauge stabilizes at its highest reading. Record the pressure reading and compare to the specification listed in **Table 3**. Press the gauge button to release pressure from the gauge.

7. If the reading is higher than normal, there may be a buildup of carbon deposits in the combustion chamber or on the piston crown. This condition can cause detonation and overheating. Service the piston as described in Chapter Four.

8. Low compression readings indicate a leaking cylinder head gasket, a leaking valve or worn, stuck or broken piston rings. To determine which, pour about a teaspoon of engine oil through the spark plug hole onto the top of the piston. Then make another compression test and record the reading. If the compression increases significantly, the valves are good but the rings are worn or damaged. If compression does not increase, the valves or the cylinder head gasket is leaking. A valve could be hanging open or a piece of carbon could be on the valve seat.

NOTE
*If worn, stuck or broken piston rings are suspected, disconnect the crankcase breather tube (**Figure 65**) while the engine is running. If there is smoke inside the tube, check for a stuck or damaged piston ring(s).*

2. Remove the left engine cover (**Figure 63**).

3. Remove the spark plug. Insert the plug into the plug cap and ground the plug against the cylinder head (**Figure 64**).

4. Install a compression gauge into the cylinder head spark plug hole. Make sure the gauge is seated properly against the hole.

5. Turn the engine stop switch off.

9. Remove the compression tester. Install the spark plug and reconnect the spark plug cap.

NOTE
If the compression is low, the engine cannot be tuned to maximum performance.

Spark Plug Removal

1. Grasp the spark plug lead as near the plug as possible and pull it off the plug. If it is stuck to the plug, twist it slightly to break it loose.

> *CAUTION*
> *Whenever the spark plug is removed, dirt around it can fall into the plug hole. This can cause engine damage.*

2. Blow away any dirt that has collected around the spark plug.
3. Remove the spark plug (**Figure 66**) with a spark plug socket.

> *CAUTION*
> *If the plug is difficult to remove, apply penetrating oil, such as WD-40 or Liquid Wrench, around the base of the plug and let it soak about 10-20 minutes.*

4. Inspect the plug carefully. Look for a broken center porcelain, excessively eroded electrodes and excessive carbon or oil fouling.

Spark Plug Gapping and Installation

Carefully adjust the electrode gap on a new spark plug to ensure a reliable, consistent spark. Use a spark plug gapping tool and a wire feeler gauge.

1. Remove the terminal nut from the end of the plug (A, **Figure 67**).
2. Insert a wire feeler gauge between the center and side electrode of the plug (**Figure 68**). The correct gap is listed in **Table 3**. If the gap is correct, a slight drag is felt while pulling the wire through. If there is no drag or the gauge does not pass through, bend the side electrode with a gaping tool (**Figure 69**) to set the proper gap.
3. Apply an antiseize compound to the plug threads before installing the spark plug. Do not use engine oil on the plug threads.
4. Screw the spark plug in by hand until it seats. Little effort should be required. If force is necessary, the plug may be cross-threaded. Unscrew it and try again.
5. Use a spark plug wrench and tighten the new spark plug to 18 N•m (159 in.-lb.). If a torque wrench is not available, tighten the plug an additional 1/4 to 1/2 turn after the gasket has made con-

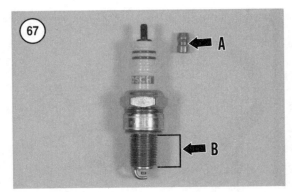

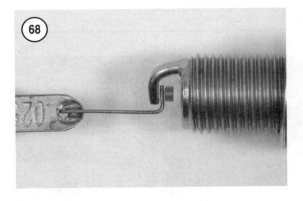

tact with the head. If installing a used spark plug, only tighten an additional 1/4 turn.

> *CAUTION*
> *Do not overtighten. This only crushes the gasket and destroys its sealing ability.*

Inspection

Reading a spark plug that has been in use can provide information about spark plug operation,

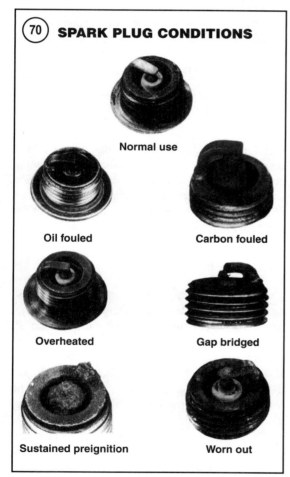

SPARK PLUG CONDITIONS

Normal use

Oil fouled

Carbon fouled

Overheated

Gap bridged

Sustained preignition

Worn out

in this section. Examine the plug and compare it to the typical plugs and conditions shown in **Figure 70**.

When reading a plug to evaluate carburetor jetting, start with a new plug and operate the ATV at the load that corresponds to the jetting information desired. For example, if the main jet is in question, operate the ATV at full throttle, shut the engine off and coast to a stop.

Heat range

Spark plugs are available in various heat ranges that are either hotter or colder than the original plugs.

Select plugs of the heat range designed for the anticipated loads and operating conditions. Use of the incorrect heat range can cause the plug to foul, overheat and cause piston damage.

In general, use a hot plug for low speeds and low temperatures. Use a cold plug for high speeds, high engine loads and high temperatures. The plug should operate hot enough to burn off unwanted deposits, but not so hot that it burns itself or causes preignition. A spark plug of the correct heat range shows a light tan color on the insulator after the plug has been in service.

The reach, or length, of a plug is also important (B, **Figure 67**). A plug that is too short causes excessive carbon buildup, hard starting and plug fouling. A plug that is too long causes overheating or may contact the top of the piston.

Table 3 lists the standard heat range spark plug.

Normal condition

If the plug has a light tan- or gray-colored deposit and no abnormal gap wear or erosion, good engine, carburetion and ignition condition are indicated. The plug in use is of the proper heat range and may be serviced and returned to use.

Carbon fouled

Soft, dry, sooty deposits covering the entire firing end of the plug are evidence of incomplete combustion. Even though the firing end of the plug is dry, the plug's insulation decreases. An electrical path is formed that lowers the voltage from the ignition system. Engine misfiring is a sign of carbon fouling.

air/fuel mixture composition and engine operating conditions (oil consumption due to wear, for example). Before checking a new spark plug, operate the ATV under a medium load for approximately 10 km (6 miles). Avoid prolonged idling before shutting off the engine. Remove the spark plug as described

Carbon fouling can be caused by one or more of the following:

1. Too rich fuel mixture.
2. Spark plug heat range too cold.
3. Clogged air filter.
4. Retarded ignition timing.
5. Ignition component failure.
6. Low engine compression.
7. Prolonged idling.

Oil fouled

The tip of an oil-fouled plug has a black insulator tip, a damp oily film over the firing end and a carbon layer over the entire nose. The electrodes should not be worn. Common causes for this condition are:

1. Incorrect carburetor jetting.
2. Low idle speed or prolonged idling.
3. Ignition component failure.
4. Spark plug heat range too cold.
5. Engine still being broken in.

An oil fouled spark plug may be cleaned in an emergency, but it is better to replace it. It is important to correct the cause of fouling before the engine is returned to service.

Gap bridging

Plugs with this condition exhibit gaps shorted out by combustion deposits between the electrodes. If this condition is encountered, check for an improper oil type or excessive carbon in the combustion chamber. Be sure to locate and correct the cause of this condition.

Overheating

Badly worn electrodes and premature gap wear, along with a gray or white blistered porcelain insulator surface are signs of overheating. The most common cause for this condition is using a spark plug of the wrong heat range (too hot). If a hotter spark plug has not been installed, but the plug is overheated, consider the following causes:

1. Lean fuel mixture.
2. Ignition timing too advanced.
3. Engine lubrication system malfunction.
4. Engine vacuum leak.
5. Improper spark plug installation (too tight).
6. No spark plug gasket.

Worn out

Corrosive gasses formed by combustion and high voltage sparks have eroded the electrodes. Spark plugs in this condition require more voltage to fire under hard acceleration. Replace with a new spark plug.

Preignition

If the electrodes are melted, preignition is almost certainly the cause. Check for carburetor mounting or intake manifold leaks and over-advanced ignition timing. It is also possible a plug of the wrong heat range (too hot) is being used. Find the cause of the preignition before returning the engine into service.

Ignition Timing

All models are equipped with a capacitor discharge ignition system (CDI). Ignition timing is not adjustable. Check the ignition timing to make sure all components within the ignition system are working correctly. If the ignition timing is incorrect, troubleshoot the ignition system as described in Chapter Two. Incorrect ignition timing can cause a drastic loss of engine performance and efficiency. It may also cause overheating.

Before starting this procedure, check all electrical connections related to the ignition system. Make sure all connections are tight and free from corrosion and that all ground connections are clean and tight.

1. Start the engine and let it warm approximately 2-3 minutes.
2. Park the ATV on level ground and apply the parking brake. Shut off the engine.
3. Remove the timing hole cap and O-ring (**Figure 71**).

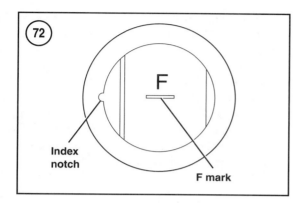

Index notch

F mark

4. Connect a portable tachometer following the manufacturer's instructions.

5. Connect a timing light following the manufacturer's instructions.

6. Restart the engine and let it run at the idle speed indicated in **Table 3**. Adjust the idle speed if necessary as described in this chapter.

7. Aim the timing light at the timing hole and pull the trigger. The *F* mark on the flywheel should align with the index mark on the rear crankcase cover as shown in **Figure 72**. If the ignition timing is incorrect, troubleshoot the ignition system as described in Chapter Two.

8. Turn the ignition switch off and disconnect the timing light and portable tachometer.

9. Install the timing hole cap and O-ring and tighten as specified in **Table 9**.

Pilot Screw Adjustment

The pilot screw does not require adjustment unless the carburetor has been overhauled or a new pilot screw was installed. To adjust the pilot screw under

these conditions, refer to *Carburetor Adjustments* in Chapter Eight.

Idle Speed Adjustment

1. Start the engine and let it warm up approximately 10 minutes.
2. Park the ATV on level ground, apply the parking brake and shut off the engine.
3. Connect a portable tachometer to the engine following the manufacturer's instructions.
4. Restart the engine and turn the idle adjust screw (**Figure 73**) to set the idle speed. Refer to **Table 3** for the idle speed specification.
5. Open and close the throttle a couple of times and check for variation in idle speed. Readjust if necessary.

> *WARNING*
> *With the engine idling, move the handlebar from side to side. If idle speed increases during this movement, the throttle cable needs adjusting or may be incorrectly routed through the frame. Correct this problem immediately. Do not ride the ATV in this unsafe condition.*

6. Turn the engine off and disconnect the portable tachometer.

STORAGE

Several months of inactivity can cause serious problems and a general deterioration of the ATV. This is especially true in extreme climates. This section describes procedures on how to prepare the ATV for storage.

Selecting a Storage Area

The most likely place to store the ATV is in a home garage or workshop. If a home garage or suitable building is not available, facilities suitable for long-term ATV storage are readily available for rent or lease in most areas. When selecting a building, consider the following:

1. The storage area must be dry. Heating is not necessary, but the building should be well insulated to minimize extreme temperature variation.

2. Buildings with large window areas should be avoided, or such windows should be masked if direct sunlight can fall on the ATV.

Preparing ATV for Storage

Careful preparation minimizes deterioration and makes it easier to restore the ATV to service later. Use the following procedure:

1. Wash the ATV completely. Make certain to remove all dirt in all the hard-to-reach areas. Completely dry all parts.

2. Run the engine long enough to warm the engine oil. Drain the oil, regardless of the time since the last oil change. Refill with the normal quantity and type of oil as described in this chapter.

3. Drain all gasoline from the fuel tank, fuel hose and carburetor. Make sure the fuel tank filler cap is tightened securely and that the vent hose is connected properly.

4. Clean and lubricate the control cables as described in this chapter.

5. Remove the spark plug and add about one tablespoon of engine oil into the cylinder. Then turn the engine over the recoil starter to distribute the oil to the cylinder wall and piston. Reinstall the spark plug and connect the spark plug cap.

6. Tape or tie a plastic bag over the end of the muffler to prevent the entry of moisture.

7. Inflate the tires to the correct pressure and move the ATV to the storage area. Support the ATV with all wheels off the ground.

8. Remove the battery and charge as described in this chapter. Then store the battery in a safe area away from freezing or excessively warm temperatures. Inspect and charge the battery once a month.

9. Clean the battery terminals, then lubricate them with dielectric grease.

10. If storing the ATV in a humid or salt-air area, spray all exposed metal surfaces with a light film of oil. Do not spray the seat, tires or any rubber part.

11. Cover the ATV with a blanket.

Restoring ATV to Service

An ATV that has been properly prepared and stored in a suitable area requires only light maintenance to service.

1. Before removing the ATV from the storage area, check air pressure in the tires and inflate the tires to the correct pressure.

2. Remove the plug from the end of the muffler.

3. When the ATV is brought to the work area, refill the fuel tank with fresh gasoline.

4. Install a fresh spark plug and start the engine.

5. Evaluate the time the ATV was in storage and the storage conditions to determine which maintenance/tune-up items require service.

6. Check the operation of the engine stop switch. Oxidation of the switch contacts during storage may make it inoperative.

7. Check the brakes and throttle controls before riding the ATV.

Table 1 MAINTENANCE AND LUBRICATION SCHEDULE

Initial maintenance: 150 km (100 miles) or 20 hours, whichever comes first	Inspect valve clearance Replace engine oil and filter Check engine idle speed Inspect brake fluid level[1] Inspect brake system Inspect reverse lock system Check for loose or missing fasteners Inspect wheels and tires
Regular maintenance: 1000 km (600 miles) or 100 hours, whichever comes first	Clean air filter[1] Drain air filter housing drain tube[1] Inspect spark plug Inspect valve clearance Replace engine oil and filter Check engine idle speed
(continued)	

Table 1 MAINTENANCE AND LUBRICATION SCHEDULE (continued)

Regular maintenance: 1000 km (600 miles)
or 100 hours, whichever comes first (continued)

Clean spark arrester
Inspect engine coolant[2]
Inspect cooling system[1]
Inspect driveshaft boots
Inspect brake system
Check for loose or missing fasteners
Check engine guard and skid plates
Inspect wheels and tires
Inspect front and rear suspension
Check toe-out

Regular maintenance: 2000 km (1200 miles)
or 200 hours, whichever comes first

Check throttle operation
Check fuel line
Check carburetor choke
Drain air filter housing drain tube[1]
Inspect spark plug
Inspect valve clearance
Replace engine oil and filter
Check engine idle speed
Clean spark arrestor
Inspect brake fluid level[1]
Inspect brake shoe wear[1]
Inspect brake system
Inspect engine coolant[2]
Inspect cooling system[1]
Inspect driveshaft boots
Check for loose or missing fasteners
Check engine guard and skid plates
Inspect wheels and tires
Inspect front and rear suspension
Check toe-out
Inspect steering shaft bearing holder
Inspect steering system
Change front differential oil[2]
Change rear final gearcase oil[2]

1. Inspect more frequently when operating in wet or muddy conditions or when riding in sand, snow or in dusty areas.
2. Replace every two years.

Table 2 TIRE INFLATION PRESSURE

	Front and rear tires psi (kPa)
Normal pressure	3.6 (25)
Minimum pressure	3.2 (22)
Maximum pressure	4.1 (28)

Table 3 TUNE-UP SPECIFICATIONS

Engine compression	608-902 kPa (88-131 psi) @ 450 rpm
Engine idle speed	1300-1500 rpm
Ignition timing (F mark)	15° @ 1400 rpm
Spark plug gap	0.8-0.9 mm (0.032-0.036 in.)

(continued)

Table 3 TUNE-UP SPECIFICATIONS (continued)

Spark plug type	
Standard	NGK IJR7A9 or Denso VX22BC
Cold weather operation*	NGK IJR6A9 or Denso VX20BC
Valve clearance	
Intake	0.15 mm (0.006 in.)
Exhaust	0.23 mm (0.009 in.)

*Below 4° C (41° F).

Table 4 BATTERY CAPACITY

Battery	
Type	Maintenance free
Capacity	12 volt, 12 amp hour

Table 5 RECOMMENDED LUBRICANTS, FLUIDS AND FUEL

Engine coolant type	Pro Honda HP or high quality ethylene-glycol*
Engine oil	
Grade	API SF or SG
Viscosity	SAE10W-40*
Differential oil	
Front and rear gearcase	Hypoid gear oil SAE 80
Air filter	Foam air filter oil
Brake fluid	DOT 3 or 4
Steering and suspension lubricant	Multipurpose grease
Fuel	Octane rating of 86 or higher

*Refer to the text for additional information.

Table 6 ENGINE OIL CAPACITY

	Liters	U.S. qt.
Oil change only	4.7	5.0
Oil and filter change	4.9	5.2
After engine disassembly	5.5	5.8

Table 7 FRONT AND REAR DIFFERENTIAL OIL CAPACITY

	ml	U.S. oz.
Front differential		
Oil change	241	8.2
After disassembly	275	9.3
Rear differential		
Oil change	90	3.0
After disassembly	100	3.4

Table 8 TOE-OUT SPECIFICATION

Toe-out	9-39 mm (0.35-1.54 in.)

Table 9 MAINTENANCE TORQUE SPECIFICATIONS

	N•m	in.-lb.	ft.-lb.
Engine oil drain bolt	25	–	18
Engine oil filter center bolt	18	159	–
Front differential gearcase			
Oil fill cap	12	106	–
Drain plug	12	106	–
Oil tank drain bolt	25	–	18
Rear differential gearcase			
Drain plug	12	106	–
Oil check plug	12	106	–
Oil fill cap	12	106	–
Spark plug	18	159	–
Tie rod locknut	54	–	40
Timing hole cap	10	88	–
Valve adjuster locknut	17	150	–
Wheel nuts (front and rear)	64	–	47

3

CHAPTER FOUR

ENGINE TOP END

The TRX500 is equipped with an overhead valve pushrod engine. The camshaft is mounted on top of the cylinder and is driven off the crankshaft by a cam chain. The camshaft operates followers, which move the pushrods against the rocker arms.

This chapter provides complete service and overhaul procedures, including information for disassembly, removal, inspection, service and reassembly of the engine top end components. These include the rocker arms, cylinder head, valves, cylinder block, piston, piston rings and camshaft. Exhaust system service is also covered. Before starting any work, read the service hints in Chapter One.

Table 1 lists general engine specifications and **Table 2** lists engine service specifications. **Table 3** lists torque specifications. **Tables 1-3** are located at the end of the chapter.

CLEANLINESS

Repairs go much faster and easier if the engine is clean before beginning work. This is important when servicing the engine's top end. Clean the engine and surrounding area before working on the engine top end.

EXHAUST SYSTEM

Refer to **Figure 1** when servicing the exhaust system in this section.

Removal/Installation

WARNING
Do not remove the exhaust pipe or muffler while they are hot.

NOTE
Although service to the muffler may be all that is required, removal of the front exhaust pipe first provides additional space to maneuver the muffler and rear exhaust during removal.

1. Remove the engine side cover (**Figure 2**).
2. Remove the side cover mounting bracket (**Figure 3**).
3. Loosen the exhaust pipe joint clamp bolts (A, **Figure 4**).
4. Remove the front exhaust pipe retaining flange nuts (**Figure 5**).
5. Move the exhaust pipe forward to disconnect it from the rear exhaust pipe section, then remove the front exhaust pipe.

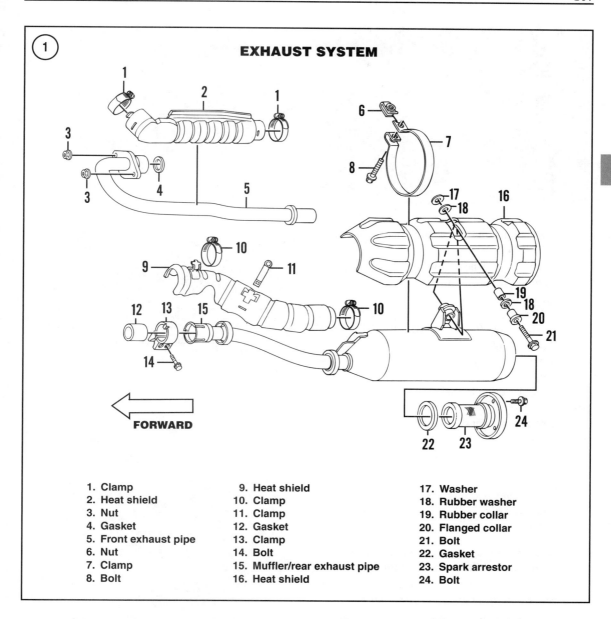

EXHAUST SYSTEM

1. Clamp
2. Heat shield
3. Nut
4. Gasket
5. Front exhaust pipe
6. Nut
7. Clamp
8. Bolt
9. Heat shield
10. Clamp
11. Clamp
12. Gasket
13. Clamp
14. Bolt
15. Muffler/rear exhaust pipe
16. Heat shield
17. Washer
18. Rubber washer
19. Rubber collar
20. Flanged collar
21. Bolt
22. Gasket
23. Spark arrestor
24. Bolt

FORWARD

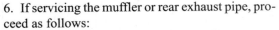

6. If servicing the muffler or rear exhaust pipe, proceed as follows:

    a. Compress and then move the breather pipe retaining clips off of the exhaust pipe bracket (B, **Figure 4**).

    b. While supporting the muffler, remove the muffler mounting bolt assembly (**Figure 6**). Refer to **Figure 1**.

    c. Remove the muffler and rear exhaust pipe assembly.

7. Replace the cylinder head exhaust gasket (**Figure 7**).

8. The exhaust gasket sleeve may remain in the rear exhaust pipe. Inspect the gasket sleeve for signs of leakage or damage and, if necessary, replace it.

NOTE
Extracting the gasket sleeve may require a puller such as a blind bearing puller.

9. Reverse the removal steps to install the exhaust pipe and muffler while noting the following:

    a. Install the exhaust pipe gasket sleeve onto the rear of the front exhaust pipe (**Figure 8**).

    b. The front exhaust pipe retaining flange has asymmetrical mounting holes. Be sure the tabs (A, **Figure 9**) on the collar fit into the notches in the flange (B).

CYLINDER HEAD COVER, ROCKER ARMS AND PUSH RODS

Removal/Installation

1. Remove the seat (Chapter Fifteen).

2. Disconnect the negative battery cable from the battery.

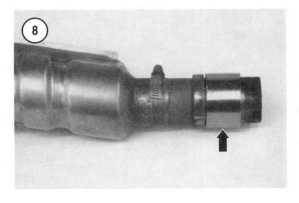

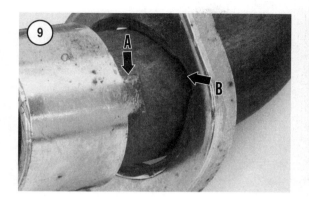

4

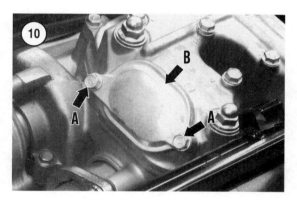

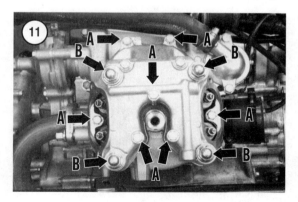

3. Remove the fuel tank and heat guard (Chapter Eight).

4. Remove the valve cover retaining bolts (A, **Figure 10**), then remove the valve cover (B) on each side.

5. Remove the seven cap bolts (A, **Figure 11**) and four cap nuts (B).

6. Remove the cylinder head cover.

7. Remove and mark each push rod (A, **Figure 12**) so it can be installed in its original location.

8. Remove the gasket (A, **Figure 13**).

9. Clean and dry the cylinder head cover. Flush the cylinder head cover oil passages and holes with compressed air.

10. Install the cylinder head cover by reversing the preceding removal steps while noting the following:

    a. If removed, install the dowels in the cylinder head as shown at B, **Figure 13**.

    b. Install a new gasket.

CAUTION
Failure to properly install the push rods may cause engine damage.

    c. Install the push rods in their original locations so each push rod rests in the respective semi-circle in the cover gasket (B, **Figure 12**).

    d. Carefully position the cylinder head cover onto the cylinder head so the push rods fit into the rocker arm push rod seats.

    e. Install sealing washers on the three inner bolts (**Figure 14**) and all cap nut studs.

    f. Apply engine oil to the cap nut threads and washers.

CAUTION
When performing substep g, if any binding or any improper operation is

noted, stop immediately and correct the cause.

g. Install the cylinder head cover fasteners finger tight. Remove the spark plug. Using the recoil starter, rotate the engine and check for proper valve operation. If the valves do not operate, remove the cylinder head cover and check for push rod dislocation.

h. Tighten the cylinder head cover fasteners in two or three steps and in a crossing pattern. Tighten the cap nuts to 53 N•m (39 ft.-lb.).

i. Install a new O-ring into the valve cover groove (**Figure 15**). Lubricate the O-ring with engine oil before valve cover installation.

Disassembly/Reassembly

Refer to **Table 2** when measuring the rocker arm components (**Figure 16**) in this section. Replace worn or damaged parts.

1. Remove the rocker shaft retaining bolt (A, **Figure 17**).

2. Extract the rocker shaft (B, **Figure 17**).

3. Remove the intake rocker arm (A, **Figure 18**) and exhaust rocker arm (B).

4. Clean and dry the rocker arm assemblies. Flush all oil passages with compressed air.

5. Inspect the rocker arm socket (A, **Figure 19**) and the adjuster pad (B). Check for cracks, uneven wear or signs of heat damage.

6. Inspect the rocker arm shaft (A, **Figure 20**) for scoring, cracks or other damage, and replace if necessary.

7. Measure the rocker arm bore inside diameter (B, **Figure 20**). If within specification, record the dimension and continue with Step 8.

8. Measure the rocker arm shaft outside diameter where the rocker arm rides. If within specification, record the dimension and perform Step 9.

9. Calculate the rocker arm-to-rocker arm shaft clearance as follows:

a. Subtract the rocker arm shaft outside diameter (Step 8) from the rocker arm bore inside diameter (Step 7) to determine rocker arm-to-shaft clearance.

b. Replace the rocker arms and/or the rocker arm shaft if the clearance is out of specification.

10. Lubricate the rocker arm bores and rocker arm shaft with engine oil.

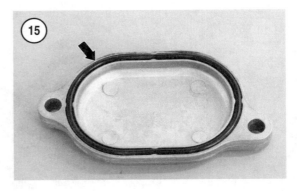

NOTE
If using the original rocker arms, install them in their original mounting positions.

11. Install the rocker arms into the cylinder head cover (**Figure 18**).

12. Install a new O-ring onto the rocker shaft, then install the rocker arm shaft (**Figure 21**) with the screwdriver slot end facing out.

13. Turn the rocker arm shaft to align the hole in the rocker arm shaft with the bolt hole in the rocker arm holder. Install the rocker arm shaft mounting bolt (A, **Figure 17**) and tighten to 7 N•m (62 in.-lb.).

14. Check that both rocker arms pivot smoothly on the rocker arm shaft.

Pushrod Inspection

Replace the pushrods (**Figure 22**) if they are excessively worn or damaged.

CAUTION
While both pushrods are identical (same part number), used pushrods must be reinstalled in their original

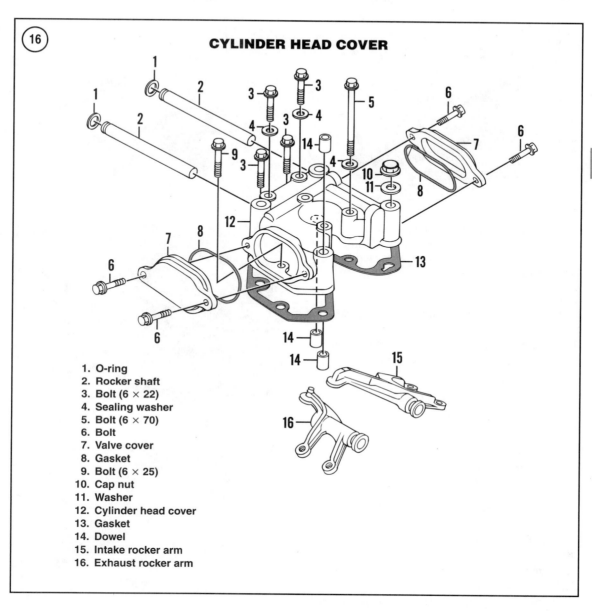

CYLINDER HEAD COVER

16

1. O-ring
2. Rocker shaft
3. Bolt (6 × 22)
4. Sealing washer
5. Bolt (6 × 70)
6. Bolt
7. Valve cover
8. Gasket
9. Bolt (6 × 25)
10. Cap nut
11. Washer
12. Cylinder head cover
13. Gasket
14. Dowel
15. Intake rocker arm
16. Exhaust rocker arm

4

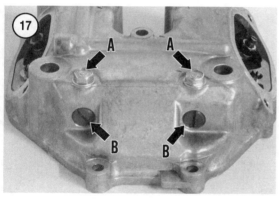

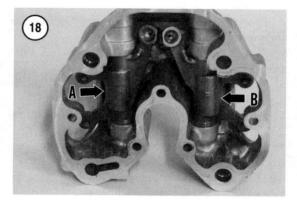

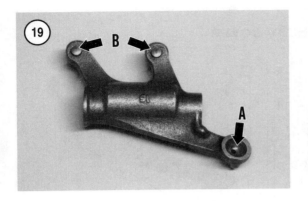

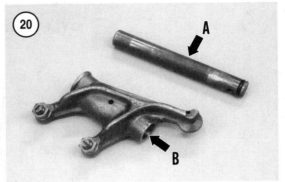

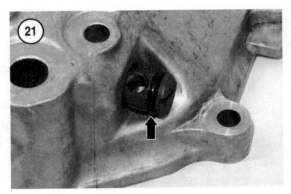

mounting position. When cleaning and inspecting the pushrods, do not remove the identification marks made during removal.

1. Clean and dry the pushrods.
2. Roll each pushrod on a flat surface and check for bending.
3. Check the pushrod ends for uneven wear, cracks or signs of heat damage (discoloration).

CYLINDER HEAD

Removal

NOTE
Perform Steps 1-6 if the engine is mounted in the frame.

1. Drain the cooling system as described in Chapter Three.
2. Remove the front exhaust pipe as described in this chapter.
3. Remove the carburetor as described in Chapter Eight. If necessary, remove the intake tube.
4. Remove the cylinder head cover as described in this chapter.
5. Detach the coolant hose (A, **Figure 23**) from the thermostat housing.
6. Detach the upper coolant bypass hose (B, **Figure 23**) from the thermostat housing.
7. Remove the fuel tank and heat guard as described in Chapter Eight.
8. Remove the upper engine hanger bolt (C, **Figure 23**).
9. Disconnect the coolant temperature sensor connector (A, **Figure 24**) from the sensor.
10. Detach the lower coolant bypass hose (B, **Figure 24**) from the thermostat housing.

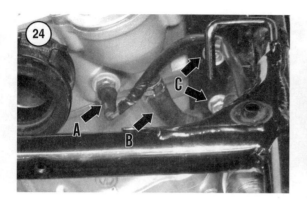

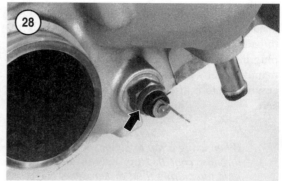

4

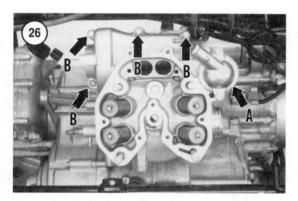

11. Remove the water pump as described in Chapter Ten.

12. Remove the upper engine mount retaining bolts (C, **Figure 24**) and remove the engine mount.

13. Remove the cylinder head cover as described in this chapter.

14. Remove the cam followers (**Figure 25**). Mark the followers so they can be reinstalled in their original locations.

15. If removing the cylinder head for service to the head, remove the thermostat housing (A, **Figure 26**) and thermostat.

16. Remove the four cylinder head retaining bolts (B, **Figure 26**).

17. Remove the cylinder head. If the head is stuck, tap the head with a plastic mallet to break it loose.

18. Remove the cylinder head gasket (A, **Figure 27**) and, if necessary, the dowel pins (B).

19. If removing the cylinder head for service to the head, remove the thermosensor (**Figure 28**).

Inspection

1. Remove all gasket residue from the cylinder head gasket surfaces. Do not scratch the gasket surface.

2. Without removing the valves, remove all carbon deposits from the combustion chamber. Use a fine wire brush dipped in solvent or make a scraper from hardwood. Do not damage the head, valves or spark plug threads.

> *CAUTION*
> *Do not clean the combustion chamber after removing the valves. The valve seat surfaces may be damaged, which may cause poor valve seating.*

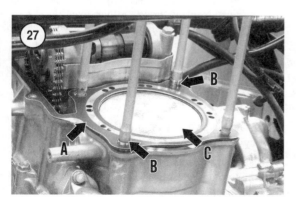

3. Examine the spark plug threads in the cylinder head for damage. If damage is minor or if the threads are dirty or clogged with carbon, use a spark plug thread tap to clean the threads following the manufacturer's instructions. If thread damage is excessive, restore the threads with a steel thread insert.

NOTE
When using a tap to clean spark plug threads, coat the tap with an aluminum tap cutting fluid or kerosene.

NOTE
Aluminum spark plug hole threads can be damaged by galling, cross-threading and overtightening. To prevent galling, apply an anti-seize compound on the plug threads before installation and do not overtighten.

4. After cleaning the combustion chamber, valve ports and spark plug thread hole, clean the entire head in solvent.

CAUTION
If the cylinder head was bead-blasted, clean the head first with solvent, and then with hot soapy water. Residue grit that seats in small crevices and other areas can be difficult to dislodge. Also chase each exposed thread with a tap to remove grit trapped between the threads. Residue grit left in the engine causes premature piston, ring and bearing wear.

5. Examine the piston crown (C, **Figure 27**). The crown must not be worn or damaged. If the crown appears pecked or spongy-looking, also check the spark plug, valves and combustion chamber for aluminum deposits. If these deposits are found, the cylinder is suffering from excessive heat caused by a lean fuel mixture or preignition.

6. Inspect the intake tube for cracks or other damage that would allow unfiltered air to enter the engine.

7. Check the exhaust pipe studs for damage. Replace the studs as described in Chapter One.

8. Inspect the combustion chamber and exhaust port for cracks.

9. Place a straightedge across the gasket surface between the bolt holes (**Figure 29**, typical). Mea-

sure for warp by inserting a feeler gauge between the straightedge and cylinder head at each location. Measure between each set of bolt holes. **Table 2** specifies the maximum allowable warp. Distortion or nicks in the cylinder head surface could cause an air leak and overheating. If the cylinder is warped, resurface or replace the cylinder head. Consult with a dealership or a machine shop for this type of work.

10. Check the cap nuts for thread damage. Discard the washers because new washers must be installed during installation.

11. To service the valves, refer to *Valves and Valve Components* in this chapter.

12. Inspect the cam followers and cylinder head cam follower bores as described under *Camshaft* in this chapter.

Installation

1. Clean the cylinder head and cylinder mating surfaces of all gasket residue.

CAUTION
Do not apply sealant onto the thermosensor head, otherwise the sensor may not operate properly.

2. If the thermosensor was removed, apply sealant to the thermosensor threads, then install the thermosensor (**Figure 28**). Tighten the thermosensor to 10 N•m (88 in.-lb.).

3. Install the two dowel pins (B, **Figure 27**) and a new cylinder head gasket (A).

4. Install the cylinder head (**Figure 26**). Be sure to seat the two dowel pins and head gasket against the cylinder head.

5. Install the four cylinder head bolts (B, **Figure 26**) fingertight. These bolts are tightened after installing the cylinder head cover.

6. Install the engine mount, then install the upper engine mount retaining bolts (C, **Figure 24**). Tighten the bolts to 32 N•m (24 ft.-lb.).

7. Install the upper engine hanger bolt (C, **Figure 23**) and tighten to 54 N•m (40 ft.-lb.).

8. Lubricate the cam followers with clean engine oil, then install them into their original positions (**Figure 25**).

9. Install the cylinder head cover as described in this chapter.

10. Tighten the four cylinder head bolts (B, **Figure 26**) to 12 N•m (106 in.-lb.).

11. If removed, install the thermostat and thermostat housing (A, **Figure 26**) as described in Chapter Ten.

12. Install the water pump as described in Chapter Ten.

13. Connect the lower coolant bypass hose (B, **Figure 24**) to the thermostat housing.

14. Connect the coolant temperature sensor connector (A, **Figure 24**) to the thermosensor.

15. Install the fuel tank and heat guard as described in Chapter Eight.

16. Connect the upper coolant bypass hose (B, **Figure 23**) to the thermostat housing.

17. Connect the coolant hose (A, **Figure 23**) to the thermostat housing.

18. If removed, install the intake tube (**Figure 30**). Be sure the notch on the underside of the tube fits around the boss on the head.

19. Install the carburetor as described in Chapter Eight.

20. Install the front exhaust pipe as described in this chapter.

21. Fill the cooling system as described in Chapter Three.

VALVES AND VALVE COMPONENTS

A complete valve job, consisting of reconditioning the valve seats and replacing the valve guides, requires specialized tools and experience. This section describes service procedures on checking the valve components for wear and how to determine what type of service is required. Refer all valve service work requiring grinding and guide replacement to a dealership or machine shop.

Special Tools

A valve spring compressor is required to remove and install the valves. This tool compresses the valve springs so the valve keepers can be released from the valve stem. Do not remove or install the valves without a valve spring compressor. Because of the limited working area found in the typical ATV cylinder head, most automotive type valve spring compressors do not work. Instead, rent or purchase a valve spring compressor designed for ATV applications.

Solvent Test

For proper engine operation, the valves must seat tightly against their seats. Any condition that prevents the valves from seating properly can cause valve burning and reduced engine performance. Before removing the valves from the cylinder head, perform the following solvent test to check valve seating:

1. Remove the cylinder head as described in this chapter.

2. Support the cylinder so the exhaust port faces up (**Figure 31**) and pour solvent or kerosene into the port. Then check the combustion chamber for fluid leaking past each exhaust valve seat.

3. Repeat Step 2 for the intake port and intake valves and seats.

4. If there is fluid leaking around a valve seat, the valve is not seating properly on its seat. The following conditions can cause poor valve seating:

   a. A bent valve stem.

   b. A worn or damaged valve seat (in cylinder head).

c. A worn or damaged valve face.

d. A crack in the combustion chamber.

Removal

A valve spring compressor is required to remove and install the valves (**Figure 32**).

1. Remove the cylinder head as described in this chapter.

2. Install a valve spring compressor squarely over the valve spring seat with the other end of tool placed against the valve head (**Figure 33**). Position the compressor head so the valve keepers can be reached and removed in Step 3.

> *NOTE*
> *When compressing the valve springs in Step 3, do not compress them any more than necessary.*

> *WARNING*
> *Wear safety glasses or goggles when performing Step 3.*

3. Tighten the valve spring compressor to remove all tension from the upper spring seat and valve keepers. Remove the valve keepers with pliers or a magnet (**Figure 34**).

4. Slowly loosen the valve spring compressor and remove it from the head.

5. Remove the valve spring retainer and both valve springs.

> *CAUTION*
> *Remove any burrs from the valve stem groove (**Figure 35**) before removing the valve; otherwise, the valve guide can be damaged as the valve stem passes through it.*

6. Remove the valve from the cylinder head.

7. Pull the valve stem seal (A, **Figure 36**) off the valve guide and discard it.

8. Remove the lower spring seat (B, **Figure 36**).

> *CAUTION*
> *Keep all parts of each valve assembly together. Do not mix components from the different valves or excessive wear may result.*

9. Repeat Steps 2-8 to remove the remaining valves.

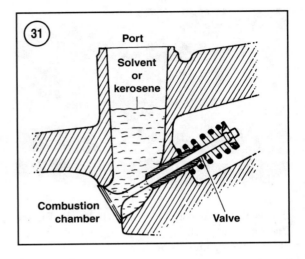

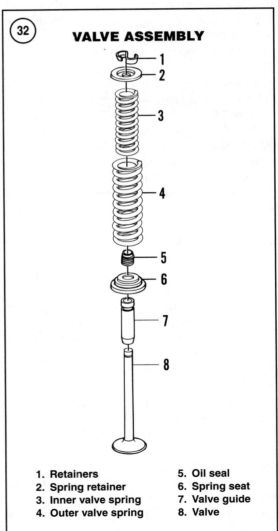

VALVE ASSEMBLY

1. Retainers
2. Spring retainer
3. Inner valve spring
4. Outer valve spring
5. Oil seal
6. Spring seat
7. Valve guide
8. Valve

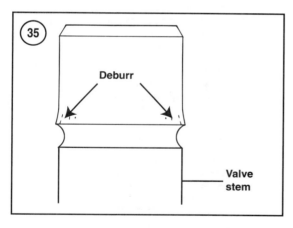

Inspection

When measuring the valve components (**Figure 32**) in this section, compare the actual measurements to the specifications in **Table 2**. Replace parts that are out of specification or show damage as described in this section.

Refer to **Figure 37** when inspecting and troubleshooting the valves in this section.

1. Clean the valves in solvent. Do not gouge or damage the valve seating surface.

2. Inspect the contact surface (**Figure 38**) of each valve for burning. Minor roughness and pitting can be removed by lapping the valve as described in this chapter. Excessive unevenness in the contact surface is an indication the valve is not serviceable.

3. Inspect the valve stems for wear and roughness. Measure the valve stem diameter for wear (**Figure 39**).

4. Remove all carbon and varnish from the valve guides with a stiff spiral wire brush before measuring wear.

> *NOTE*
> *If the required measuring tools are not available, proceed to Step 7.*

5. Measure each valve guide at its top, center and bottom inside diameter with a small hole gauge. Then measure the small hole gauge with a micrometer to determine the valve guide inside diameter.

6. Subtract the measurement made in Step 3 from the measurement made in Step 5. The difference is the valve stem-to-guide clearance. Replace any guide or valve that is not within tolerance. Refer valve guide replacement to a dealership.

7. If a small hole gauge is not available, insert each valve in its guide. Hold the valve just slightly off its seat and rock it sideways (**Figure 40**). If the valve rocks more than slightly, the guide is probably worn. However, as a final check, take the cylinder head to a dealership and have the valve guides measured.

8. Check the inner and outer valve springs as follows:

    a. Check each valve spring for visual damage.

    b. Use a square and check each spring for distortion or tilt (**Figure 41**).

    c. Measure the valve spring free length with a vernier caliper (**Figure 42**).

    d. Replace worn or damaged springs as a set.

(37)

VALVE TROUBLESHOOTING

| Valve deposits | Check:
• Worn valve guide
• Carbon buildup from incorrect tuning
• Carbon buildup from incorrect carburetor adjustment
• Dirty or gummed fuel
• Dirty engine oil |

| Valve sticking | Check:
• Worn valve guide
• Bent valve stem
• Deposits collected on valve stem
• Valve burning or overheating |

| Valve burning | Check:
• Valve sticking
• Cylinder head warped
• Valve seat distorted
• Valve clearance incorrect
• Incorrect valve spring
• Valve spring worn
• Valve seat worn
• Carbon buildup in engine
• Engine ignition and/or carburetor adjustments incorrect |

| Valve seat/face wear | Check:
• Valve burning
• Incorrect valve clearance
• Abrasive material on valve face and seat |

| Valve damage | Check:
• Valve burning
• Incorrectly installed or serviced valve guides
• Incorrect valve clearance
• Incorrect valve, spring seat and retainer assembly
• Detonation caused by incorrect ignition and/or carburetor adjustments |

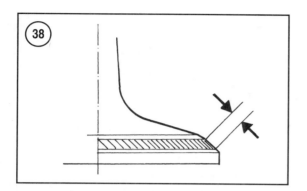

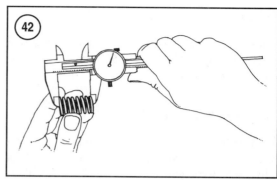

4

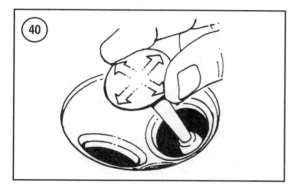

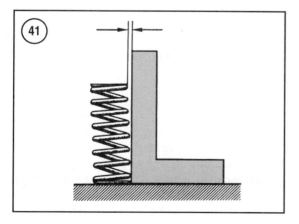

9. Check the valve spring seats and valve keepers for cracks or other damage.

10. Inspect the valve seats (**Figure 43**) for burning, pitting, cracks, excessive wear or other damage. If worn or burned, they may be reconditioned as described in this chapter. Seats and valves in near-perfect condition can be reconditioned by lapping with fine carborundum paste. Check as follows:

a. Clean the valve seat and valve mating areas with contact cleaner.

b. Coat the valve seat with machinist's blue.

c. Install the valve into its guide and rotate it against its seat with a valve lapping tool. Refer to the *Valve Lapping* section in this chapter.

d. Lift the valve out of the guide and measure the seat width (**Figure 44**) with a vernier caliper.

e. The seat width for intake and exhaust valves should measure within the specifications listed in **Table 2** all the way around the seat. If the seat width exceeds the service limit, have a dealership machine the seats.

f. Remove all machinist's blue residue from the seats and valves.

Valve Guide Replacement

Refer valve guide replacement to a dealership or machine shop. Otherwise, a 5.5 mm valve guide reamer is required.

Valve Seat Reconditioning

The valve seats are an integral part of the cylinder head and cannot be replaced separately. Minor valve seat wear and damage can be repaired by regrinding. Refer this service to a dealership or machine shop. If the necessary tools and expertise are available, refer to **Figure 45** for the valve seat angles required. Refer to **Table 2** for valve seat width dimensions.

Valve Lapping

Valve lapping can restore the valve seal without machining (if the amount of wear or distortion is not too great).

Only perform this procedure after determining the valve seat width and outside diameter are within specifications. Refer to the *Inspection* procedure in this section.

1. Smear a light coating of fine grade valve lapping compound on the valve face seating surface.
2. Insert the valve into the head.
3. Wet the suction cup of the lapping stick and stick it onto the head of the valve. Lap the valve to the seat by spinning the lapping stick in both directions. Every 5 to 10 seconds, rotate the valve 180° in the valve seat. Continue this action until the mating surfaces on the valve and seat are smooth and equal in size.
4. Closely examine the valve seat in the cylinder head. It should be smooth and even with a polished seating ring.
5. Thoroughly clean the valves and cylinder head in solvent and then with hot soapy water to remove all lapping compound. Any compound left on the valves or the cylinder head contaminates the engine oil and causes excessive wear and damage. After drying the cylinder head, lubricate the valve guides with engine oil to prevent rust.
6. After installing the valves into the cylinder, test the valve seat seal as described in the *Solvent Test* in this section. If fluid leaks past the seat, remove the valve assembly and repeat the lapping procedure until there is no leakage. When there is no leakage,

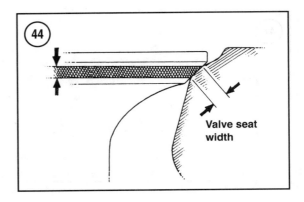

Valve seat width

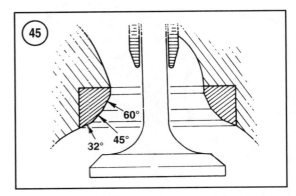

60°
32° 45°

remove all valve sets and reclean the cylinder head assembly as described in Step 5.

Valve Installation

1. Clean and dry all parts. If the valve seats were reground or lapped or the valve guides replaced, thoroughly clean the valves and cylinder head in solvent and then with hot soapy water to remove all lapping and grinding compound. Any abrasive residue left on the valves or in the cylinder head con-

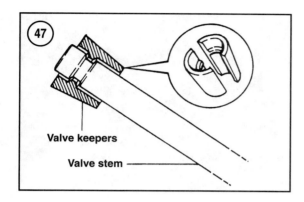

Valve keepers

Valve stem

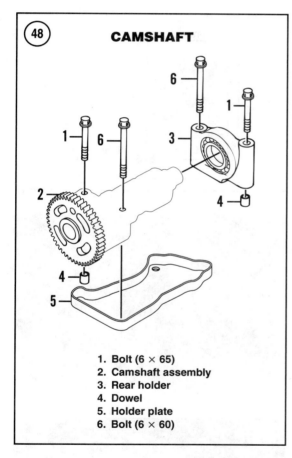

CAMSHAFT

6
1
1
6
3
2
4
4
5

1. Bolt (6 × 65)
2. Camshaft assembly
3. Rear holder
4. Dowel
5. Holder plate
6. Bolt (6 × 60)

taminates the engine oil and causes excessive wear and damage. After drying the cylinder head, lubricate the valve guides with engine oil to prevent rust.

2. Install the spring seat (B, **Figure 36**).

3. Install new valve seals as follows:

NOTE
New valve seals must be installed whenever the valves are removed.

a. Lubricate the inside of each new valve seal with molybdenum disulfide paste.

b. Install the new valve seal onto the valve guide and seat it into place (A, **Figure 36**).

4. Coat a valve stem with molybdenum disulfide paste and install it into its correct guide.

NOTE
*Install both valve springs so the ends with the closer wound coils (**Figure 46**) face toward the cylinder head.*

5. Install the inner and outer valve springs.

6. Install the valve spring retainer.

WARNING
Wear safety glasses or goggles when performing Step 7.

7. Install the valve spring compressor (**Figure 33**). Push down on the upper valve seat and compress the springs, then install the valve keepers (**Figure 47**). Release tension from the compressor and check that the keepers seat evenly around the end of the valve. Tap the end of the valve stem with a soft-faced hammer to ensure the keepers are properly seated.

8. Repeat Steps 2-7 for the remaining valves.

9. After installing the cylinder head cover onto the engine, adjust the valve clearance. Refer to Chapter Three.

CAMSHAFT

The camshaft (**Figure 48**) can be removed with the engine mounted in the frame. Because of the engine's position in the frame, some of the following illustrations show the engine removed for clarity.

Camshaft Removal

1. Remove the cylinder head as described in this chapter.

2. Remove the camshaft chain tensioner sealing bolt (**Figure 49**).

3. Make a tensioner holding tool using 1.0 mm thick metal to the dimensions shown in **Figure 50**.

4. Insert the holding tool (**Figure 51**) and turn the internal tensioner bolt fully clockwise. Insert the tool farther so it engages the slots in the tensioner body and holds the tensioner bolt so it cannot turn.

5. Remove the camshaft mounting bolts (A, **Figure 52**).

> *NOTE*
> *When removing the camshaft, do not allow the cam chain to fall into the crankcase.*

6. Lift up the holder plate (B, **Figure 52**) so the dowel pins disengage from the cylinder, detach the camshaft sprocket from the cam chain and remove the camshaft with the holder plate.

7. Attach a wire to the cam chain and hold up the chain so it cannot fall into the crankcase.

8. Separate the holder plate from the camshaft.

> *NOTE*
> *Do not remove the dowel pins from the camshaft holders unless they are damaged and require replacement.*

Camshaft Inspection

Refer to **Table 2** when measuring the camshaft components (**Figure 48**) in this section. Replace parts that are out of specification or damaged.

1. Clean and dry the camshaft assembly. Lubricate the bearings with engine oil.

2. Turn the camshaft bearings by hand. The bearings must turn without roughness, catching, binding or excessive play. If either bearing is damaged, replace the camshaft assembly or the rear camshaft holder.

3. Examine the cam lobes (**Figure 53**) for scoring or other damage.

4. Measure each cam lobe height with a micrometer (**Figure 54**). Replace the camshaft if either lobe is out of specification.

5. Check the decompressor cam operation as follows:

   a. Press on the decompressor cam as shown in **Figure 55**. When doing so, the decompressor cam should move and lock above the exhaust base.

   b. Press on the opposite side of the decompressor cam. When doing so, the decompressor lobe should move below the exhaust base.

6. If the camshaft, bearings or decompressor cam fail to operate properly or are excessively worn, replace the camshaft assembly. The front bearing and decompressor cam are not available separately.

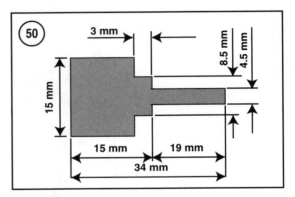

4

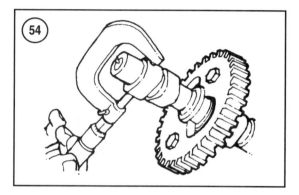

Cam Follower Inspection

Refer to **Table 2** when measuring the cam followers and cam follower bores in this section. Replace parts that are out of specification or damaged.

> *CAUTION*
> *The cam followers must not be interchanged when cleaning them in Step 1. Each cam follower should be installed in its original operating position.*

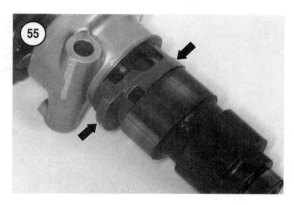

1. Clean and dry the cam followers.

2. Inspect the cam followers (**Figure 56**) for scoring, cracks or other damage.

3. Inspect the cam follower bores in the cylinder head (**Figure 57**) for scoring, excessive wear or other damage.

4. Measure the cam follower outside diameter. Record the dimension. Replace the cam follower if out of specification.

5. Measure the cam follower bore inside diameter. Record the dimension. Replace the cylinder head if the bore is out of specification.

6. If the cam followers and cam follower bore inside diameters are within specifications, determine the cam follower-to-bore clearance as follows:

    a. Subtract the dimension in Step 5 from the dimension in Step 4. The result is cam follower-to-bore operating clearance. Repeat for both cam followers.

    b. If out of specification, replace the cam follower and then remeasure. If the operating clearance is still out of specification, replace the cylinder head.

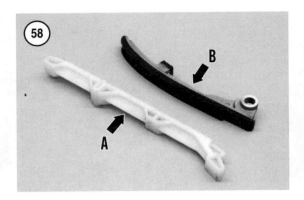

Camshaft Chain and Sprocket Inspection

1. Inspect the sprocket on the camshaft for broken or chipped teeth. Also check the teeth for cracks or other damage.

2. Inspect the cam chain for excessive wear, loose or damaged pins, cracks or other damage. Replace if damaged.

3. If the camshaft sprocket is damaged, also inspect the drive sprocket on the crankshaft. The drive sprocket may be viewed either through the cam chain compartment after removing the cylinder or by removing the clutch. If the drive sprocket on the crankshaft is damaged, replace the crankshaft assembly. Refer to Chapter Five.

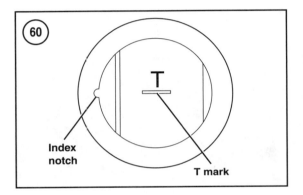

Cam Chain Guides

The right cam chain guide (A, **Figure 58**) may be inspected and removed after removing the cylinder as described in this chapter. The left guide (B, **Figure 58**) may be inspected after removing the cylinder, but removal requires removal of the clutch for access to the guide retaining bolt.

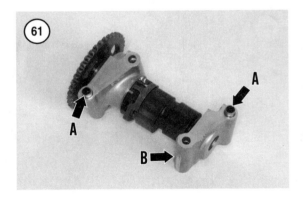

Camshaft Installation

1. Remove the timing plug (**Figure 59**).

2. Using the recoil starter, rotate the crankshaft so the *T* mark on the flywheel aligns with the index notch in the rear crankcase cover (**Figure 60**).

CAUTION
Make sure the crankshaft does not rotate while performing camshaft installation.

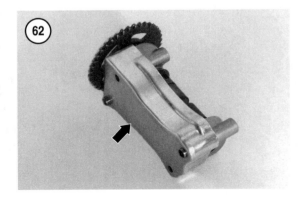

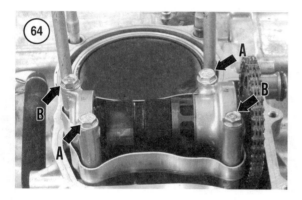

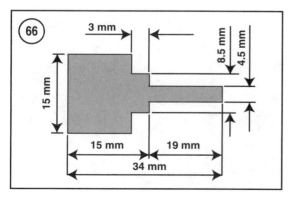

3. If removed, install the dowel pins into the bearing holders (A, **Figure 61**).

4. Install the rear bearing holder (B, **Figure 61**) onto the camshaft.

5. Apply molybdenum disulfide grease to the camshaft lobes.

6. Lubricate the camshaft bearings with engine oil.

7. Install the holder plate onto the camshaft holders (**Figure 62**).

NOTE
Make sure the camshaft chain is installed on the crankshaft drive sprocket when installing the camshaft.

8. Position the camshaft sprocket so the timing mark (**Figure 63**) is parallel to the cylinder top surface.

9. Install the camshaft chain onto the camshaft sprocket.

10. Install the camshaft so the dowel pins fit into the holes in the cylinder. Make sure the camshaft sprocket timing mark is aligned with the cylinder top surface (**Figure 63**).

11. Install the camshaft holder retaining bolts. Note the position of the short bolts (A, **Figure 64**) and long bolts (B). Tighten the bolts to 12 N•m (106 in.-lb.).

12. Remove the tool from the cam chain tensioner (**Figure 51**), then install the sealing bolt (**Figure 49**).

13. Install the timing plug (**Figure 59**) and tighten to 10 N•m (88 in.-lb.).

14. Install the cylinder head as described in this chapter.

CAMSHAFT CHAIN TENSIONER

Removal/Installation

1. Remove the front exhaust pipe section as described in this chapter.

2. Remove the camshaft chain tensioner sealing bolt (A, **Figure 65**).

3. Make a tensioner holding tool using 1.0 mm thick metal to the dimensions shown in **Figure 66**.

4. Insert the holding tool (**Figure 67**) and turn the internal tensioner bolt fully clockwise to retract the tensioner pushrod. Insert the tool farther so it engages the slots in the tensioner body and holds the tensioner bolt so it cannot turn.

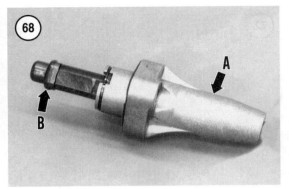

5. Remove the bolts and washers (B, **Figure 65**) securing the tensioner to the cylinder head. Remove the tensioner and gasket.

6. Install by reversing the preceding removal steps while noting the following:

    a. Retract the tensioner pushrod using the tool before installation. Remove the tool to release the pushrod after installation.

    b. Install a new gasket.

    c. Tighten the bolts to 10 N•m (88 in.-lb.).

Inspection

The camshaft chain tensioner (A, **Figure 68**) cannot be rebuilt or serviced.

1. Move the tensioner pushrod (B, **Figure 68**) in and out by hand. The pushrod must move with no roughness or binding. Replace the camshaft chain tensioner if necessary.

2. Remove all gasket residue from the tensioner housing.

CYLINDER

The alloy cylinder has a pressed-in cast iron cylinder liner. Oversize piston and ring sizes are available.

The cylinder and piston can be serviced with the engine mounted in the frame. Because of the engine's mounting position in the frame, some of the following illustrations depict the engine removed for clarity.

Removal

1. Remove the cam chain tensioner as described in this chapter.

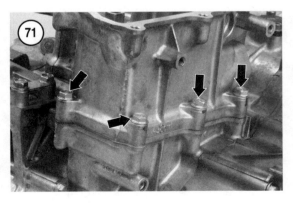

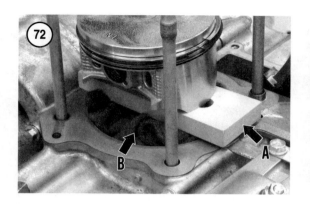

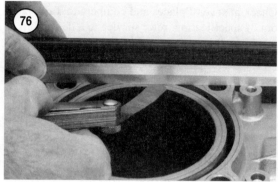

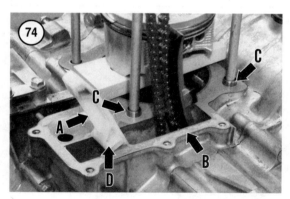

2. Remove the camshaft as described in this chapter.

3. Disconnect the crankcase breather hose from the cylinder (**Figure 69**).

4. If not removed during the water pump removal, remove the water pump outlet pipe and O-ring (**Figure 70**).

5. Remove the four cylinder retaininer bolts (**Figure 71**).

6. Loosen the cylinder by tapping around the perimeter with a rubber or plastic mallet.

7. Pull the cylinder straight up and off the crankcase.

8. Install a piston holding fixture under the piston (A, **Figure 72**). This can be a purchased unit or a homemade unit (**Figure 73**).

9. Remove the right cam chain guide (A, **Figure 74**).

10. Remove and discard the base gasket (B, **Figure 74**).

11. If necessary, remove the piston as described in the *Piston and Piston Rings* section in this chapter.

12. If necessary, remove the two dowel pins (C, **Figure 74**).

13. Cover the crankcase opening (B, **Figure 72**) to prevent objects from falling into the crankcase.

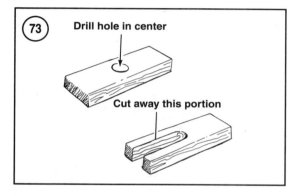

Inspection

Refer to **Table 2** when measuring the cylinder in this section.

1. Remove all gasket residue from the top and bottom cylinder block gasket surfaces.

2. Wash the cylinder block (**Figure 75**) in solvent. Dry with compressed air.

3. Check the dowel pin holes for cracks or other damage.

4. Check the cylinder block for warp with a feeler gauge and straightedge as shown in **Figure 76**.

Check at several places and compare to **Table 2**. If out of specification, refer service to a dealership or machine shop.

> *NOTE*
> *Unless the precision measuring equipment and expertise are available, have the cylinder bore measured by a Honda dealership or machine shop.*

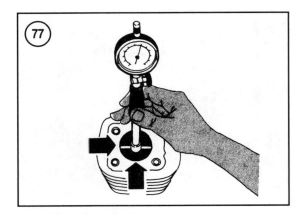

5. Measure the cylinder bore with a bore gauge or inside micrometer (**Figure 77**) at the points shown in **Figure 78**. Make six measurements aligned with the piston pin and three at 90° to the pin. Use the maximum bore dimension to determine cylinder wear. Average the other measurements to determine taper and out-of-round. If any dimension is out of specification (**Table 2**), the cylinder must be rebored and a new piston and ring assembly installed. Refer this service to a dealership or machine shop.

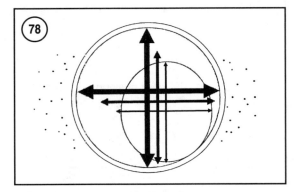

> *NOTE*
> *To determine piston clearance, refer to the **Piston and Piston Rings** in this chapter.*

6. If the cylinder is not worn past the service limit, check the bore for scratches or gouges. The bore still may require boring and reconditioning.

> *NOTE*
> *The cylinder contains oil and coolant passages. When performing Step 7 be sure to clean and remove obstructions in these passages.*

7. After servicing the cylinder, wash the bore in hot soapy water. This is the only way to clean the cylinder wall of the fine grit material left from the bore or honing job. After washing the cylinder wall, run a clean white cloth through it. The cylinder must be free of all grit and other residue. If the rag is dirty, rewash the cylinder wall again and recheck with the white cloth. Repeat until the cloth comes out clean. When the cylinder is clean, lubricate it with engine oil to prevent the cylinder liner from rusting.

> *CAUTION*
> *The soap and water described in Step 7 is the only solution that can wash the fine grit residue out of the cylinder crevices. Solvent and kerosene cannot*

do this. Grit residue left in the cylinder acts like a grinding compound and causes rapid and premature wear to the contact surfaces of the piston rings, cylinder bore and piston.

Installation

1. Check that the top and bottom cylinder surfaces are clean of all gasket residue.

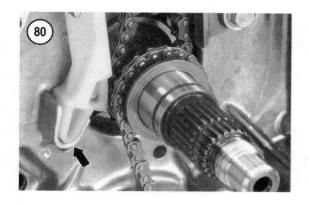

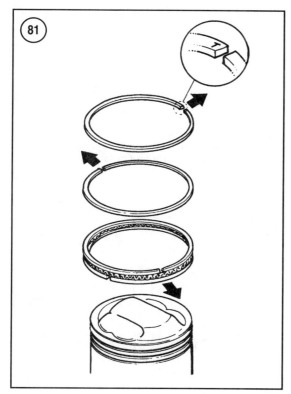

2. If removed, install the piston and rings as described in the *Piston and Piston Rings* in this chapter.

> *CAUTION*
> *Make sure to install and secure the piston pin circlips.*

3. Install the two dowel pins into the crankcase (C, **Figure 74**).
4. Install a new base gasket onto the crankcase (B, **Figure 74**). Make sure all holes align.
5. Install the cam chain guide so the triangular-shaped end (**Figure 79**) fits into the receptacle on the side of the crankcase as shown in **Figure 80**.
6. Lubricate the cylinder wall, piston and rings with engine oil.
7. Stagger the piston rings around the piston as shown in **Figure 81**.
8. Look down into the crankcase through the cam chain compartment and verify the cam chain fits properly on the drive sprocket (**Figure 82**). Maintain tension on the cam chain so it remains on the sprocket.
9. Position the cylinder onto the retaining studs and route the cam chain through the cylinder. Hold the cam chain so it cannot fall into the engine.

> *NOTE*
> *It is easier to install the cylinder over the piston by first compressing the rings with a ring compressor. As the cylinder is installed over the piston, the rings pass into the cylinder compressed and then expand out once they are free of the ring compressor. A hose clamp works well for this. Before using a ring compressor or hose clamp, lubricate its ring contact side with engine oil. When using a ring compressor or hose clamp, do not overtighten. The tool should be able to slide freely as the cylinder pushes against it.*

> *NOTE*
> *Make sure the bosses on the cam chain guide (D, **Figure 74**) fit into the corresponding recesses in the cylinder while installing the cylinder.*

10A. Compress the rings with a ring compressor or appropriate size hose clamp. Then align the cylinder with the piston and carefully slide it down past

the rings. When all of the rings are installed in the cylinder, hold the cylinder and remove the ring compressor or hose clamp.

10B. If not using a ring compressor or hose clamp, align the cylinder with the piston and install the cylinder. Compress each ring by hand as the ring enters the cylinder.

11. Remove the piston holding fixture and slide the cylinder all the way down.

12. While holding the cylinder down with one hand, operate the recoil starter. The piston must move up and down in the bore with no binding or roughness.

> *CAUTION*
> *If the piston does not move smoothly, one of the piston rings may have slipped out of its groove when the cylinder was installed. Lift the cylinder and piston up together so there is space under the piston. Install a clean rag under the piston to catch any pieces from a broken piston ring, then remove the cylinder.*

13. Install the four cylinder head retaining bolts (**Figure 83**) and tighten finger tight.

14. Install the camshaft and cylinder head as described in this chapter.

15. After installation of the cylinder head cover, tighten the four cylinder head bolts (**Figure 83**) to 12 N•m (106 in.-lb.).

PISTON AND PISTON RINGS

The piston (**Figure 84**) is made of an aluminum alloy. The piston pin is made of steel and is a precision fit in the piston. The piston pin is held in place by a clip at each end.

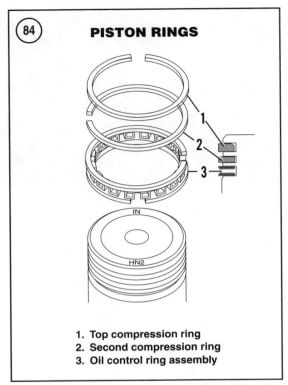

PISTON RINGS

1. Top compression ring
2. Second compression ring
3. Oil control ring assembly

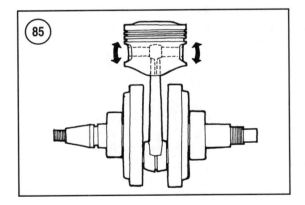

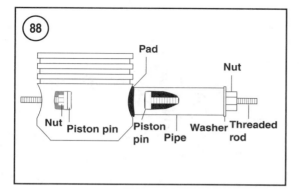

Piston Removal/Installation

1. Remove the cylinder as described in this chapter.
2. Cover the crankcase below the piston to prevent the piston pin circlips from falling into the crankcase.
3. Before removing the piston, hold the rod and rock the piston (**Figure 85**). Any rocking motion (do not confuse with the normal sliding motion) indicates wear on the piston pin, rod bore, pin bore or a combination of all three.

> *WARNING*
> *Wear safety glasses or goggles when removing the circlips in Step 4.*

4. Remove the circlips from the piston pin bore grooves (**Figure 86**).

> *CAUTION*
> *Discard the piston circlips. Install new circlips during reassembly.*

5. Push the piston pin (**Figure 87**) out of the piston by hand. If the pin is tight, use a homemade tool (**Figure 88**) to remove it. Do not drive the piston pin out because the force may damage the piston pin, connecting rod or piston.
6. Lift the piston off the connecting rod.
7. Inspect the piston as described in this chapter.

Piston Inspection

1. Remove the piston rings as described in this chapter.
2. Clean the carbon from the piston crown (**Figure 89**) with a soft scraper. Large carbon accumulations reduce piston cooling and cause detonation and piston damage.

> *CAUTION*
> *Do not clean the piston skirt using a wire brush.*

3. After cleaning the piston, examine the crown. The crown must show no signs of wear or damage. If the crown appears pecked or spongy-looking, also check the spark plug, valves and combustion chamber for aluminum deposits. If these deposits are found, the engine is overheating.
4. Examine each ring groove (**Figure 90**) for burrs, dented edges or other damage. Pay particular attention to the top compression ring groove because it

usually wears more than the others. Because the oil rings are bathed in oil, their rings and grooves wear less than compression rings and their grooves. If there is evidence of oil ring groove wear or if the oil ring is tight and difficult to remove, the piston skirt may have collapsed due to excessive heat. Replace the piston.

5. Check the piston oil control holes for carbon or oil sludge buildup. Clean the holes with wire.

6. Inspect the piston skirt (**Figure 91**) for cracks or other damage. If the piston shows signs of partial seizure (bits of aluminum on the piston skirt), replace the piston.

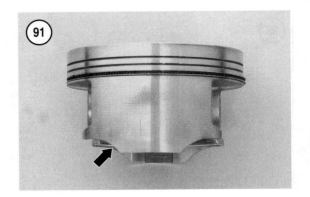

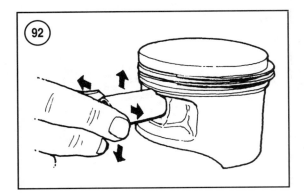

> *NOTE*
> *If the piston skirt is worn or scuffed unevenly from side to side, the connecting rod may be bent or twisted.*

7. Check the piston circlip grooves for wear, cracks or other damage. If a circlip groove is worn, replace the piston.

8. Measure piston-to-cylinder clearance as described in the *Piston Clearance* section in this section.

Piston Pin Inspection

Refer to **Table 2** when measuring the piston pin components in this section. Replace parts that are out of specification or show damage.

1. Clean and dry the piston pin.

2. Inspect the piston pin for chrome flaking, cracks or signs of heat damage.

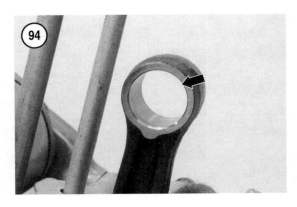

3. Lubricate the piston pin and install it in the piston. Slowly rotate the piston pin and check for excessive play as shown in **Figure 92**.

4. Measure the piston pin bore diameter (**Figure 93**) in the piston. If within specification, record the dimension and continue with Step 5.

5. Measure the piston pin outside diameter. If within specification, record the dimension and continue with Step 6.

6. Subtract the measurement made in Step 5 from the measurement made in Step 4 to determine the piston-to-piston pin clearance. Replace the piston and/or piston pin if the clearance is excessive.

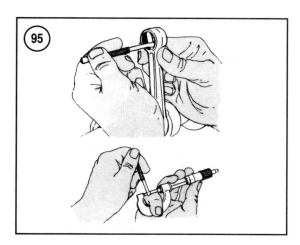

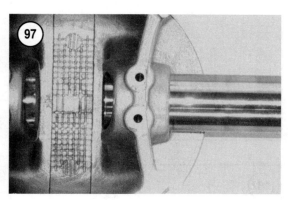

Specified distance

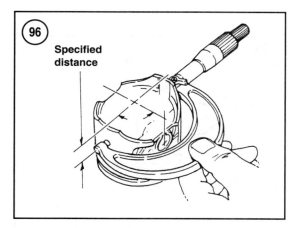

Connecting Rod Small End Inspection

1. Inspect the connecting rod small end (**Figure 94**) for cracks or signs of heat damage.

2. Measure the connecting rod bore diameter with a snap gauge (**Figure 95**). Then measure the snap gauge with a micrometer and compare with the di-

mension in **Table 2**. If the bore wear is excessive, replace the crankshaft assembly. The connecting rod cannot be replaced separately.

Piston Clearance

Unless precision measuring equipment and expertise are available, have this procedure performed by a dealership or machine shop.

1. Make sure the piston and cylinder walls are clean and dry.

2. Measure the cylinder bore with a bore gauge or inside micrometer (**Figure 77**) at the points shown in **Figure 78**. Measure aligned with the piston pin and 90° to the pin. This measurement determines the cylinder bore diameter. Write down the bore diameter measurement.

3. Measure the piston diameter with a micrometer at a right angle to the piston pin bore (**Figure 96**). Measure 15 mm (0.6 in.) from the bottom edge of the piston skirt (**Figure 96**). Write down the piston diameter measurement.

4. Subtract the piston diameter from the largest bore diameter; the difference is piston-to-cylinder clearance. If clearance exceeds the service limit in **Table 2**, the cylinder must be bored and a new piston/ring assembly installed.

Piston Installation

1. Install the piston rings onto the piston as described in this chapter.

2. Coat the connecting rod bore, piston pin and piston with engine oil.

3. Slide the piston pin into the piston until its end is flush with the piston pin boss as shown in **Figure 97**.

4. Place the piston onto the connecting rod so the IN mark (**Figure 98**) on the piston crown faces toward the intake side of the engine.

5. Align the piston pin with the hole in the connecting rod. Push the piston pin (**Figure 87**) through the connecting rod and into the other side of the piston and center it in the piston.

6. Cover the crankcase opening with clean rags.

> *WARNING*
> *Wear safety glasses or goggles when installing the piston pin circlips in Step 7.*

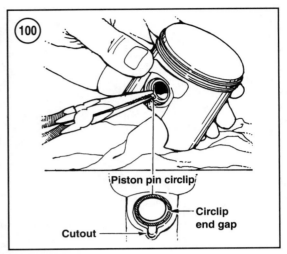

Piston pin circlip

Circlip
end gap

Cutout

7. Install new piston pin circlips (**Figure 99**) in both ends of the piston pin bore (**Figure 100**). Make sure the circlips seat in the piston clip grooves completely. Turn the circlips so their end gaps do not align with the cutout in the piston (**Figure 100**).

8. Install the cylinder as described in this chapter.

Piston Ring Inspection and Removal

A three-ring type piston and ring assembly is used (**Figure 101**). The top and second rings are compression rings. The lower ring is an oil control ring assembly (consisting of two ring rails and an expander spacer).

1. Measure the side clearance of each compression ring in its groove with a flat feeler gauge (**Figure 102**) and compare with the specifications in **Table 2**. If the clearance is greater than specified, replace the rings. If the clearance is still excessive with the new rings, replace the piston.

> *WARNING*
> *The edges of all piston rings are very sharp. Be careful when handling them to avoid cut fingers.*

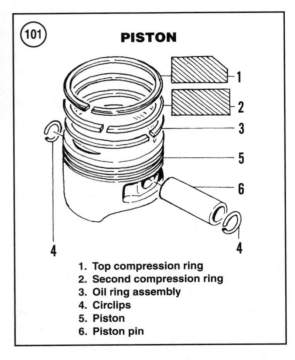

PISTON

1. Top compression ring
2. Second compression ring
3. Oil ring assembly
4. Circlips
5. Piston
6. Piston pin

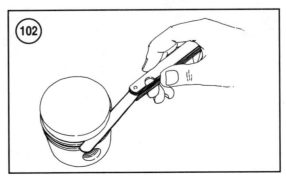

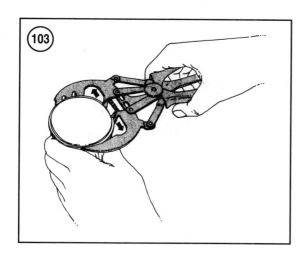

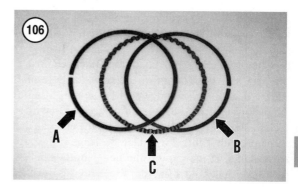

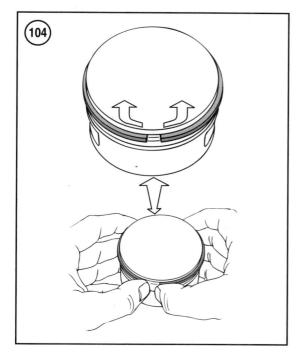

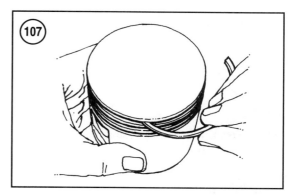

NOTE
Store the rings in order of removal.

2. Remove the compression rings with a ring expander tool (**Figure 103**) or spread the ring ends with your thumbs and lift the rings out of their grooves and up over the piston (**Figure 104**).

3. Remove the oil ring assembly (**Figure 105**) by first removing the upper (A, **Figure 106**) and then the lower (B) ring rails. Then remove the expander spacer (C, **Figure 106**).

CAUTION
When cleaning the piston ring grooves in Step 4, use the same type of ring that operates in the groove. Using a ring that is dissimilar to the groove damages the groove.

4. Using a broken piston ring, remove carbon and oil residue from the piston ring grooves (**Figure 107**).

CAUTION
Do not remove aluminum material from the ring grooves because this increases ring side clearance.

5. Inspect the ring grooves for burrs, nicks or broken or cracked lands. Replace the piston if necessary.

6. Check the end gap of each ring. To check, insert the ring into the bottom of the cylinder bore and square it with the cylinder wall by tapping it with the piston (**Figure 108**). Measure the end gap with a feeler gauge (**Figure 108**). Compare the end gap dimension with **Table 2**. Replace the rings if the gap is too large. If the gap on the new ring is smaller than specified, hold a fine-cut file in a vise. File the ends of the ring to enlarge the gap.

NOTE
*When measuring the oil control ring end gap, measure the upper and lower ring rail end gaps only. Do not measure the expander spacer (C, **Figure 106**).*

7. Roll each ring around its piston groove (**Figure 109**) to check for binding. Repair minor binding with a fine-cut file.

Piston Ring Installation

1. Hone or deglaze the cylinder before installing new piston rings. This machining process helps the new rings seat in the cylinder. If necessary, refer this job to a dealership or machine shop. After honing, measure the end gap of each ring and compare to the dimensions in **Table 2**.

2. Clean the piston and rings with hot soapy water, then dry with compressed air.

3. If the cylinder was honed, clean the cylinder as described under *Cylinder Inspection* in this chapter.

4. Clean the piston and rings in solvent. Dry with compressed air.

NOTE
*The top and second compression rings are different. Refer to **Figure 106** to identify the rings.*

5. Install the piston rings as follows:

NOTE
Install the piston rings—first the bottom, then the middle, then the top ring—by spreading the ring ends with your thumbs or a ring expander tool, then slip the rings over the top of the piston.

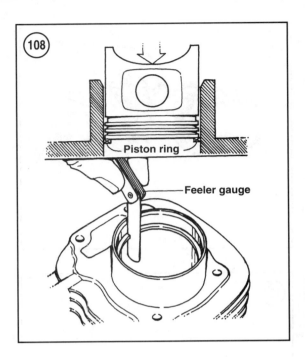

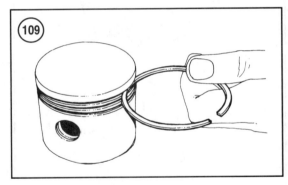

a. Install the oil ring assembly into the bottom ring groove. First install the expander spacer, then the bottom and top ring rails (**Figure 106**).

b. Install the compression rings with the manufacturer's marks facing up.

NOTE
On original equipment pistons, the top compression ring is thinner than the second compression ring.

c. Install the second compression ring.
d. Install the top compression ring.

6. Position the end gaps around the piston as shown in **Figure 81**. Check that the piston rings rotate freely.

Table 1 GENERAL ENGINE SPECIFICATIONS

Engine	4-stroke, overhead valve pushrod engine
Displacement	499 cc (30.4 cu.-in)
Bore	92 mm (3.62 in.)
Stroke	75 mm (2.95 in.)
Compression ratio	9.2:1
Cooling system	Liquid cooled
Valve timing*	
Intake valve opens	8° BTDC
Intake valve closes	35° ABDC
Exhaust valve opens	5° BBDC
Exhaust valve closes	40° ATDC

*Specified at 1 mm (0.039 in.) lift.

Table 2 ENGINE TOP END SERVICE SPECIFICATIONS

	New mm (in.)	Service limit mm (in.)
Cam follower bore diameter	22.510-22.526 (0.8862-0.8868)	22.54 (0.887)
Cam follower-to-bore clearance	0.028-0.059 (0.0011-0.0023)	0.07 (0.003)
Cam follower outside diameter	22.467-22.482 (0.8845-0.8851)	22.46 (0.884)
Cam lobe height		
Intake	33.9602-34.1202 (1.3370-1.3433)	33.790 (1.3303)
Exhaust	34.1959-34.3559 (1.3463-1.3526)	33.946 (1.3365)
Connecting rod small end inside diameter	20.020-20.041 (0.7882-0.7890)	20.07 (0.790)
Connecting rod-to-piston pin clearance	0.020-0.047 (0.0008-0.0019)	0.10 (0.004)
Cylinder bore diameter (standard bore)	92.00-92.01 (3.6220-3.6224)	92.10 (3.626)
Cylinder head warp limit	– –	0.10 (0.004)
Cylinder out-of-round limit	– –	0.10 (0.004)
Cylinder taper limit	–	0.10 (0.004)
Cylinder warp limit	–	0.10 (0.004)
Piston diameter (standard piston)	91.965-91.985 (3.6207-3.6214)	91.90 (3.618)
Piston diameter measuring point	see text	–
Piston-to-cylinder clearance	0.015-0.045 (0.0006-0.0018)	0.10 (0.004)
Piston pin bore diameter	20.002-20.008 (0.7875-0.7877)	20.04 (0.789)
Piston pin outside diameter	19.994-20.000 (0.7872-0.7874)	19.96 (0.786)
Piston-to-piston pin clearance	0.002-0.014 (0.0001-0.0006)	0.08 (0.003)
Piston ring end gap		
Top compression ring	0.15-0.30 (0.006-0.012)	0.5 (0.02)

(continued)

Table 2 ENGINE TOP END SERVICE SPECIFICATIONS (continued)

	New mm (in.)	Service limit mm (in.)
Piston ring end gap (continued)		
Second compression ring	0.30-0.45 (0.012-0.018)	0.6 (0.02)
Oil ring (side rails)	0.20-0.70 (0.008-0.028)	–
Piston ring side clearance		
Top & second compression ring	0.03-0.06 (0.001-0.002)	0.09 (0.004)
Rocker arm bore inside diameter	12.000-12.018 (0.4724-0.4731)	12.05 (0.474)
Rocker arm shaft outside diameter	11.964-11.984 (0.4710-0.4718)	11.92 (0.469)
Rocker arm-to-shaft clearance	0.016-0.054 (0.0006-0.0021)	0.08 (0.003)
Valve clearance		
Intake	0.15 (0.006)	–
Exhaust	0.23 (0.009)	–
Valve guide Inside diameter	5.500-5.512 (0.2165-0.2170)	5.53 (0.218)
Valve seat width	1.0-1.1 (0.039-0.043)	–
Valve spring free length		
Inner	38.82 (1.528)	37.8 (1.49)
Outer	51.17 (2.015)	49.0 (1.93)
Valve stem diameter		
Intake	5.475-5.490 (0.2156-0.2161)	5.45 (0.215)
Exhaust	5.455-5.470 (0.2148-0.2154)	5.43 (0.214)
Valve stem-to-guide clearance		
Intake	0.010-0.037 (0.0004-0.0015)	0.12 (0.005)
Exhaust	0.030-0.057 (0.0012-0.0022)	0.14 (0.006)

Table 3 ENGINE TOP END TORQUE SPECIFICATIONS

	N•m	in.-lb.	ft.-lb.
Cylinder head cap nuts	53	–	39
Cylinder head bolts	12	106	–
Exhaust system			
Exhaust pipe joint bolts	23	–	17
Front exhaust pipe heat shield clamp screws	3	27	–
Rear exhaust pipe heat shield			
Center clamp screw	3	27	–
End clamp screws	6	53	–
Muffler mounting bolt	23	–	17
Muffler heat shield clamp screws	3	27	–
Rocker arm shaft mounting bolt	7	62	–
Thermosensor	10	88	–
Upper engine hanger bolt	54	–	40
Upper engine hanger bracket bolts	32	–	24

CHAPTER FIVE

ENGINE LOWER END

This chapter describes service procedures for the following lower end components:

1. Recoil starter.
2. Alternator cover.
3. Flywheel and starter clutch.
4. Crankcase and crankshaft.
5. Oil pump.
6. Oil strainer screen.

One of the most important aspects of a successful engine overhaul is preparation. Before removing the engine and disassembling the crankcase, degrease the engine and frame. Have all the necessary hand and special tools available. Make sure the work area is clean and well lit. Identify and store individual parts and assemblies in appropriate storage containers.

Throughout the text there is frequent mention of the front and rear sides of the engine. This refers to the engine as it sits in the frame, not as it sits on the workbench. Likewise, the references to the left and right sides of the engine refer to the engine as it is mounted in the frame.

Specifications are in **Tables 1-3** at the end of this chapter.

SERVICING ENGINE IN FRAME

The following components can be serviced with the engine mounted in the frame:
1. Cylinder head cover.
2. Cylinder head.
3. Cylinder and piston.
4. Clutch.
5. Recoil starter.
6. Carburetor.

ENGINE

Refer to **Figure 1** when removing and installing the engine in the frame.

Removal/Installation

1. Park the ATV on a level surface and set the parking brake.
2. Before disassembling the engine, perform a compression test (Chapter Three) and leakdown test (Chapter Two). Record the readings for future use.
3. Remove the seat (Chapter Fifteen).
4. Disconnect the negative battery cable from the battery (Chapter Three).

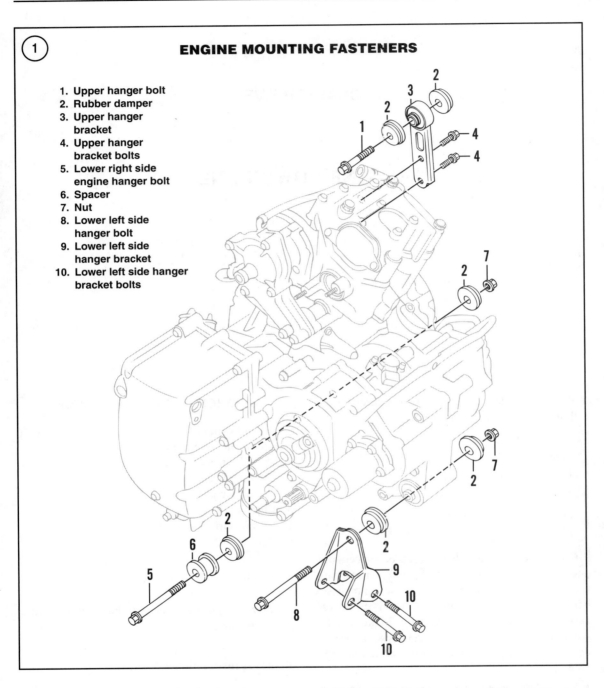

ENGINE MOUNTING FASTENERS

1. Upper hanger bolt
2. Rubber damper
3. Upper hanger bracket
4. Upper hanger bracket bolts
5. Lower right side engine hanger bolt
6. Spacer
7. Nut
8. Lower left side hanger bolt
9. Lower left side hanger bracket
10. Lower left side hanger bracket bolts

5. Drain the engine oil (Chapter Three).

6. Drain the cooling system (Chapter Three).

7. Remove the center mud guards on both sides (Chapter Fifteen).

8. Remove the front mud guards on both sides (Chapter Fifteen).

9. Remove the right front inner fender (Chapter Fifteen).

10. Remove the exhaust system (Chapter Four).

11. Remove the fuel tank and heat guard (Chapter Eight).

12. Remove the carburetor (Chapter Eight).

13. Detach the ground terminal from the engine (**Figure 2**).

14. Push back the rubber boot, then disconnect the starter cable from the starter terminal (A, **Figure 3**).

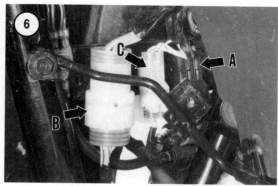

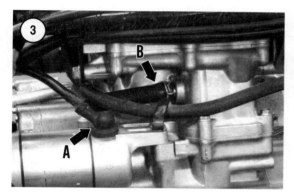

15. Detach the crankcase breather hose from the cylinder (B, **Figure 3**).

16. Disconnect the shift motor connector (**Figure 4**) and release the motor cable from the wiring clamps.

17. Disconnect the angle sensor connector (**Figure 5**) and release the angle sensor wire from the wiring clamps.

18. Refer to **Figure 6**, then disconnect the following electrical connectors and release the wires from any wiring clamps:

    a. Speed sensor connector (A, **Figure 6**).

    b. Alternator/pulse generator connector (B, **Figure 6**).

    c. Gear position switch connector (C, **Figure 6**).

19. Disconnect the spark plug wire.

20. Detach the coolant hose from the water pump (**Figure 7**).

21. Detach the upper coolant hose from the thermostat housing (A, **Figure 8**).

22. Disconnect the oil thermosensor connector (**Figure 9**), then remove the thermosensor to prevent damage.

23. Disconnect the coolant thermosensor connector (A, **Figure 10**).

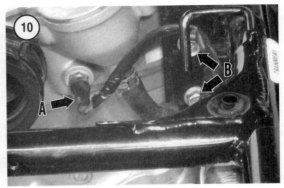

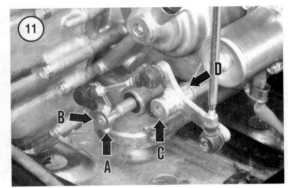

24. Make sure the transmission shift lever is in neutral.

25. Remove the pinch bolt (A, **Figure 11**) on the gearshift arm (B). Remove the pivot bolt (C, **Figure 11**) and washer (D). Remove the gearshift arm from the gearshift spindle, then move the shift linkage out of the way.

26. Remove the oil pipe retaining bolt (**Figure 12**) and separate the oil pipe from the oil tank. Repeat for the remaining oil pipe. Cover the pipe ends and oil tank openings to prevent oil leakage and contamination.

27. Remove the brake pedal as described in Chapter Fourteen.

28. Loosen the rear driveshaft boot clamp screw (**Figure 13**) and move the boot off the engine.

29. Remove the lower front differential mounting bolt (**Figure 14**).

30. Remove the upper front differential mounting bolt (A, **Figure 15**) and spacer (B).

31. Remove the front differential front mounting bracket bolts (**Figure 16**).

32. Push the front differential forward, then pull the front driveshaft forward so it disconnects from the engine output shaft (**Figure 17**).

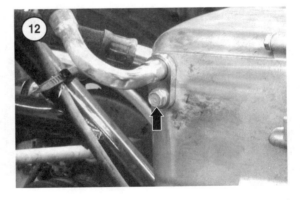

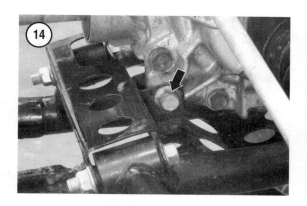

5

33. Remove the engine upper hanger bolt (B, **Figure 8**).

34. Remove the engine upper hanger bracket bolts (B, **Figure 10**) and the upper hanger assembly.

35. Support the engine with just enough force to remove weight from the lower engine hanger mounting bolts when removing them in the following steps. Make sure to protect the frame and engine cases.

36. Remove the left lower engine hanger bolt (A, **Figure 18**).

37. Remove the mounting bracket bolts, then remove the mounting bracket (B, **Figure 18**).

38. Remove the right lower engine hanger bolt (A, **Figure 19**) and spacer (B).

> *WARNING*
> ***Table 1*** *lists the approximate weight of an assembled engine. Two people may be required to safely remove the engine from the frame.*

39. Move the engine forward to disconnect the universal joint from the rear driveshaft. Tip the engine to the right to lower the cylinder head, then remove

the engine from the left side of the frame. Support the engine on a workbench.

40. Install the engine in the frame by reversing the preceding steps while noting the following:

  a. Install a new O-ring onto the front engine output shaft (**Figure 20**).

  b. Lubricate the universal joint, engine and driveshaft splines with molybdenum disulfide grease.

  c. Make sure the splines on the engine rear output shaft and the rear driveshaft universal joint fit properly. Cocking prevents the engine from sitting correctly in the frame.

  d. Replace damaged engine mount fasteners.

  e. Apply an antiseize compound to the shoulders on each engine mount bolt. This helps prevent rust and corrosion.

  f. Install the lower rubber mounting dampers so the larger diameter side faces the engine (C, **Figure 18**).

  g. Tighten the lower mounting bracket (B, **Figure 18**) bolts to 32 N•m (24 ft.-lb.).

  h. Install the spacer on the right lower hanger bolt so the spacer is in front of the engine (B, **Figure 19**). Tighten the lower engine hanger bracket bolts (A, **Figure 18** and **Figure 19**) to 54 N•m (40 ft.-lb.).

  i. Tighten the upper engine hanger bracket bolts (B, **Figure 10**) to 32 N•m (24 ft.-lb.).

  j. Tighten the upper engine hanger bolt (B, **Figure 8**) to 54 N•m (40 ft.-lb.).

  k. Tighten the front differential mounting bracket bolts (**Figure 16**) to 22 N•m (16 ft.-lb.).

  l. Tighten the front differential lower mounting bolt (**Figure 14**) to 44 N•m (33 ft.-lb.).

  m. Install the spacer on the front differential upper mounting bolt as shown in B, **Figure 15**. Tighten the mounting bolt to 44 N•m (33 ft.-lb.).

  n. Install the gearshift arm (B, **Figure 11**) so the master splines on the arm and gearshift spindle are aligned. Install new O-rings and apply grease onto the pivot bolt (C, **Figure 11**).

  o. Tighten the oil thermosensor to 18 N•m (159 in.-lb.).

  p. Check the electrical connectors for corrosion. Pack the connectors with dielectric grease before reconnecting them.

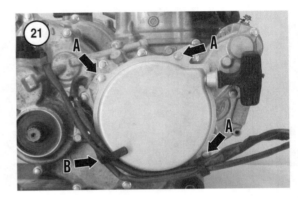

  q. Fill the engine with the recommended type and quantity of oil. Refer to Chapter Three.

  r. Fill and bleed the cooling system as described in Chapter Three.

  s. Check throttle operation (Chapter Three).

  t. Check brake pedal free play (Chapter Three).

RECOIL STARTER

The recoil starter can be removed and installed with the engine mounted in the frame. The following procedures are shown with the engine removed for clarity.

Removal/Installation

1. If the engine is mounted in the frame, remove the airbox as described in Chapter Eight. Remove any wires or cables from the guides mounted on the recoil starter assembly.

2. Remove the four bolts and the recoil starter assembly (A, **Figure 21**).

3. Install the recoil starter assembly by reversing the removal step while noting the following:

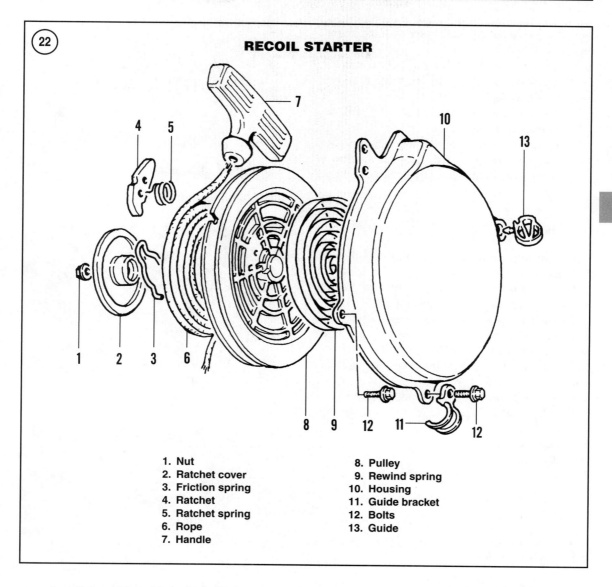

RECOIL STARTER

1. Nut
2. Ratchet cover
3. Friction spring
4. Ratchet
5. Ratchet spring
6. Rope
7. Handle

8. Pulley
9. Rewind spring
10. Housing
11. Guide bracket
12. Bolts
13. Guide

a. Install the cable guide in the hole shown at B, **Figure 21**.

b. Tighten the recoil starter assembly mounting bolts securely.

c. Pull the recoil starter handle to check operation.

Disassembly

Refer to **Figure 22**.

WARNING
The rewind spring is under pressure and may jump out when the starter is serviced in the following steps. Wear safety glasses and gloves when disassembling the starter.

1. Remove the starter housing as described in this chapter.

2. Remove the nut (A, **Figure 23**) and ratchet cover (B).

3. Remove the ratchet (A, **Figure 24**) and spring (A, **Figure 25**).

4. Untie the starter rope and remove the starter handle (C, **Figure 23**), then release the starter rope slowly and allow the drive pulley to unwind. Re-

move the drive pulley (D, **Figure 23**) and starter rope assembly.

5. Remove the starter rope from the drive pulley.

6. If necessary, remove the rewind spring from the housing as follows:

    a. Place the starter housing on the floor with the spring side facing down.

    b. Tap on the top of the housing with a plastic hammer while holding the housing firmly against the floor. The spring should fall out and unwind inside the housing.

Inspection

Replace worn or damaged parts as described in this section.

1. Clean and dry all parts. Do not clean the drive pulley, rope and ratchet cover in solvent.

2. Check the starter shaft in the starter housing. Replace the starter housing if the starter shaft is excessively worn or damaged.

3. Check the drive pulley for excessive wear or damage.

4. Check the ratchet and ratchet spring for damage.

5. Check the rewind spring (**Figure 26**) for cracks or damaged ends.

6. Check the starter rope for tearing, fraying or other damage.

7. Check the ratchet cover and spring for damage.

Assembly

1. If removed, install the rewind spring into the starter housing as follows:

> *WARNING*
> *The rewind spring is put under pressure when installing it in the following steps. Safety glasses and gloves must be worn when installing the rewind spring and assembling the starter assembly.*

    a. Before installing the rewind spring, wipe some grease onto a clean rag, then slide the spring against the rag to lubricate it with grease. Wipe off any excess grease.

    b. Lubricate the starter housing shaft with the same type of grease.

    c. Hook the outer end of the rewind spring onto the spring guide as shown in **Figure 27**.

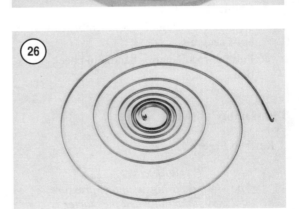

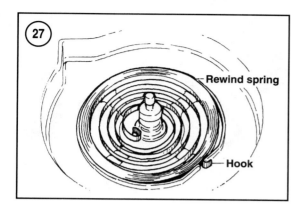

Figure 27 — Rewind spring, Hook

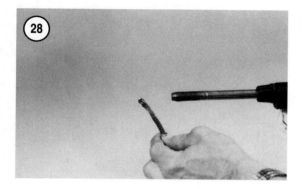

Figure 28

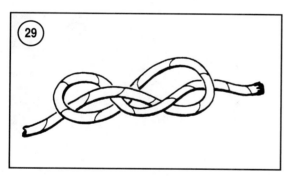

Figure 29

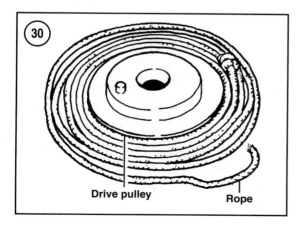

Figure 30 — Drive pulley, Rope

Figure 31

d. Wind the rewind spring counterclockwise working from the outside of the spring into the starter housing. Push down the end of the spring so it contacts the starter housing shaft (**Figure 27**).

e. Compare the rewind spring ends with **Figure 27**, then confirm that the spring lies flat in the housing.

2. Before installing the rope, check the rope ends for fraying. Apply heat with a heat gun (**Figure 28**) to tighten loose or frayed rope ends. Do not overheat.

3. To install the rope, perform the following:

a. Tie a knot in one end of the rope (**Figure 29**).

b. Insert the rope through the hole in the drive pulley. Pull the rope tight so the knot enters the raised shoulder on the pulley (**Figure 30**).

c. With the ratchet side of the drive pulley facing up, wind the rope clockwise around the drive pulley as shown in **Figure 30**.

4. Grease the drive pulley shaft bore.

5. Install the drive pulley into the starter housing as follows:

a. Align the hook in the bottom of the drive pulley with the end of the rewind spring and install the drive pulley into the housing.

b. Rotate the drive pulley slightly until it drops into place, indicating the hook in the drive pulley meshes with the rewind spring end.

6. Extend the rope, then catch the rope in the drive pulley notch (B, **Figure 25**).

7. Rotate the drive pulley 2 1/2 turns clockwise and hold in this position. Do not let go of the drive pulley.

8. Feed the rope through the starter housing rope hole and secure it in place with a pair of locking pliers (**Figure 31**). Slip the rope out of the drive pulley notch.

9. Insert the starter handle onto the rope. Tie a knot in the end of the rope (**Figure 32**).

10. Remove the locking pliers and allow the drive pulley to unwind in the housing while pulling the rope into the housing (**Figure 33**).

11. Grease the ratchet spring and ratchet.

12. Install the end of the ratchet spring into the hole in the drive pulley. Refer to A, **Figure 25**.

13. Install and hook the ratchet against the ratchet spring as shown in B, **Figure 24**.

14. If removed, install the friction spring (A, **Figure 34**) onto the back of the ratchet cover (B).

15. Grease the friction spring and ratchet cover surfaces.

16. Install the ratchet cover (**Figure 35**). Make sure the ratchet aligns with the friction spring.

17. Install and tighten the nut (A, **Figure 23**).

18. Pull the starter handle and confirm the ratchet extends as shown in **Figure 35**. If the ratchet does not extend, remove the ratchet cover and reassemble the parts.

DRIVEN PULLEY

It is necessary to hold the driven pulley when removing or installing the pulley retaining bolt. Honda tool Part no. 07SMB-HM70100 may be used to hold the pulley or a holding tool may be made using a piece of 3/8-inch bar stock that is bent as needed.

Removal/Installation

1. Remove the recoil starter assembly as described in this chapter.

> *CAUTION*
> *If using a fabricated tool to hold the driven pulley in Step 2, make sure it does not damage the pulley flanges.*

2. Loosen and remove the driven pulley bolt (A, **Figure 36**). To prevent pulley rotation, insert a tool between the flanges as shown in **Figure 37**.

3. Remove the driven pulley (B, **Figure 36**).

4. Inspect the driven pulley for cracks or other damage. Replace if necessary.

5. Inspect the O-ring (**Figure 38**) on the bolt and replace if damaged.

6. Install the driven pulley by reversing the preceding removal steps while noting the following:

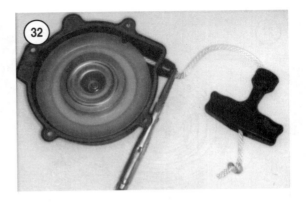

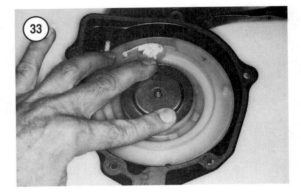

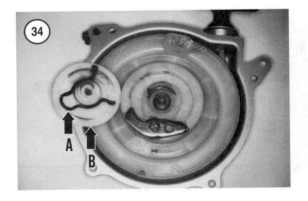

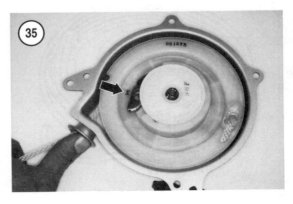

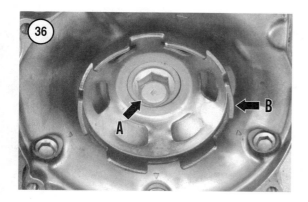

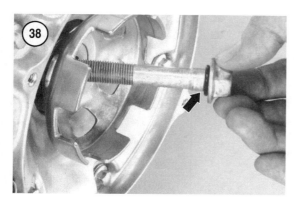

a. Apply engine oil to the driven pulley shaft and the seal in the alternator cover.

b. Align the master spline on the end of the driven pulley with the corresponding spline in the flywheel, then install the driven pulley.

c. Lubricate the O-ring with engine oil and install it onto the driven pulley bolt.

d. Secure the driven pulley with the same tool used during removal.

e. Apply engine oil to the bolt threads and seating surface, then install the driven pulley bolt and tighten to 108 N•m (80 ft.-lb.).

ALTERNATOR COVER

The stator coil assembly and ignition pulse generator are mounted on the alternator cover.

Removal/Installation

1. Remove the swing arm as described in Chapter Thirteen.

> *NOTE*
> *The starter gears may fall out of the rear crankcase cover when removing the alternator cover in Step 2.*

2. Remove the driven pulley as described in this chapter.

3. Remove the bolts and the alternator cover (A, **Figure 39**).

4. Remove the gasket and, if necessary, the dowel pins.

> *NOTE*
> *The alternator cover is pulled with considerable magnetic force toward the engine during installation. Make sure no wires or other objects can be trapped while installing the cover.*

5. Install the alternator cover by reversing the preceding removal steps while noting the following:

a. If removed, install the dowel pins into the holes (**Figure 40**) in the rear crankcase cover.

b. Apply Yamabond No. 4 (or equivalent) onto the grommet in the alternator cover (**Figure 41**).

c. Install new sealing washers on the lower bolts (B, **Figure 39**).

d. Install and tighten the alternator cover mounting bolts securely.

Oil Seal Inspection/Replacement

1. Inspect the alternator cover oil seal (**Figure 42**) for leaks, wear or damage.
2. Replace the alternator cover oil seal as follows:
   a. Pry the oil seal out of the cover with a wide-blade screwdriver. Pad the bottom of the screwdriver to prevent it from damaging the alternator cover.
   b. Pack the lips of the new oil seal with grease.
   c. Press in the oil seal with the flat side (**Figure 42**) facing out.

Disassembly/Reassembly

Perform these steps to remove the stator coil, ignition pulse generator or neutral/reverse switch assembly.

1. Disconnect the connector from the top of the ignition pulse generator (B, **Figure 41**).
2. Remove the ignition pulse generator (B, **Figure 41**) and wire clamp (C) mounting bolts. Remove the ignition pulse generator.
3. Remove the stator mounting bolts (**Figure 43**), then remove the stator assembly.
4. Inspect the starter shaft bearing (A, **Figure 44**). If the bearing is excessively worn or damaged, use a blind bearing puller to extract the bearing. Refer to Chapter One for bearing removal/installation information.
5. Install by reversing the preceding removal steps while noting the following:
   a. Tighten the stator mounting bolts (**Figure 43**) to 10 N•m (88 in.-lb.).
   b. Remove all threadlock residue from the ignition pulse generator mounting bolt threads.
   c. Apply a medium strength threadlock onto the ignition pulse generator mounting bolts. Install and tighten the bolts to 6 N•m (53 in.-lb.).
   d. Be sure the ignition pulse generator wire is routed under the wire clamp (B, **Figure 41**) and ignition pulse generator.
   e. Apply Yamabond No. 4 (or equivalent) onto the grommet (A, **Figure 41**) and be sure it is properly seated in the notch in the alternator cover.

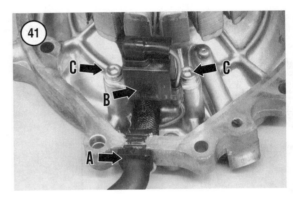

44

45

46

47

STARTER REDUCTION GEARS

Removal/Installation

1. Remove the alternator cover as described in this chapter.

2. Remove the gear A (A, **Figure 45**) and shaft (B).

3. Remove the washer (C, **Figure 45**) and gear C (D).

4. Remove the reduction shaft and gear (**Figure 46**).

5. Inspect the gears and shaft. Inspect the splines on the gear shaft (A, **Figure 47**) and gear C. Make sure the snap ring (B, **Figure 47**) fits securely in the shaft groove.

6. Inspect the shaft bearing bores in the alternator cover (B, **Figure 44**) and the rear crankcase cover. If the bores are excessively worn or damaged, replace the cover.

7. Install the starter reduction gears by reversing the removal steps.

REAR CRANKCASE COVER

The rear crankcase cover houses the following components:

1. Sub-transmission bearings.

2. Final driveshaft seal and bearing.

3. Gear position switch.

4. ATV speed sensor.

Removal/Installation

The rear crankcase cover can be removed with the flywheel installed on the engine.

1. Remove the engine as described in this chapter.

2. Remove the starter as described in Chapter Nine.

3. Remove the alternator cover as described in this chapter.

4. Remove the starter reduction gears as described in this chapter.

5. Remove the speed sensor as described in Chapter Nine.

6. Remove the gear position switch as described in Chapter Nine.

7. If not previously removed, remove the left engine side cover mounting bracket.

8. Remove the 11 rear cover bolts (**Figure 48**).

9. Remove the rear crankcase cover.

10. Remove the oil tube and O-ring (**Figure 49**).

5

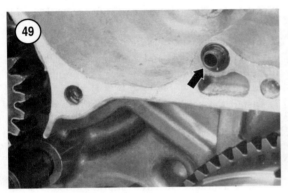

11. If necessary, remove the two dowel pins (A, **Figure 50**).

12. Remove all gasket material from the rear crankcase cover and engine mating surfaces.

13. Inspect the rear crankcase cover assembly as described in this section.

14. Install the rear crankcase cover assembly by reversing the preceding removal steps while noting the following:

a. Pack the driveshaft oil seal lips with grease.

b. The transmission must be in neutral, which is indicated by the position of the slot on the shift drum (A, **Figure 51**). The slot must be aligned with the bolt hole (B, **Figure 51**) on the crankcase.

c. Make sure the washers are installed on the countershaft and reverse idle shaft (B, **Figure 50**).

d. Thoroughly clean the mating surfaces of the crankcase and crankcase cover. Apply a bead of Yamabond No. 4 (or equivalent) to the rear crankcase cover mating surface.

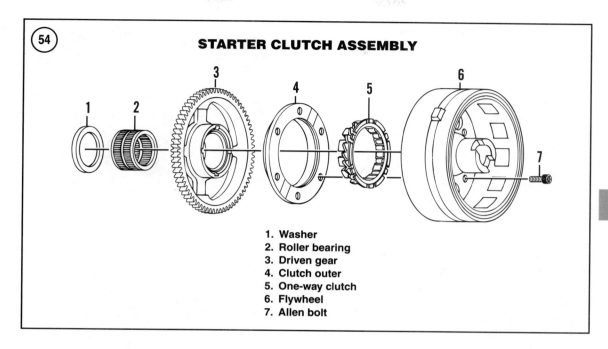

STARTER CLUTCH ASSEMBLY

1. Washer
2. Roller bearing
3. Driven gear
4. Clutch outer
5. One-way clutch
6. Flywheel
7. Allen bolt

e. Install the middle length bolt in hole A, **Figure 52** and the longest cover retaining bolts in holes B, **Figure 52**.

f. Tighten the rear crankcase cover bolts in a crossing pattern and in two or three steps. Tighten all cover bolts to 12 N•m (106 in.-lb.).

Inspection

1. Clean and dry the rear crankcase cover.

2. Inspect the final driveshaft oil seal (A, **Figure 53**) for leaks or damage. When replacing the oil seal, note the following:

a. Remove the clip (B, **Figure 53**) before removing the final driveshaft oil seal.

b. Remove the oil seal by prying it out of the cover with a wide-blade screwdriver.

c. Check the oil seal mounting bore for cracks or other damage.

d. Pack the lip of the new oil seal with grease.

e. Install the oil seal with the flat side facing out.

f. Install the clip (B, **Figure 53**), making sure it seats in the groove completely.

3. Check the driveshaft bearing (C, **Figure 53**) for roughness and end play by rotating it slowly by hand. Replace the bearing if it turns roughly or has excessive play. Refer to Chapter One for general

bearing replacement. Install the bearing with the marked side up.

FLYWHEEL AND STARTER CLUTCH

This section describes service to the flywheel and starter clutch assembly.

Refer to **Figure 54** when performing the following procedures.

Flywheel Puller

A flywheel puller is required to remove the flywheel from the crankshaft. Use one of the following pullers:

1. Honda flywheel puller (part No. 07933-3950000).

2. K&L universal rotor puller (part No. 35-9456).

Removal

1. Remove the alternator cover as described in this chapter.

2. If not previously removed, remove the starter reduction gears as described in this chapter.

CAUTION
Apply grease to the puller threads and the tip of the puller stem.

3. Install the flywheel puller into the flywheel (**Figure 55**).

> *CAUTION*
> *Do not remove the flywheel without a puller. Any attempt to do so damages the crankshaft and flywheel.*

> *CAUTION*
> *If normal flywheel removal attempts fail, do not force the puller. Excessive force strips the flywheel threads, causing damage. Take the engine to a dealership or machine shop and have them remove the flywheel.*

4. Hold the flywheel and gradually tighten the flywheel puller (**Figure 55**) until the flywheel pops off the crankshaft taper.

5. Remove the puller from the flywheel.

6. Remove the flywheel and the starter clutch assembly (**Figure 56**).

7. Remove the needle bearing (A, **Figure 57**) and washer (B).

8. If necessary, remove the Woodruff key (C, **Figure 57**) from the crankshaft keyway.

9. Inspect the flywheel, starter clutch and starter reduction gear assembly as described in this section.

Starter Clutch Removal/Inspection/Installation

Refer to **Figure 54**.

1. Check the one-way clutch operation as follows:
   a. Place the flywheel and starter clutch on the workbench so the driven gear faces up as shown in **Figure 58**.
   b. Hold the flywheel and try to turn the driven gear clockwise and then counterclockwise. The driven gear should only turn clockwise as viewed in **Figure 58**.
   c. If the driven gear turns counterclockwise, the one-way clutch is damaged and must be replaced as described in this procedure.

2. Remove the driven gear (**Figure 58**) from the one-way clutch assembly.

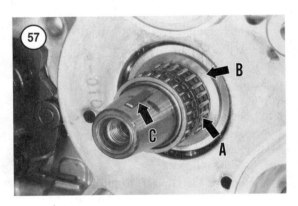

3. Inspect the driven gear (A, **Figure 59**) for the following conditions:
   a. Worn or damaged gear teeth.
   b. Worn or damaged bearing shoulder.
   c. Measure the outside diameter of the bearing surface (B, **Figure 59**) and refer to **Table 2**.

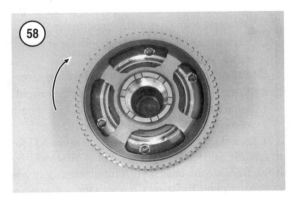

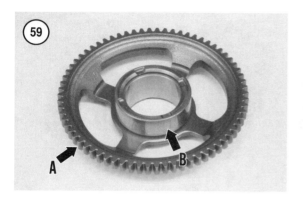

4. Inspect the one-way clutch (**Figure 60**) for the following conditions:

    a. Excessively worn or damaged one-way clutch rollers.

    b. Loose one-way clutch Torx bolts.

5. To replace the one-way clutch (**Figure 60**), perform the following:

    a. Secure the flywheel with a strap or band wrench.

    b. Using an impact driver, remove the one-way clutch mounting bolts (**Figure 61**).

    c. Separate the clutch outer race (A, **Figure 62**) and the sprag clutch (B).

    d. Install the sprag clutch into the outer race so the flange on the sprag fits into the recess in the outer race as shown in **Figure 63**.

    e. Apply a medium strength threadlock to the threads of each mounting bolt.

    f. Install the one-way clutch mounting bolts finger-tight, then tighten to 30 N•m (22 ft.-lb.).

6. Inspect the needle bearing (A, **Figure 57**). The needles should be smooth and polished with no flat spots, cracks or other damage. Inspect the bearing cage for cracks or other damage. Replace the bearing if necessary.

7. Inspect the washer (B, **Figure 57**) for cracks, scoring or other damage.

Flywheel Inspection

1. Clean and dry the flywheel (**Figure 56**).

2. Check the flywheel for cracks or breaks.

> *WARNING*
> *Replace a cracked or chipped fly-*
> *wheel. A damaged flywheel can fly*
> *apart at high rpm, throwing metal*

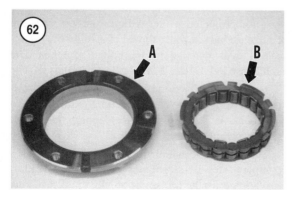

fragments into the engine. Do not re-pair a damaged flywheel.

3. Check the flywheel tapered bore and the crankshaft taper for damage.

4. Replace damaged parts as required.

Installation

1. Apply engine oil to the one-way clutch rollers and the driven gear shoulder.

2. To install the driven gear:
   a. Place the flywheel on the workbench so the one-way clutch faces up.
   b. Rotate the driven gear clockwise and slide it into the one-way clutch (**Figure 58**).

3. Apply engine oil onto the washer and needle bearing before installing them onto the crankshaft.

4. Install the washer (B, **Figure 57**) and the needle bearing (A) onto the crankshaft.

5. If removed, install the Woodruff key (C, **Figure 57**) into the crankshaft keyway.

6. Align the keyway in the flywheel with the Woodruff key in the crankshaft and install the flywheel (**Figure 64**).

> *NOTE*
> *Performing Step 7 seats the flywheel on the crankshaft taper. If the flywheel is not secured in this manner, magnetic force pulls the flywheel off the crankshaft when the stator coil (alternator cover assembly) is installed.*

7. Secure the flywheel to the crankshaft as follows:
   a. Temporarily install the recoil starter pulley (**Figure 65**, typical) and the mounting bolt.
   b. Hold the flywheel and tighten the mounting bolt sufficiently to seat the flywheel on the taper.
   c. Remove the mounting bolt and recoil starter pulley.

8. Install the starter reduction gears as described in this chapter.

9. Install the alternator cover as described in this chapter.

CRANKCASE AND CRANKSHAFT

The crankcase is made in two halves of thin-wall, precision diecast aluminum alloy. To avoid damage,

do not hammer or pry on any of the interior or exterior projected walls. A liquid gasket seals the crankcase halves while dowel pins align the crankcase halves when they are bolted together. The crankcase halves can be replaced separately.

The crankshaft assembly consists of two full-circle flywheels pressed together on a crankpin. Two ball bearings in the crankcase support the crankshaft assembly.

The procedure which follows is presented as a complete, step-by-step major lower end overhaul. If servicing only the transmission, the crankcase may

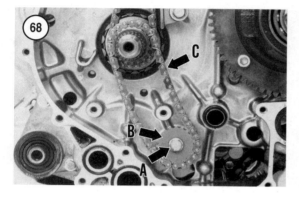

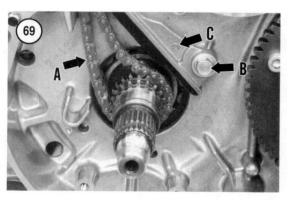

be disassembled and reassembled without removing the crankshaft.

References to the front and rear side of the engine, as used in the text, refer to the engine as it sits in the frame, not as it sits on a workbench.

Special Tools

A press is required to remove the crankshaft from the crankcase.

To install the crankshaft into the crankcase, a number of Honda crankshaft installation tools or their equivalents are required. These tools and part numbers are called out during the crankshaft installation procedure.

Crankcase Disassembly

This procedure describes disassembly of the crankcase halves and removal of the transmission and internal shift mechanism. Crankshaft removal is covered in a separate procedure.

Chapter Seven describes transmission and internal shift mechanism service procedures.

1. Remove all exterior engine assemblies as described in this chapter and other related chapters:
   a. Cylinder head (Chapter Four).
   b. Cylinder and piston (Chapter Four).
   c. Recoil starter (this chapter).
   d. Flywheel and starter clutch (this chapter).
   e. Starter (Chapter Nine).
   f. Clutch (Chapter Six).
   g. Sub-transmission and gearshift linkage (Chapter Seven).

2. If not previously removed, refer to Chapter Nine and remove the angle sensor.

3. Remove the angle sensor joint (**Figure 66**).

4. Remove the oil separate plate retaining bolts (A, **Figure 67**), then remove the plate (B).

5. Remove the oil pump sprocket retaining bolt (A, **Figure 68**), sprocket (B) and drive chain (C).

6. Remove the cam chain (A, **Figure 69**).

7. Remove the chain guide retaining bolt (B, **Figure 69**), guide (C), washer and collar.

8. Remove the primary driven gear from the transmission using the following procedure:
   a. Install the clutch drum (A, **Figure 70**).
   b. Place gear holder (Honda part No. 07724-001A100) between the primary drive gear on

the clutch housing and the primary driven gear (**Figure 71**).

> *NOTE*
> *If a gear holder tool is not available, a copper penny may be placed between the gear teeth to prevent gear rotation.*

c. Remove the primary driven gear retaining Allen bolts (B, **Figure 70**).

d. Remove the clutch drum, then remove the primary driven gear.

e. Remove the dowel pin (A, **Figure 72**) in the transmission drive flange.

9. Remove the oil pickup bolt (A, **Figure 73**) and remove the pickup (B).

10. Remove the oil strainer screen bolt (C, **Figure 73**) and remove the strainer screen (D).

11. Remove the engine dampers and bushings (**Figure 74**).

12. Remove the rear crankcase bolts (**Figure 75**) in a crossing pattern.

13. Position the engine so the front side (clutch side) is accessible.

14. Remove the front crankcase mounting bolts (**Figure 76**) in a crossing pattern.

> *CAUTION*
> *Perform this operation over and close to the work bench because the crankcase halves may easily separate. Do not hammer on the crankcase halves.*

> *CAUTION*
> *Do not pry between the crankcase mating surfaces when separating the crankcase halves. Doing so may cause an oil leak.*

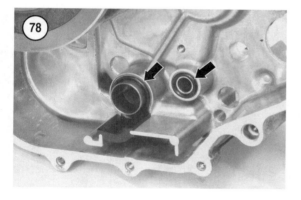

15. Position the crankcase on wooden blocks so the crankshaft is vertical and the front side is up.

16. Tap on the front crankcase half using a soft-faced hammer while lifting it off the engine. Rotate the transmission drive flange (B, **Figure 72**) as needed so it clears the crankcase half during removal.

17. Remove the main bearing inner race (**Figure 77**).

NOTE
The main bearing inner race may remain in the main bearing.

18. Remove the O-rings (**Figure 78**).

19. If necessary, remove the dowel pins (A, **Figure 79**).

NOTE
Steps 10-14 describe removal of the transmission assembly.

20. Remove the five transmission mounting bolts, then remove the transmission (B, **Figure 79**). Set aside the transmission unit (**Figure 80**).

21. Remove the dowel pin (**Figure 81**).

22. If necessary, remove the oil pump as described in this chapter.

23. If necessary, remove the crankshaft and balancer shaft as described in the following section.

Crankshaft/Balancer Shaft Removal

Remove the crankshaft (A, **Figure 82**) and balancer shaft (B) as follows:

1. Support the rear crankcase in a press.

> *CAUTION*
> *When supporting the rear crankcase in the press, confirm there is adequate room to press the crankshaft out without the connecting rod hitting against the press bed. If this happens, a bent connecting rod may result. Check the setup carefully before applying pressure to the crankshaft.*

> *CAUTION*
> *Catch the crankshaft and balancer shaft once the crankshaft is free of the rear crankcase half. Otherwise these parts can fall to the floor, causing damage.*

2. Center the crankshaft under the press arm (**Figure 83**) and press the crankshaft out of the crankcase.

3. Remove the crankshaft and balancer shaft (A and B, **Figure 82**) from the crankcase half.

4. Remove the rear crankcase from the press.

Crankcase Inspection

1. Remove all gasket residue from the crankcase mating surfaces.

2. Pry out the output shaft oil seal (**Figure 84**) from the front crankcase half using a wide-blade screwdriver. Pad the bottom of the screwdriver to prevent crankcase damage.

> *CAUTION*
> *When drying the crankcase bearings in Step 3, do not allow the inner bearing races to spin. The bearings are not lubricated and damage may result. When drying the bearings with compressed air, do not allow the air jet to spin the bearing. The air jet can rotate the bearings at excessive speeds.*

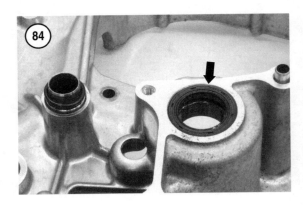

3. Clean both crankcase halves and all crankcase bearings with solvent. Thoroughly dry with compressed air.

4. Flush all crankcase oil passages with compressed air.

5. Lightly oil all of the crankcase bearings with engine oil before checking the bearings in Step 6.

6. Check the bearings for roughness, pitting, galling and play by rotating them slowly by hand. Replace any bearing that turns roughly or has excessive play (**Figure 85**).

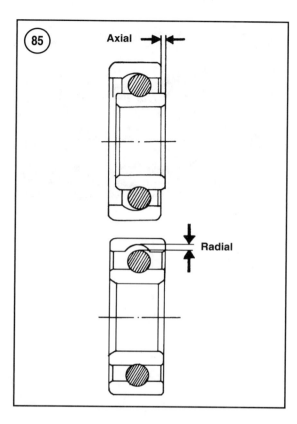

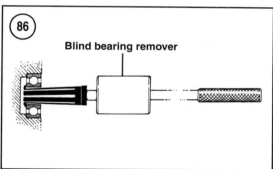

7. Replace any worn or damaged bearings as described under *Crankcase Bearing Replacement* in this section.

NOTE
Always replace the opposing bearing
at the same time.

8. Carefully inspect the case halves for cracks and fractures, especially in the lower areas where they are vulnerable to rock damage.
9. Check the areas around the stiffening ribs, around bearing bosses and threaded holes for dam-

age. Refer crankcase repair to a shop specializing in the repair of precision aluminum castings.
10. Check the threaded holes in both crankcase halves for thread damage, dirt or oil buildup. If necessary, clean or repair the threads with the correct size metric tap. Coat the tap threads with kerosene or an aluminum tap fluid before use.
11. Install the output shaft oil seal with the flat side (**Figure 84**) facing out. Pack the lips of the new oil seal with grease.

Crankcase Bearing Replacement

The crankcase contains bearings for the crankshaft, transmission and balancer shaft. Note that the front crankshaft main bearing includes a separate inner race. The race may be found on the crankshaft (**Figure 77**) or in the bearing. When replacing bearings, note the following:
1. Before removing the bearings, note and record the direction in which the bearings size codes face for proper reinstallation.
2. Refer to the general bearing replacement procedures in Chapter One and replace the bearings as described. Use a blind bearing remover to remove bearings installed in blind holes (**Figure 86**).

Crankshaft Inspection

Handle the crankshaft carefully when performing the following cleaning and inspection procedures. Individual crankshaft components are not available separately. If the crankshaft is excessively worn or damaged or if any measurement is out of specification, replace the crankshaft as an assembly.
1. Clean the crankshaft thoroughly with solvent. Clean the crankshaft oil passageway with compressed air. Dry the crankshaft with compressed air, then lubricate all bearing surfaces with a light coat of engine oil.
2. Check the crankshaft journals for scratches, heat discoloration or other defects.
3. Check the flywheel taper, threads and keyway for damage.
4. Check the connecting rod big end for signs of damage as well as bearing or thrust washer damage.
5. Check the connecting rod small end for signs of excessive heat (blue coloration) or other damage.
6. Measure the connecting rod small end inside diameter (**Figure 87**) with a snap gauge or an inside

5

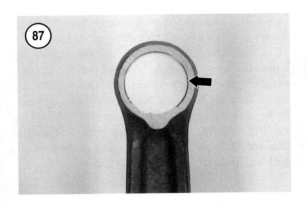

micrometer and compare with the dimension in **Table 2**.

7. Slide the connecting rod to one side and check the connecting rod side clearance with a flat feeler gauge (**Figure 88**) and compare with the dimension in **Table 2**.

8. Place the crankshaft on a set of V-blocks and measure runout with a dial indicator at the points listed in **Table 2**. If the runout exceeds the service limit, take the crankshaft to a Honda dealership for service or replacement.

9. Place the crankshaft on a set of V-blocks and measure the connecting rod big end radial clearance with a dial indicator. Measure in the two directions shown in **Figure 89** and compare with the dimension in **Table 2**.

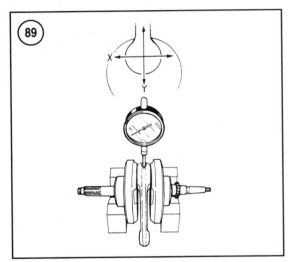

Balancer Shaft Inspection

1. Inspect the balancer shaft bearing journals (**Figure 90**) for deep scoring, excessive wear, heat discoloration or cracks.

2. Replace the balancer shaft if necessary.

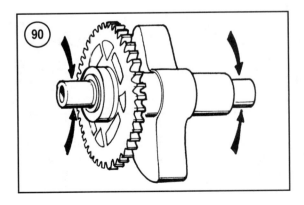

Final Drive Shaft and Gear Inspection

Refer to Chapter Seven for all disassembly, inspection and reassembly procedures.

Crankshaft and Balancer Shaft Installation

Transmission Inspection

Refer to Chapter Seven for all disassembly, inspection and reassembly procedures.

1. Use the following Honda tools (or equivalent) to install the crankshaft and balancer shaft into the rear crankcase.

   a. Threaded adapter (part No. 07931-KF00200): A, **Figure 91**.

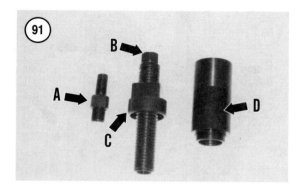

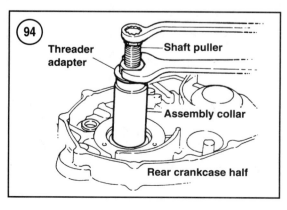

Threader adapter — Shaft puller — Assembly collar — Rear crankcase half

b. Shaft puller (part No. 07931-ME4010B USA only or 07965-VM00200): B, **Figure 91**.

c. Threaded adapter (part No. 07931-HB3020A): C, **Figure 91**.

d. Assembly collar (part No. 07965-VM00100): D, **Figure 91**.

NOTE
Before ordering these tools, confirm the tool part numbers with a Honda dealership.

2. Lubricate the crankshaft and balancer shaft bearings with oil.

3. Align the timing marks on the crankshaft and balancer shaft (**Figure 92**) and install both parts into the rear crankcase half. Recheck the timing mark alignment.

4. Install the threaded adapter into the end of the crankshaft (**Figure 93**).

5. Install the crankshaft puller assembly (**Figure 94**) onto the end of the crankshaft and thread it into the threaded adapter. Center the tool assembly on the main bearing inner race.

CAUTION
When installing the crankshaft in Step 5, position the connecting rod at the TDC or BDC position. Otherwise the connecting rod may contact the side of the crankcase, causing expensive connecting rod and crankcase damage.

6. Hold the threaded adapter and turn the shaft puller (**Figure 94**) to pull the crankshaft into the main bearing. When installing the crankshaft, frequently check that it is going straight into the bearing and not binding to one side.

7. Continue to turn the shaft puller until the crankshaft bottoms against the main bearing. Remove the crankshaft tools and turn the crankshaft (**Figure 93**). The crankshaft must turn with no binding or roughness.

8. Make sure the index marks on the crankshaft and balancer shaft align as shown in **Figure 92**.

CAUTION
Engine damage occurs if the crankshaft and balancer shaft index marks do not align.

Crankcase Assembly

1. Install the crankshaft and balancer shaft into the rear crankcase as described in this chapter.
2. Lightly oil all of the crankcase bearings.
3. Install the dowel pin (**Figure 95**).
4. Install the oil pump as described in this chapter.
5. Install the transmission (A, **Figure 96**). Tighten the retaining bolts to 12 N•m (106 in.-lb.).
6. Install the dowel pins (B, **Figure 96**).
7. Lubricate and install the O-rings (**Figure 97**).
8. Install the main bearing inner race (**Figure 98**) so the flanged side contacts the crankshaft.
9. Lubricate all shafts, gears and bearings with engine oil.
10. Thoroughly clean the mating surfaces of the crankcases halves. Apply a bead of Yamabond No. 4 or equivalent to the front crankcase half mating surface.
11. Align the front crankcase half with the crankshaft and transmission and install it onto the rear crankcase half. Rotate the transmission drive flange as needed so it clears the crankcase half during installation. Push the crankcase down squarely into place until it engages the dowel pins and then seats completely against the rear crankcase half.

CAUTION
Force is not required to mate the crankcase halves. If the crankcase halves do not fit together completely, do not pull them together with the crankcase bolts. Remove the front crankcase half and investigate the cause of the interference. If the crankshaft was removed, confirm it is installed and seated properly in the rear crankcase main bearing.

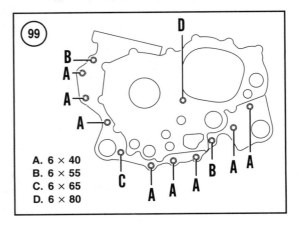

A. 6 × 40
B. 6 × 55
C. 6 × 65
D. 6 × 80

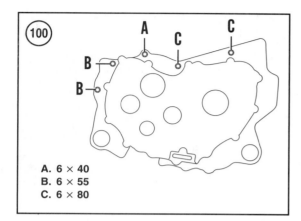

A. 6 × 40
B. 6 × 55
C. 6 × 80

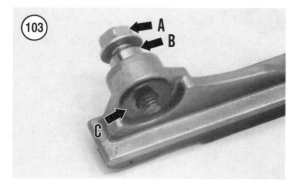

5

12. Verify that each rotating assembly turns freely with no binding. If everything turns properly, continue with Step 13.

13. Install the front crankcase mounting bolts. Refer to **Figure 99** for bolt length and location. Tighten the crankcase mounting bolts in three steps in a crossing pattern to 12 N•m (106 in.-lb.).

14. Install the rear crankcase mounting bolts. Refer to **Figure 100** for bolt length and location. Tighten the crankcase mounting bolts in a crossing pattern to 12 N•m (106 in.-lb.).

15. Rotate the transmission shafts and crankshaft to ensure there is no binding. If there is any binding, disassemble the engine as needed and correct the problem.

16. Install the primary driven gear onto the transmission drive flange using the following procedure:

    a. Install the dowel pin (**Figure 101**) in the transmission drive flange.

    b. Install the primary driven gear onto the transmission drive flange (**Figure 102**). Install the bolts finger tight.

    c. Temporarily install the clutch drum.

    d. Using the holding device used in Step 8 of the *Crankcase Disassembly* procedure, lock the gears and tighten the primary driven gear retaining bolts in three steps to 17 N•m (150 in.-lb.).

    e. Remove the clutch drum.

17. Install the camshaft chain guide. Install the retaining bolt (A, **Figure 103**), collar (B) and washer (C) as shown.

18. Install the cam chain (**Figure 104**) so it meshes with the drive sprocket on the crankshaft.

19. Install the oil pump drive chain (A, **Figure 105**) so it meshes with the drive sprocket on the crankshaft. Install the oil pump sprocket into the

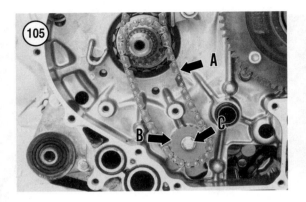

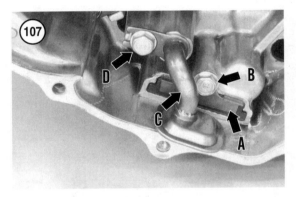

chain, then install the sprocket onto the oil pump shaft (B, **Figure 105**).

20. Apply medium strength threadlock to the oil pump sprocket retaining bolt. Install the bolt (C, **Figure 105**) and tighten to 12 N•m (106 in.-lb.).

21. Install the oil separate plate (**Figure 106**) and retaining bolts.

22. Install the strainer screen (A, **Figure 107**) and bolt (B).

23. Install a new O-ring onto the oil pickup tube (**Figure 108**). Install the oil pickup (C, **Figure 107**) and bolt (D).

24. Install the angle sensor joint (**Figure 109**).

25. Inspect the engine mounting dust seal and bushing (**Figure 110**) sets for wear or damage.

26. Install the bushing sets so the outer dust seal lips face out as shown in **Figure 111**.

27. Install all exterior engine assemblies as described in this chapter and other related chapters.

LUBRICATION SYSTEM

The lubrication system consists of the oil tank, oil pump, relief valve, check valve, thermosensor, oil strainer screens, oil filter, oil cooler and engine oil passages. Servicing these items (except the thermosensor, oil filter and oil cooler) is described in this chapter. Service the engine oil and oil filter as described in Chapter Three. Service the oil cooler as described in Chapter Ten. Refer to Chapter Nine for thermosensor service information.

OIL STRAINER SCREENS

Two oil strainer screens are installed in the engine; one in the oil tank and one in the crankcase. Inspect the oil strainer screens whenever servicing

5

those components. Refer to the *Oil Tank* or *Crankcase and Crankshaft* in this chapter.

OIL TANK

Removal/Installation

1. Drain the engine oil (Chapter Three).
2. Remove the right front mud guard (Chapter Fifteen).
3. Remove the right front inner fender (Chapter Fifteen).
4. Disconnect the oil thermosensor connector (**Figure 112**), then remove the thermosensor to prevent damage.
5. Remove the oil pipe retaining bolt (**Figure 113**) and separate the oil pipe from the oil tank. Repeat for the remaining oil pipe. Cover the pipe ends and oil tank openings to prevent oil leakage and contamination.

> *CAUTION*
> *The oil tank retaining bolts are different lengths. Note the bolt locations during disassembly.*

6. Remove the oil tank retaining bolts (**Figure 114** and **Figure 115**), then remove the oil tank.
7. Remove the oil port O-ring (**Figure 116**).
8. Remove the oil pipe (**Figure 117**), then remove the O-rings.
9. Reverse the removal procedure to install the oil tank while noting the following:
   a. Lubricate the O-rings with clean engine oil.
   b. Install new O-rings onto the oil pipe (**Figure 117**).
   c. Install a new O-ring (**Figure 116**) onto the front crankcase cover.

d. Install a new O-ring onto each oil pipe (**Figure 118**).

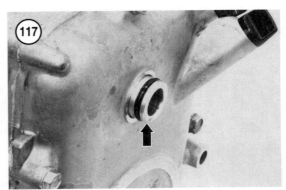

Disassembly/Inspection/Reassembly

1. Remove the cover retaining bolts (**Figure 119**).
2. Invert the oil tank, then remove the remaining bolts (**Figure 120**). Separate the cover from the oil tank.
3. Remove and clean the oil screen (**Figure 121**).
4. Remove the O-ring (A, **Figure 122**).
5. Remove the plate retaining bolts (B, **Figure 122**) and remove the plate.
6. Clean the oil tank and cover.
7. Reverse the disassembly steps to reassemble the oil tank while noting the following:
   a. Install a new O-ring onto the plate tube (A, **Figure 122**). Lubricate the O-ring with clean engine oil.
   b. Thoroughly clean the mating surfaces of the oil tank and cover. Apply a bead of Yamabond No. 4 (or equivalent) to oil tank mating surface.

OIL PUMP

Removal/Installation

1. Separate the crankcase as described under *Crankcase and Crankshaft* in this chapter.
2. Remove the oil pump mounting bolts (A and B, **Figure 123**), then remove the oil pump from the crankcase half.
3. Replace the O-rings (**Figure 124**). Lubricate the O-rings with clean engine oil.
4. Install the oil pump by reversing the removal procedure. Note the location of the short mounting

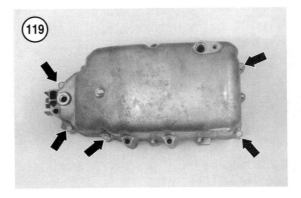

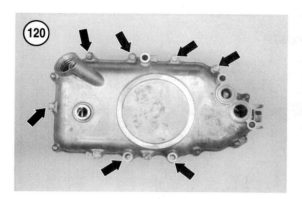

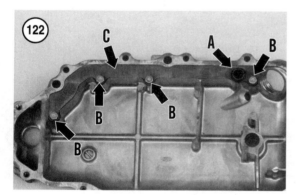

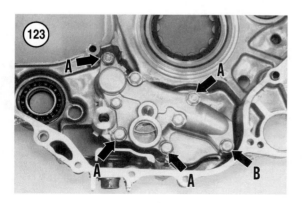

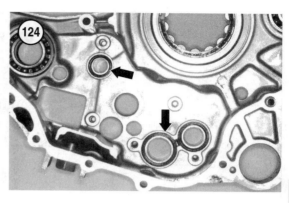

bolt (B, **Figure 123**). Tighten the bolts to 12 N•m (106 in.-lb.).

Disassembly/Inspection/Assembly

Refer to **Figure 125**.

> *CAUTION*
> *Install the pump rotors in their original positions. Some rotors are marked with a punch mark for identification (**Figure 126**), otherwise, mark the rotor.*

1. Remove the pump bolts (A, **Figure 127**), then remove pump body C (B, **Figure 127**).
2. Remove the spring seat (A, **Figure 128**), spring (B) and relief valve (C).
3. Remove the outer rotor (A, **Figure 129**) and inner rotor (B).
4. Remove the drive pin (**Figure 130**).
5. Remove the spacer (**Figure 131**).
6. Remove the outer rotor (A, **Figure 132**) and inner rotor (B).
7. Remove the drive pin (**Figure 133**).
8. Remove the dowel pins (**Figure 134**).
9. Remove the pump body B (A, **Figure 135**) from the pump body A (B). Remove the pump shaft assembly (C, **Figure 135**) from pump body A (B).
10. Remove the inner rotor (A, **Figure 136**) and drive pin (B) from the pump shaft.

Cleaning and Inspection

An excessively worn or damaged oil pump does not maintain sufficient oil pressure. Inspect the oil pump carefully when troubleshooting a lubrication or oil pressure problem.

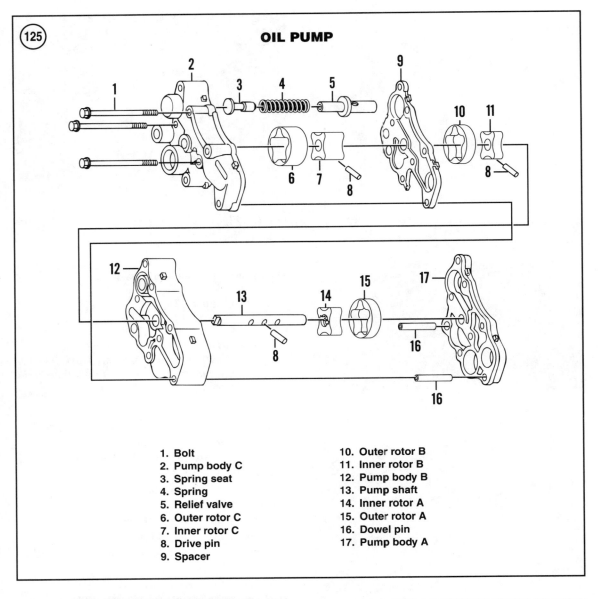

OIL PUMP

1. Bolt
2. Pump body C
3. Spring seat
4. Spring
5. Relief valve
6. Outer rotor C
7. Inner rotor C
8. Drive pin
9. Spacer
10. Outer rotor B
11. Inner rotor B
12. Pump body B
13. Pump shaft
14. Inner rotor A
15. Outer rotor A
16. Dowel pin
17. Pump body A

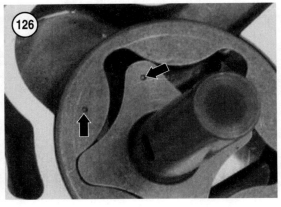

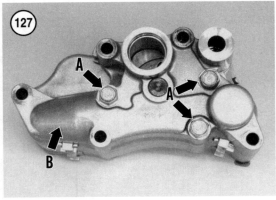

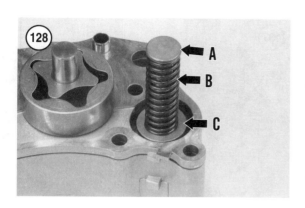

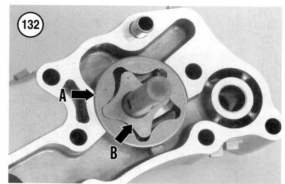

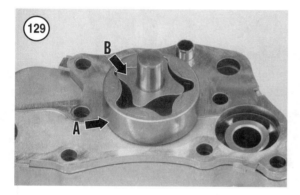

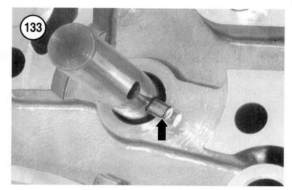

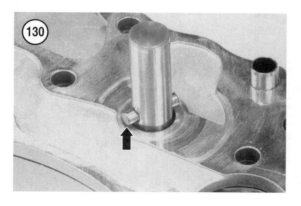

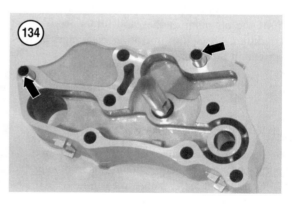

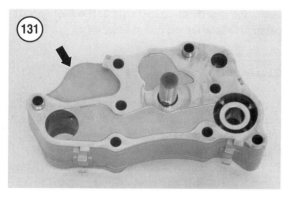

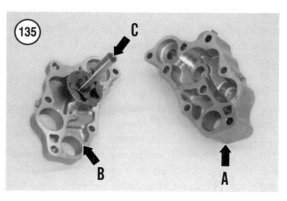

5

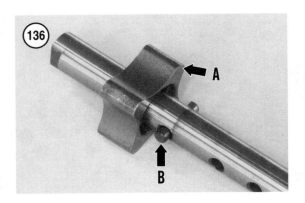

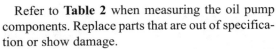

Refer to **Table 2** when measuring the oil pump components. Replace parts that are out of specification or show damage.

1. Clean and dry all parts. Place the parts on a clean, lint-free cloth.

2. Check the pump shaft for scoring, cracks or signs of heat discoloration.

3. Check the oil pump body for:
   a. Warped or cracked mating surfaces.
   b. Rotor bore damage.

4. Check the oil pump rotors for:
   a. Cracked or damaged outer surface.
   b. Worn or scored inner mating surfaces.

5. If the oil pump bodies and rotors are in good condition, check the operating clearances as described in Step 6 and Step 7.

> *NOTE*
> *The pump rotors are sold separately.*
> *The pump bodies, pump shaft and spacer are not.*

6. Install a set of inner and outer rotors and the pump shaft into the corresponding pump body.

7. Using a flat feeler gauge, measure the clearance between the outer rotor and the oil pump body (**Figure 137**, typical) and refer to the body clearance specification in **Table 2**. If out of specification, replace the outer rotor and remeasure. If still out of specification, replace the oil pump assembly.

8. Using a flat feeler gauge, measure the clearance between the inner rotor tip and the outer rotor (**Figure 138**, typical) and refer to the tip clearance specificationin **Table 2**. If out of specification, replace the inner and outer rotors.

9. Using a flat feeler gauge and straightedge, measure the side clearance between the body surface and rotors (**Figure 139**, typical) and refer to the end

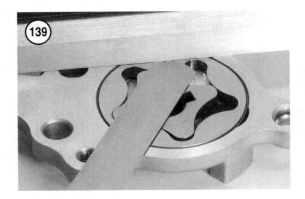

clearance specification in **Table 2**. If out of specification, replace the oil pump assembly.

Reassembly

1. If necessary, reclean the parts as described in the previous section. Lubricate the rotors and body rotor bore with engine oil when installing them in the following steps.

2. Install the pump shaft (A, **Figure 140**) into pump body A with the stepped end inserted first.

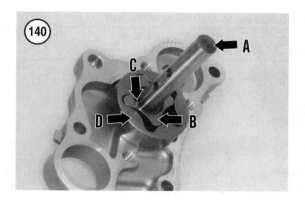

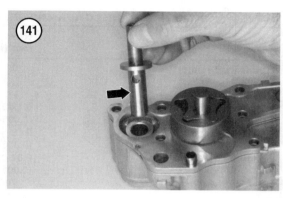

3. Install the inner rotor (B, **Figure 140**) so the drive slot is out, then install the drive pin (C). Install the outer rotor (D, **Figure 140**). If installing the original rotors, install them with their original sides facing up as identified during disassembly.

4. Install pump body B (B, **Figure 135**) onto pump body A (A).

5. Install the dowel pins (**Figure 134**).

6. Install the drive pin (**Figure 133**), then install the inner and outer rotors (**Figure 132**). Make sure the drive slot in the inner rotor fits against the drive pin.

7. Install the spacer (**Figure 131**).

8. Install the drive pin (**Figure 130**), then install the inner and outer rotors (**Figure 129**). Make sure the drive slot in the inner rotor fits against the drive pin.

9. Insert the relief valve (**Figure 141**), then install the spring (B, **Figure 128**) and spring seat (A).

10. Install pump body C (B, **Figure 127**).

11. Install the oil pump bolts (A, **Figure 127**) and tighten to 12 N•m (106 in.-lb.).

12. Turn the pump shaft. If there is any roughness or binding, disassemble the oil pump and check it for damage.

13. Store the oil pump in a plastic bag until installation.

ENGINE BREAK-IN

If the piston rings or a new piston were installed, the cylinder was honed or rebored or major lower end work was performed, break in the engine as if new. The performance and service life of the engine depends greatly on a careful and sensible break-in.

For the first 5-10 hours of operation, use no more than one-third throttle and vary the speed as much as possible within the one-third throttle limit. Avoid prolonged or steady running at one speed as well as hard acceleration.

Table 1 GENERAL ENGINE SPECIFICATIONS

Crankshaft type	Two main journals, unit type
Engine weight (approximate)	63 kg (139 lb.)
Lubrication system	Dry sump, forced pressure

Table 2 ENGINE LOWER END SERVICE SPECIFICATIONS

	New mm (in.)	Service limit mm (in.)
Connecting rod big end radial clearance	0.006-0.018 (0.0002-0.0007)	0.05 (0.002)
Connecting rod side clearance	0.05-0.65 (0.002-0.026)	0.8 (0.03)
Connecting rod small end inside diameter	20.020-20.041 (0.7882-0.7890)	20.07 (0.790)
	(continued)	

Table 2 ENGINE LOWER END SERVICE SPECIFICATIONS (continued)

	New mm (in.)	Service limit mm (in.)
Crankshaft runout*	– –	0.05 (0.002)
Oil pump		
Body clearance	0.12-0.22 (0.005-0.009)	0.25 (0.010)
End clearance	0.15 (0.006)	0.20 (0.008)
Side clearance	0.02-0.09 (0.001-0.004)	0.11 (0.004)
Starter driven gear boss OD	51.705-51.718 (2.0356-2.0361)	51.705 (2.0356)

*Measure crankshaft runout at each end at a point 6 mm (0.24 in.) in from either crankshaft end.

Table 3 ENGINE LOWER END TORQUE SPECIFICATIONS

	N•m	in.-lb.	ft.-lb.
Crankcase bolts	12	106	–
Driven pulley mounting bolt	108	–	80
Engine mounts			
Lower engine mounting through bolts			
Left and right side	54	–	40
Upper engine mounting through bolt	54	–	40
Engine mounting brackets			
Upper hanger bolts	32	–	24
Lower support bolts	32	–	24
Front differential			
Mounting bracket bolts	22	–	16
Lower mounting bolt	44	–	33
Upper mounting bolt	44	–	33
Gearshift arm pinch bolt	26	–	19
Ignition pulse generator mounting bolts	6	53	–
Oil pump assembly bolts	12	106	–
Oil pump drive sprocket bolt	12	106	–
Oil pump mounting bolts	12	106	–
Oil thermosensor	18	159	–
Rear crankcase cover bolts	12	106	–
Starter one-way clutch Allen bolts	30	–	22
Stator mounting bolts	10	88	–
Transmission primary driven gear bolts	17	150	–
Transmission retaining bolts	12	106	–

CHAPTER SIX

CLUTCH AND PRIMARY DRIVE GEAR

This chapter describes service procedures for the following subassemblies:

1. Clutch cover.
2. Centrifugal clutch.
3. Primary drive gear.

The primary drive gear is an integral part of the centrifugal clutch drum. The clutch cover, clutch and primary drive gear can be serviced with the engine mounted in the frame. However, because of the mounting position of the engine in the frame, some of the illustrations included in this chapter depict the engine removed from the frame for clarity.

Service specifications are listed in **Table 1** and **Table 2**. The tables are located at the end of this chapter.

CLUTCH COVER

Clutch Cover Removal/Installation

1. If the engine is mounted in the frame, perform the following steps:
   a. Park the ATV on level ground and set the parking brake.
   b. Drain the engine oil as described in Chapter Three.
   c. Remove the front mud guards as described in Chapter Fifteen.

   d. Remove the inner fender panels as described in Chapter Fifteen.
   e. Remove the front driveshaft as described in Chapter Twelve.
   f. Remove the external gearshift linkage as described in Chapter Seven.
   g. Remove the external oil tank as described in Chapter Five.
   h. Remove the left engine side cover (**Figure 1**).
   i. Remove the left engine side cover support (**Figure 2**).

2. Remove the oil passage plug (**Figure 3**), then remove the internal oil feed pipe (**Figure 4**).

3. Before removing the clutch cover mounting screws, draw an outline of the cover on a piece of cardboard. Punch holes along the outline for the placement of each mounting screw.

NOTE
If the oil filter has not been previously removed, a considerable amount of oil drains out of the clutch cover oil passages when it is handled.

4. Remove the clutch cover as follows:
   a. Remove the shift control motor mounting bolts (A, **Figure 5**) and remove the shift control motor (B).

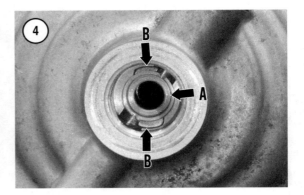

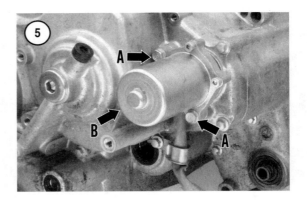

b. Remove the 12 remaining cover mounting screws and remove the clutch cover (**Figure 6**).

5. If necessary, remove both dowel pins (A, **Figure 7**).

6. Remove the O-ring (B, **Figure 7**) from the oil pipe.

7. Remove all sealant residue from the clutch cover and crankcase mating surfaces.

8. Inspect and, if necessary, replace the gearshift seal in the cover (**Figure 8**).

9. If necessary, remove the oil pressure check valve assembly using the following procedure:

a. Remove the oil passage plug (**Figure 9**).

b. Remove the spring and check valve (**Figure 10**).

c. Inspect the components and replace if necessary.

d. Clean the oil passage in the clutch cover.

e. Install the oil pressure check valve assembly by reversing the removal steps.

f. Install the check valve so the pin end is out (**Figure 11**), then install the spring onto the check valve.

g. Install a new sealing washer on the plug. Tighten the plug to 34 N•m (25 ft.-lb.).

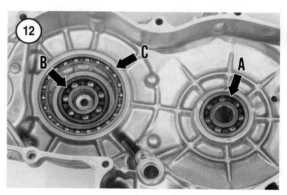

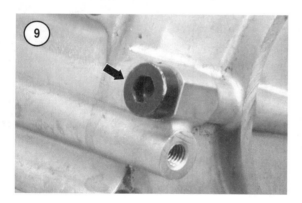

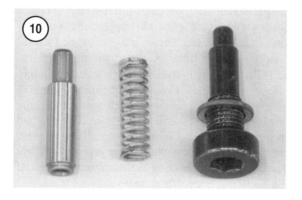

10. If the clutch cover is going to be serviced and/or cleaned in solvent, perform the *Clutch Cover Cleaning* procedure in this section. Otherwise, store the clutch cover in a plastic bag until reassembly.

11. Check the crankshaft end bearing (A, **Figure 12**), small transmission bearing (B) and large transmission bearing (C) as described in this section.

12. Install the clutch cover by reversing the preceding steps, while noting the following:

   a. Lubricate the crankshaft end bearing (A, **Figure 12**) and transmission bearings (B and C) with engine oil.

   b. Replace all O-rings if worn or damaged. Lubricate the O-rings with engine oil.

   c. Lubricate the reduction gear shaft (**Figure 13**) with engine oil.

   d. Apply Yamabond No. 4 (or equivalent) to the mating surface of the clutch cover.

   e. Tighten all of the clutch cover mounting bolts securely. Tighten all cover mounting screws, including the shift control motor mounting bolts, in two or three steps.

   f. Install an O-ring onto the oil feed pipe (A, **Figure 14**) and oil passage plug (B). Install the oil feed pipe so the tab on the pipe (C, **Figure 14**) fits into one of the notches in the cover hole (B, **Figure 4**).

g. Tighten the oil passage plug (**Figure 3**) to 18 N•m (159 in.-lb.).

Clutch Cover Cleaning

1. If not previously removed, remove the oil filter.
2. Clean the clutch cover and the oil passages with solvent. Clean the crankshaft and transmission bearings while submerged in solvent. Dry the clutch cover, oil passages and bearings with compressed air.

> *WARNING*
> *Do not spin the bearings with compressed air. Doing so may damage the bearing.*

3. Lubricate the bearings with engine oil.

Crankshaft End Bearing
Inspection and Replacement

The bearing installed in the clutch cover supports the front crankshaft end. This bearing must be in good condition and fit tightly in the mounting bore.

1. Hold the clutch cover and slowly turn the crankshaft end bearing (A, **Figure 12**) inner race. Check for roughness, play or noise. If the bearing feels gritty, clean the bearing as described in *Clutch Cover Cleaning* and then recheck it for wear and damage. If any of these conditions are present, the bearing is probably damaged. Replace the bearing as described in Step 3. If the bearing is good, lubricate it with engine oil.

2. Check that the bearing outer race is a tight fit in the mounting bore. If the bearing is a loose fit, the mounting bore is probably cracked or excessively worn. If the mounting bore is damaged, replace the clutch cover.

3. Replace the bearing as follows:

a. Clean the clutch cover in solvent and dry with compressed air.

b. Remove the bearing using a blind bearing remover. Refer to Chapter One.

c. Position the new bearing so the sealed side is toward the cover, then press or drive the new bearing into the mounting bore until it bottoms. Refer to Chapter One.

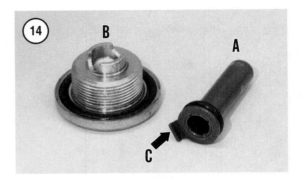

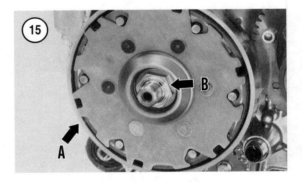

Transmission Bearing
Inspection and Replacement

The transmission bearings installed in the clutch cover (B and C, **Figure 12**) support the transmission shaft and case. The bearings must be in good condition and fit tightly in the mounting bores.

1. Hold the clutch cover and slowly turn the inner race of each bearing. Check for roughness, excessive play or noise. If the bearing feels gritty, clean the bearing as described in *Clutch Cover Cleaning* and then recheck it for wear and damage. If any of these conditions are present, the bearing is probably damaged. Replace the bearing as described in Step 3. If the bearing is good, lubricate it with engine oil.

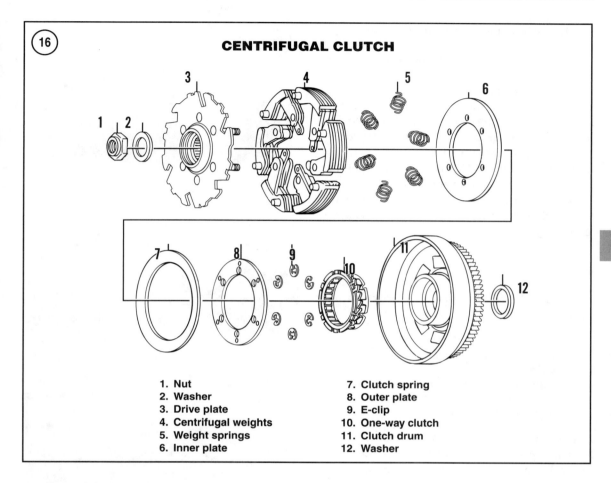

CENTRIFUGAL CLUTCH

1. Nut
2. Washer
3. Drive plate
4. Centrifugal weights
5. Weight springs
6. Inner plate
7. Clutch spring
8. Outer plate
9. E-clip
10. One-way clutch
11. Clutch drum
12. Washer

2. Check that the bearing outer race is a tight fit in the mounting bore. If the bearing is a loose fit, the mounting bore is probably cracked or excessively worn. If the mounting bore is damaged, replace the clutch cover.

3. Replace each bearing as follows:

WARNING
Wear gloves when handling the heated cover and bearing.

NOTE
In some instances, in may be possible to invert the cover after heating and tap the cover so the bearing dislodges. If not, use a bearing removal tool.

CAUTION
Do not heat the cover with a propane or acetylene torch. Never bring a flame into contact with the bearing or cover. The direct heat destroys the

case hardening of the bearing and likely warps the cover.

a. Heat the area around the bearing using a heat gun, then remove the bearing with a blind bearing remover. Refer to Chapter One.

b. Heat the clutch cover again, then press the new bearing into the mounting bore until it bottoms. Install the bearing with the manufacturer's numbers facing out.

CENTRIFUGAL CLUTCH AND PRIMARY DRIVE GEAR

The primary drive gear is an integral part of the centrifugal clutch drum. The centrifugal clutch (A, **Figure 15**) can be removed with the engine installed in the frame. The engine was removed for improved clarity in the following illustrations.

Refer to **Figure 16**.

Special Tools and Replacement Parts

Before removing the clutch locknut, note the following:

1. The clutch drum must be locked in place when loosening and tightening the clutch locknut (B, **Figure 15**). The recommended clutch holder tool is Honda part No. 07ZMB-HN2A1000 (A, **Figure 17**).

2. The Honda clutch puller (part No. 07933-HB3000A [B, **Figure 17**]) is required to pull the centrifugal clutch off the crankshaft.

3. The clutch locknut (B, **Figure 15**) is staked to a notch in the crankshaft. Purchase a new locknut for reassembly.

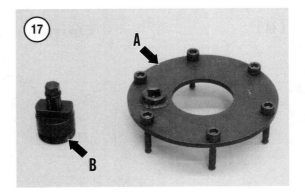

Removal/Installation

1. Remove the clutch cover as described in this chapter.

> *CAUTION*
> *Make sure to unstake the clutch locknut where it contacts the crankshaft. This prevents the nut from damaging the crankshaft threads as the nut is being removed.*

2. Using a die grinder, unstake the clutch locknut from the groove in the crankshaft (**Figure 18**). Cover the parts so metal particles do not enter the clutch or engine.

3. Secure the clutch drum with the clutch holder tool as shown in **Figure 19**. Loosen and remove the clutch locknut and washer. Discard the clutch locknut.

4. Thread the clutch puller (**Figure 20**) into the drive plate threads. Hold the clutch puller body with a wrench and then turn the end bolt to pull the centrifugal clutch assembly off the crankshaft. Refer to **Figure 21**.

5. If necessary, remove the washer.

6. Inspect the centrifugal clutch and primary drive gear as described in this section.

7. Install the centrifugal clutch by reversing the preceding removal steps, while noting the following:

    a. Lubricate the crankshaft, centrifugal clutch bore and washer with engine oil.

    b. Lubricate the clutch weight linings (**Figure 22**) with engine oil.

    c. Install the centrifugal clutch by first aligning the drive plate splines with the crankshaft

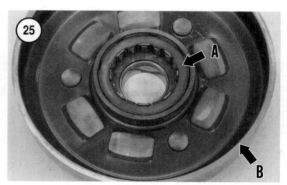

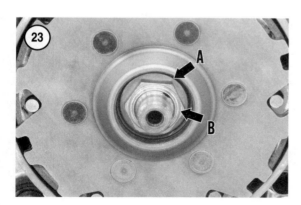

6

splines, then rotate the clutch drum and engage the primary gear teeth with the transmission driven gear teeth.

  d. Lubricate the washer (A, **Figure 23**) and the threads of a new clutch locknut (B) with engine oil and install them.

  e. Secure the clutch drum with the tool used during removal, then tighten the centrifugal clutch locknut to 118 N•m (87 ft.-lb.). Stake the edge of the clutch locknut to the notch in the crankshaft (**Figure 18**).

Clutch Drum and One-Way Clutch Inspection

Refer to **Table 1** when measuring the clutch drum components (**Figure 16**) in this section. Replace parts that are out of specification or show damage.

1. Check one-way clutch operation as follows:

  a. Place the assembled clutch assembly on the workbench as shown in **Figure 24**.

  b. Hold the clutch drum (A, **Figure 24**) and turn the drive plate assembly (B).

  c. The drive plate assembly should only turn counterclockwise (**Figure 24**). If the drive plate turns clockwise, the one-way clutch is faulty and must be replaced as described in this procedure.

2. Remove the drive plate assembly from the clutch drum.

3. Remove the one-way clutch (A, **Figure 25**) from the clutch drum. Inspect the one-way clutch for signs of heat damage, cracks or other damage. Replace the one-way clutch if there is visible damage or if it failed to operate as described in Step 1.

4. Check the drive plate boss (**Figure 26**) for scoring, excessive wear or damage. Check for signs of overheating.

5. Check the exterior of the clutch drum (B, **Figure 25**) for cracks or damage. Check the clutch drum inside diameter for excessive wear or damage. Measure the clutch drum inside diameter (**Figure 27**) with a caliper and compare to the service limit in **Table 1**.

6. Inspect the clutch drum bushing (A, **Figure 28**). Measure the bushing inside diameter (B, **Figure 28**) with a caliper and compare to the service limit in **Table 1**. The bushing is not renewable. Replace the clutch drum if the bushing is excessively worn or damaged.

7. Inspect the clutch support surface on the crankshaft (**Figure 29**). Measure the crankshaft outside diameter and compare to the service limit in **Table 1**. Replace the crankshaft if it is excessively worn or damaged.

8. Check the primary drive gear (**Figure 30**) for worn or damaged gear teeth. If damaged, replace the clutch drum.

9. Lubricate the one-way clutch and the clutch drum bore with engine oil, then install the one-way clutch in the clutch drum with the OUTSIDE mark (**Figure 31**) facing out.

10. Inspect and service the centrifugal weight assembly as described in this section.

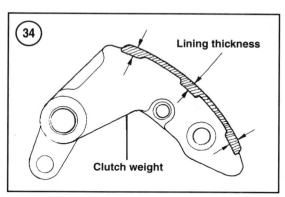

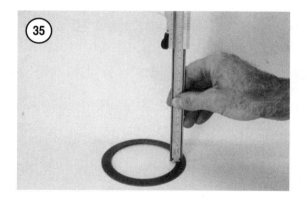

Centrifugal Weight Assembly Disassembly/Inspection/Reassembly

Refer to **Table 1** when measuring the centrifugal weight components (**Figure 16**) in this section. Replace parts that are out of specification or damaged.

1. Disassemble the centrifugal weight assembly as follows:

    a. Remove the E-clips (**Figure 32**), outer plate, spring plate and inner plate.

    b. Remove the weight springs (A, **Figure 33**) and clutch weights (B).

2. Measure the thickness of each weight lining at the points shown in **Figure 34**. If out of specification, replace all of the clutch weight arms as a set.

3. Inspect the clutch spring plate (**Figure 35**) for cracks or signs of heat damage. Measure the height of the spring plate with a vernier caliper (**Figure 35**). Replace the spring plate if the height is not as specified in **Table 1**.

4. Inspect the weight springs (A, **Figure 33**) for cracks or stretched coils. Measure the free length of each spring with a vernier caliper. If out of specification, replace all of the springs as a set.

5. Examine the outer and inner plates and replace if cracked or damaged.

6. Inspect the drive plate for damaged splines, warpage or damaged clutch weight pins. Check the E-clip groove in the end of each pin for damage.

7. Reassemble the clutch weight assembly as follows:

    a. Lubricate the drive plate pins with engine oil.

    b. Install the clutch weights and weight springs. Install the weight springs with the open ends facing down.

    c. Install the inner plate (A, **Figure 36**) with the lip facing up.

    d. Install the spring plate (B, **Figure 36**) with the cupped side facing in.

e. Install the outer washer (A, **Figure 37**) with the locating pins facing out.

f. Secure the drive plate in a vise by applying just enough pressure to compress the spring plate and expose the clip grooves in the end of each drive plate pin. Install the E-clips with the open end of each E-clip toward the corresponding locating pin on the outer washer (B, **Figure 37**). Check that each E-clip seats in its groove completely.

g. Remove pressure from the drive plate and check that the outer washer seats evenly against each E-clip.

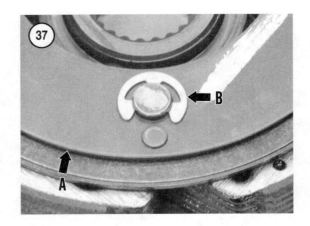

Table 1 CLUTCH SERVICE SPECIFICATIONS

	New mm (in.)	Service mm (in.)
Clutch drum bushing inside diameter	29.000-29.020 (1.1417-1.1425)	29.05 (1.144)
Clutch drum inside diameter	150.0-150.2 (5.906-5.913)	150.4 (5.92)
Clutch spring plate height	3.72 (0.146)	3.6 (0.14)
Clutch weight spring free length	23.2 (0.91)	24.1 (0.95)
Clutch weight lining thickness	3.0 (0.12)	2.0 (0.08)
Crankshaft outside diameter at drive gear	28.959-28.980 (1.1401-1.1409)	28.93 (1.139)

Table 2 CLUTCH TORQUE SPECIFICATIONS

	N•m	in.-lb.	ft.-lb.
Clutch locknut	118	–	87
Oil passage plug (check valve)	34	–	25
Oil passage plug (oil feed pipe)	18	159	–

TRANSMISSIONS AND SHIFT MECHANISM

The ATV is equipped with an automatic transmission contained within the crankcase and a sub-transmission located behind the rear crankcase cover. The automatic transmission is controlled electrically while the sub-transmission is controlled by an external shift mechanism.

Automatic transmission service requires engine removal and crankcase separation (Chapter Five). The sub-transmission is accessible after removing the rear crankcase cover.

Table 1 lists transmission general specifications. **Table 2** lists sub-transmission service specifications. **Tables 1-3** are located at the end of this chapter.

SHIFT MECHANISM

The sub-transmission is controlled by the mechanical linkage described in this section. The automatic transmission is controlled using an electromechanical system described under *Automatic Transmission* in this chapter.

Neutral Adjustment

The neutral position of the gearshift control lever (**Figure 1**) must be synchronized with the gearshift arm (A, **Figure 2**) neutral position to ensure the sub-transmission is in neutral.

If the ATV is not in neutral when the gearshift control lever is positioned in neutral, use the following procedure to adjust the gearshift linkage:

> *CAUTION*
> *The rod ends are permanently attached to the gearshift arm and pivot arm. Do not detach the rod ends from the arms.*

> *NOTE*
> *The front driveshaft has been removed for illustrative purpose. It is not neces-*

sary to remove the front driveshaft to perform this procedure.

1. Remove the left front mud guard as described in Chapter Fifteen.

2. Remove the left side cover as described in Chapter Fifteen.

3. Move the gearshift control lever (**Figure 1**) so the ATV is in neutral.

> *NOTE*
> *The locknuts at the lower ends of the tie rods have left-hand threads.*

4. Measure the length of the lower tie rod (B, **Figure 2**) as shown in **Figure 3**. Refer to **Table 2** for the specified length. If incorrect, loosen the locknuts on the tie rod and turn the tie rod until the specified length is obtained. Tighten the locknuts.

5. Measure the length of the upper tie rod (C, **Figure 2** and A, **Figure 4**) as shown in **Figure 3**. Refer to **Table 2** for the specified length. If incorrect, loosen the locknuts on the tie rod and turn the tie rod until the specified length is obtained. Tighten the locknuts.

6. Remove the cotter pin (B, **Figure 4**) and washer (C). Position the gearshift lever (**Figure 1**) so it is centered in the neutral detent. The slide shaft (A, **Figure 5**) should be centered in the slot (B). If not, loosen the upper tie rod locknuts and turn the tie rod as needed. Tighten the locknuts to 10 N•m (88 in.-lb.).

7. Check the operation of the gearshift linkage, and readjust if necessary.

Removal/Installation

> *NOTE*
> *The front driveshaft has been removed for illustrative purposes. It is not neces-*

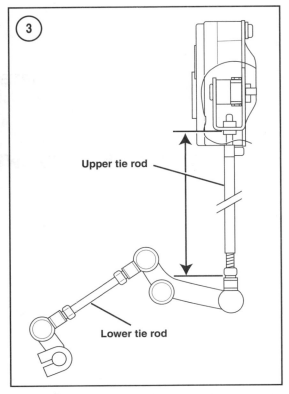

Upper tie rod

Lower tie rod

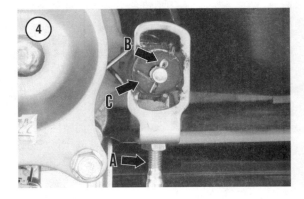

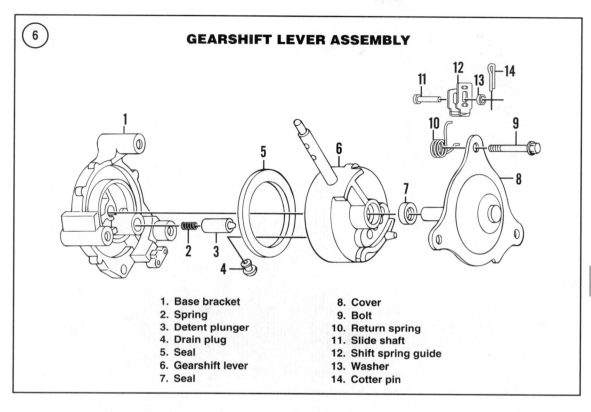

⑥ GEARSHIFT LEVER ASSEMBLY

1. Base bracket
2. Spring
3. Detent plunger
4. Drain plug
5. Seal
6. Gearshift lever
7. Seal
8. Cover
9. Bolt
10. Return spring
11. Slide shaft
12. Shift spring guide
13. Washer
14. Cotter pin

7

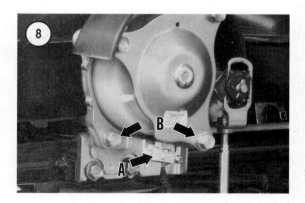

sary to remove the front driveshaft to perform this procedure.

Refer to **Figure 6**.

1. Shift the sub-transmission into neutral.

2. Remove the left front mud guard and front fender as described in Chapter Fifteen.

3. Remove the pivot bolt (A, **Figure 7**) and washer.

4. Remove the gearshift arm pinch bolt (B, **Figure 7**), then detach the gearshift arm (C) from the gearshift shaft.

5. Remove the reverse switch mounting bolt, then remove the reverse switch (A, **Figure 8**).

6. Remove the gearshift lever assembly mounting bolts (B, **Figure 8**), then remove the entire gearshift linkage assembly.

7. Reverse the removal procedure to install the gearshift linkage assembly while noting the following:

    a. Install new O-rings onto the pivot bolt. Lubricate the bolt and O-rings with molybdenum grease.

    b. Tighten the pivot bolt to 26 N•m (19 ft.-lb.).

    c. When installing the reverse switch, make sure the locating pin on the switch body fits into the hole on the lever base bracket.

d. Perform the neutral adjustment procedure previously described in this chapter.

Inspection

1. Loosen the locknut and remove the tie rod from the gearshift lever guide (A, **Figure 9**).

2. Remove the cover retaining bolts (B, **Figure 9**) and remove the cover (C).

3. Remove the detent plunger (**Figure 10**) and inspect the plunger, spring and bracket bore. The plunger must move smoothly in the bore.

4. Actuate the plunger in the lever and be sure the lock pin (A, **Figure 11**) moves smoothly. The plunger, spring and lock pin are not available separately.

5. Inspect the oil seals (B, **Figure 11** and **Figure 12**). Replace if damaged.

6. Replace the return spring (A, **Figure 12**) if damaged.

7. Apply molybdenum grease to all moving parts and contact surfaces, then reassemble the gearshift lever assembly.

8. Inspect the pivot bolt (A, **Figure 13**) and pivot arm bore (B). Replace either part if it is excessively worn or damaged.

9. Replace the O-rings (C, **Figure 13**) on the pivot bolt.

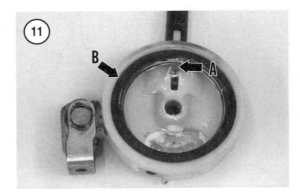

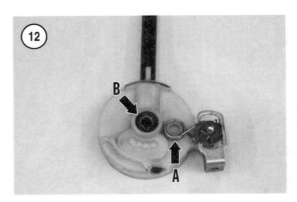

SUB-TRANSMISSION

The sub-transmission serves as a high-low range transmission and provides reverse for all shifting modes. The gearshift lever on the left side of the front fender (**Figure 1**) operates the sub-transmission. The sub-transmission is contained behind the rear crancase cover.

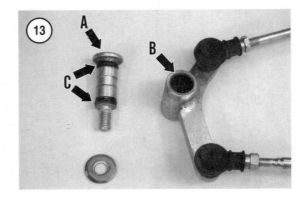

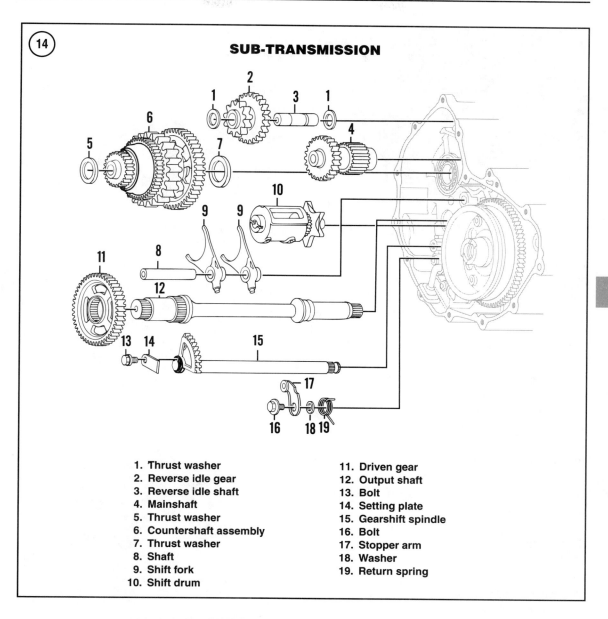

SUB-TRANSMISSION

1. Thrust washer
2. Reverse idle gear
3. Reverse idle shaft
4. Mainshaft
5. Thrust washer
6. Countershaft assembly
7. Thrust washer
8. Shaft
9. Shift fork
10. Shift drum
11. Driven gear
12. Output shaft
13. Bolt
14. Setting plate
15. Gearshift spindle
16. Bolt
17. Stopper arm
18. Washer
19. Return spring

Troubleshooting

Refer to Chapter Two.

Removal/Installation

Refer to **Figure 14**.

1. Remove the rear crankcase cover as described in Chapter Five.

2. Remove the driven gear (A, **Figure 15**) and output shaft (B).

3. Remove the shift fork shaft (A, **Figure 16**) and the shift forks (B).

4. Using a screwdriver, push back the stopper arm (A, **Figure 17**) and remove the shift drum (B). Rotate the shift drum as needed to clear the detent lobes.

5. Remove the setting plate retaining bolt (A, **Figure 18**) and remove the setting plate (B).

6. Remove the gearshift spindle (C, **Figure 18**).

7. Remove the stopper arm retaining bolt (D, **Figure 18**), stopper arm (E), spring and washer.

8. Remove the mainshaft (A, **Figure 19**) from the automatic transmission.

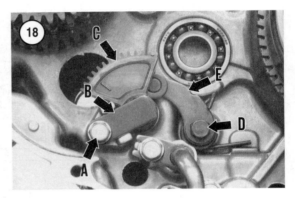

9. Remove the washers (B, **Figure 19**) on the countershaft and reverse idle shaft.

10. Remove the countershaft assembly (A, **Figure 20**) and the reverse gear (B) together.

11. Remove the reverse idle gear shaft (A, **Figure 21**) and washer (B).

12. Remove the O-ring on the automatic transmission shaft (**Figure 22**).

13. Disassemble and inspect the sub-transmission components as described in the following section.

14. Install the sub-transmission by reversing the removal steps while noting the following:

    a. Lubricate all components with clean engine oil.

    b. Lubricate and install a new O-ring onto the automatic transmission shaft (**Figure 22**).

    c. Install the countershaft assembly and reverse gear together.

    d. Make sure to install the washer on the backside of the stopper arm.

    e. Install the spring (**Figure 23**) onto the stopper arm as shown.

    f. Apply a medium strength threadlocker to the threads of the stopper arm bolt (D, **Figure 18**). Tighten the bolt to 12 N•m (106 in.-lb.).

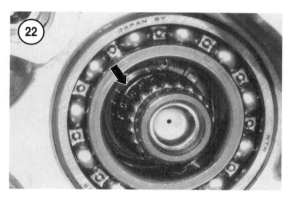

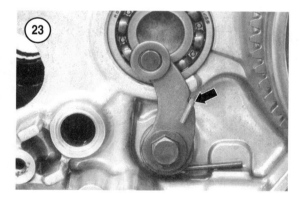

g. Install the shift drum so the index mark on the gearshift spindle sector (A, **Figure 24**) aligns with the boss (B) on the shift drum.

h. Install the shift forks so the mark on each fork faces out (**Figure 25**).

i. Note that the hub webs on the output driven gear are recessed farther inward on one side. Install the gear so the side with less recess is out (**Figure 15**).

Countershaft/Reverse Idle Components Disassembly/Inspection/Assembly

Refer to **Table 2** when measuring the components (**Figure 26**) in this section. Replace parts that are out of specification or damaged. It is a good practice to replace mating gears even though one gear may not show as much wear or damage.

NOTE
It is not necessary to disassemble the shifter assemblies except for service.

1. Refer to **Figure 26** and disassemble the countershaft components.

NOTE
Unless the special washer (A, Figure 27) or countershaft replacement is required, leave the washer on the end of the countershaft. If the special washer or countershaft replacement is required, carefully remove the special washer from the end of the countershaft. Discard the special washer if removed.

2. Clean and dry all parts.

3. Inspect the countershaft (B, **Figure 27**) for:

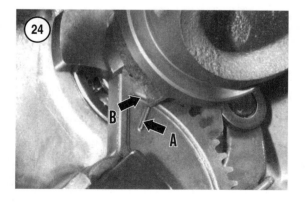

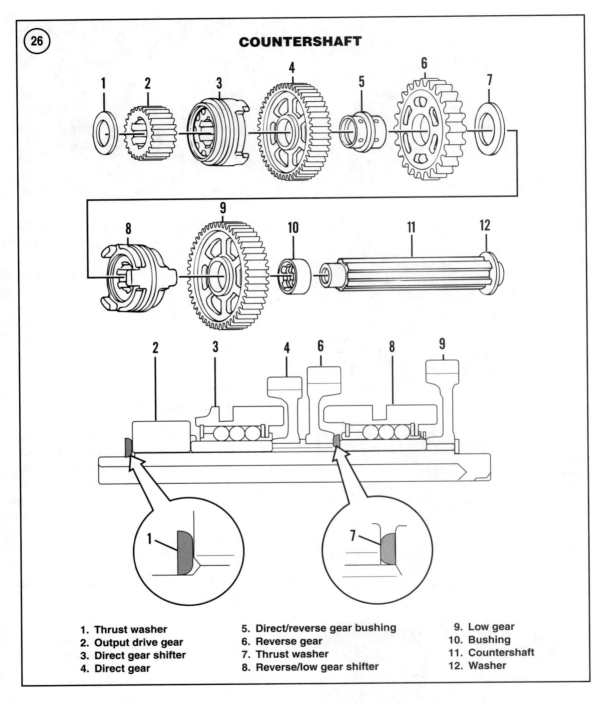

COUNTERSHAFT

1. Thrust washer
2. Output drive gear
3. Direct gear shifter
4. Direct gear
5. Direct/reverse gear bushing
6. Reverse gear
7. Thrust washer
8. Reverse/low gear shifter
9. Low gear
10. Bushing
11. Countershaft
12. Washer

   a. Worn or damaged splines.
   b. Excessively worn or damaged bearing surfaces.
4. Check each gear for:
   a. Missing, broken or chipped teeth.
   b. Worn, damaged or rounded gear lugs.
   c. Worn or damaged splines.

   d. Cracked or scored gear bore.
5. Check each bushing for:
   a. Excessively worn or damaged bearing surface.
   b. Worn or damaged splines.
   c. Cracked or scored gear bore.

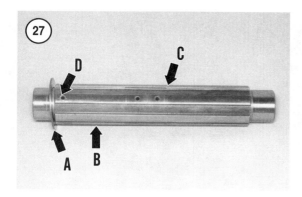

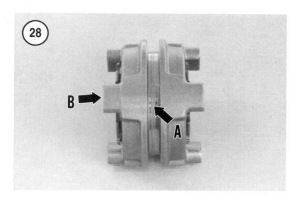

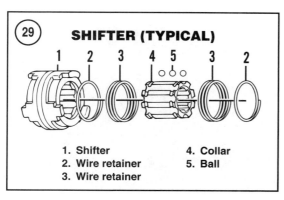

SHIFTER (TYPICAL)

1 2 3 4 5 3 2

1. Shifter
2. Wire retainer
3. Wire retainer
4. Collar
5. Ball

6. Check each shifter (**Figure 28**) for smooth operation. Inspect the shifter groove (A, **Figure 28**) for excessive wear or damage. Inspect for worn, damaged or rounded gear lugs (B, **Figure 28**). If necessary, refer to **Figure 29** and disassemble the shifter as follows:

    a. Hold the shifter over a container that catches the loose balls. Each shifter contains 27 balls.

    b. Remove the wire retainer in either end and separate the inner and outer shifter parts.

    c. Inspect the ball grooves for excessive wear and damage.

    d. Reassemble the shifter. Install nine balls in each ball groove. Make sure the wire retainers fit properly in their grooves.

7. Measure the countershaft outside diameter at the bushing contact surface (C, **Figure 27**) and record the dimension. Compare the dimension with the service limit in **Table 2**.

8. Measure the direct/reverse gear bushing (A, **Figure 30**) inside and outside diameters and record the dimensions.

9. Measure the direct and reverse gear inside diameters (B, **Figure 30**) and record the dimensions.

10. Using the dimensions recorded in Steps 7-9, determine the gear-to-bushing and bushing-to-shaft clearances and compare with the service limits specified in **Table 2**.

11. Measure the inside diameter of the low gear and the outside diameter of the low gear bushing. Calculate the bushing-to-shaft clearance and compare with the service limit specified in **Table 2**.

12. Measure the reverse idle gear (A, **Figure 31**) inside diameter and record the dimension.

13. Measure the reverse idle gear shaft (B, **Figure 31**) outside diameter and record the dimension.

14. Using the dimensions recorded in Step 12 and Step 13, determine the gear-to-shaft clearances and compare with the service limits in **Table 2**.

7

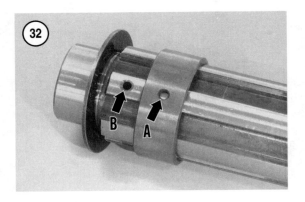

15. Reassemble the countershaft using the following procedure:

    a. If removed, press a new special washer (A, **Figure 27**) onto the end of the countershaft nearer the oil feed hole (D). Seat the washer against the countershaft shoulder.

    b. Install the spline bushing so the oil hole in the bushing (A, **Figure 32**) aligns with the oil hole in the shaft (B).

    c. Install low gear so the flat side is toward the end of the shaft and the exposed hub (**Figure 33**) is toward the shifter.

    d. Install the reverse/low shifter (A, **Figure 34**).

    e. Install the thrust washer (B, **Figure 34**) so the flat edge is toward the shifter as shown in **Figure 26**.

    f. Install the reverse gear (A, **Figure 35**) and ribbed bushing (B). The flat side of the gear must be toward the bushing rib.

    g. Install the direct gear (**Figure 36**) so the flat side is toward the bushing rib and the exposed hub is toward the shifter.

    h. Install the direct gear shifter so the lugs (A, **Figure 37**) are toward the direct gear (B).

    i. Install the output drive gear (A, **Figure 38**) and thrust washer (B). Install the thrust washer so the flat edge is toward the end of the shaft as shown in **Figure 26**.

Shift Components
Disassembly/Inspection/Reassembly

Refer to **Table 2** when measuring the components (**Figure 14**) in this section. Replace parts that are out of specification or damaged.

1. Clean and dry all parts.

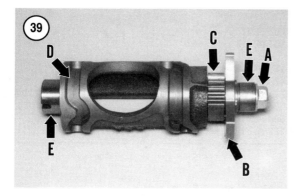

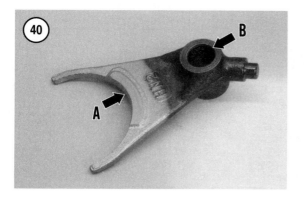

2. If necessary, remove the detent plate retaining bolt (A, **Figure 39**). Remove the detent plate (B, **Figure 39**) and shifter gear (C).

3. Inspect the shift drum for excessively worn or damaged cam grooves (D, **Figure 39**) or bearing surfaces (E). Replace the shift drum if necessary.

4. Inspect each shift fork (**Figure 40**) for signs of wear or damage. Examine the shift forks at the points where they contact the shifter gear (A, **Figure 40**). These surfaces must be smooth with no signs of wear, bending, cracks, heat discoloration or other damage.

5. Check each shift fork for arc-shaped wear or burn marks. These marks indicate the shift fork has contacted the gear.

6. Check the shift fork shaft for bending or other damage. Install each shift fork on the shaft and slide it back and forth. Each shift fork must slide smoothly with no binding or tight spots. If both shift forks bind on the shaft, check the shaft closely for bending. If only one shift fork binds on the shaft, check that shift fork closely.

7. Measure the shift fork thickness (A, **Figure 40**).

8. Measure the shift fork inside diameter (B, **Figure 40**) with a snap gauge. Then measure the snap gauge with a micrometer.

9. Measure the shift fork shaft outside diameter at three different points on the shaft.

10. If disassembled, install the dowel pin, shifter gear (C, **Figure 39**), detent plate (B) and bolt (A) onto the shift drum. Apply medium strength threadlocker to the bolt threads. Tighten the bolt to 26 N•m (19 ft.-lb.).

AUTOMATIC TRANSMISSION

Operation

The automatic, main transmission is a hydraulic type that uses engine oil supplied by the engine oil pump. The transmission consists of a pump, motor and moveable swashplate to transmit power from the engine to the sub-transmission. The pump and motor are each equipped with axial pistons and radial valves that pressurize and distribute oil to rotate the output shaft. The moveable swashplate determines the stroke of the motor pistons which affects oil volume, thereby also determining output shaft speed. The swashplate rotates, and when the swashplate angle changes, the stroke distance for each piston also changes. A screw shaft connected to the swashplate carrier is used to change the swashplate angle. The shift control motor rotates the screw shaft through a set of gears. The engine control module (ECM) controls the shift control motor, using input from sensors to determine transmission operation. Refer also to Chapter Nine.

Removal/Installation

The crankcase must be split for access to the transmission. Refer to the *Crankcase And Crankshaft* section in Chapter Five for removal and installation procedures.

Inspection

1. Inspect the bearing contact surfaces for damage (A, **Figure 41**).
2. Inspect the splines (B, **Figure 41**) for damage.

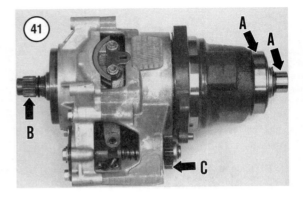

3. Rotate the shift control gear (C, **Figure 41**). The screw shaft and swashplate assemblies must move smoothly without binding.
4. Do not disassemble any components of the transmission for further inspection. The transmission is only available as a unit assembly.

Table 1 TRANSMISSION GENERAL SPECIFICATIONS

Main transmission	Automatic
Sub-transmission	Constant mesh, two forward gears & one reverse gear
Primary reduction ratio	1.045 (70/67)
Secondary reduction ratio	2.000 (40/20)
Final reduction ratio	
Front	3.231 (42/13)
Rear	3.154 (41/13)
Automatic transmission ratio (low-overdrive)	
2001-2003	3.13-0.84
2004-on	3.47-0.93
Sub-transmission gear ratios	
Drive	1.583 (38/24)
Low	2.500 (45/18)
Reverse	3.222 (29/18 × 28/14)

Table 2 SUB-TRANSMISSION SERVICE SPECIFICATIONS

	New mm (in.)	Service limit mm (in.)
Bushing-to-shaft clearance	0.020-0.054 (0.0008-0.0021)	0.10 (0.004)
Countershaft outside diameter	24.959-24.980 (0.9826-0.9835)	24.93 (0.981)
Gear bushing inside diameter	25.000-25.013 (0.9843-0.9848)	25.04 (0.986)
Gear bushing outside diameters		
Low gear	27.984-28.005 (1.1017-1.1026)	27.93 (1.100)
Direct and reverse gears	27.979-28.000 (1.1015-1.1024) (continued)	27.93 (1.100)

Table 2 SUB-TRANSMISSION SERVICE SPECIFICATIONS (continued)

	New mm (in.)	Service limit mm (in.)
Gear inside diameter		
Direct, low and reverse gears	28.020-28.041 (1.1031-1.1040)	28.07 (1.105)
Reverse idle gear	14.00-14.018 (0.5512-0.5519)	14.04 (0.553)
Gear-to-bushing clearance		
Low gear	0.015-0.057 (0.0006-0.0022)	0.10 (0.004)
Direct and reverse gears	0.020-0.062 (0.0008-0.0024)	0.10 (0.004)
Gearshift tie rod length		
Lower tie rod	58.0-59.0 (2.28-2.323)	
Upper tie rod	328.5-329.5 (12.93-12.97)	
Reverse idle gear shaft outside diameter	13.966-13.984 (0.5498-0.5506)	13.93 (0.548)
Reverse idle gear-to-shaft clearance	0.016-0.052 (0.0006-0.0020)	0.10 (0.004)

7

Table 3 TRANSMISSION TORQUE SPECIFICATIONS

	N•m	in.-lb.	ft.-lb.
Pivot bolt	26	–	19
Stopper arm bolt	12	106	
Shift drum bolt	26	–	19
Tie rod locknuts	10	88	–

CHAPTER EIGHT

FUEL SYSTEM

The fuel system consists of the carburetor, fuel tank, fuel shutoff valve and air filter.

This chapter includes service procedures for all parts of the fuel system. Routine air filter service is covered in Chapter Three.

Table 1 and **Table 2** list carburetor specifications. **Tables 1-3** are located at the end of this chapter.

CARBURETOR

Removal/Installation

> *WARNING*
> *Due to the close proximity of the exhaust, perform this procedure when the engine is cold.*

1. Park the ATV on level ground and set the parking brake.

2. Remove the air box as described in this chapter.

3. Disconnect the negative battery cable from the battery (Chapter Three).

4. Detach the carburetor heater wire from the retaining clamp, then disconnect it from the connector (**Figure 1**).

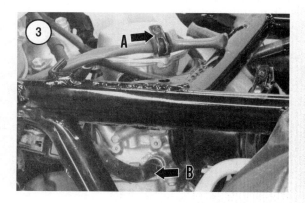

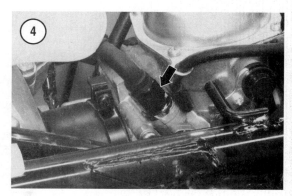

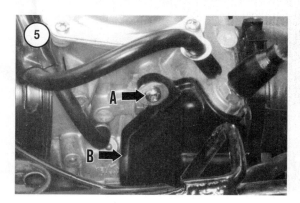

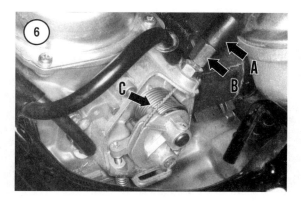

5. Detach the carburetor drain hose from the retaining clamp.

6. Disconnect the throttle position sensor (TPS) connector (**Figure 2**), then detach the sensor wire lead from the retaining clamp (A, **Figure 3**).

7. Pull back the rubber boot, loosen the starting enrichment (SE) valve nut (**Figure 4**) and remove the SE valve from the carburetor.

8. Turn the fuel shutoff valve off. Detach the fuel hose from the carburetor fitting (B, **Figure 3**).

9. Disconnect the throttle cable as follows:

   a. Remove the carburetor cover screw (A, **Figure 5**) and cover (B).

   b. Slide the boot (A, **Figure 6**) away from the throttle cable adjuster (B) on the carburetor.

   c. Loosen the throttle cable locknut and unscrew the adjuster from the carburetor.

   d. Disconnect the throttle cable (C, **Figure 6**) from the throttle pulley.

10. Loosen the intake tube hose clamp screw (**Figure 7**).

11. Pull back the carburetor to remove it from the intake tube, then remove the carburetor.

12. Install the carburetor by reversing the preceding removal steps while noting the following:

   a. When installing the carburetor, align the boss on the carburetor rim with the intake tube slot (**Figure 8**).

   b. Apply a dab of grease onto the end of the throttle cable before connecting it onto the throttle pulley.

   c. When connecting the throttle cable and threading the adjuster (B, **Figure 6**) into the carburetor, do not twist or kink the cable.

   d. When installing the throttle cable cover, be sure the tab at the lower end fits the slot in the carburetor (**Figure 9**).

e. Apply some multi-purpose grease inside the SE valve nut at the point shown in A, **Figure 10**. Install and tighten the SE valve nut securely. Operate the choke cable by hand, making sure the SE valve moves with no binding or roughness.

> *CAUTION*
> *Wipe off any grease that may contact the SE valve (B, **Figure 10**). Otherwise the grease may plug the choke opening and cause the system to malfunction during engine starting.*

f. Check and adjust the throttle cable adjustment (Chapter Three).

Disassembly

Refer to **Figure 11**.

> *NOTE*
> *The throttle position sensor (A, **Figure 12**) is mounted on a bracket, which is attached to the carburetor body. The throttle position sensor on the bracket is preset by the manufacturer. Do not remove the throttle position sensor from the bracket unless it requires replacement. Removal of the sensor requires adjustment as described in Chapter Nine.*

1. Remove the throttle position sensor bracket screws (B, **Figure 12**), then remove the throttle position sensor and bracket assembly.
2. Note the location of the vent and drain hoses in **Figure 13** and **Figure 14**, then detach the hoses from the carburetor.
3. Unscrew and remove the carburetor heater (A, **Figure 15**). Also remove the collar (B, **Figure 15**).
4. Remove the screws and top cover (A, **Figure 16**). Note the location of the hose clamp (B, **Figure 16**) and hose guides (C).
5. Remove the spring (**Figure 17**) and vacuum piston assembly (**Figure 18**).
6. Remove the jet needle (**Figure 19**) as follows:
   a. Turn the jet needle holder (**Figure 20**) counterclockwise to release it from the vacuum piston.
   b. Remove the jet needle holder, spring, jet needle and washer.

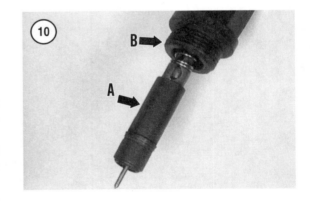

> *NOTE*
> *Before removing the jet needle, first record the clip position and compare it to the clip position listed in **Table 1**.*

7. Remove the screws, primer valve assembly (**Figure 21**) and spring (**Figure 22**).
8. Remove the screw, retainer plate (A, **Figure 23**) and air joint (B).
9. Remove the float bowl screws (**Figure 24**), float bowl and gasket.
10. Remove the main jet baffle (**Figure 25**).

CARBURETOR

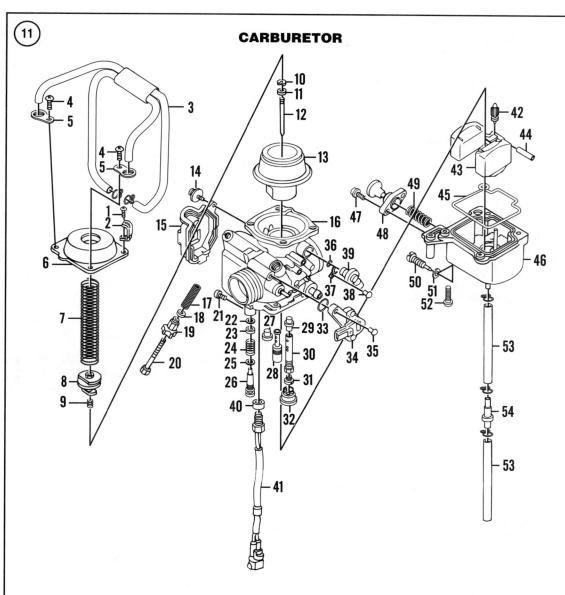

1. Screw	15. Side cover	29. Needle jet	42. Fuel inlet valve
2. Clamp	16. Body	30. Needle jet holder	43. Float
3. Hoses	17. Spring	31. Main jet	44. Float pin
4. Screw	18. Washer	32. Baffle	45. Gasket
5. Hose guide	19. Idle speed knob	33. O-ring	46. Float bowl
6. Top cover	20. Bolt	34. Throttle position sensor	47. Screw
7. Spring	21. Starter jet	35. Screw	48. Primer
8. Jet needle holder	22. O-ring	36. O-ring	49. Spring
9. Spring	23. Washer	37. Retainer	50. Drain screw
10. E-clip	24. Spring	38. Screw	51. O-ring
11. Washer	25. O-ring	39. Vent joint	52. Screw
12. Jet needle	26. Pilot screw	40. Spacer	53. Hose
13. Vacuum cylinder	27. Plug	41. Carburetor heater	54. One-way valve
14. Screw	28. Slow jet		

8

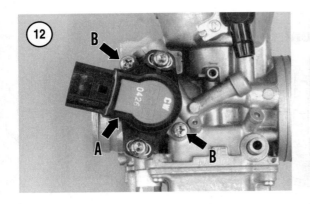

11. Remove the float pin (**Figure 26**), float and fuel valve (**Figure 27**).

12. Remove the plug (**Figure 28**).

13. Remove the starter jet (**Figure 29**).

14. Remove the slow jet (**Figure 30**).

15. Remove the main jet (A, **Figure 31**).

16. Remove the needle jet holder (B, **Figure 31**).

17. Turn the carburetor so the top side faces up, and tap the body to remove the needle jet (**Figure 32**). If the needle jet does not fall out, gently push it out with a plastic rod.

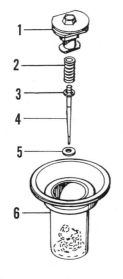

⑲ JET NEEDLE ASSEMBLY

1. Jet needle holder
2. Spring
3. E-clip
4. Jet needle
5. Washer
6. Vacuum cylinder

8

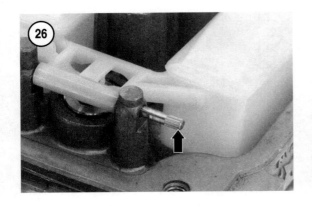

18. While counting the number of turns, rotate the pilot screw in until lightly seated. Record the number of turns during reassembly. Back out the pilot screw and remove it from the carburetor (A, **Figure 33**).

19. Unscrew and remove the idle speed adjusting screw (A, **Figure 34**) and spring.

20. Remove the drain screw (**Figure 35**) and O-ring from the float bowl.

> *NOTE*
> *Further disassembly is neither necessary nor recommended. Do not remove the choke shaft or plate because these parts are not available separately.*

21. Clean and inspect all parts as described in this section.

Cleaning and Inspection

1. Clean and dry the carburetor parts.

> *CAUTION*
> *Do not dip the carburetor body or any of the O-rings in a carburetor cleaner*

8

or other solution that damages the rubber parts and seals.

CAUTION
Do not use wire or drill bits to clean jets because minor gouges in the jet can alter the flow rate and change the air/fuel mixture.

2. Clean the float bowl overflow tube with compressed air.

3. Replace the float bowl O-ring if leaking or damaged.

4. Inspect the fuel valve assembly as follows:

   a. Inspect the end of the fuel valve (**Figure 36**) for steps, excessive wear or damage.

   b. Inspect the fuel valve seat in the carburetor for steps, uneven wear or other damage.

5. Inspect the pilot screw (**Figure 37**) and spring for damage. Replace the screw if damaged. Replace both pilot screw O-rings.

6. Inspect the float (**Figure 38**) for deterioration or damage. Check the float by submersing it in a container of water. If water enters the float, replace it.

7. Move the throttle pulley from stop-to-stop and check for free movement. If it does not move freely, replace the carburetor body.

8. Make sure all openings in the carburetor body are clear. Clean with compressed air.

9. Inspect the vacuum piston diaphragm (**Figure 39**) for cracks, deterioration or other damage.

10. Inspect the primer valve assembly (**Figure 40**) for wear, damage or deterioration. Inspect the rubber diaphragm (**Figure 41**) for cracks or other damage.

11. Make sure all jet openings are clear. Replace any jet that cannot be cleaned.

Assembly

Refer to **Figure 11**.

1. Install the drain screw (**Figure 35**) and O-ring into the float bowl. Tighten the drain screw securely.

2. Install the idle speed adjusting screw (A, **Figure 34**) and spring.

3. Install the two O-rings, spring and flat washer onto the pilot screw (**Figure 37**).

4. Install the pilot screw (A, **Figure 33**). Turn it in until it is lightly seated. Back the screw out the number of turns recorded during removal, or set it to the number of turns listed in **Table 1**.

5. Install the needle jet (**Figure 32**) with the chamfered end facing toward the needle jet holder, and install the needle jet holder. Tighten the needle jet holder (B, **Figure 31**) securely.

6. Install the main jet (A, **Figure 31**).

7. Install the slow jet (**Figure 30**).

8. Install the starter jet (**Figure 29**).

9. Install the plug (**Figure 28**).

10. Install the fuel valve onto the float, and then install the fuel valve into the fuel valve seat (**Figure 27**). Insert the float pin (**Figure 26**) through the pedestal arms and float.

11. Check the float level as described in the *Carburetor Float Level Adjustment* in this chapter.

12. Install the main jet baffle (**Figure 25**).

13. Install the O-ring into the float bowl groove (**Figure 42**). Install the float bowl and secure it with the mounting screws (**Figure 24**).

14. Install a new O-ring onto the air joint, then install the air joint (B, **Figure 23**), retainer plate (A) and screw.

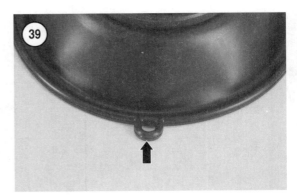

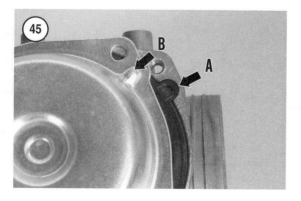

15. Install the primer valve spring (**Figure 22**) and primer valve (**Figure 21**) into the float bowl. Tighten the screws securely.

16. Assemble the vacuum piston and install the jet needle (**Figure 19**) as follows:

    a. If removed, install the E-clip into the jet needle clip groove recorded during disassembly or refer to the stock clip position in **Table 1**.

    b. Install the washer onto the bottom of the jet needle and seat it against the E-clip.

    c. Install the jet needle and washer (**Figure 43**) into the vacuum piston.

    d. Insert the spring in the end of the jet needle holder.

    e. Insert the jet needle holder (**Figure 20**) into the vacuum piston and turn it 90° clockwise to lock it in place.

17. Install the vacuum piston into the carburetor body. Align the tab on the diaphragm (**Figure 39**) with the hole (**Figure 44**) in the carburetor body.

18. Install the spring into the vacuum piston (**Figure 17**).

19. Align the tab on the vacuum piston diaphragm (A, **Figure 45**) with the raised boss (B) on the top cover. Install the top cover.

20. Install the hose clamp (B, **Figure 16**) and hose guides (C), then install and tighten the cover screws securely.

21. Connect the hoses to the carburetor. Install the overflow hose so the small end of the one-way valve installed in the hose is toward the carburetor (**Figure 46**).

22. Install the carburetor heater (A, **Figure 15**) and collar (B). The stepped end of the collar must be toward the carburetor.

23. If the throttle position sensor and bracket were removed, install a new O-ring on the carburetor (A,

Figure 47). Align the throttle shaft flats (B, **Figure 47**) with the slot in the sensor and install the throttle position sensor and bracket (**Figure 48**). Tighten the bracket screws securely.

> *NOTE*
> *If the throttle position sensor was sep-arated from the bracket, refer to Chapter Nine and adjust the throttle position sensor position.*

24. Install the carburetor as described in this chapter.

25. Adjust the pilot screw as described in the *Carburetor Adjustments* section in this chapter.

CARBURETOR FLOAT LEVEL ADJUSTMENT

The fuel valve and float maintain a constant fuel level in the carburetor float bowl. Because the float level affects the fuel mixture throughout the engine's operating range, this level must be within specifications in **Table 2**.

1. Remove the carburetor as described in this chapter.

2. Remove the float bowl mounting screws and float bowl (**Figure 49**). Do not remove the O-ring from the float bowl groove.

3. Hold the carburetor so the fuel valve just touches the float arm without pushing it down. Measure the distance from the carburetor body gasket surface to the float (**Figure 50**) using a float level gauge, ruler or vernier caliper.

4. The float is non-adjustable. If the float level is incorrect, check the float pin and fuel valve for damage. If these parts are in good condition, replace the float and remeasure the float level.

5. Install the float bowl, O-ring and the mounting screws (**Figure 49**). Tighten the mounting screws securely.

6. Install the carburetor as described in this chapter.

CARBURETOR ADJUSTMENTS

Idle Speed Adjustment

Refer to Chapter Three.

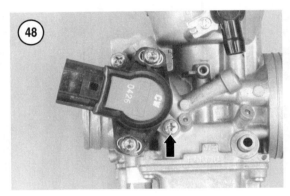

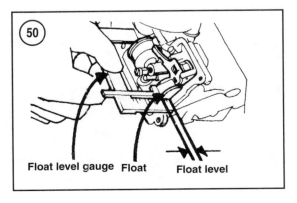

Float level gauge Float Float level

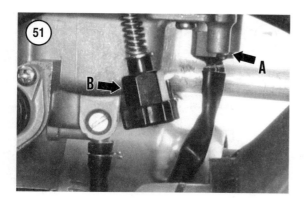

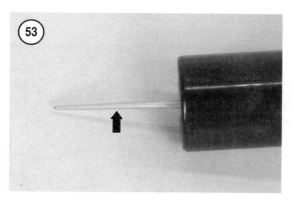

Pilot Screw Adjustment

The pilot screw (A, **Figure 51**) is preset. Routine adjustment is not necessary unless the pilot screw was removed or replaced or the carburetor was overhauled.

WARNING
Do not run the engine in an enclosed area when adjusting the pilot screw in this procedure. Carbon monoxide gas

can cause loss of consciousness and death in a short time.

1. Clean the air filter as described in Chapter Three.
2. Connect a tachometer to the engine following the manufacturer's instructions.

NOTE
To accurately detect speed changes during this adjustment, use a tachometer with graduations of 50 rpm or smaller.

3. Turn the pilot screw (A, **Figure 51**) clockwise until it lightly seats, then back out the number of turns specified in **Table 1**.
4. Start the engine and warm to normal operating temperature.
5. Open and release the throttle lever (**Figure 52**) a few times, making sure it returns to the closed position. If necessary, turn the engine off and adjust the throttle cable as described in Chapter Three.
6. With the engine idling, turn the idle speed screw (B, **Figure 51**) to set the engine idle speed to the rpm listed in **Table 1**.
7. Turn the pilot screw (A, **Figure 51**) in or out to obtain the highest engine idle speed.
8. Turn the idle speed screw (B, **Figure 51**) to reset the engine idle speed to the rpm listed in **Table 1**.
9. While reading the tachometer, turn the pilot screw (A, **Figure 51**) in slowly until the engine speed drops 100 rpm.
10. Turn the pilot screw (A, **Figure 51**) out one turn.
11. Open and close the throttle lever a few times while checking the idle speed reading. The engine must idle within the speed range listed in **Table 1**. If necessary, readjust the idle speed with the idle speed screw (B, **Figure 51**).
12. Turn the engine off and remove the tachometer.

Jet Needle Adjustment

The jet needle (**Figure 53**) controls the fuel mixture between 1/4 and 3/4 throttle openings. Changing the jet needle position affects the air/fuel mixture.

1. Remove the carburetor as described in this chapter.

2. Remove the vacuum piston and then remove the jet needle (**Figure 43**) as described in *Carburetor Disassembly* in this chapter.

> *NOTE*
> *Record the jet needle clip position before removing it. Refer to **Table 1** for the standard jet needle clip position.*

3. Raising the needle (lowering the clip) enriches the mixture between 1/4 and 3/4 throttle openings, while lowering the needle (raising the clip) leans the mixture. Refer to **Figure 54**.

4. Install the jet needle and vacuum piston as described in *Carburetor Assembly* in this chapter.

High Altitude Adjustment

Honda specifies two different jetting specifications for the TRX500 models-standard and high altitude. Use the standard jetting when operating the ATV below 1500 m (5000 ft.). Use the high altitude jetting when operating the ATV between 1500-2500 m (3000-8000 ft.).

1. Remove the carburetor as described in this chapter.

2. Remove the float bowl mounting screws and float bowl (**Figure 49**). Do not remove the gasket from the float bowl groove.

3. Remove the standard main jet (A, **Figure 55**) and install the correct size main jet for high altitude operation as listed in **Table 1**.

4. Turn the pilot screw (B, **Figure 55**) clockwise 7/8 turn.

5. Reassemble and install the carburetor.

6. Adjust the idle speed as described in Chapter Three. The idle speed is the same for standard and high altitude carburetor settings.

> *CAUTION*
> *When operating the ATV below 1000 m (3000 ft.) with the high altitude jetting, engine overheating may occur. If operating below this elevation, install the standard main jet and adjust the pilot screw setting as described in **Pilot Screw Adjustment** section.*

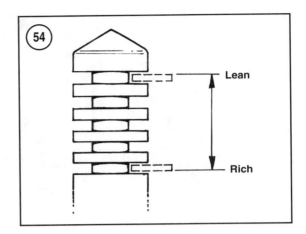

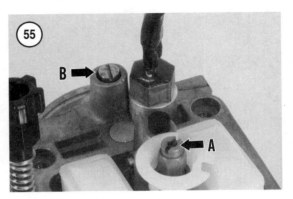

CARBURETOR HEATER

Carburetor Heater Testing

The carburetor heater may be tested while it is installed on the carburetor or removed from the carburetor.

1. To test the carburetor heater while installed on the ATV, remove the right side cover as described in Chapter Fifteen.

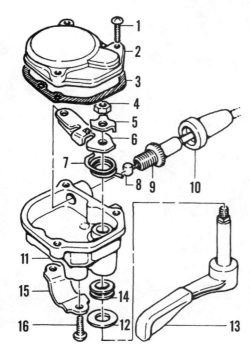

THROTTLE HOUSING AND CABLE

1. Screw
2. Cover
3. Gasket
4. Nut
5. Lockwasher
6. Throttle arm
7. Spring
8. Throttle cable
9. Cable adjuster
10. Rubber boot
11. Housing
12. Nylon washer
13. Throttle lever
14. Dust seal
15. Clamp
16. Screw

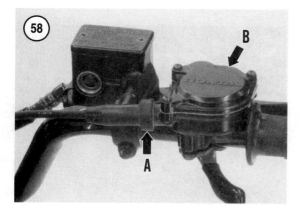

2. Disconnect the electrical lead from the carburetor heater connector (**Figure 56**).

3. Connect ohmmeter leads to the two terminals of the carburetor heater connector lead.

Replace the heater if the resistance is outside the range specified in **Table 4**.

4. If the heater tests correctly, verify the presence of 12 volts at the wiring harness heater connector using a voltmeter. Turn the ignition switch on. Connect the positive tester lead to the black/green wire terminal. Connect the negative tester lead to the green wire terminal. The voltmeter should indicate 12 volts. If not, refer to Chapter Nine and determine the cause.

THROTTLE HOUSING AND CABLE

Refer to **Figure 57**.

**Throttle Housing
Disassembly/Inspection/Reassembly**

1. Park the ATV on level ground and set the parking brake.

2. Slide the rubber boot (A, **Figure 58**) off the cable adjuster.

3. Remove the throttle housing cover screws and cover (B, **Figure 58**). Remove the dowel pins, if used.

4. Loosen the throttle cable adjuster locknut (A, **Figure 59**) and loosen the adjuster.

5. Pry the lockwasher tabs away from the throttle arm pivot nut (B, **Figure 59**).

6. Remove the throttle arm pivot nut (B, **Figure 59**) and lockwasher, and then remove the throttle lever and its plastic washer (**Figure 60**).

7. Disconnect the throttle cable from the throttle arm (A, **Figure 61**), and then remove the throttle arm and spring (B, **Figure 61**).

8. Clean and dry the throttle housing and all parts.

9. Replace the throttle housing dust seal (14, **Figure 57**) if damaged.

10. Inspect the throttle lever assembly (**Figure 62**) for:

   a. Weak or damaged spring.

   b. Damaged throttle arm.

   c. Corroded or damaged throttle arm.

   d. Worn or damaged plastic washer.

11. Replace the throttle housing cover gasket if damaged.

NOTE
Use a lithium based multipurpose grease (NLGI #2 or equivalent) in Step 12 and Step 16.

12. Lubricate the dust seal (14, **Figure 57**) with grease.

13. Connect the throttle cable ball into the end of the throttle arm (A, **Figure 61**).

14. Connect the spring to the throttle arm. Then install the spring and throttle arm into the throttle housing. Make sure the spring engages with the throttle arm and against the throttle housing as shown in **Figure 63**.

15. Install the plastic washer (**Figure 60**) onto the throttle lever.

16. Lubricate the throttle lever shaft with grease.

17. Install the throttle lever shaft through the dust seal and throttle arm.

18. Install a new lockwasher as shown in **Figure 64**.

19. Install and tighten the throttle arm nut (B, **Figure 59**). Bend the lockwasher tab against the nut.

20. Install the throttle housing dowel pins, if used.

21. Install the throttle housing cover (B, **Figure 58**) and gasket, and then install and tighten the cover screws.

22. Adjust the throttle cable as described in Chapter Three.

NOTE
*After adjusting the throttle cable, make sure to tighten the throttle cable adjuster locknut (A, **Figure 59**) and slide the rubber boot (A, **Figure 58**) over the adjuster.*

Throttle Cable Replacement

1. Park the ATV on level ground and set the parking brake.
2. Remove the fuel tank as described in this chapter.
3. Disconnect the throttle cable at the throttle housing as described in this section.
4. Disconnect the throttle cable at the carburetor as described in *Carburetor Removal* in this chapter.
5. Disconnect the throttle cable from any retainers holding the cable to the frame.
6. Remove the throttle cable.
7. Install the new throttle cable through the frame, routing it from the handlebar to the carburetor. Secure the cable in the cable retainers.
8. Connect the throttle cable to the carburetor as described in *Carburetor Installation* in this chapter.
9. Reconnect the throttle cable at the throttle housing as described in this section.
10. Operate the throttle lever and make sure the carburetor throttle pulley is operating correctly. If throttle operation is sluggish, check that the cable is attached correctly and there are no tight bends in the cable.
11. Adjust the throttle cable as described in Chapter Three.
12. Test ride the ATV and make sure the throttle is operating correctly.

FUEL TANK

Table 3 lists fuel tank specifications.

Removal/Installation

1. Park the ATV on level ground and set the parking brake.
2. Turn off the fuel valve.
3. Remove the seat as described in Chapter Fifteen.
4. Disconnect the negative battery cable from the battery.
5. Remove the fuel tank cover as described in Chapter Fifteen.
6. Remove the air intake duct and air intake guide plate as described in this chapter.
7. Detach the fuel tank holder bands (**Figure 65**).
8. Remove the front fuel tank mounting bolts (**Figure 66**).
9. Disconnect the fuel hose from the carburetor (**Figure 67**).
10. Remove the fuel tank.

11. To remove the heat guard, perform the following:
   a. Remove the trim clips (A, **Figure 68**).
   b. Detach the throttle and choke cables from the retaining tabs.
   c. Detach the coolant hose from the retaining arms.
   d. Remove the heat guard (B, **Figure 68**).
   e. Reverse the previous steps to install the heat guard.
12. Install the fuel tank by reversing the preceding removal steps while noting the following:
   a. Replace missing or damaged fuel tank dampers or holder bands.
   b. Tighten the fuel tank mounting bolts securely.
   c. Turn the fuel valve on and check for leaks.

FUEL VALVE

Removal/Installation

1. Remove the fuel tank as described in this chapter.
2. Drain the fuel tank of all gas. Store the gas in a can approved for gasoline storage.
3. Remove the screws securing the fuel valve to the bottom of the fuel tank (**Figure 69**).
4. Clean the strainer screen in a high-flash point solvent, then inspect the screen (A, **Figure 70**). Replace the strainer screen if damaged.
5. Install a new fuel valve O-ring (B, **Figure 70**).
6. Install the fuel valve by reversing the preceding removal steps. Turn on the fuel valve and check the fuel valve and hose for leaks.

AIR BOX

Removal/Installation

Refer to **Figure 71**.
1. Park the ATV on level ground and set the parking brake.
2. Remove the seat, side covers and fuel tank cover (Chapter Fifteen).
3. Disengage the trim clips (**Figure 72**).
4. Remove the left engine side cover (**Figure 73**).
5. Loosen the clamp screw at the air box (A, **Figure 74**) and separate the intake duct (B) from the air box.
6. Loosen the carburetor hose clamp at the air box (**Figure 75**).
7. Disengage the breather hose retaining clips from the muffler bracket (**Figure 76**). Disconnect the breather hose from the air box.

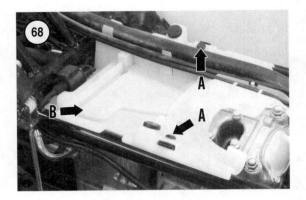

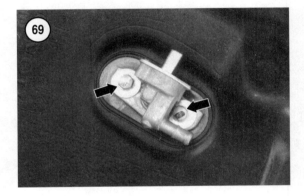

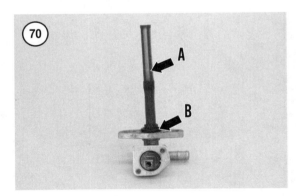

8. Disconnect the breather hose from the air box (**Figure 77**).
9. Detach the vent hose from the carburetor (**Figure 78**).
10. Remove the air box assembly.
11. Cover the carburetor opening.
12. Install by reversing the preceding removal steps while noting the following:
   a. Check the air box intake hose for loose parts or other debris before connecting it to the carburetor.
   b. Check all the hoses for proper routing.

AIR BOX ASSEMBLY

71

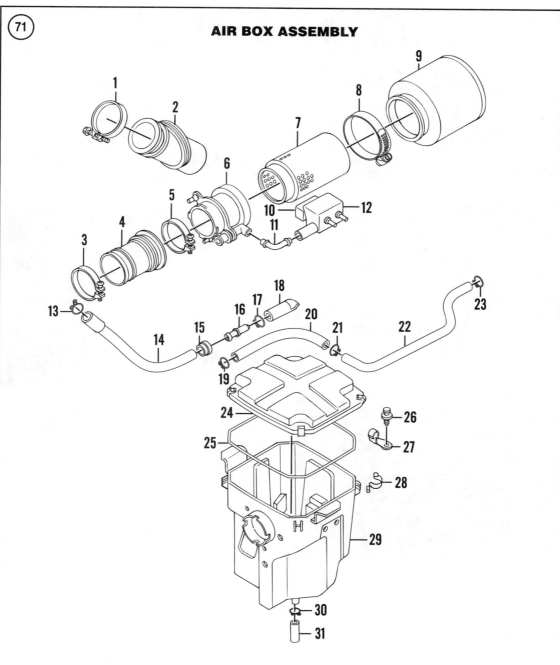

1. Clamp
2. Air intake duct tube
3. Clamp
4. Intake hose
5. Clamp
6. Tube
7. Element core
8. Clamp

9. Filter element
10. Breather filter element
11. Tube
12. Breather joint
13. Clip
14. Vent tube
15. Grommet
16. Fitting

17. Clip
18. Vent air filter element
19. Clip
20. Crankcase
     breather hose
21. Clip
22. Tube
23. Clip

24. Cover
25. Gasket
26. Trim clip
27. Bracket
28. Clamp
29. Air box
30. Clip
31. Drain tube

8

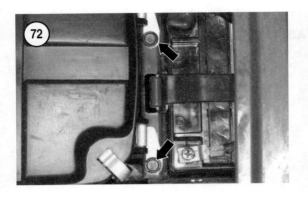

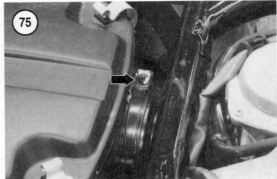

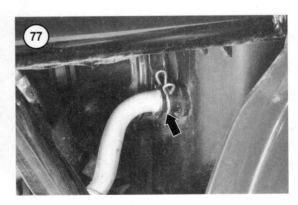

AIR INTAKE DUCT

Removal/Installation

1. Remove the front fender as described in Chapter Fifteen.

2. Loosen the rear clamp screw (A, **Figure 74**).

3. Disengage the guide notch on the intake duct from the retaining post on the frame (A, **Figure 79**).

4. Separate the front duct end from the air intake guide (B, **Figure 79**) and remove the air intake duct.

5. If necessary, detach the resonator (A, **Figure 80**) from the duct (B). Note the index tabs when installing the resonator onto the duct.

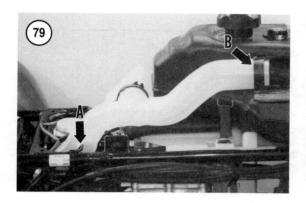

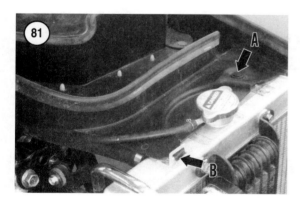

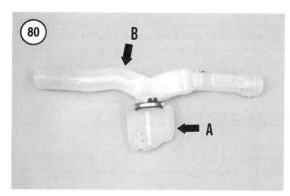

6. Reverse the removal steps to install the air intake duct.

AIR INTAKE GUIDE PLATE

Removal/Installation

1. Remove the front fender as described in Chapter Fifteen.

2. Remove the trim clip (A, **Figure 81**).

3. Remove the air intake guide plate by disengaging the plate hook from the retaining bracket (B, **Figure 81**) and moving the plate assembly backward and upward.

4. Reverse the preceding steps to install the air intake guide plate. Make sure the air intake duct fits properly into the guide plate retaining tube (B, **Figure 79**).

CHOKE CABLE REPLACEMENT

1. Remove the fuel tank as described in this chapter.

2. Make a diagram of the choke cable routing path from the handlebar to the carburetor.

3. Remove any cable guides from the choke cable.

4. Detach the choke cable from the front retaining bracket as follows:

    a. Loosen the retaining nut (A, **Figure 82**).

    b. Detach the cable from the bracket (B, **Figure 82**).

5. Loosen the starting enrichment (SE) valve nut (**Figure 83**) and remove the SE valve from the carburetor.

6. Remove the choke cable.

7. Reverse the preceding steps to install the choke cable. Position the cable so it lies in the channel in the heat guard plate. After installation, check the choke operation.

8

Table 1 CARBURETOR SPECIFICATIONS

Type	Vacuum piston
Throttle bore size	36 mm (1.4 in.)
Identification number	
2001-2003	VE6AB
2004	VE6AC
Main jet	
Standard	158
High altitude	152
Pilot jet	45
Jet needle clip position	2nd groove from top
Idle speed	1300-1500 rpm
Pilot screw adjustment (turns out)*	
2001-2003	2 5/8
2004	2 3/4
Heater resistance	13-15 ohms

*Initial adjustment only. Refer to the text for procedure and final pilot air screw adjustment (turns out).

Table 2 CARBURETOR FLOAT LEVEL

Float level	
2001-2003	18.5 mm (0.73 in.)
2004	15.9 mm (0.63 in.)

Table 3 FUEL TANK SPECIFICATIONS

	Liters	U.S. gal.
Fuel tank capacity	14.0	3.7
Reserve capacity	3.8	1.0

ELECTRICAL SYSTEM

This chapter contains service and test procedures for electrical and ignition components. Maintenance specific information for the battery and spark plug are in Chapter Three.

All models are equipped with electric shifting and a digital combination meter mounted above the handlebar. TRX500FGA models are equipped with a global positioning system (GPS).

Specifications are in **Tables 1-6** at the end of this chapter.

RESISTANCE AND PEAK VOLTAGE TESTING

Resistance readings vary with temperature. The resistance increases when the temperature increases and decreases when the temperature decreases.

Specifications for resistance are based on tests performed at a specific temperature (20° C [68° F]). If a component is warm or hot let it cool to room temperature. If a component is tested at a temperature that varies from the specification test temperature, a false reading may result.

To measure peak voltage, use a tester capable of measuring peak voltage or a voltmeter that has a minimum input impedance of 10M ohms/DCV and is coupled to a peak voltage adapter. An equivalent tool is the Motion Pro IgnitionMate (part No. 08-0193).

Make sure the battery of any tester being used is in good condition. The battery of an ohmmeter is the source for the current that is applied to the circuit being tested. Accurate results depend on the battery having sufficient voltage.

All peak voltage specifications are minimum values. If the measured voltage meets or exceeds the specifications, the test results are acceptable.

> *NOTE*
> *When using an analog ohmmeter, always calibrate the meter between each resistance test by touching the test leads together and zeroing the meter.*

ELECTRICAL COMPONENT REPLACEMENT

Most motorcycle dealerships and parts suppliers do not accept the return of any electrical part. If the *exact* cause of any electrical system malfunction cannot be determined, have a Honda dealership retest that specific system to verify the test results. If you purchase a new electrical component(s), install it, and then find that the system still does not work properly, you will probably be unable to return the unit for a refund.

Consider any test results carefully before replacing a component that tests only *slightly* out of specification, especially resistance. A number of variables can affect test results dramatically. These include the testing meter's internal circuitry, ambient temperature and conditions under which the machine has been operated. All instructions and specifications have been checked for accuracy; however, successful test results depend to a great degree upon individual accuracy.

ELECTRICAL CONNECTORS

Service

The position of the connectors may have been changed during previous repairs. Always confirm the wire colors to and from the connector and follow the wiring harness to the various components when performing tests.

> *CAUTION*
> *Connector internal pins are easily damaged and dislodged, which may cause a malfunction. Exercise care when handling or testing the connectors.*

Under normal operating conditions the connectors are weather-tight. If continuous operation in adverse operating condition is expected, the connectors may be packed with dielectric grease to prevent the intrusion of water or other contaminants. To prevent moisture from entering into the various connectors, it is a good practice to disconnect them, and after making sure the terminals are clean, pack the connector with dielectric grease. Do not use a substitute that may interfere with current flow. Dielectric grease is specifically formulated to seal the connector and not increase current resistance. For best results, the compound should fill the entire inner area of the connector. It is recommended that each time a connector is unplugged, it be cleaned and sealed with dielectric grease.

Ground connections are often overlooked when troubleshooting. Make sure they are corrosion free and tight. Apply dielectric grease to the terminals before reconnecting them.

Removal/Disassembly

To remove a connector (**Figure 1** or **Figure 2**) from the mounting bracket, use a thin screwdriver

or other tool to disengage the mounting tang on the bracket from the tab on the connector.

> *NOTE*
> *It is necessary to remove large rectangular connectors from the mounting bracket for disassembly. The mounting bracket tang also locks together the connector halves. The connector must be free from the mounting bracket to disassemble or assemble the connector.*

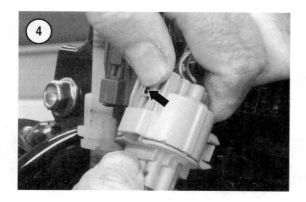

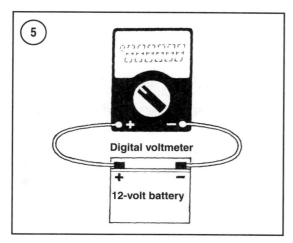

Small connectors and large round connectors may be disassembled by pulling or prying out the retaining tab at the lower end of the outer half (**Figure 3**) and pulling out the inner connector half. Large rectangular connectors are equipped with a locking tab on the outer body (**Figure 4**). Depress the tab, then pull out the inner half. It may be necessary to remove an adjacent connector from the mounting bracket to gain sufficient space to remove

the desired connector. The following connectors must be removed from the mounting bracket for disassembly or assembly:
1. Handlebar switch connector (**Figure 1**).
2. Meter connector (**Figure 2**).

CHARGING SYSTEM

The charging system consists of the battery, alternator and a voltage regulator/rectifier. A 30-amp main fuse protects the circuit.

Alternating current generated by the alternator is rectified to direct current. The voltage regulator maintains the voltage to the battery and additional electrical loads at a constant voltage despite variations in engine speed and load.

Troubleshooting

Refer to Chapter Two.

Battery Voltage Check

To obtain accurate charging system test results, the battery must be fully charged. Check battery voltage as follows:
1. Remove the seat (Chapter Fifteen).
2. Connect a digital voltmeter between the battery negative and positive terminals and measure the battery voltage (**Figure 5**). A fully charged battery reads between 13.0-13.2 volts. If the voltage reading is less than this amount, recharge the battery as described in Chapter Three.

Charging System Current Draw Test

Perform this test before performing the charging voltage test:
1. Remove the seat (Chapter Fifteen).
2. Turn the ignition switch off.
3. Disconnect the negative battery cable from the battery (**Figure 6**).

CAUTION
Before connecting the ammeter into the circuit in Step 4, set the meter to its highest amperage scale. This prevents a large current flow from damaging the meter or blowing the meter's fuse, if so equipped.

4. Connect an ammeter between the battery ground cable and the negative battery terminal.

5. Switch the ammeter between its highest and lowest amperage scale while reading the ammeter scale. The ammeter reading should be less than 0.1 mA.

6. A current draw higher than 0.1 mA may indicate a short circuit and a continuous battery discharge. Dirt and/or electrolyte on top of the battery or a crack in the battery case can cause this type of problem by providing a path for battery current to follow. Remove and clean the battery as described in Chapter Three. Reinstall the battery and retest.

7. If the current draw is still excessive, consider the following probable causes:

    a. Damaged battery.

    b. Short circuit in system.

8. To find the short circuit, refer to the appropriate wiring diagram at the end of the manual. Measure the current draw while disconnecting each charging system connector one by one. When the current draw returns to normal, the circuit with the short circuit is identified. Test the circuit further to find the problem.

9. Disconnect the ammeter from the battery and battery cable.

10. Reconnect the negative battery cable to the battery.

11. Install the seat (Chapter Fifteen).

Charging Voltage Test

This procedure tests charging system operation. It does not measure maximum charging system output. **Table 1** lists charging system specifications.

To obtain accurate test results, the battery must be fully charged. Measure battery voltage as described in this section.

1. Start and run the engine until it reaches normal operating temperature, then turn the engine off.

2. Connect a tachometer to the engine following its manufacturer's instructions.

3. Connect a DC voltmeter to the battery terminals as shown in **Figure 5**.

4. Start the engine and allow it to run at idle speed.

5. Gradually increase engine speed idle to 5000 rpm and read the regulated voltage reading on the voltmeter. Compare to the regulated voltage reading in **Table 1**. If the regulated voltage is higher than 15.5 volts, check for a shorted wiring harness, damaged ignition switch or a faulty regulator/recti-

fier. Perform the *Regulator/Rectifier Wiring Test* in this section. If the regulated voltage reading is correct but there is a problem in the charging system, the battery may be faulty.

6. Disconnect the voltmeter and tachometer.

7. Install the seat (Chapter Fifteen).

Regulator/Rectifier Wiring Harness Test

1. Disconnect the regulator/rectifier electrical connector (A, **Figure 7**).

> *NOTE*
> *Make all of the tests (Steps 2-4) at the wiring harness connector, not at the regulator/rectifier.*

2. Check the battery charge lead as follows:

    a. Connect a voltmeter between the red (+) and green (−) connectors.

    b. With the ignition switch off, the voltmeter should read 13.0-13.2 volts (battery voltage).

    c. If the battery voltage is less than specified, check both wires for damage.

    d. Disconnect the voltmeter leads.

3. Check the ground wire as follows:

    a. Connect an ohmmeter between the green wire and a good engine ground.

    b. The ohmmeter must read continuity.

    c. If there is no continuity, check the green wire for damage.

4. Check the charge coil wires as follows:

    a. Using an ohmmeter measure the resistance between each yellow wire.

    b. The ohmmeter must read 0.1-1.0 ohms at 20° C (68° F). An infinity reading indicates an open

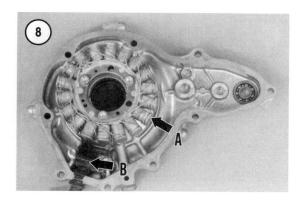

circuit. Test the stator coil resistance as described in this section.

  c. If the resistance reading is excessive, check for dirty or loose-fitting terminals or damaged wires.

5. If any regulator/rectifier measurement is out of specification, replace the regulator/rectifier as described in this chapter.

6. Reconnect the regulator/rectifier electrical connector (A, **Figure 7**).

Regulator/Rectifier Removal/Installation

1. Remove the seat.

2. Disconnect the negative battery cable from the battery (**Figure 6**).

3. Disconnect the regulator/rectifier unit electrical connector (A, **Figure 7**).

4. Remove the bolts securing the regulator/rectifier (B, **Figure 7**) to the frame and remove it.

5. Install by reversing the preceding removal steps.

ALTERNATOR

The alternator consists of the flywheel and stator coil assembly. Flywheel and stator removal and installation procedures are covered in Chapter Five.

Flywheel Testing

The flywheel is permanently magnetized and cannot be tested except by replacing it with a known good one. The rotor can lose magnetism over time or a sharp hit, such as dropping it onto the floor. Replace the flywheel if defective or damaged.

Stator Coil Resistance Test

NOTE
The stator coil is also referred to as the charge coil.

The stator coil (A, **Figure 8**) is mounted inside the alternator cover. The stator coil can be tested with the alternator cover mounted on the engine.

1. Disconnect the alternator/pulse generator connector (**Figure 9**).

2. Measure the resistance between each yellow wire at the alternator end of the connector. **Table 1** lists the specified stator coil resistance.

3. If the resistance is within specification, the stator coil is good. If the resistance is higher than specified, the coil is damaged. Replace the stator assembly.

4. Check the continuity from each yellow wire terminal in the alternator stator end of the connector and to ground. Replace the stator coil if any yellow terminal has continuity to ground. Continuity indicates a short within the stator coil winding.

NOTE
Before replacing the stator assembly, check the electrical wires to and within the electrical connector for any open or poor connections.

5. If the stator coil (A, **Figure 8**) fails either of these tests, replace it as described under *Alternator Cover* in Chapter Five.

6. Apply a dielectric grease to the stator coil connector before reconnecting it. This helps seal out moisture. Make sure the O-ring is mounted on the stator coil connector.

7. Reconnect the alternator/pulse generator connector.

IGNITION SYSTEM

All models are equipped with a capacitor discharge ignition system.

Servicing Precautions

Protect the ignition system as follows:
1. Never disconnect any of the electrical connections while the engine is running.
2. Apply dielectric grease to all electrical connectors before reconnecting them. This helps seal out moisture.
3. The electrical connectors must be free of corrosion and properly connected.
4. The ignition control module (ICM) unit is part of the engine control module (ECM) which is mounted in a rubber mount. If removed, make sure to reinstall it into its rubber mount.

Troubleshooting

Refer to Chapter Two.

Pulse Generator

The pulse generator is mounted inside the alternator cover (B, **Figure 8**). The pulse generator may be tested with the alternator cover mounted on the engine.

Peak voltage test

The following test checks the condition of the pulse generator, wiring and connections. A peak voltage tester or adapter is required to measure the peak voltage.
1. Detach the right ECM connector (**Figure 10**) from the ECM module.
2. Connect the positive voltmeter lead to the blue/yellow wire terminal in the connector.
3. Connect the negative voltmeter lead to ground.
4. Turn the ignition switch on.
5. Push the starter button and operate the starter motor while observing the voltmeter.
6. The voltage reading should be at least 0.7 volts.

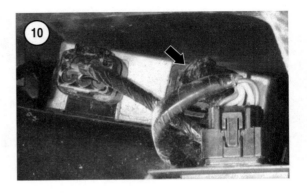

NOTE
Slow cranking speed may produce a low voltage reading. If the voltmeter indicates at least one reading that is at least 0.7 volts, then the voltmeter reading is correct.

7. If the voltage reading is less than 0.7 volts, proceed as follows:
   a. Disconnect the alternator connector (**Figure 9**).
   b. Connect the positive voltmeter lead to the blue/yellow wire terminal in the alternator end of the connector.
   c. Ground the negative voltmeter lead to the engine.

d. Turn the ignition switch on.

e. Push the starter button and operate the starter motor while observing the voltmeter.

f. The voltage reading should be at least 0.7 volts.

8. If the voltage reading is abnormal in Step 6, but satisfactory in Step 7, check for faulty wiring or connections.

9. If the voltage reading is abnormal in Step 6 and Step 7, the pulse generator is faulty.

Removal/installation

1. Remove the alternator cover as described in Chapter Five.

2. Remove the pulse generator mounting bolts (A, **Figure 11**).

3. Disconnect the wire lead (B, **Figure 11**) from the pulse generator and remove the pulse generator.

4. Reverse the removal steps to install the pulse generator. Apply threadlocker to the mounting bolts and tighten to 6 N•m (53 in.-lb.).

Ignition Control Module

No test specifications are available for the ignition control module (ICM). The ICM is part of the engine control module (ECM). Only replace the ECM after all other components, including wiring and connections, have been eliminated Refer to Chapter Two.

Removal/Installation

Refer to the *Engine Control Module* section in this chapter.

Ignition Coil

The ignition coil is mounted on the front upper frame rail (**Figure 12**). The ignition coil may be tested without removing it.

Primary peak voltage test

1. Remove the left side cover as described in Chapter Fifteen.

2. Remove the left engine side cover (**Figure 13**).

3. Disconnect the spark plug cap (**Figure 14**).

> *NOTE*
> *A grounding device may be used as described in Chapter One instead of grounding a spark plug as described in the following steps.*

4. Connect a new spark plug to the plug cap.

5. Ground the spark plug to the crankcase.

> *WARNING*
> *High voltage is present during ignition system operation. Do not touch ignition components, wires or test leads while cranking or running the engine.*

> *NOTE*
> *A peak voltage tester or adapter is required to measure the peak voltage. All peak voltage specifications are minimum values. If the measured voltage meets or exceeds the specification, the test results are satisfactory.*

6. Check the peak voltage by performing the following:

> *NOTE*
> *Do not disconnect the wires from the ignition coil when performing the following test. If it is not possible to con-*

9

tact the coil terminal with the tester probe, pierce the wire using a needle probe.

a. Remove the fuel tank as described in Chapter Eight.

b. Connect the positive test probe to the black/yellow wire or terminal on the ignition coil (**Figure 15**) and connect the negative test probe to ground.

c. Turn the ignition switch on.

d. Press the starter button and crank the engine for a few seconds while reading the meter. Record the highest meter reading. The minimum peak voltage is 100 volts.

7. If the peak voltage reading is less than specified, perform the troubleshooting procedure described in Chapter Two to determine the cause for the low voltage reading.

> *NOTE*
> *Before replacing an ignition coil, have it checked by a dealership on an ignition coil testing machine.*

Removal/Installation

1. Remove the fuel tank as described in Chapter Eight.

2. Remove the left engine side cover (**Figure 13**).

3. Disconnect the spark plug cap (**Figure 14**) from the spark plug and disengage the spark plug wire from the retaining clips.

4. Disconnect the two primary wires from the ignition coil (A, **Figure 16**).

5. Remove the ignition coil and rubber holder (B, **Figure 16**) from the frame.

6. Remove the rubber holder from the old ignition coil and install it onto the new coil.

7. Install the ignition coil by reversing the preceding removal steps. Make sure all electrical connections are tight and free of corrosion.

ELECTRIC STARTING SYSTEM

The starting system consists of the starter, starter gears, solenoid and the starter button.

Table 3 lists starter service specifications.

The starter gears are covered in Chapter Five.

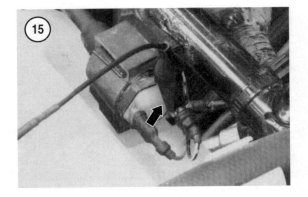

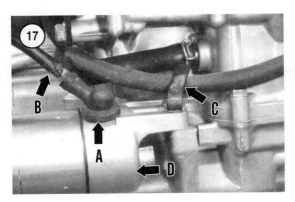

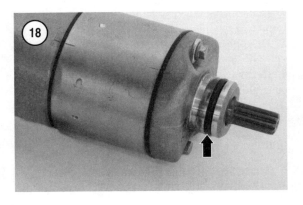

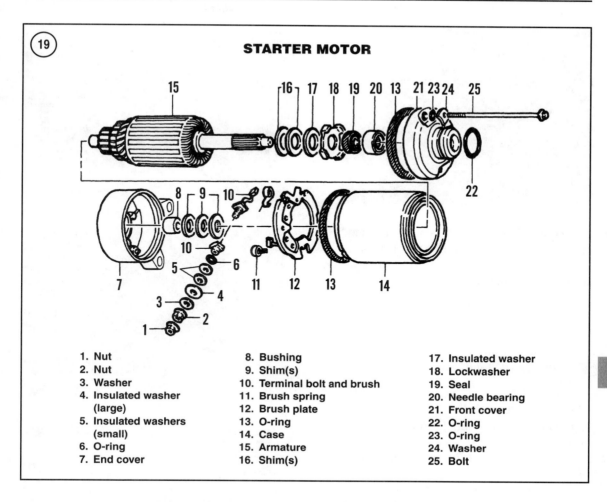

STARTER MOTOR

1. Nut
2. Nut
3. Washer
4. Insulated washer (large)
5. Insulated washers (small)
6. O-ring
7. End cover
8. Bushing
9. Shim(s)
10. Terminal bolt and brush
11. Brush spring
12. Brush plate
13. O-ring
14. Case
15. Armature
16. Shim(s)
17. Insulated washer
18. Lockwasher
19. Seal
20. Needle bearing
21. Front cover
22. O-ring
23. O-ring
24. Washer
25. Bolt

CAUTION
Do not operate the starter for more than 5 seconds at a time. Let it cool approximately 10 seconds before operating it again.

Troubleshooting

Refer to Chapter Two.

Starter Removal/Installation

1. Remove the seat.

2. Remove the recoil starter cover (Chapter Fifteen).

3. Disconnect the negative battery cable from the battery (**Figure 6**).

4. Push back the rubber cap (A, **Figure 17**), then remove the nut and the starter cable (B) from the starter.

5. Pull back the hose retaining clamp (C, **Figure 17**) and remove the two starter mounting bolts.

6. Remove the starter (D, **Figure 17**).

7. If necessary, service the starter as described in this chapter.

8. Install the starter by reversing the preceding removal steps, plus the following:

　a. Lubricate the starter O-ring (**Figure 18**) with grease.

　b. Clean any rust or corrosion from the starter cable eyelet.

　c. Tighten the starter mounting bolts securely.

Disassembly

Refer to **Figure 19**.

1. Find the alignment marks on the case and both end covers. If necessary, scribe new marks.

2. Remove the two case bolts, washers, lockwashers and O-rings (**Figure 20**).

> *NOTE*
> *Record the thickness and alignment of each shim and washer removed during disassembly. The number of shims used in each starter varies.*

3. Remove the front cover (**Figure 21**) and lockwasher (**Figure 22**).

4. Remove the front shims (**Figure 23**) from the armature shaft.

5. Remove the case (**Figure 24**) and end cover (**Figure 25**).

6. Remove the rear shim set (**Figure 26**).

7. Clean all grease, dirt and carbon from the armature, case and end covers.

> *CAUTION*
> *Do not immerse the wire windings in the case or the armature coil in solvent because the insulation may be damaged. Wipe the windings with a cloth lightly moistened with solvent.*

Inspection

1. Pull the brush plate (A, **Figure 27**) out of the end cover.

2. Pull the spring away from each brush and pull the brushes (B, **Figure 27**) out of their guides.

3. Measure the length of each brush (**Figure 28**). If the length is less than the service limit in **Table 3**, replace both brushes as a set. When replacing the brushes, note the following:

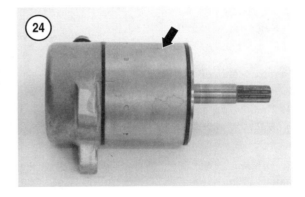

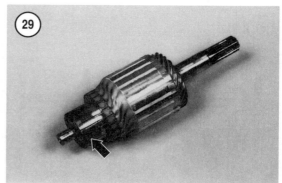

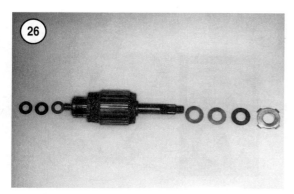

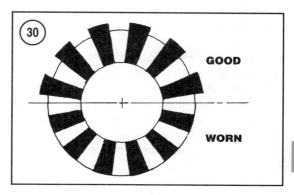

9

a. Soldering is not necessary when replacing the starter motor brushes.

b. Replace the terminal bolt and brush as an assembly. Remove the terminal bolt (C, **Figure 27**) and brush and replace them. Be sure to install the washer set in the order shown in **Figure 19**.

c. The brush plate (A, **Figure 27**) and brush are replaced as a set. Remove the brush plate and brush and replace them.

4. Inspect the brush springs and replace them if weak or damaged. To replace the brush springs, perform the following:

a. Make a drawing that shows the location of the brush springs on the brush holder. Also indicate the direction in which each spring coil turns.

b. Remove and replace both brush springs as a set.

5. Inspect the commutator (**Figure 29**). The mica must be below the surface of the copper bars. On a worn commutator the mica and copper bars may be worn to the same level (**Figure 30**). If necessary, have the commutator serviced by a dealership or electrical repair shop.

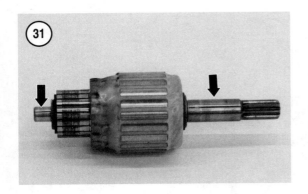

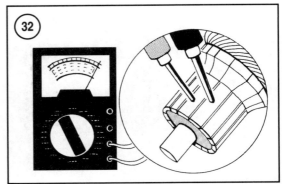

6. Inspect the commutator copper bars for discoloration. A discolored pair of bars indicates grounded armature coils.

7. Inspect the armature shaft (**Figure 31**) for excessive wear, scoring or other damage.

8. Use an ohmmeter and perform the following:

    a. Check for continuity between the commutator bars (**Figure 32**). There should be continuity between pairs of bars.

    b. Check for continuity between the commutator bars and the shaft (**Figure 33**). There should be no continuity.

    c. If the armature fails either of these tests, replace the starter assembly.

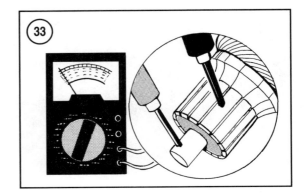

9. Use an ohmmeter and perform the following:

    a. Check for continuity between the starter cable terminal and the end case cover (**Figure 34**). There should be no continuity.

    b. Check for continuity between the starter cable terminal and the brush black wire terminal (**Figure 35**). There should be continuity.

    c. If the unit fails either of these tests, replace the starter assembly.

10. Inspect the front cover seal and needle bearing (**Figure 36**). Replace the front cover if either part is excessively worn or damaged.

11. Inspect the rear cover bushing. Replace the rear cover if the bushing is damaged.

12. Inspect the case (**Figure 37**) for cracks or other damage. Inspect for loose, chipped or damaged magnets.

13. Inspect the O-rings and replace them if worn or damaged.

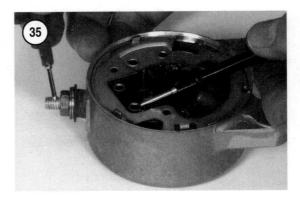

Assembly

1. If removed, install the brushes into their holders and secure the brushes with the springs.

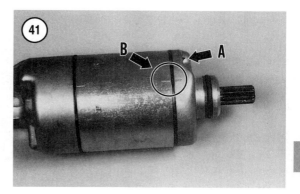

2. Align the brush plate arm with the notch in the end cover and install the brush plate (**Figure 37**).

3. Install the rear shims (**Figure 26**) on the armature shaft next to the commutator.

4. Insert the armature coil assembly into the rear cover (**Figure 25**). Turn the armature during installation so the brushes engage the commutator properly. Make sure the armature is not turned upside down or the shims could slide off the end of the shaft. Do not damage the brushes.

5. Install the two O-rings (**Figure 38**) onto the case, then slide the case over the armature (**Figure 24**). Align the mark on the case and end cover (**Figure 39**).

6. Install the front shims (**Figure 23**) onto the armature shaft.

7. Install the lockwasher (**Figure 22**) onto the front cover so the lockwasher tabs engage the cover slots (**Figure 40**).

8. Install the front cover (A, **Figure 41**) onto the armature shaft. Align the marks on the front cover and the case (B, **Figure 41**).

9. Lubricate the O-rings (23, **Figure 19**) with oil.

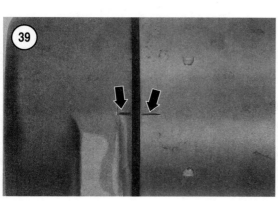

10. Install the bolts, washers and O-rings (**Figure 20**) and tighten the bolts securely.

> *NOTE*
> *If one or both bolts do not pass through the starter, the end covers and/or brush plate are installed incorrectly.*

STARTER RELAY

System Test

Refer to *Electric Starting System* in Chapter Two.

Operation Check

1. Remove the seat (Chapter Fifteen), then remove the lid above the battery.

2. Turn the ignition switch on and depress the starter button. The starter relay (**Figure 42**) should click. If the starter relay did not click, perform the *Voltage Test* in this section.

3. Turn the ignition switch off and install the seat (Chapter Fifteen).

Voltage Test

1. Remove the seat (Chapter Fifteen), then remove the lid above the battery.

2. Disconnect the starter relay connector (**Figure 43**).

3. Connect a voltmeter between the starter relay connector yellow/red (+) and green/red (−) wire terminals at the wiring harness end of the connector.

4. Shift the transmission into neutral and turn the ignition switch on, then depress the starter button. The voltmeter should read battery voltage. If the voltmeter reading is incorrect, perform the *Continuity Test* in this section.

5. Turn the ignition switch off.

Continuity Test

1. Remove the starter relay as described in this chapter.

2. Connect an ohmmeter to the starter relay—battery and starter motor terminals (**Figure 44**).

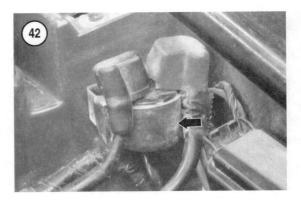

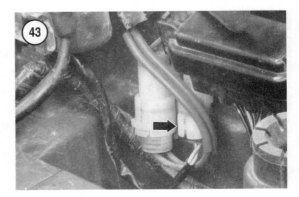

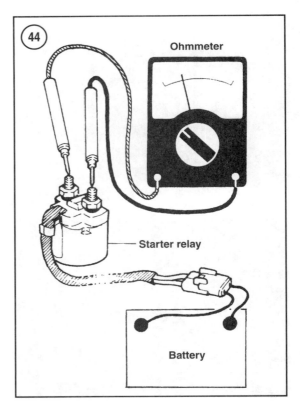

Ohmmeter

Starter relay

Battery

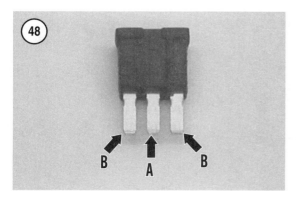

B A B

3. Momentarily connect a 12-volt battery to the starter relay terminals as shown in **Figure 44** while reading the resistance on the ohmmeter.

4. The ohmmeter must show continuity when battery voltage is applied and no continuity when the battery voltage is removed.

5. If either reading is incorrect, replace the starter relay and retest.

Removal/Installation

1. Remove the seat (Chapter Fifteen), then remove the lid above the battery.

2. Disconnect the negative battery cable from the battery (**Figure 6**).

3. Disconnect the starter relay connector (**Figure 43**).

4. Slide the two covers away from the terminals on top of the starter relay.

5. Disconnect the battery and starter motor cables from the starter relay (**Figure 45**).

6. Remove the starter relay and the rubber mount from the frame.

7. Install the starter relay by reversing the preceding removal procedures.

START CIRCUIT DIODE

A diode is installed in the starting circuit. Refer to the wiring diagrams at back of this manual.

Removal/Testing/Installation

1. Remove the seat (Chapter Fifteen), then remove the lid above the battery.

2. Remove the fuse box cover (**Figure 46**).

3. Pull out the diode (**Figure 47**).

4. Test the diode as follows:

    a. Check for continuity between the middle terminal on the diode (A, **Figure 48**) and one of the end terminals (B). Reverse the ohmmeter leads and recheck for continuity between the same terminals. The ohmmeter must read continuity during one test and no continuity (infinite resistance) with the leads reversed.

    b. Repeat substep a by checking for continuity between the middle terminal and the remaining end terminal.

    c. Replace the diode if it fails the continuity tests.

9

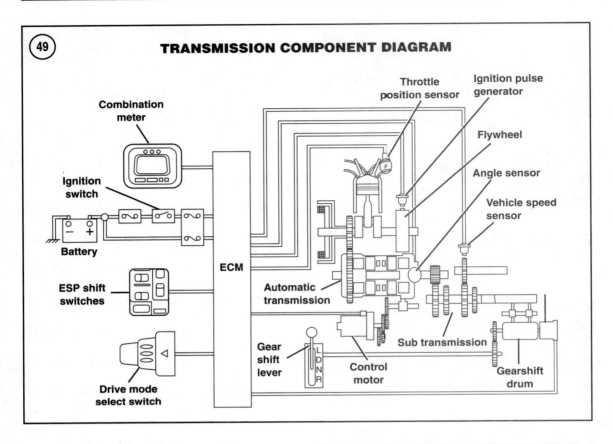

TRANSMISSION COMPONENT DIAGRAM

Throttle position sensor

Ignition pulse generator

Combination meter

Flywheel

Ignition switch

Angle sensor

Vehicle speed sensor

Battery

ECM

Automatic transmission

ESP shift switches

Gear shift lever

Sub transmission

Drive mode select switch

Control motor

Gearshift drum

5. Reverse Steps 1-3 to install the diode.

AUTOMATIC TRANSMISSION (HONDAMATIC)

The TRX500 is equipped with the Hondamatic automatic transmission. The engine control module (ECM) controls transmission operation. When in automatic mode, the ECM controls transmission output speed based on input from switches and sensors mounted on the powertrain components. Refer to **Figure 49**. The ECM operates the shift control motor, which drives a set of reduction gears to rotate the transmission screw shaft gear.

Operation

The control motor (**Figure 50**) may rotate in either direction. Rotation transfers through the gear reduction assembly to the transmission screw shaft gear. The screw shaft gear rotates the screw shaft, which determines the position of the transmission swashplate. Also refer to Chapter Five.

maximum power, while the D2 position provides maximum torque.

The gear position indicator switch sends a signal to the ECM to indicate the position of the sub-transmission shift drum. The ECM adjusts the transmission output ratio according to the engaged sub-transmission gear, low or direct.

The ignition pulse generator and the speed sensor provide the ECM with engine and ATV speed signals. The throttle position sensor indicates to the ECM the carburetor throttle opening. The ignition pulse generator, speed sensor and throttle position sensor are covered elsewhere in this chapter.

The automatic transmission may also be operated manually using the Electric Shift Program (ESP), which is described in this chapter.

The automatic transmission does not contain a reverse gear. Operation in reverse is provided by the reverse gears in the sub-transmission.

Initial Setting Procedure

Perform the following initial setting procedure if the ECM, throttle position sensor or angle sensor is replaced. Also perform the procedure if the throttle cable is disconnected.

The angle sensor converts transmission screw shaft motion into electrical signals that are sent to the ECM to inform the ECM of the transmission's position.

The ECM converts the input signals from the switches and sensors into directional signals for the motor circuit, which powers the control motor. The ECM also contains a self-diagnostic circuit that stops automatic operation if it detects an error (the ATV still operates).

> *NOTE*
> *If the automatic system malfunctions, turn off the ignition switch, wait a short time, then turn it back on. If the automatic system malfunction remains, refer to Chapter Two and follow the troubleshooting procedure.*

The ECM provides two selectable programs: maximum torque or maximum power. The operator may select the desired setting using the drive mode select switch (**Figure 51**). The D1 position provides

> *NOTE*
> *Make sure the throttle cable freeplay is correct before performing this procedure. Refer to Chapter Three.*

1. Set the mode selector switch (**Figure 52**) in the D1 mode.
2. Move the gearshift lever (**Figure 53**) to neutral, then start the engine and let it idle for approximately 30 seconds.
3. Move the gearshift lever to the D position [the gear indicator on the combination meter (**Figure 54**) should display D].
4. Let the ATV run slowly forward approximately 5 feet, then move the gearshift lever back to the neutral position. The gear indicator on the combination meter should display N.
5. Turn the ignition switch off.
6. Turn the ignition switch on while simultaneously holding in the UP and DOWN electric shift switches (**Figure 55**). Immediately release the shift switches.
7. Push and release the UP, DOWN and UP switches in that order. Push each switch individu-

ally just long enough to make good contact. Do not hold in the switch.

> *NOTE*
> *If the meter continues to display the N symbol in Step 8, repeat the procedure starting at Step 5.*

8. The gear position indicator on the combination meter should display a constant dash (–) symbol. After the symbol appears, move the throttle lever from the fully closed to fully open and back to fully closed positions. The shift control motor should operate (listen for motor noise) to adjust the angle sensor.

9. The gear position indicator on the combination meter changes from the dash (–) symbol to the N indicator when the initial setting procedure is successful.

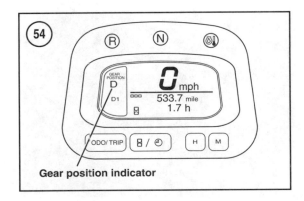

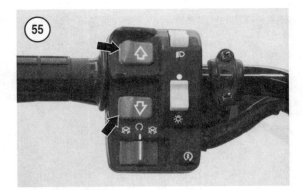

Gear position indicator

Engine Control Module (ECM)

Troubleshooting

Test procedures are not available for the ECM. Refer to Chapter Two and determine if the ECM is faulty by eliminating other possible causes for a malfunction.

Removal/installation

> *CAUTION*
> *The ECM may be damaged by stray voltage. Make sure the ignition switch is off before detaching the electrical connectors.*

> *CAUTION*
> *The ECM may be damaged if dropped or struck. Use care when handling the ECM.*

1. Remove the rear fender as described in Chapter Fifteen.

2. Disconnect the electrical connectors (**Figure 56**) from the ECM.

3. Remove the ECM.

4. Inspect the rubber retaining straps and replace if damaged.

5. Reverse the removal steps to install the ECM.

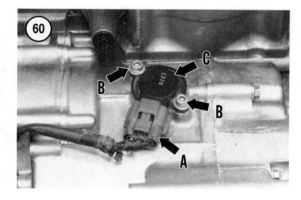

Control Motor

Testing

CAUTION
Do not attempt to jump the shift control motor with the motor circuit intact. Doing so may damage the ECM.

To test the shift control motor, proceed as follows:

1. Remove the motor as described in the following section.
2. Connect a 12-volt battery to the terminals of the shift motor connector. Replace the motor if it does not operate. Individual parts are not available.

Removal/installation

1. Remove the left front mud guard as described in Chapter Fifteen.
2. Remove the left front inner fender as described in Chapter Fifteen.
3. Make sure the ignition switch is off.
4. Disconnect the control motor electrical connector (**Figure 57**) on the left front frame downtube. Detach the wire clamps securing the wire to the frame.
5. Remove the control motor mounting bolts (A, **Figure 58**), then remove the control motor (B).
6. Inspect the O-ring (**Figure 59**) and replace if damaged or hard.
7. Reverse the removal steps to install the control motor while noting the following:
   a. Apply engine oil to the O-ring.
   b. Tighten the mounting bolts securely.

Angle Sensor

Testing/replacement

1. Make sure the ignition switch is off.
2. Remove the front section of the exhaust pipe as described in Chapter Four.
3. Clean the area around the angle sensor.
4. Disconnect the angle sensor connector (A, **Figure 60**).
5. Remove the angle sensor mounting bolts (B, **Figure 60**), then remove the sensor (C).
6. Connect an ohmmeter to the end terminals (A and B, **Figure 61**). The ohmmeter should read 1600-2400 ohms.

7. Connect an ohmmeter to the center terminal (C, **Figure 61**) and end terminal (B).

> *CAUTION*
> *Do not damage the sensor shaft hole when turning the shaft in Step 7.*

8. Rotate the sensor shaft (A, **Figure 62**) slowly while watching the ohmmeter. The ohmmeter reading should change smoothly from 0 ohms to 1600-2400 ohms.

9. Inspect the sensor shaft hole for damage or excessive wear.

10. Reverse the removal procedure to install the angle sensor while noting the following:

   a. Install a new O-ring onto the angle sensor (B, **Figure 62**).

   b. Clean any dirt or debris off the sensor joint (**Figure 63**).

   c. Align the tabs on the sensor shaft (A, **Figure 60**) with the flats on the sensor joint (**Figure 63**) when installing the angle sensor onto the crankcase. The sensor position is different than its original position (**Figure 64**, typical). Rotate the sensor clockwise so the mounting holes align with the crankcase holes (**Figure 65**).

   d. Apply threadlocker to the sensor mounting bolts.

   e. Tighten the sensor mounting bolts to 6 N•m (53 in.-lb.).

Gear Position Switch

The gear position switch is mounted on the outside of the rear crankcase cover (A, **Figure 66**).

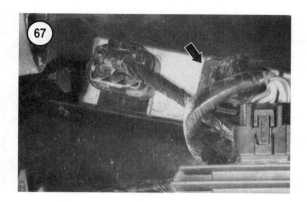

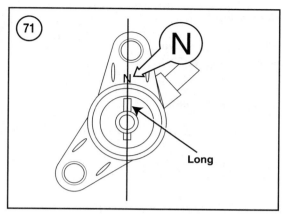

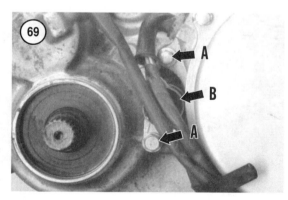

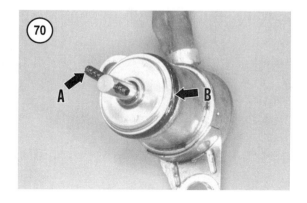

Testing/replacement

1. Disconnect the right ECM connector (**Figure 67**).

2. Move the sub-transmission gear selector into each gear. Using an ohmmeter, check for continuity between the wire terminals identified in the wiring diagrams in Chapter Seventeen and ground. If incorrect readings are noted, proceed to Step 3.

3. Disconnect the gear position switch connector (**Figure 68**). Repeat Step 2 at the gear position switch connector.

4. If the readings in Step 2 are incorrect, but the readings in Step 3 are correct, check the wires and terminals for open or short circuits. If the readings are incorrect in Step 2 and Step 3, replace the gear position switch:

> *NOTE*
> *The engine is removed for illustrative clarity.*

a. Place the sub-transmission gear selector in neutral.

b. Remove the recoil starter cover.

c. Separate the wires from the guides and move them away from the switch.

d. Remove the gear position switch retaining bolts (A, **Figure 69**), then remove the switch (B).

e. Note that the switch drive pin has a long end (A, **Figure 70**). During installation position the drive pin so the long end points toward the N on the mounting flange (**Figure 71**).

f. Install a new O-ring (B, **Figure 70**) onto the switch. Lubricate the O-ring with clean engine oil.

g. Tighten the mounting bolts securely.

Mode Select Switch

The mode select switch is mounted on the handlebar cover (**Figure 72**).

Testing/replacement

1. Disconnect the right ECM connector (**Figure 67**).
2. Move the mode selector switch to each switch position. Using an ohmmeter, check for continuity between the wire terminals identified in the wiring diagrams in Chapter Seventeen. If incorrect readings are noted, proceed to Step 3.
3. Remove the right inner fender as described in Chapter Fifteen. Disconnect the mode select switch connector (**Figure 73**). Repeat Step 2 at the mode select switch connector.
4. If the readings in Step 2 are incorrect, but the readings in Step 3 are correct, check the wires and terminals for open or short circuits. If the readings are incorrect in Step 2 and Step 3, replace the mode select switch as follows:

   a. Release the mode select switch wire from the retaining clamps.
   b. Remove the handlebar cover as described in Chapter Fifteen.
   c. Remove the switch retaining bolts (A, **Figure 74**) and bracket (B).
   d. Push in the switch tabs (C, **Figure 74**) and remove the switch.
   e. Reverse the removal steps to install the switch. Make sure to position the alignment tab on the switch with the slot in the handlebar cover.

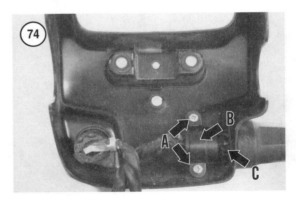

Electric Shift System

The electric shift system may be used to select a specific transmission speed. The engine control module (ECM) controls transmission operation. When in automatic mode, the ECM controls transmission output speed. When the electric shift system is selected, the rider can determine the transmission output speed. To use the electric shift system the mode select switch (**Figure 72**) must be rotated to the ESP position. In the ESP position, the ECM uses input signals from the electric shift switches (**Figure 75**) to control transmission output

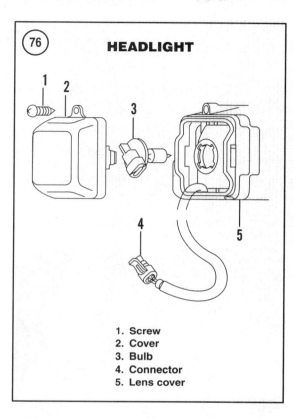

HEADLIGHT

1. Screw
2. Cover
3. Bulb
4. Connector
5. Lens cover

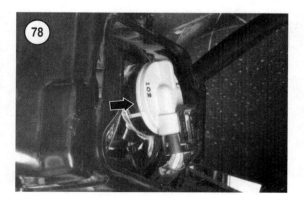

speed using the shift control motor. Also refer to *Automatic Transmission* in this chapter.

Refer to *Switches* in this chapter for the electric shift switches.

LIGHTING SYSTEM

The lighting system consists of a headlight, assist headlight, taillight and indicator lights. **Table 4** lists replacement bulbs for these components.

Always use the correct wattage bulb listed in **Table 4**. Using the wrong size bulb produces a dim light or causes the bulb to burn out prematurely.

Headlight Bulb Replacement

WARNING
If the headlight just burned out or was just turned off, it is hot! Do not touch the bulb until it cools.

Refer to **Figure 76**.
1. Remove the screw and the headlight bulb cover (**Figure 77**).
2. Turn the bulb (**Figure 78**) counterclockwise and remove it.
3. Disconnect the electrical lead from the bulb.
4. Install the new bulb by reversing the removal procedure. Make sure the rubber seal ring on the electrical connector is in good condition.
5. Check headlight operation.

Headlight Lens Removal/Installation

Refer to **Figure 79**.
1. Remove the headlight bulb as described in this section.
2. Remove the headlight aim adjusting screw (A, **Figure 80**).
3. Remove the lower mounting bolt (B, **Figure 80**).
4. Remove the four retaining screws (C, **Figure 80**), then remove the headlight.
5. Disengage the lens tabs from the headlight housing slots and separate the lens from the housing (**Figure 81**).
6. Install the headlight lens and housing by reversing the preceding removal steps. Check headlight operation. Adjust the headlight as described in this chapter.

9

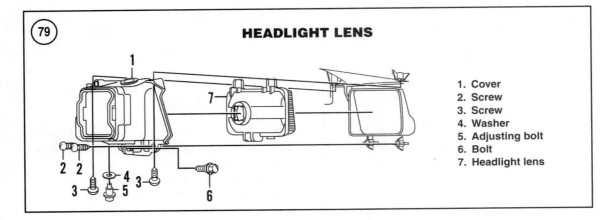

HEADLIGHT LENS

1. Cover
2. Screw
3. Screw
4. Washer
5. Adjusting bolt
6. Bolt
7. Headlight lens

Headlight Adjustment

The headlight is equipped with only a vertical aiming adjust screw located at the bottom of the headlight (A, **Figure 80**).

To adjust the headlight vertically, turn the screw clockwise to aim the light lower and counterclockwise to direct the light upward.

Assist Headlight Bulb Replacement

1. Remove the headlight upper cover retaining screw (**Figure 82**).

2. Disengage the upper cover from the lower cover by disengaging the tabs at the mating surfaces. Push in the lower cover while pulling out the upper cover.

3. Remove the headlight mounting bolt on each side (**Figure 83**).

4. Disconnect the electrical connector (**Figure 84**) from the bulb and remove the headlight assembly.

> *CAUTION*
> *All models use a quartz-halogen bulb (**Figure 85**). Because traces of oil on this type of bulb reduces the life of the bulb, do not touch the bulb glass. Clean any traces of oil or other contamination from the bulb with a cloth moistened in alcohol or lacquer thinner.*

5. Unhook the bulb retainer (A, **Figure 86**) and remove the bulb (B).

6. Install the bulb by reversing the preceding removal steps, while noting the following:

    a. Align the tabs on the bulb with the notches in the bulb holder and install the bulb.

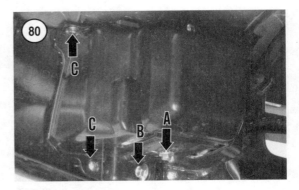

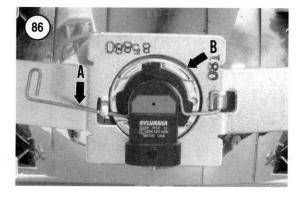

b. Start the engine and check the assist headlight operation.

Taillight Bulb Replacement

1. Turn the bulb holder (**Figure 87**) counterclockwise and remove it from the lens housing.
2. Remove the old bulb from the bulb holder.
3. Reverse the removal steps to install the taillight. Be sure the bulb holder gasket is in good condition.

Indicator Bulb Replacement

Indicator bulbs for coolant temperature, reverse gear and neutral are mounted on the circuit board contained in the combination meter. Refer to *Combination Meter* in this chapter.

COMBINATION METER

All models are equipped with a digital display combination meter (**Figure 88**).

Troubleshooting

Refer to Chapter Two.

Removal/Installation

1. Remove the assist headlight as described in this chapter.
2. Disconnect the meter connector (**Figure 89**).
3. Detach the meter wire from the retaining clip on the steering shaft holder.
4. Remove the meter retaining nuts (**Figure 90**), then remove the meter (**Figure 91**).
5. Install the combination meter by reversing the preceding removal steps.
6. Start the engine and check the meter operation.

Digital Meter Panel
Removal/Installation

> *NOTE*
> *The digital meter panel is available only as part of the digital combination meter assembly.*

1. Remove the combination meter.
2. Remove the four meter cover retaining screws (**Figure 92**).
3. Carefully remove the outer housing to expose the digital meter panel unit (**Figure 93**).

SWITCHES

Testing

Test switches for continuity using an ohmmeter (see Chapter One) or a self-powered test light. Test at the switch connector by operating the switch in each of its operating positions and comparing the results with its switch continuity diagram. For example, refer to the ignition switch continuity diagram in **Figure 94**.

When the ignition switch key is turned on, there is continuity between the red/black and pink wire terminals and between the red and black wire terminals (**Figure 94**). The wires joining the terminals show continuity (**Figure 94**). An ohmmeter connected between these terminals shows no resistance or a test light lights. When the ignition switch is turned off, there is no continuity between the same terminals.

When testing switches, note the following:

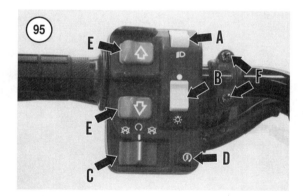

IGNITION SWITCH

	BAT2	DC	BAT1	BAT
On	•———•		•———•	
Off				
Color	R/B	P	R	B

R = Red
B = Black
P = Pink

4. When separating two connectors, pull on the connector housings and not the wires.

5. After finding a defective circuit, check the connectors to make sure they are clean and properly connected. Check all wires going into a connector housing for loose connections or damage.

6. When joining two connectors, push them until they click or snap into place.

If a switch or button does not perform properly, replace the switch as described in this section.

Refer to the wiring diagrams at the back of this manual for continuity diagrams.

Left Handlebar Switch Housing Replacement

All models are equipped with the left handlebar switch housing shown in **Figure 95**.

1. The left handlebar switch is equipped with the following switches:

    a. Lighting switch (A).

    b. Dimmer switch (B).

    c. Engine stop switch (C).

    d. Starter switch (D).

    e. Gearshift switches (E).

NOTE
The switches mounted in the left handlebar switch housing are not available separately. If one switch is damaged, replace the switch housing assembly.

2. Remove the left inner front fender panel as described in Chapter Fifteen.

3. Disconnect the green handlebar switch connector (**Figure 96**).

4. Detach the wiring retaining clips on the steering shaft holder and frame.

1. Check the fuses as described in this chapter.

2. Check the battery as described in Chapter Three. Charge the battery to the correct state of charge, if required.

3. Before testing the switches, disconnect the negative battery cable from the battery (Chapter Three) and disconnect the switch electrical connector.

CAUTION
Do not start the engine with the negative battery cable disconnected.

5. Remove the rear (parking) brake lever clamp screws (F, **Figure 95**), remove the clamp and move the brake lever assembly out of the way.

6. Remove the switch housing screws and separate the switch halves. Remove the switch and its wiring harness from the frame.

7. Install the switch housing by reversing the preceding removal steps, while noting the following:

   a. Install the switch housing, but do not tighten the screws.

   b. Install the brake lever assembly while inserting the tab on the brake lever (**Figure 97**) into the slot in the switch housing.

   c. Install the brake lever clamp so the punch mark is up (**Figure 98**). Position the clamp so the inner edge aligns with the punch mark (**Figure 99**) on the handlebar. Tighten the upper clamp screw first, then tighten the lower clamp screw.

   d. Tighten the upper switch housing screw first, then the lower screws.

8. Start the engine and check the switch in each of its operating positions.

Ignition Switch Replacement

The ignition switch is mounted in the handlebar cover (**Figure 100**).

1. Remove the left inner fender panel as described in Chapter Fifteen.

2. Disconnect the white ignition switch connector (**Figure 101**).

3. Detach the wiring retaining clips on the steering shaft holder and frame.

4. Remove the handlebar cover as described in Chapter Fifteen.

5. Depress the ignition switch tabs (A, **Figure 102**, typical), then remove the ignition switch (B) by pushing it from the bottom side.

6. Install the ignition switch by reversing the preceding steps while noting the following:

   a. Install the new switch by aligning the two plastic guide strips on the switch housing with the notch in the switch mounting hole. Push the switch into place.

   b. Turn the ignition switch on and check operation.

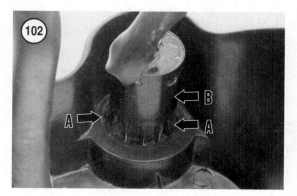

Front Brake Light Switch Testing/Replacement

The front brake switch (A, **Figure 103**) is mounted on the front master cylinder assembly.

1. Disconnect the two electrical connectors (B, **Figure 103**) from the front brake light switch.

2. Connect ohmmeter leads between the two front brake light switch terminals.

3. Read the ohmmeter while pulling in and releasing the front brake lever. Note the following:
   a. There must be continuity with the front brake lever pulled in and no continuity with the lever released.
   b. Replace the front brake light switch if it fails to operate as described.

4. To remove the brake switch, remove the mounting screw (C, **Figure 103**) and brake switch.

5. Reconnect the two electrical connectors to the front brake light switch.

6. Turn on the ignition switch and apply the front brake lever. Make sure the brake light illuminates.

Reverse Switch

The reverse switch signals the engine control module (ECM) when the sub-transmission is in reverse gear. The reverse switch is mounted on the gearshift body (A, **Figure 104**).

1. Remove left inner fender panel as described in Chapter Fifteen.

2. Remove the left side cover as described in Chapter Fifteen.

3. Disconnect the reverse switch connector (**Figure 105**) located on a bracket behind the gearshift.

4. Connect ohmmeter leads to the switch connector terminals.

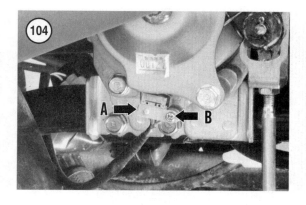

9

5. Read the ohmmeter scale while moving the gear-shift lever. Note the following:

    a. There must be continuity with the gearshift lever in the reverse position and no continuity with the lever in any other position.

    b. Replace the reverse switch if it fails to operate as described.

6. To remove the reverse switch, remove the mounting screw (B, **Figure 104**) and reverse switch. Make sure to insert the pin on the switch into the hole of the bracket during installation.

7. Reconnect the electrical connector.

THROTTLE POSITION SENSOR

Removal/Installation

The throttle position sensor (TPS) is mounted on a bracket that is attached to the carburetor. If only TPS removal is required, the TPS must be adjusted after installation. If the TPS and bracket are removed as a unit, TPS adjustment is not required.

1. Disconnect the negative battery cable.

2. Remove the left side cover as described in Chapter Fifteen.

3. Remove the left engine cover (**Figure 106**).

4. Make sure the fuel valve is off, then disconnect the catch fuel remaining in the hose from the carburetor (A, **Figure 107**).

5. Disconnect the black, three-wire TPS electrical connector (B, **Figure 107**).

6A. If removing the TPS and bracket as a unit, proceed as follows:

    a. Remove the bracket mounting screws (A, **Figure 108**).

    b. Remove the bracket and TPS as a unit.

    c. If necessary, install a new O-ring onto the carburetor.

    d. Install the TPS and bracket so the slot in the TPS engages the tang on the carburetor shaft. Tighten the screws securely.

6B. If removing only the TPS, proceed as follows:

    a. Remove the throttle position sensor Torx mounting screws (B, **Figure 108**), then remove the throttle position sensor.

    b. If necessary, install a new O-ring onto the bracket.

    c. Install the TPS so the slot in the TPS engages the tang on the carburetor shaft.

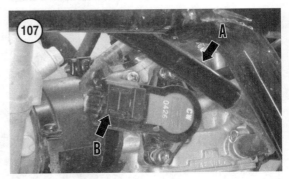

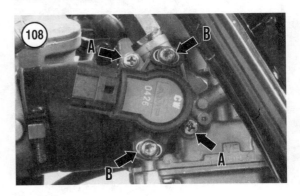

    d. Apply threadlocker to the TPS mounting screws and install the screws loose.

    e. Adjust the TPS position as described in this chapter.

7. Connect the TPS connector.

8. Reconnect the fuel hose.

9. Install the left engine cover.

10. Install the left side cover.

11. Reconnect the negative battery cable.

Throttle Position Sensor Test

1. Remove the left side cover as described in Chapter Fifteen.

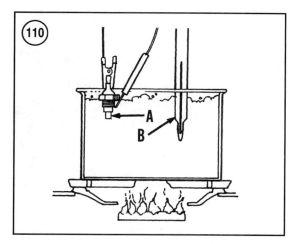

2. Disconnect the black, three-wire TPS electrical connector (B, **Figure 107**).

3. Using an ohmmeter, check the resistance between the yellow/white wire terminal on the sensor and the green/yellow wire terminal on the sensor. The specified resistance is 3500-5500 ohms.

4. Connect the ohmmeter leads to the yellow/black wire terminal on the sensor and the green/yellow wire terminal on the sensor.

5. Operate the throttle while watching the ohmmeter readings. The ohmmeter reading should increase smoothly from closed to full throttle. The specified resistance is 580-620 ohms at closed throttle to 3500-5500 ohms at full throttle.

6. If the ohmmeter reading is erratic or not within specification, the sensor is defective and must be replaced.

7. Turn the ignition switch on.

8. Connect a DC voltmeter to the sensor wire connector. Connect the positive lead to the yellow/white terminal and the negative lead to the

green/yellow terminal. The specified voltage is 4.7-5.3 volts.

9. Connect the TPS electrical connector.

10. Install the left side cover.

Adjustment

1. Verify the engine idles at the desired idle speed. If not, adjust as needed. Turn off the engine.

2. Remove the left side cover as described in Chapter Eight.

3. Disconnect the TPS connector (B, **Figure 107**).

4. Loosen the throttle position sensor Torx mounting screws (B, **Figure 108**).

5. Connect an ohmmeter to the yellow/black wire terminal and the green/yellow wire terminal on the TPS.

6. Slowly rotate the TPS until the ohmmeter reading is 580-620 ohms.

7. Tighten the mounting screws securely.

8. Connect the TPS connector.

9. Install the left side cover.

10. Perform the ECM initial setting procedure as described in this chapter.

OIL THERMOSENSOR

The oil thermosensor (**Figure 109**) is located on the lower, front of the oil tank.

Testing

1. Remove the oil thermosensor as described in this section.

WARNING
Wear eye protection and gloves during this test. Keep all flammable materials away from the burner.

2. Use an ohmmeter with an alligator clip on one test lead end. Attach one of the alligator clips to the electrical connector on the sensor.

3. Suspend the thermosensor in a small container filled with engine oil (A, **Figure 110**).

4. Place a thermometer in the pan of oil (B, **Figure 110**). Do not let the sensor or the thermometer touch the pan or a false reading results.

5. Heat the oil and place the remaining ohmmeter test lead against the threads on the thermosensor body.

6. Check the resistance readings at the temperatures listed below:

    a. At 150° C (302° F), the ohmmeter should read 306-340 ohms.

    b. At 170° C (338° F), the ohmmeter should read 209-231 ohms.

7. If the resistance readings are incorrect, replace the thermosensor.

8. Install the oil thermosensor as described in this section.

Removal/Installation

1. Drain the engine oil (Chapter Three).

2. Disconnect the connector from the thermosensor and remove the thermosensor (**Figure 109**).

3. Reverse Step 1 and Step 2 to install the thermosensor while noting the following:

    a. Install a new sealing washer.

    b. Tighten the oil thermosensor to 18 N•m (159 in.-lb.).

    c. After starting the engine, check for oil leaks.

COOLANT THERMOSENSOR

The coolant thermosensor (**Figure 111**) is located on the cylinder head adjacent to the thermostat housing.

Testing

1. Remove the coolant thermosensor as described in this section.

> *WARNING*
> *Wear eye protection and gloves during this test. Keep all flammable materials away from the burner.*

2. Use an ohmmeter with an alligator clip on one test lead end. Attach one of the alligator clips to the electrical connector on the sensor.

3. Suspend the thermosensor in a small container filled with coolant (A, **Figure 110**).

4. Place a thermometer in the pan of coolant (B, **Figure 110**). Do not let the sensor or the thermometer touch the pan or a false reading results.

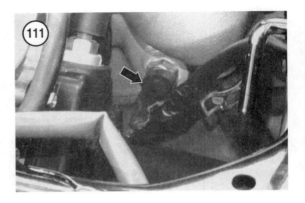

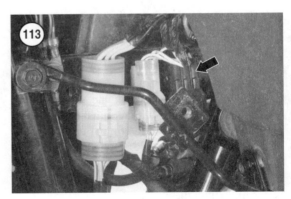

5. Heat the coolant and place the remaining ohmmeter test lead against the threads on the thermosensor body.

6. Check the resistance readings at the temperatures listed below:

    a. At 80° C (176°F), the ohmmeter should read 47-67 ohms.

    b. At 120° C (248° F), the ohmmeter should read 14-18 ohms.

7. If the resistance readings are incorrect, replace the thermosensor.

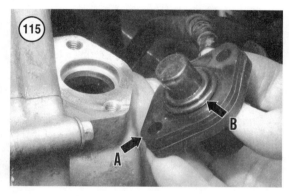

8. Install the coolant thermosensor as described in this section.

Removal/Installation

1. Drain the engine coolant (Chapter Three).

2. Remove the air intake duct as described in Chapter Eight.

3. Disconnect the connector from the thermosensor and remove the thermosensor (**Figure 111**).

4. Reverse Step 1 and Step 2 to install the thermosensor while noting the following:
   a. Apply threadlocker to the thermosensor threads. Do not allow threadlocker on the sensor portion.
   b. Tighten the coolant thermosensor to 10 N•m (88 in.-lb.).
   c. Check for coolant leaks.

COOLANT FAN MOTOR

Refer to Chapter Two.

SPEED SENSOR UNIT

All models are equipped with a speed sensor unit. The speed sensor unit is mounted in the rear crankcase cover (**Figure 112**).

Testing

Refer to *Combination Meter* in Chapter Two.

Removal/Installation

1. Disconnect the speed sensor electrical connector (**Figure 113**).
2. Remove the left side cover as described in Chapter Fifteen.
3. Remove the left engine cover (**Figure 114**).
4. Remove the sensor mounting bolts, then remove the speed sensor (**Figure 112**) and insulator.
5. Install by reversing the preceding removal steps while noting the following:
   a. Install the insulator (A, **Figure 115**) onto the sensor.
   b. Lubricate a new O-ring with engine oil and install it onto the speed sensor (B, **Figure 115**).
   c. Tighten the mounting bolts securely.

FUSES

Whenever a fuse blows, determine the reason for the failure before replacing the fuse. Usually the trouble is a short circuit in the wiring, which may be caused by worn-through insulation or a disconnected wire touching ground.

All fuses are contained in the fuse box located adjacent to the battery (**Figure 116**).

9

Refer to **Table 5** for fuse ratings.

Fuse Removal/Installation

1. Turn the ignition switch off.
2. Remove the seat (Chapter Fifteen), then remove the lid above the battery.

> *CAUTION*
> *If a fuse is replaced with the ignition switch turned on, an accidental short circuit could damage the electrical system.*

3. Remove the fuse box cover. Remove the fuse (**Figure 117**). Replace the fuse if blown (**Figure 118**).

> *NOTE*
> *The size and function of each fuse is listed on a label inside the fuse box cover (**Figure 119**). Always carry spare fuses.*

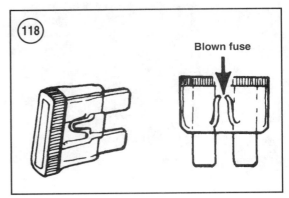

4. Install by reversing the preceding removal steps.

GPS

TRX500FGA models are equipped with a global positioning system (GPS) that provides location information on the combination meter display. The GPS system consists of a receiver unit, which is adjacent to the combination meter, and the combination meter.

Troubleshooting

Refer to Chapter Two.

Removal/Installation

1. Remove the assist headlight as described in this chapter.
2. Disconnect the GPS electrical connector.
3. Remove the receiver mounting bolts, then remove the receiver.
4. If necessary, remove the combination meter as described in this chapter.

5. No service is possible for the receiver or combination meter. Either component must be replaced as a unit.
6. Reverse the removal steps to install the combination meter and receiver.

WIRING DIAGRAMS

Wiring diagrams for all models are located in Chapter Seventeen.

Table 1 CHARGING SYSTEM SPECIFICATIONS

Alternator	
Capacity	0.33 kW at 5000 rpm
Stator coil resistance*	0.1-1.0 ohms
Regulator/rectifier	
Type	Triple phase/full-wave rectification
Regulated voltage	14.7-15.5 volts at 5000 rpm

*Perform tests at 20° C (68° F). Do not test if the engine or component is hot.

Table 2 IGNITION SYSTEM SPECIFICATIONS

Ignition coil peak voltage	100 volts minimum
Ignition pulse generator peak voltage	0.7 volts minimum

Table 3 STARTER MOTOR SERVICE SPECIFICATIONS

	New mm (in.)	Service limit mm (In.)
Starter motor brush length	12.5 (0.49)	9.0 (0.35)

Table 4 REPLACEMENT BULBS

	Voltage-wattage
Assist headlight	12V-45W
Headlight	12V-30/30W
Taillight	12V-5W
Indicator lights	LED

Table 5 FUSES

	Fuse rating
Main fuse	30 amp
Shift control motor	30 amp
Sub-fuses located in fuse box	
Accessories	10 amp
Fan motor	15 amp
Ignition	10 amp
Lights	15 amp

Table 6 ELECTRICAL SYSTEM TORQUE SPECIFICATIONS

	N•m	in.-lb.	ft-lb.
Angle sensor	6	53	–
Coolant thermosensor	10	88	–
Ignition pulse generator Allen bolts	6	53	–
Oil thermosensor	18	159	–

CHAPTER TEN

COOLING SYSTEM

This chapter describes the repair and replacement of cooling system components, including the engine oil cooler. **Table 1** and **Table 2** at the end of this chapter list cooling system specifications. For electrical test procedures, refer to Chapter Nine. For routine cooling system maintenance, refer to Chapter Three.

COOLANT

Coolant Type

Refer to Chapter Three for the coolant type recommended for use in the TRX500.

Coolant Level

Refer to Chapter Three.

Coolant Test

1. Remove the radiator cap cover (**Figure 1**) in the front fender.

WARNING
Do not remove the radiator cap when the engine is hot. The coolant is hot and under pressure. Severe scalding may result if hot coolant contacts skin.

2. Remove the radiator cap (**Figure 2**).
3. Test the specific gravity of the coolant with an antifreeze tester to ensure adequate temperature and corrosion protection. A 50:50 mixture is recommended. Never allow the mixture to become less than 40 percent antifreeze. Refer to *Coolant Type* in Chapter Three.
4. Reinstall the radiator cap. Turn the radiator cap clockwise to the first stop. Then push the cap down and turn it clockwise until it stops.
5. Reinstall the cover.

Coolant Change and Air Bleeding

Drain and refill the cooling system at the intervals listed in Chapter Three.

It is sometimes necessary to drain the cooling system when performing a service on some part of the engine. If the coolant is still in good condition, the

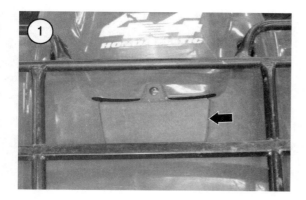

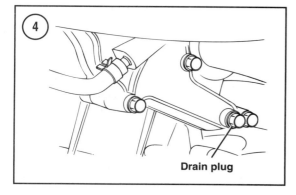

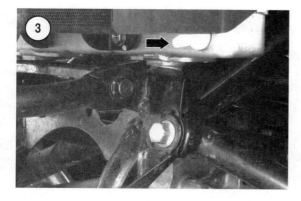

Drain plug

coolant can be reused. Drain the coolant into a clean pan and pour the coolant into a clean container for storage.

WARNING
Waste antifreeze is toxic and may never be discharged into storm sewers, septic systems, waterways or onto the ground. Place used antifreeze in the original container and dispose of it according to local regulations. Do not store coolant where it is accessible to children or pets.

WARNING
*Do not remove the radiator cap (**Figure 2**) if the engine is hot. The coolant is hot and under pressure. Severe scalding may result if hot coolant contacts skin.*

CAUTION
Be careful not to spill antifreeze on painted surfaces because it damages the surface. Wash immediately with soapy water and rinse thoroughly.

Perform the following procedure when the engine is cold:

1. Park the ATV on level ground.
2. Remove the radiator cap cover (**Figure 1**) in the front fender.
3. Remove the radiator cap (**Figure 2**).
4. Place a drain pan under the radiator. Remove the radiator drain plug (**Figure 3**) and allow the coolant to drain into the drain pan.
5. Inspect the rubber washer on the drain plug and, if necessary, replace it. Reinstall the drain plug.
6. Remove the right side cover as described in Chapter Fifteen.
7. Place a drain pan under the engine. Remove the drain bolt (**Figure 4**) and sealing washer from the water pump. Allow the coolant to drain into the pan.
8. Reinstall the drain bolt and sealing washer on the water pump. Replace the sealing washer if it is leaking or damaged. Tighten the coolant drain bolt securely.
9. Install the right side cover as described in Chapter Fifteen.
10. Drain the coolant reserve tank as follows:
   a. Place a drain pan underneath the coolant reserve tank.
   b. Remove the reserve tank cap (**Figure 5**).

10

c. Disconnect the radiator siphon tube (**Figure 6**) from the reserve tank and drain the coolant into the drain pan.

d. Rinse the inside of the coolant reserve tank with water and allow it to drain.

e. Reconnect the siphon tube and secure it with its clamp.

CAUTION
Do not use a higher percentage of anti-freeze-to-water solution than is recommended. A higher concentration of coolant decreases the performance of the cooling system.

11. Place a funnel in the radiator filler neck and slowly refill the radiator and engine with a mixture of 50 percent antifreeze and 50 percent distilled water. Add the mixture slowly so it expels as much air as possible from the cooling system. Refer to *Coolant Type* in Chapter Three before purchasing and mixing the coolant. **Table 1** lists engine coolant capacity.

12. Sit on the ATV and slowly rock it from side to side to help expel air bubbles from the engine and coolant hoses.

13. Fill the coolant reserve tank to the UPPER level line (**Figure 7**).

WARNING
Do not start and run the ATV in an enclosed area. The exhaust gasses contain carbon monoxide, a colorless, odorless, poisonous gas. Carbon monoxide levels build quickly in an enclosed area and can cause unconsciousness and death.

14. After filling the radiator, leave the radiator cap off and bleed the cooling system as follows:

a. Start the engine and allow it to idle for 2 to 3 minutes.

b. Snap the throttle a few times to bleed air from the cooling system. When the coolant level drops in the radiator, add coolant to bring the level to the bottom of the filler neck.

c. When the radiator coolant level has stabilized, perform Step 15.

15. Install the radiator cap (**Figure 2**). Turn the radiator cap clockwise to the first stop. Then push the cap down and turn it clockwise until it stops.

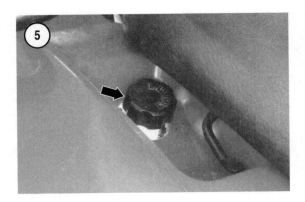

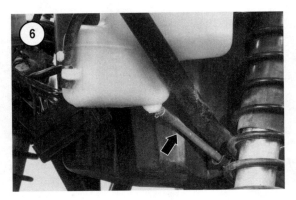

16. Start the engine and let it run at idle speed until the engine reaches normal operating temperature. Make sure there are no air bubbles in the coolant and that the coolant level in the coolant reserve tank stabilizes at the correct level. Add coolant to the coolant reserve tank, as necessary.

17. Test ride the ATV and readjust the coolant level in the reserve tank as required.

COOLING SYSTEM INSPECTION

The pressurized cooling system consists of the radiator, water pump, radiator cap, thermostat, electric cooling fan and coolant reservoir.

WARNING
*Do not remove the radiator cap (**Figure 2**) when the engine is hot. The coolant is very hot and is under pressure. Severe scalding could result if the coolant contacts skin.*

CAUTION
Drain and flush the cooling system at the interval listed in Chapter Three.

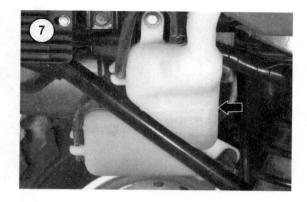

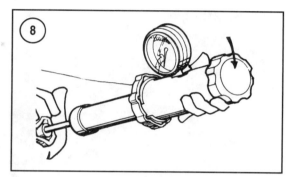

2. If the level is low, remove the reservoir tank cap (**Figure 5**) and add coolant to the reservoir, not to the radiator.

3. Check the coolant hoses and clamps for looseness or damage.

4. Start the engine and allow it to idle. If steam is observed at the muffler, a head gasket might be damaged. If enough coolant leaks into the cylinder, the cylinder could hydrolock, thus preventing the engine from being cranked. Coolant may also be present in the engine oil. If the oil on the dipstick is foamy or milky-looking, there is coolant in the oil. If so, correct the problem before returning the motorcycle to service.

> *CAUTION*
> *If the engine oil is contaminated with coolant, change the oil and filter after performing the repair.*

5. Check the radiator for clogged or damaged fins. Refer radiator repair to a dealership or a radiator repair shop.

6. Check all coolant hoses for cracks or damage. Replace all questionable parts. Make sure the hose clamps are tight, but not so tight they cut the hoses. Refer to the *Hoses and Hose Clamps* in this chapter.

7. When troubleshooting the cooling system for loss of coolant, pressure test the system as described in this section.

10

Pressure Test

A cooling system tester is required to make the following tests.

> *WARNING*
> *Do not remove the radiator cap when the engine is hot.*

1. Remove the radiator cap cover (**Figure 1**).
2. Remove the radiator cap (**Figure 2**).
3. Pressure test the radiator cap (**Figure 8**) using a cooling system tester. Refer to the manufacturer's instructions when making the tests. The specified radiator cap pressure is 108-137 kPa (16-20 psi). Replace the radiator cap if it does not hold pressure or if the relief pressure is too high or too low.

> *CAUTION*
> *Excessive pressure can damage the radiator or other cooling system com-*

Refill with a mixture of Pro Honda HP or ethylene glycol antifreeze (formulated for aluminum engines) and distilled water. Do not reuse the old coolant because it deteriorates with use. Do not operate the cooling system with only distilled water, even in climates where antifreeze protection is not required. Doing so promotes internal engine corrosion. Refer to **Coolant Change and Air Bleeding** *in this chapter.*

> *NOTE*
> *Waste antifreeze is toxic and may never be discharged into storm sewers, septic systems or onto the ground. Place used antifreeze in the original container and dispose of it according to local regulations. Do not store coolant where it is accessible to children or pets.*

It is important to keep the coolant level between the UPPER and LOWER marks on the coolant reserve tank. Refer to **Figure 7**.

1. Check the level with the engine at normal operating temperature and the ATV upright.

*ponents. Do not exceed the pressure
specified in Step 4.*

4. Leave off the radiator cap and pressure test the
cooling system up to 137 kPa (20 psi). The cooling
system must be able to hold this pressure. If there is
a leak, locate and replace the damaged component.

5. Reinstall the radiator cap and cover.

HOSES AND HOSE CLAMPS

Hoses deteriorate with age. Replace them periodically or whenever they show signs of cracking or
leakage. To be safe, replace the hoses every two
years. The spray of hot coolant from a cracked hose
can injure the rider. Loss of coolant can also cause
the engine to overheat and cause damage.

Whenever any component of the cooling system
is removed, inspect the hoses and clamps to determine if replacement is necessary.

Inspection

1. With the engine cool, check the cooling hoses
for brittleness, hardness or cracks. Replace hoses in
this condition.

2. With the engine hot, examine the hoses for
swelling along the entire hose length. Replace hoses
that show signs of swelling.

3. Check the area around each hose clamp. Signs of
rust around clamps indicate possible hose leakage
from a damaged or over-tightened clamp.

Replacement

Perform hose replacement when the engine is
cool.

1. Drain the cooling system as described in *Coolant Change* in this chapter.

2. Loosen the hose clamps from the hose to be replaced. Slide the clamps along the hose and out of
the way.

3. Twist the hose end to break the seal and remove
it from the connecting joint. If the hose has been on
for some time, it may have become fused to the
joint. If so, insert a small screwdriver or pick tool
between the hose and joint. While working the tool
around the joint, carefully pry the hose loose with a
thin screwdriver.

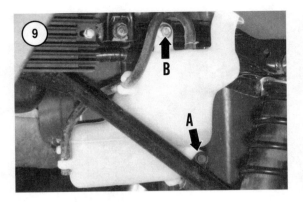

CAUTION
*Do not apply excessive force to a hose
when attempting to remove it. Many
of the hose connectors are fragile and
can be easily damaged.*

4. Examine the connecting joint for cracks or other
damage. Repair or replace parts as required. Remove rust and corrosion with a wire brush.

5. Inspect the hose clamps and replace if necessary.
The hose clamps are as important as the hoses. If
they do not hold the hose in place tightly, coolant
leaks.

6. Slide the hose clamp over the outside of the hose
and install the hose over its connecting joint. Make
sure the hose clears all obstructions and is routed
properly.

NOTE
*If it is difficult to install a hose on a
joint, apply some antifreeze into the
end of the hose where it seats onto its
connecting joint. This usually aids installation.*

7. With the hose positioned correctly on the joint,
position the clamp back away from end of the hose

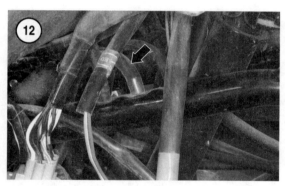

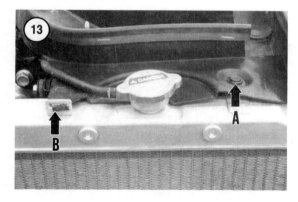

slightly. Tighten the clamp securely, but not so much the hose is damaged.

NOTE
If installing coolant hoses onto the engine while it is removed from the frame, check the position of the hose clamp(s) to make sure it can be loosened when installed in the frame.

8. Refill the cooling system as described in *Coolant Change and Air Bleeding* in this chapter. Start

the engine and check for leaks. Retighten hose clamps as necessary.

COOLANT RESERVE TANK

Removal/Installation

1. Place a drain pan underneath the coolant reserve tank.
2. Remove the reserve tank cap (**Figure 5**).
3. Disconnect the radiator siphon tube (**Figure 6**) from the reserve tank and drain the coolant into the drain pan.
4. Remove the trim clip (A, **Figure 9**). Refer to Chapter Fifteen.
5. Remove the mounting bolt (B, **Figure 9**), then remove the reserve tank.
6. Rinse the inside of the coolant reservoir tank with water and allow to drain.
7. Install the coolant reservoir tank by reversing the preceding removal steps while noting the following:
   a. Do not overtighten the mounting bolt.
   b. Refill the coolant reservoir tank with a 50:50 mixture of antifreeze and distilled water as described in Chapter Three.
   c. Check the hoses for leaks.

RADIATOR

Removal/Installation

The radiator and fan are removed as an assembly.
1. Drain the cooling system as described in Chapter Three.
2. Disconnect the negative battery cable at the battery.
3. Remove the oil cooler as described in this chapter.
4. Remove the fuel tank as described in Chapter Eight to the fan motor electrical connector.
5. Disconnect the fan motor electrical connector (**Figure 10**).
6. Detach the headlight electrical connector from the mounting bracket (A, **Figure 11**).
7. Detach the vent hose from the frame tube (**Figure 12**).
8. Remove the trim clip (see Chapter Fifteen) that secures the air guide plate to the radiator (A, **Figure 13**).

10

9. Disengage the tab on the air guide plate from the slot on the radiator (B, **Figure 13**).

10. Detach the siphon tube from the radiator filler neck (A, **Figure 14**).

11. Disconnect the upper hose (B, **Figure 14**) from the radiator.

12. Disconnect the lower hose (**Figure 15**) from the radiator.

13. Remove the retaining bolts on each side (B, **Figure 11**) securing the radiator brackets.

14. Carefully move the radiator up so the lower mounting pins disengage, then remove the radiator.

15. Install by reversing the preceding removal steps while noting the following:

    a. Make sure the rubber grommets and flange collars are in place in the radiator mounting brackets. These help to prevent road shocks and vibration from damaging the mounting brackets.

    b. Fill and bleed the cooling system as described in this chapter.

    c. Check the hoses for leaks.

Inspection

1. Inspect the radiator cap top and bottom seals (**Figure 16**) for deterioration or damage. Check the spring for damage. Pressure test the radiator cap as described in *Cooling System Inspection* in this chapter. Replace the radiator cap if necessary.

2. Flush off the exterior of the radiator with a water hose on low pressure. Spray both the front and the back to remove all dirt and debris. Carefully use a whiskbroom or stiff paintbrush to remove any stubborn debris.

> *CAUTION*
> *Do not press too hard on the cooling fins and tubes because they may be damaged and cause a leak.*

3. Carefully straighten any bent cooling fins with a broad-tipped screwdriver.

4. Check for cracks or coolant leaks (usually a moss-green colored residue) at the various hose fittings and tank seams (**Figure 17**).

5. Check the mounting brackets for cracks or damage.

6. To prevent oxidation to the radiator, touch up any area where the paint is worn off. Use good-quality spray paint. Do not apply heavy coats

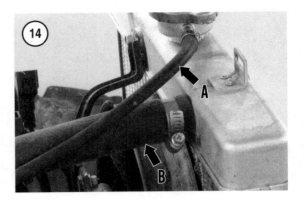

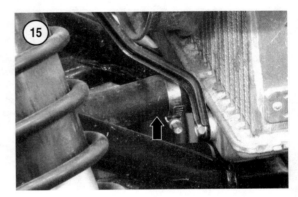

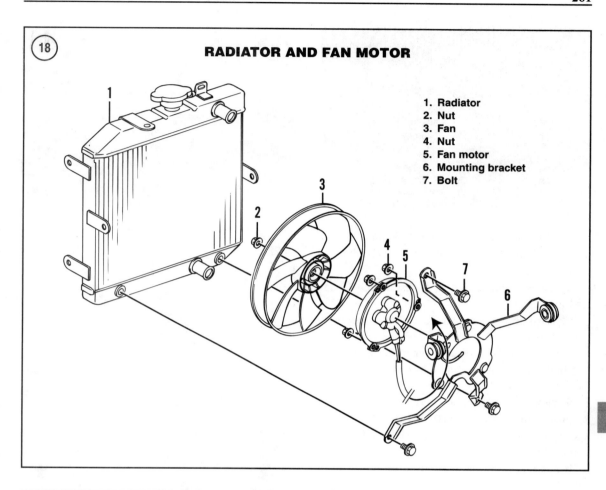

18

RADIATOR AND FAN MOTOR

1. Radiator
2. Nut
3. Fan
4. Nut
5. Fan motor
6. Mounting bracket
7. Bolt

10

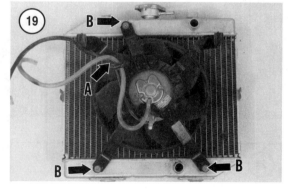

19

because this decreases the cooling efficiency of the radiator.

COOLING FAN

The cooling fan is mounted on the backside of the radiator. Refer to **Figure 18**.

Removal/Installation

1. Remove the radiator as described in this chapter.
2. Detach the fan wire and vent hose from the locating clamp (A, **Figure 19**). Detach the vent hose from the motor.
3. Remove the bolts (B, **Figure 19**), then remove the fan motor assembly from the radiator.
4. To separate the motor from the bracket unit, proceed as follows:
   a. Remove the fan retaining nut.
   b. Remove the retaining nuts, then separate the motor from the bracket.
5. Install by reversing the preceding removal steps.

THERMOSTAT

Removal/Installation

1. Drain the cooling system as described in *Coolant Change* in this chapter.

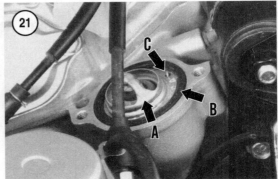

2. Remove the seat as described in Chapter Fifteen.

3. Remove the fuel tank cover as described in Chapter Fifteen.

4. Remove the intake air duct as described in Chapter Eight.

5. Remove the thermostat cover retaining bolts (**Figure 20**).

6. Separate the thermostat cover from the thermostat housing to expose the thermostat (A, **Figure 21**).

7. Remove the thermostat and rubber seal.

8. Inspect the rubber seal (B, **Figure 21**). If damaged, remove the rubber seal and install a new rubber seal.

9. If necessary, test the thermostat as described in this chapter.

10. Install the thermostat by reversing the removal steps while noting the following:

    a. Install the thermostat so the air bleed hole (C, **Figure 21**) faces toward the right side.

    b. Tighten the thermostat cover bolts to 12 N•m (106 in.-lb.).

    c. Refill the cooling system with the recommended type and quantity of coolant as described in *Coolant Change and Air Bleeding* in this chapter.

Inspection

Test the thermostat to ensure proper operation as follows:

NOTE
Do not allow the thermometer or thermostat to touch the sides or bottom of the pan or a false reading results.

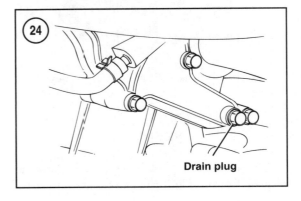

Drain plug

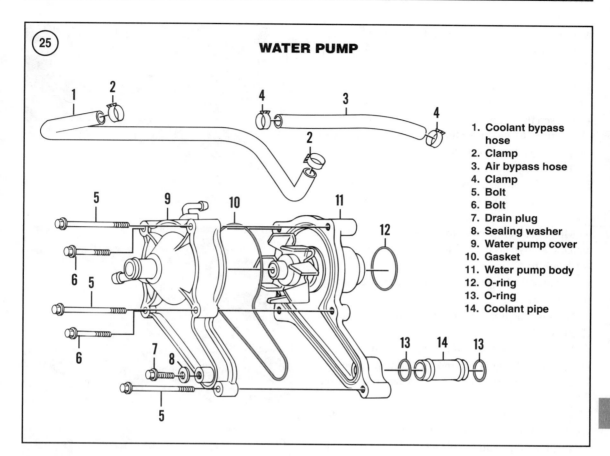

WATER PUMP

1. Coolant bypass hose
2. Clamp
3. Air bypass hose
4. Clamp
5. Bolt
6. Bolt
7. Drain plug
8. Sealing washer
9. Water pump cover
10. Gasket
11. Water pump body
12. O-ring
13. O-ring
14. Coolant pipe

1. Suspend the thermostat in a pan of water (**Figure 22**) and place a thermometer in the pan of water. Use a thermometer rated higher than the test temperature.

2. Gradually heat the water and continue to gently stir the water until it reaches the temperature specified in **Table 1**. At this temperature, the thermostat should start to open.

3. Continue to heat the water to the fully open temperature. The minimum valve lift is 8 mm (0.3 in.) at 95° C (203° F).

4. Replace the thermostat if it remains open at normal room temperature or stays closed after the specified temperature has been reached during the test procedure. Make sure the replacement thermostat has the same temperature rating.

NOTE
After the specified temperature is reached, it may take 3 to 5 minutes for the valve to open completely.

WATER PUMP

Pre-inspection

NOTE
These pre-inspection steps can be performed with the water pump installed.

1. Check the water pump inspection hole (**Figure 23**) for leaks. If coolant leaks from the passage, an internal seal is damaged. Replace the water pump unit. If there is no indication of coolant leakage from the inspection hole, pressure test the cooling system as described in the *Cooling System Inspection* in this chapter.

2. Check the drain bolt and sealing washer (**Figure 24**) for leaks. If necessary, replace the sealing washer and tighten the bolt securely.

Removal/Installation

Refer to **Figure 25**.

1. Remove the seat as described in Chapter Fifteen.

2. Remove the right side cover as described in Chapter Fifteen.

3. Drain the cooling system as described in *Coolant Change and Air Bleeding* in this chapter.

4. Loosen the clamp screw on the water pump hose (A, **Figure 26**) and move the clamp back off the water pump neck. Detach the hose from the water pump.

5. Move the clamp away from the hose end and detach the bypass hose (B, **Figure 26**) from the water pump.

6. Move the clamp away from the hose end and detach the air bypass hose (**Figure 27**) from the cylinder head fitting.

7. Remove the lower bolts securing the water pump (**Figure 28**).

8. Remove the upper bolt securing the water pump (**Figure 29**).

9. Remove the water pump from the cylinder.

10. Inspect the area around the coolant pipe (A, **Figure 30**) for signs of leaks. If necessary, remove the coolant pipe.

11. Reverse the removal procedure to install the water pump while noting the following:

   a. Clean the seating surface of the pipe and install a new O-ring (B, **Figure 30**) onto the coolant pipe. Install new O-rings at both ends of the pipe if it was removed.

   b. Clean the seating surface of the water pump and install a new O-ring (A, **Figure 31**) onto the water pump.

   c. Install the water pump so the drive lug (B, **Figure 31**) on the pump shaft fits into the slot in the end of the camshaft (**Figure 32**).

   d. Refill the cooling system with the recommended type and quantity of coolant as described in *Coolant Change* in this chapter.

CAUTION
Do not install the bolts until the water pump is completely seated. Do not try to force the pump into place using the mounting bolts because the water pump may be damaged.

   e. Tighten the water pump mounting bolts to 12 N•m (106 in.-lb.).

   f. Start the engine and check for leaks.

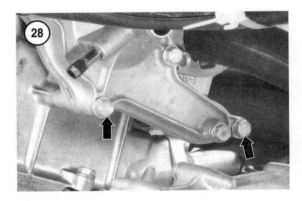

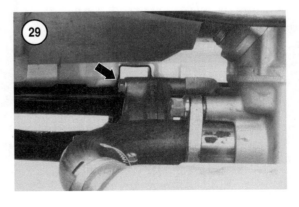

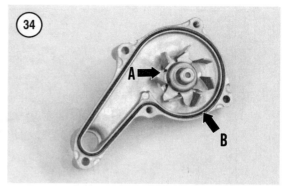

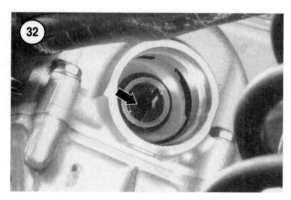

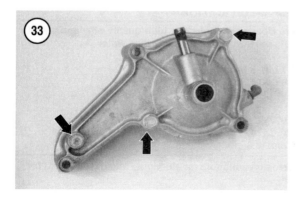

Disassembly/Inspection/Assembly

Refer to **Figure 25**.

1. Detach the air bypass hose (C, **Figure 31**) from the water pump.

2. Remove the water pump cover retaining bolts (**Figure 33**) and remove the cover.

3. Inspect the water pump assembly for wear or damage. Rotate the impeller (A, **Figure 34**) to make sure the bearings are not worn or damaged. If the bearings are damaged, the assembly must be replaced because it cannot be serviced.

4. Check the impeller blades. Straighten any bent blades.

5. Remove the O-ring seal (B, **Figure 34**) from the cover. This seal must be replaced each time the water pump is removed to prevent an oil leak. Install a new O-ring seal.

6. Install the cover and tighten the screws securely.

OIL COOLER

Removal/Installation

1. Remove the front fender as described in Chapter Fifteen.

2. Remove the trim clips (Chapter Fifteen) on each side of the radiator grille (**Figure 35**), then remove the grille.

3. Place drain pan under the oil cooler.

4. Remove the oil pipe retaining bolt and separate the oil pipe from the oil cooler. Repeat for the remaining oil pipe. Cover the pipe ends and oil cooler openings to prevent oil leaks and contamination.

5. Hold the oil cooler, unscrew the mounting bolts and remove the oil cooler. Drain out any residual coolant and engine oil.

10

6. Install by reversing the preceding removal steps. Install a new O-ring (**Figure 36**) onto each oil pipe and lubricate it with engine oil.

Inspection

1. Make sure the oil cooler inlet and outlet fittings (**Figure 37**) are clear. Clean out with low-pressure air if necessary.
2. Inspect the bolt hole threads for damage. Clean out if necessary.
3. Clean the exterior of the cooler. Carefully use a whiskbroom or stiff paintbrush to remove any stubborn debris.

> *CAUTION*
> *Do not press too hard on the cooling fins and tubes because they may be damaged and cause a leak.*

4. Check for cracks or signs of leakage.

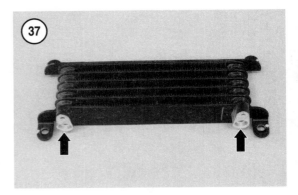

5. Check the mounting brackets for cracks or damage.

THERMOSENSORS

Refer to Chapter Nine for the coolant thermosensor and oil thermosensor.

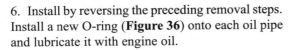

Table 1 COOLING SYSTEM SPECIFICATIONS

Coolant type	Pro Honda HP coolant or high-quality ethylene glycol*
Standard concentration	50% mixture coolant and purified water
Coolant capacity	
Radiator and engine	1.7 L (1.8 US qt.)
Reserve tank	0.4 L (0.42 US qt.)
Radiator cap pressure relief	108-137 kPa (16-20 psi)
Thermostat	
Begins to open	73-77° C (163-171° F)
Fully open	95° C (203° F)
Minimum valve lift @ 90° C (194° F)	8 mm (0.3 in.)

* Use a high quality ethylene glycol coolant containing corrosion inhibitors for aluminum engines. See text for further information.

Table 2 COOLING SYSTEM TORQUE SPECIFICATIONS

Item	N•m	in.-lb.	ft.-lb.
Thermostat housing cover bolts	12	106	–
Water pump cover bolt	10	88	–
Water pump mounting bolts	12	106	–

10

CHAPTER ELEVEN

FRONT SUSPENSION AND STEERING

This chapter describes repair and maintenance of the front wheels, suspension arms and steering components.

Refer to **Table 1** for general front suspension and steering specifications. **Tables 2-4** list service specifications and torque specifications. **Tables 1-4** are located at the end of this chapter.

WARNING
Self-locking nuts are used to secure some of the front suspension components. Honda recommends discarding all self-locking nuts after removal. The self-locking portion of the nut is weakened once the nut has been removed and no longer properly locks onto the mating threads. Never reinstall a used nut once it has been removed.

FRONT WHEEL

Removal/Installation

1. Park the ATV on level ground and set the parking brake.

NOTE
Mark the tires for location and direction before removing them.

2. Loosen the front wheel lug nuts (**Figure 1**).
3. Support the ATV with the front wheels off the ground.
4. Place wooden blocks(s) under the frame to support the ATV securely with the front wheels off the ground.
5. Remove the wheel nuts and front wheel (**Figure 1**).
6. Inspect the nuts and replace them if damaged.
7. Inspect the wheels and replace if damaged. Refer to *Tires and Wheels* in this chapter.
8. Install the front wheel by reversing the preceding removal steps, while noting the following:
   a. Install the wheel nuts (**Figure 2**) with the curved side facing toward the wheel. First install the wheel nuts finger-tight and check that the wheel sits squarely against the front hub.
   b. Lower the ATV so both front wheels are on the ground.
   c. Tighten the wheel nuts in a crossing pattern to 64 N•m (47 ft.-lb.).

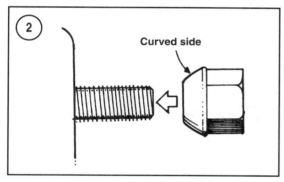

Curved side

d. Support the ATV again so both front wheels are off the ground.

e. Rotate the wheels and then apply the front brake. Repeat this step several times to make sure each wheel rotates freely and the brake is working properly.

TIRES AND WHEELS

The TRX500 is equipped with tubeless, low-pressure tires designed specifically for off-road use. Rapid tire wear occurs if the ATV is ridden on paved surfaces.

Tire Changing

A bead breaker, tire irons, rim protectors and tire lubricant are required to change a tire.

NOTE
*Tire bead and wheel separation can be extremely difficult. K&L Supply Co. offers a heavy-duty tire break-down tool (**Figure 3**) that is available through motorcyle dealerships.*

NOTE
If the tire is difficult to remove or install using the proper tools, do not take a chance on damaging the tire or rim sealing surface. Take the tire and rim to a dealership and have it service the tire.

1. Remove the valve stem cap and core and deflate the tire. Do not reinstall the core at this time.

2. Lubricate the tire bead and rim flanges with a rubber tire lubricant. Press the tire sidewall/bead down to allow the lubricant to run into and around the bead area. Also apply lubricant to the area where the bead breaker arm contacts the tire sidewall.

3. Position the wheel into the bead breaker tool (**Figure 4**).

4. Slowly work the bead breaker tool, making sure the tool arm seats against the outside of the rim, and break the tire bead away from the rim.

5. Apply hand pressure against the tire on either side of the tool to break the rest of the bead free from the rim.

6. If the rest of the tire bead cannot be broken loose, raise the tool, rotate the tire/rim assembly and

11

repeat Step 4 and Step 5 until the entire bead is broken loose from the rim.

7. Turn the wheel over and repeat the preceding steps to break the opposite side loose.

CAUTION
When using tire irons in the following steps, work carefully so the tire or rim sealing surfaces are not damaged. Damage to these areas may cause an air leak and require tire ir rim replacement.

8. Lubricate the tire beads and rim flanges as described in Step 2. Pry the bead over the rim with two tire irons (**Figure 5**). Take small bites with the tire irons. Place rim protectors between the tire irons and the rim.

9. When the upper tire bead is free, lift the second bead up into the center rim well and remove it as described in Step 8.

10. Clean and dry the rim.

11. Inspect the sealing surface on both sides of the rim (**Figure 6**). If the rim is bent, it may leak air.

12. To replace the air valve, perform the following:

   a. Support the rim and pull the valve stem out of the rim. Discard the valve stem.

   b. Lubricate the new valve stem with tire lubricant.

   c. Pull a new valve stem into the rim, from the inside out, until it snaps into place (**Figure 7**).

NOTE
Special tools are available for installing this type of valve stem.

13. Inspect the tire for cuts, tears, abrasions or any other defects.

14. Clean the tire and rim of any lubricant used during removal.

WARNING
When mounting the tire, use only clean water as a tire lubricant. Other lubricants may leave a slippery residue on the tire that would allow the tire to slip on the rim, causing a loss of air pressure.

WARNING
The tire tread pattern on the original equipment tires is directional. Position the tire onto the rim so the rotation arrow on the tire sidewall

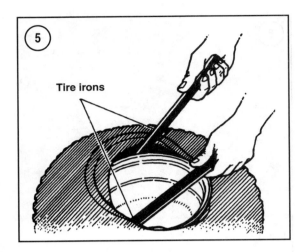

Tire irons

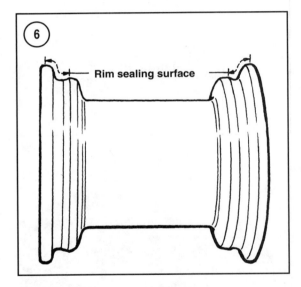

Rim sealing surface

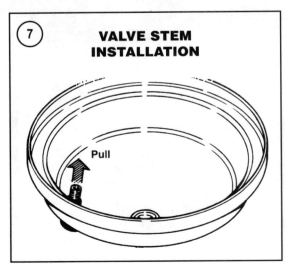

VALVE STEM INSTALLATION

Pull

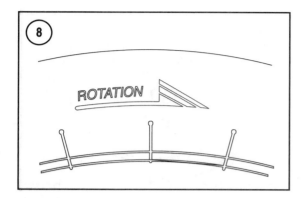

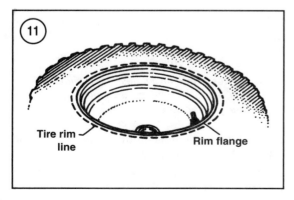

Tire rim line — Rim flange

(**Figure 8**) *faces in the correct direction of wheel rotation.*

NOTE
If the tire is difficult to install, place the tire outside in the sun (or in the trunk of a car). The higher temperatures soften the tire and help with installation.

15. Install the tire onto the rim starting with the side opposite the valve stem. Push the first bead over the rim flange. Force the bead into the center of the rim to help installation (**Figure 9**).

16. Install the rest of the bead with tire irons (**Figure 10**).

17. Repeat the preceding steps to install the second bead onto the rim.

18. Install the valve stem core, if necessary.

WARNING
Never exceed the maximum inflation pressure specified on the tire sidewall.

19. Apply water to the tire bead and inflate the tire to seat the tire onto the rim. Check that the rim lines on both sides of the tire are parallel with the rim flanges as shown in **Figure 11**. If the rim flanges are not parallel, deflate the tire and break the bead. Then lubricate the tire with water again and re-inflate the tire.

20. When the tire is properly seated, remove the air valve to deflate the tire and wait 1 hour before putting the tire into service. After 1 hour, inflate the tire to the operating pressure listed in **Table 4**.

21. Check for air leaks and install the valve cap.

Cold Patch Repair

Use the manufacturer's instructions for the tire repair kit. If there are no instructions, use the following procedure:

1. Remove the tire as described in this chapter.

2. Before removing the object that punctured the tire, mark the puncture location with chalk or a crayon. Remove the object.

3. Working on the inside of the tire, roughen the area around the hole larger than the patch (**Figure 12**). Use the cap from the tire repair kit or a pocket knife. Do not scrape too vigorously or additional damage may occur.

11

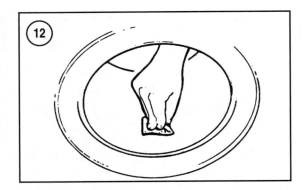

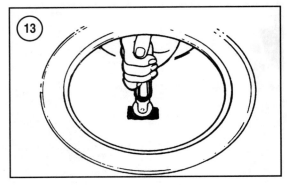

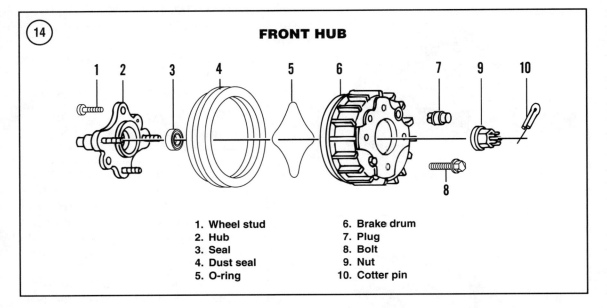

FRONT HUB

1. Wheel stud
2. Hub
3. Seal
4. Dust seal
5. O-ring
6. Brake drum
7. Plug
8. Bolt
9. Nut
10. Cotter pin

4. Clean the area with a non-flammable solvent. Do not use an oil base solvent because it leaves a residue rendering the patch useless.

5. Apply a small amount of special cement to the puncture and spread it evenly.

6. Allow the cement to dry until tacky, usually 30 seconds or so is sufficient.

7. Remove the backing from the patch.

CAUTION
Do not touch the newly exposed rubber or the patch does not stick firmly.

8. Center the patch over the hole. Hold the patch firmly in place for about 30 seconds to allow the cement to dry. If available, use a roller to press the patch into place (**Figure 13**).

9. Dust the area with talcum powder.

FRONT HUB

Refer to **Figure 14**.

Removal/Installation

1. Remove the front wheel as described in this chapter.

WARNING
Do not inhale brake dust. It may contain asbestos, which can cause lung injury and cancer.

2A. To remove the brake drum only, remove the bolts (A, **Figure 15**) and brake drum.

2B. To remove the brake drum and front hub at the same time, perform the following:

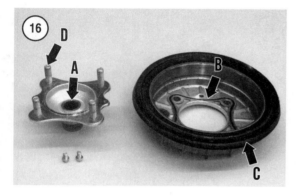

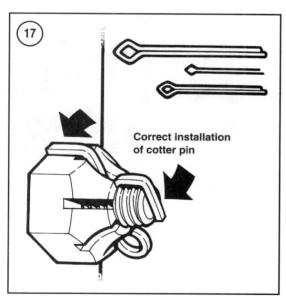

Correct installation
of cotter pin

a. Remove and discard the axle nut cotter pin
(B, **Figure 15**).

b. Remove the axle nut and front hub assembly
(C, **Figure 15**).

3. Inspect the front hub as described in this chapter.

4. Refer to Chapter Fourteen to service the brake
drum and brake drum seal (A, **Figure 16**).

5. Install the front hub by reversing the preceding
removal steps, while noting the following:

    a. If the brake drum was removed from the front
hub, install the O-ring (B, **Figure 16**) into the
brake drum groove.

    b. If the brake drum was removed from the front
hub, install the brake drum and tighten the
mounting bolts (A, **Figure 15**) to 10 N•m (88
ft.-lb.).

    c. Install and tighten the axle nut (B, **Figure 15**)
to 78 N•m (58 ft.-lb.).

NOTE
*If necessary, tighten the axle nut to
align it with the cotter pin hole in the
axle. Do **not** loosen the axle nut to
align it with the hole.*

WARNING
Always install a new cotter pin.

    d. Install a new cotter pin through the nut groove
and axle hole and then spread the ends to lock
it in place (**Figure 17**).

Inspection

1. Inspect the dust seal (C, **Figure 16**) and replace
if damaged.

2. Inspect the studs (D, **Figure 16**) and replace if
damaged.

3. Clean and dry the hub splines.

4. Check the hub for cracks or other damage.

5. Service the dust seal (C, **Figure 16**) and brake
drum as described in the *Brake Drum* section in
Chapter Thirteen.

SHOCK ABSORBERS

Removal/Installation

1. Support the ATV with the front wheels off the
ground.

2. Remove the lower shock absorber locknut and
bolt and remove the shock absorber (**Figure 18**).
Discard the locknuts.

3. Inspect the shock absorber as described in this
section.

11

4. Install the shock absorber by reversing the preceding removal steps, while noting the following:

    a. Install new shock locknuts.

    b. Tighten the upper and lower shock absorber locknuts to 44 N•m (33 ft.-lb.).

Inspection

1. Clean and dry the shock absorber (**Figure 19**).

2. Check the damper unit for leaks or other damage. Inspect the damper rod for bending.

3. Inspect the upper rubber bushing (**Figure 20**). Replace an excessively worn or damaged upper bushing.

4. Remove one of the dust seals (A, **Figure 21**) and inspect the bearing (B) and bushing (C) in the lower end of the shock absorber. Replace the bearing and bushing if corroded or damaged.

5. Inspect the spring for damage.

6. If the damper unit or spring is damaged, replace the entire shock absorber unit. Other than the end bushings, bearing and seals, individual components are not available.

TIE RODS

The tie rods consist of an inner end and outer end. Individual parts that make up the tie rod assembly (**Figure 22**) are available.

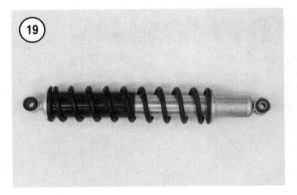

Removal

1. Support the ATV with the front wheels off the ground.

2. Remove the cotter pins from both tie rod ends. Refer to A, **Figure 23** and A, **Figure 24**.

3. Hold the flat on each tie rod stud with a wrench, (B, **Figure 23** or B, **Figure 24**) and remove the tie rod nuts, then remove the tie rod.

Inspection

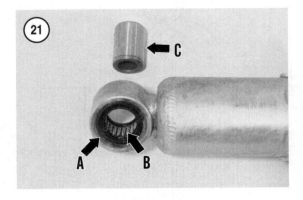

> *CAUTION*
> *When cleaning the tie rods, do not immerse the ball joints in any type of chemical that could contaminate the grease and/or damage the rubber boots.*

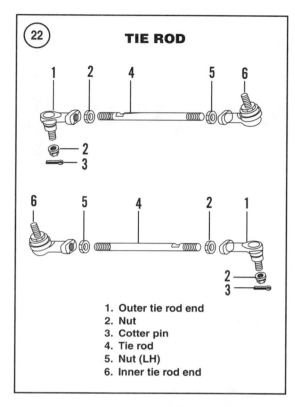

TIE ROD

1. Outer tie rod end
2. Nut
3. Cotter pin
4. Tie rod
5. Nut (LH)
6. Inner tie rod end

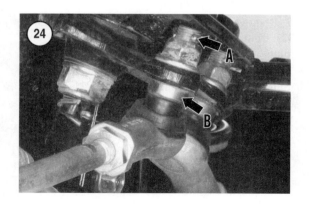

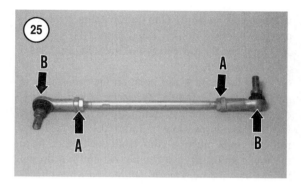

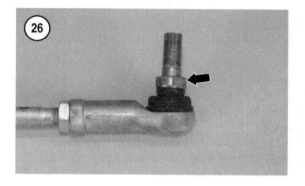

1. Inspect the tie rod shaft (**Figure 25**) and replace if damaged.

2. Inspect the rubber boot at each end of the tie rod end swivel joint (**Figure 26**). The swivel joints are permanently packed with grease. Replace the ball joint if excessively worn or if the rubber boot is damaged. Refer to *Tie Rod Disassembly/Reassembly* in the following procedure.

3. Pivot the tie rod end (**Figure 26**) back and forth by hand. If the tie rod end moves roughly or with excessive play, replace it as described in the following procedure.

Tie Rod Disassembly/Reassembly

If the tie rod ends are to be replaced, refer to **Figure 22** and perform the following:

1. Loosen the locknuts (A, **Figure 25**) securing the tie rod ends. The locknut securing the inner tie rod end has left-hand threads.

2. Unscrew the damaged tie rod end(s) (B, **Figure 25**).

3. Clean the mating shaft and tie rod end threads with contact cleaner.

4. The inner tie rod is marked with an L (**Figure 27**). Install this tie rod onto the end of the tie rod

without the flat on it. This tie rod has a silver colored nut.

5. The outer tie rod end is not marked, but uses a gold colored nut.

6. Refer to **Table 1** and position the rod ends and nuts as shown in **Figure 28**. After tie rod and toe-out adjustment, the maximum difference allowable for the locknut positions is 3 mm (0.12 in.). The tie rod end studs must be 180° from each other. Turn the locknuts up against the tie rod end but do not tighten at this time. They are tightened when checking the wheel alignment in Chapter Three.

Installation

1. Install the tie rod with the flat on the shaft (**Figure 29**) nearer the steering knuckle.

2. Attach the tie rod assembly to the steering shaft and steering knuckle. Refer to **Figure 25** and **Figure 26**.

3. Thread the castle nut onto each ball joint stud.

4. Hold the flat on each tie rod stud with a wrench and tighten the tie rod nuts to 54 N•m (40 ft.-lb.). Tighten the nut(s), if necessary, to align the cotter pin hole with the nut slot. Do not loosen the nut to align the hole and slot.

5. Install new cotter pins through all ball joint studs. Spread the cotter pin arms to lock them in place.

6. Check the toe-in adjustment as described in the *Toe-in Adjustment* in Chapter Three. If the tie rod ends were replaced, their locknuts are tightened during the adjustment procedure.

STEERING KNUCKLE

Removal/Installation

Refer to **Figure 30**.

1. Remove the front hub as described in this chapter.

2. Remove the boot protector (**Figure 31**).

3. Detach the brake vent hose and brake hose from the mounting brackets on the upper suspension arm.

> *CAUTION*
> *It is not necessary to disconnect the brake hose in Step 3. Do not allow the brake panel to hang from the brake hose.*

4. Remove the brake panel (Chapter Fourteen) and hang the panel so it is out of the way.

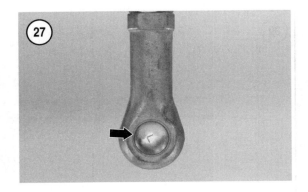

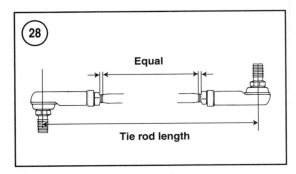

Equal

Tie rod length

5. Disconnect the tie rod from the steering knuckle as described in this chapter.

6. Remove the cotter pins and castle nuts (**Figure 32**) from the upper and lower control arm ball joints.

7. Disconnect the upper and lower control arm ball joints using the ball joint remover (Honda part No. 07MAC-SL00200 or equivalent [**Figure 33**]). Perform the following:

> *CAUTION*
> *Do not strike the ball joint or its stud when removing it. Otherwise the ball joint may be damaged.*

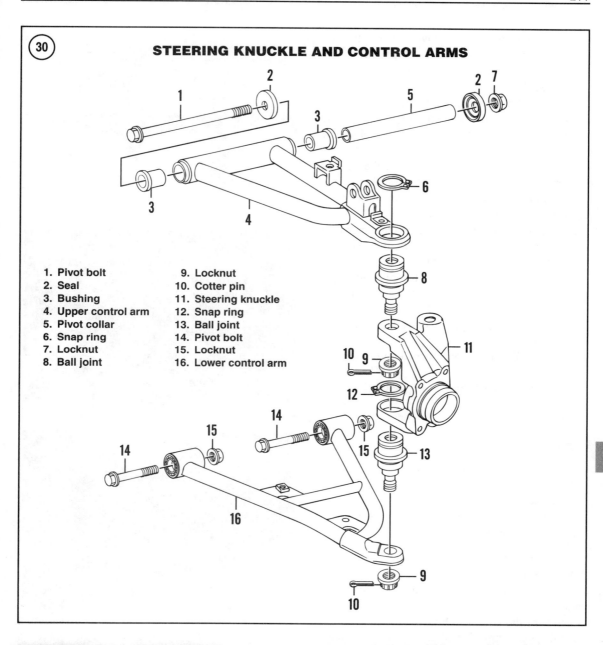

30

STEERING KNUCKLE AND CONTROL ARMS

1. Pivot bolt
2. Seal
3. Bushing
4. Upper control arm
5. Pivot collar
6. Snap ring
7. Locknut
8. Ball joint
9. Locknut
10. Cotter pin
11. Steering knuckle
12. Snap ring
13. Ball joint
14. Pivot bolt
15. Locknut
16. Lower control arm

11

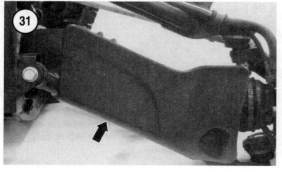

31

32

a. Mount the ball joint remover between the ball joint upper arm as shown in **Figure 34**.

b. Operate the tool and break the upper ball joint loose from the upper arm.

c. Repeat for the lower control arm.

8. Remove the steering knuckle (**Figure 35**) while being careful not to damage the axle splines or boots.

9. Inspect the steering knuckle as described in this chapter.

10. Install the steering knuckle by reversing these removal steps, plus the following:

a. Lubricate the steering knuckle seal lips with a waterproof grease, then insert the axle into the steering knuckle (**Figure 35**).

b. Install the steering knuckle onto the upper and lower control arms. Install the castle nuts and tighten to 29 N•m (22 ft.-lb.).

c. Install new cotter pins and bend the ends over completely.

d. Check front brake operation before riding the ATV.

e. Install the brake hose clamps and tighten to 12 N•m (106 in.-lb.).

Inspection

> *CAUTION*
> *When cleaning the steering knuckle, do not wash the ball joint in solvent. The ball joint cover may be damaged or the grease contaminated.*

1. Clean and dry the steering knuckle assembly (**Figure 36**).

2. Inspect the steering knuckle and replace if damaged.

3. Examine the holes (A, **Figure 36**) where the tie rod and upper control arm attach. Check for elongation and fractures.

4. Inspect the ball joint and rubber boot (B, **Figure 36**). Pivot the ball joint by hand. It should move freely. The ball joint is permanently packed with grease. If the rubber boot is damaged, dirt and moisture can enter the ball joint and damage it. If the ball joint or boot is damaged, replace the steering knuckle assembly.

5. Check the hole at the end of the ball joint where the cotter pin fits. Make sure there are no fractures or cracks leading out toward the end of the ball

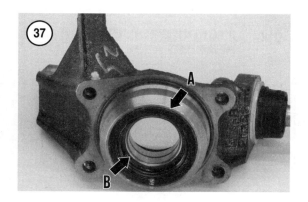

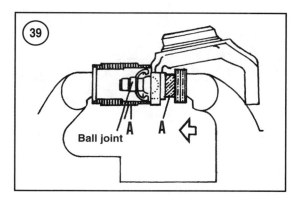

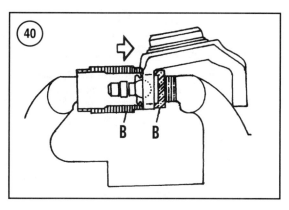

Ball joint   A   A

joint. If any are present, replace the steering knuckle.

6. Check the inner (C, **Figure 36**) and outer (A, **Figure 37**) dust seals for excessive wear or damage. If necessary, replace the oil seals as described in this section.

7. Turn the inner and outer bearings (B, **Figure 37**) with a finger. Both bearing races should turn freely and without any sign of roughness, catching or excessive noise. Replace the damaged bearings as described in this section.

Lower Ball Joint Replacement

> *CAUTION*
> *Ball joint removal and installation require special tools. Do not try to replace the ball joints without these tools because the steering knuckle may be damaged.*

1. Remove the snap ring (**Figure 38**) securing the lower ball joint to the steering knuckle.

2. Position the special tools (Honda part No. 07JMF-HC50110 or equivalent), with the A mark facing the ball joint and install the special tools and the steering knuckle in a vise (**Figure 39**).

3. Slowly tighten the vise and press the ball joint out of the steering knuckle.

4. Remove the special tools, steering knuckle and ball joint form the vise.

5. Clean the ball joint receptacle in the steering knuckle with solvent and thoroughly dry.

6. Correctly position the new ball joint into the steering knuckle and use the same special tools used for removal. Position the special tools with the B mark facing toward the ball joint.

7. Install the special tools and the steering knuckle in a vise (**Figure 40**).

> *CAUTION*
> *While tightening the vise, if there is a strong resistance or if the vise stops moving, stop immediately. There probably is an alignment problem with either the ball joint or the special tool. Realign the ball joint and special tools and try again. The ball joint should press in with a minimum amount of resistance.*

11

8. Slowly tighten the vise and press the ball joint straight into the steering knuckle. Press the ball joint in until it bottoms.

9. Remove the special tools and the steering knuckle from the vise.

10. Make sure the snap ring groove is completely visible to accept the snap ring. Press the ball joint in farther if necessary.

11. Install the snap ring so the flat side is out. Make sure the snap ring seats correctly.

Steering Knuckle Dust Seal and Bearing Replacement

Refer to **Figure 41**.

1. Remove the inner (C, **Figure 36**) and outer (A, **Figure 37**) dust seals. Discard both dust seals.

NOTE
If only replacing the dust seals, go to Step 10.

2. Remove the snap ring (4, **Figure 41**).

3. Support the steering knuckle and press or drive out the bearing.

4. If the bearing was a loose fit in the steering knuckle, check the bearing bore for cracks or excessive wear.

5. Clean the bearing bore.

6. Check the snap ring groove for cracks or other damage.

7. Pack the new bearing with grease.

8. Press or drive the new bearing into the steering knuckle. Press or drive against the marked side of the bearing. Force the bearing in until it is fully seated. Refer to *Ball Bearings* in Chapter One for bearing installation information.

9. Install a new snap ring (4, **Figure 41**) with the flat side out. Make sure it seats in the groove completely.

10. Install the dust seals as follows:

   a. Pack the lip of each dust seal with grease.

   b. Install both dust seals with the closed side facing out.

   c. Press both dust seals into the steering knuckle

CONTROL ARMS

Refer to **Figure 30**.

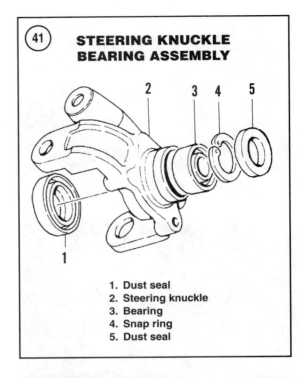

STEERING KNUCKLE BEARING ASSEMBLY

1. Dust seal
2. Steering knuckle
3. Bearing
4. Snap ring
5. Dust seal

Removal/Installation

1. Remove the steering knuckle as described in this chapter.

2. Remove the upper control arm as follows:

   a. Remove the locknut and bolt (A, **Figure 42**) securing the shock absorber to the upper control arm.

   b. Remove the brake hose and breather tube clamp bolt (B, **Figure 42**) from the upper control arm.

   c. Remove the locknut and bolt, then remove the upper control arm (A, **Figure 43**).

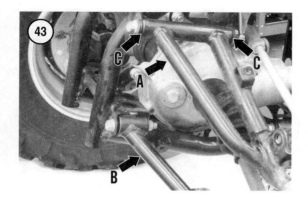

3. Remove the locknuts and bolts and the lower control arm (B, **Figure 43**).

4. Discard all of the control arm and lower shock absorber locknuts removed in Step 2 and Step 3.

5. Inspect the upper and lower control arms as described in this section.

NOTE
Install new upper and lower control arm locknuts when performing Step 7 and Step 8 and tighten them finger-tight. These locknuts are tightened to their final torque specifications after the front wheels are installed and with the ATV resting on the ground.

NOTE
Install all control arm mounting bolts so the bolt head is toward the front of the ATV.

6. Install the lower control arm (B, **Figure 43**) onto the frame and secure it with bolts and new locknuts.

7. Apply mulltipurpose grease to the pivot collar and install it into the upper control arm.

8. Position the cup seals onto the ends of the upper control arm (2, **Figure 30**) and install the upper control arm. Secure it with the bolt and a new locknut.

9. Install the shock absorber lower mounting bolt and a new locknut (A, **Figure 42**). Tighten the locknut to 44 N•m (33 ft.-lb.).

10. Install the brake hose and breather tube clamp bolt (B, **Figure 42**).

11. Install the steering knuckle as described in this chapter.

12. Install the front wheels as described in this chapter.

13. Lower the ATV so all four wheels are on the ground.

14. Tighten the upper control arm locknut to 34 N•m (25 ft.-lb.).

15. Tighten the lower control arm locknuts to 44 N•m (33 ft.-lb.).

Inspection

CAUTION
*When cleaning the upper control arm, do not wash the ball joint (**Figure 44**) in solvent. The ball joint boot may be damaged or the grease contaminated.*

1. Clean and dry the control arms.

2. Examine both control arms for bending, cracks or other damage. Replace if necessary.

3. Inspect the upper control arm ball joint and rubber boot (**Figure 44**). Pivot the ball joint by hand. It should move freely. The ball joint is permanently packed with grease. If the rubber boot is damaged, dirt and moisture can enter the ball joint and destroy it. If the ball joint or boot is damaged, replace the ball joint as described in this chapter.

4. Inspect the pivot bolts and replace them if excessively worn or damaged.

5. Inspect the pivot bushings (**Figure 45**) for excessive wear or other damage. The flanged bushings in the upper control arm may be replaced using a suitable driver or puller. The bushings in the lower control arm are not available separately. If the bushings are damaged, replace the lower control arm.

11

Upper Control Arm Ball Joint Replacement

> *NOTE*
> *The lower ball joint is installed on the steering knuckle.*

> *CAUTION*
> *Ball joint removal and installation require special tools. Do not try to replace the ball joints without these tools because the control arm may be damaged.*

1. Remove the upper control arm as described in this chapter.
2. Remove the snap ring (**Figure 46**) securing the upper ball joint to the upper control arm.
3. Position the special tools (Honda part No. 07WMF-HN00100 or equivalent), with the A mark facing the ball joint and install the special tools and the control arm in a vise (**Figure 47**) or press.
4. Slowly press the ball joint out of the control arm.
5. Remove the special tools, control arm and ball joint from the vise.
6. Clean the ball joint receptacle in the control arm with solvent and thoroughly dry.
7. Correctly position the new ball joint into the control arm and use the same special tools used for removal. Position the special tools with the B mark facing toward the ball joint.
8. Install the special tools and the control arm in a vise (**Figure 48**) or press.

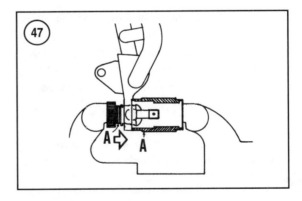

> *CAUTION*
> *While tightening the vise, if there is a strong resistance or if the vise stops moving, stop immediately. There probably is an alignment problem with either the ball joint or the special tool. Realign the ball joint and special tools and try again. The ball joint should press in with a minimum amount of resistance.*

9. Slowly press the ball joint straight into the control arm. Press the ball joint in until it bottoms.
10. Remove the special tools and the control arm from the vise.
11. Make sure the snap ring groove is completely visible to accept the snap ring. Press the ball joint in farther if necessary.
12. Install the snap ring so the flat side is out. Make sure the snap ring seats correctly.

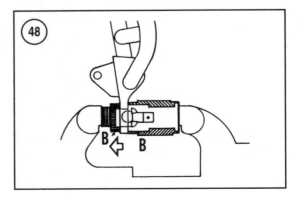

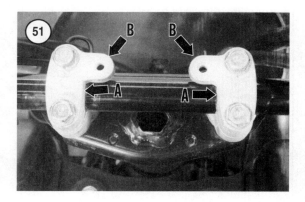

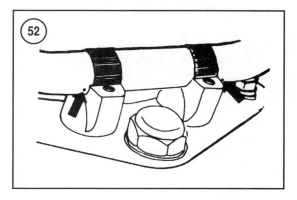

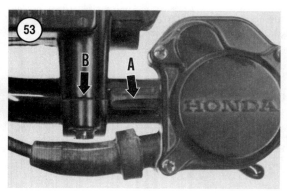

HANDLEBAR

Removal

1. Remove the handlebar cover (Chapter Fifteen).

2. Remove the wire retaining bands securing the wiring harness to the handlebar.

3. Remove the throttle housing screws, clamp and throttle housing (**Figure 49**).

4. Remove the front master cylinder as described in Chapter Thirteen.

5. Remove the screws and the rear brake lever clamp (**Figure 50**).

6. Remove the switch housing as described in the *Left Handlebar Switch Housing Replacement* in Chapter Nine.

7. Remove the upper handlebar holder mounting bolts, holders (A, **Figure 51**) and handlebar.

Installation

1. Position the handlebar on the lower handlebar holders and hold it in place.

2. Install the upper handlebar holders with the cover bolt holes (B, **Figure 51**) toward the front.

3. Align the punch mark on the handlebar with the top surface of the lower holders (**Figure 52**).

4. Install the handlebar holder bolts. Tighten the forward bolts first and then the rear bolts. Tighten each bolt securely.

5. Install the switch housing and rear brake lever assembly as described in the *Left Handlebar Switch Housing Replacement* in Chapter Nine.

6. Install the master cylinder as described in Chapter Thirteen.

7. Install the throttle housing by aligning the lug on the throttle housing (A, **Figure 53**) with the mating

surfaces of the master cylinder and clamp (B). Install the clamp and screws and tighten securely.

8. Secure the wiring harness to the handlebar with the wire bands.

9. Check all cable adjustments as described in Chapter Three.

10. Check that the front brake works properly.

11. Check that each handlebar switch works properly.

12. Install the handlebar cover (Chapter Fifteen).

STEERING SHAFT

Refer to **Figure 54**.

Removal

1. Remove the front fender and inner fender panels (Chapter Fifteen).

2. Remove the combination meter and assist headlight as described in Chapter Nine.

3. Remove both front wheels as described in this chapter.

4. Remove the lower handlebar holder nuts and washers (**Figure 55**). Disengage the wires and cables from the retaining guides and clamps. Move the handlebar assembly out of the way while being careful not to damage the brake hose, cables or wiring harness.

5. Detach both inner tie rod ends (A, **Figure 56**) from the steering shaft as described in the *Tie Rods* section in this chapter.

6. Remove the cotter pin and nut at the bottom of the steering shaft (B, **Figure 56**).

7. Remove the steering shaft holder bolts (A, **Figure 57**) and holder assembly (B).

8. Remove the steering shaft and steering arm assembly from the frame.

Inspection

Replace excessively worn or damaged parts as described in this section.

1. Clean and dry all parts.

2. Remove the set ring (**Figure 58**) and the steering shaft bushing from the steering shaft. Check both parts for excessive wear or damage.

3. Check the steering shaft for bending and spline or thread damage.

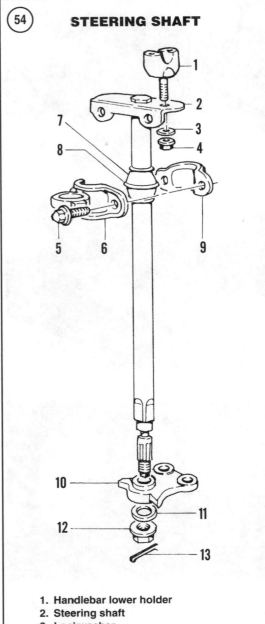

54 **STEERING SHAFT**

1. Handlebar lower holder
2. Steering shaft
3. Lockwasher
4. Handlebar lower holder locknut
5. Steering shaft holder mounting bolt
6. Steering shaft outer holder
7. Bushing
8. Set ring
9. Steering shaft inner holder
10. Steering arm
11. Washer
12. Steering shaft nut
13. Cotter pin

4. Examine the cotter pin hole at the end of the steering shaft. Make sure no fractures or cracks are leading out toward the end of the steering shaft. If any are present, replace the steering shaft.

5. Inspect the steering arm for cracks, spline or other damage.

6. Check the bushing for excessive wear or damage.

7. Inspect the steering bearing (A, **Figure 59**) by turning the inner race with a finger. Replace the bearing if it turns roughly or has excessive play.

8. Inspect the dust seals (B, **Figure 59**) for excessive wear or other damage.

9. Replace the dust seals and bearing as described in the following procedure.

Dust Seal and Bearing Replacement

The steering shaft bearing is pressed into the frame. Do not remove the bearing unless it requires replacement.

1. Remove the dust seals from both sides of the bearing.

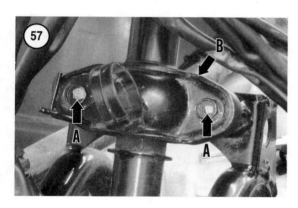

NOTE
If only replacing the dust seals, go to Step 10.

2. Remove the snap ring (**Figure 60**) from the bearing bore groove.

3. Before removing the bearing, check that its outer race is a tight fit in the bearing bore. If the bearing is loose, check the bearing bore for cracks or other damage.

4. Drive the bearing up and out of the frame.

5. Clean the bearing bore and check it for cracks or other damage.

6. Install the new bearing so the marked side faces up.

7. Tap the bearing squarely on the outer race only and into place. Use a socket or bearing driver that matches the outer race diameter. Do not tap on the inner race or the bearing might be damaged. Install the bearing so it is fully seated below the snap ring groove in the bearing bore.

8. Install the snap ring into the bearing bore groove. Make sure the snap ring seats in the groove completely.

9. Pack the lips of the new dust seals with grease, then install each dust seal so its closed side faces out.

Installation

1. Lubricate the steering shaft bushing with grease and install it onto the steering shaft so the UP mark (**Figure 61**) faces toward the handlebar. Install the set ring (**Figure 58**) into the bushing groove.

2. Install the steering shaft into the frame.

3. Install the inner and outer (B, **Figure 57**) steering shaft holders around the bushing and install the bolts (A). Tighten the steering shaft holder bolts to 32 N•m (24 ft.-lb.).

4. Lubricate the steering shaft splines with grease.

5. Align the master spline on the steering shaft (**Figure 62**) with the master spline on the steering arm splines (**Figure 63**).

6. Lubricate the steering shaft nut flange and threads with grease. Install the steering shaft nut (B, **Figure 56**) and washer and tighten to 108 N•m (80 ft.-lb.). Secure the nut with a new cotter pin and bend the ends over completely.

7. Reattach both inner tie rod ends to the steering shaft (A, **Figure 56**) as described in the *Tie Rods* section in this chapter.

8. Install the handlebar assembly onto the steering shaft. Check the routing of the brake hose, cables and wiring harness.

9. Install new handlebar lower holder locknuts (**Figure 55**) and tighten to 39 N•m (29 ft.-lb.).

10. Install both front wheels as described in this chapter.

11. Install the assist headlight and combination meter as described in Chapter Nine.

12. Install the front fender and inner fender panels (Chapter Fifteen).

13. Check that the handlebar turns properly and the throttle returns to its closed position after releasing it.

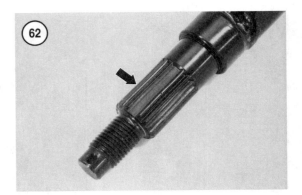

Table 1 STEERING AND FRONT SUSPENSION SPECIFICATIONS

Front suspension type	Double wish-bone
Front wheel travel	170 mm (6.7 in.)
Front damper type	Double tube
Toe-out	9-39 mm (0.35-1.54 in.)
Caster angle	3°
Camber angle	0°
Trail length	12 mm (0.5 in.)
Tie rod distance between ball joints*	381-383 mm (15.0-15.1 in.)
Tie rod locknut position*	5.5 mm (0.22 in.)
*Refer to *Figure 28* and text.	

Table 2 TIRE AND WHEEL SPECIFICATIONS

Tires	
Type	
Front	Bridgestone Dirt Hooks 15
Rear	Bridgestone Dirt Hooks 14
Size	
Front	AT25 × 8-12
Rear	AT25 × 10-12
Wheels	
Front rim size	12 × 6.0 AT
Rear rim size	12 × 7.5 AT

Table 3 TIRE INFLATION PRESSURE

	Front and rear tires psi (kPa)
Normal pressure	3.6 (25)
Minimum pressure	3.2 (22)
Maximum pressure	4.1 (28)

Table 4 FRONT SUSPENSION AND STEERING TORQUE SPECIFICATIONS

	N•m	in.-lb.	ft.-lb.
Ball joint nut	29	–	22
Brake drum mounting bolts	10	88	–
Brake hose clamps	12	106	–
Front wheel axle nut	78	–	58
Front wheel nuts	64	–	47
Handlebar lower holder locknuts	39	–	29
Shock absorber locknut	44	–	33
Steering shaft holder flange bolt	32	–	24
Steering shaft nut	108	–	80
Throttle case cover screws	4	35	–
Tie rod nut	54	–	40
Control arms			
Lower	44	–	35
Upper	34	–	25

11

CHAPTER TWELVE

FRONT DRIVE MECHANISM

This chapter describes repair and replacement procedures for the front drive mechanism. This includes the front drive axles, front driveshaft and front differential gearcase.

Refer to **Table 1** for front drive specifications. **Table 2** lists torque specifications for the front drive mechanism assembly. **Table 1** and **Table 2** are located at the end of this chapter.

FRONT DRIVE AXLES

Removal/Installation

1. Detach the lower end of the shock absorber for the side being serviced (Chapter Eleven). Raise the shock absorber out of the way.

NOTE
It is not necessary to remove the brake panel when performing Step 2.

2. Separate the lower ball joint from the lower control arm (Chapter Eleven) for the side being serviced.

3. Raise the steering knuckle assembly and remove the outer axle end from the steering knuckle (**Figure 1**). Support the steering knuckle assembly so it is out of the way.

CAUTION
When removing the front axle, be careful not to damage the rubber boots.

CAUTION
To avoid damage to the front differential oil seal and splines, pull the inboard joint straight out of the front differential.

4. Hold the inboard joint and pull the driveshaft (**Figure 2**) out of the differential. It may be necessary to use a screwdriver to pry the axle loose.

5. Perform the inspection procedures described in this section.

6. Install the front axle by reversing the preceding removal steps while noting the following:

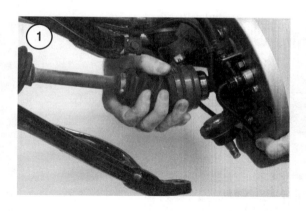

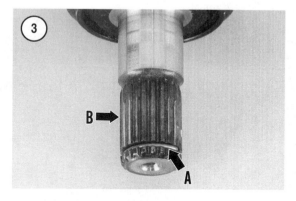

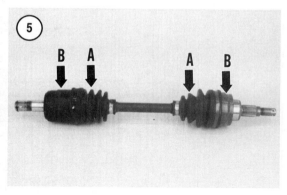

a. Install a new stopper ring (A, **Figure 3**) in the groove in the inboard joint. Make sure it is properly seated in the axle groove.

b. Lubricate the front axle seal (**Figure 4**) and inner splines (B, **Figure 3**) with molybdenum disulfide grease.

c. Carefully guide the front axle into the gearcase (**Figure 2**). Push it in all the way until it bottoms. Pull the inboard joint a little to make sure the stopper ring locks into the front differential side gear groove.

d. Install the steering knuckle and shock absorber (Chapter Eleven).

Inspection

1. Inspect the rubber boots (A, **Figure 5**) for wear, cuts or damage. Damaged boots allow dirt, mud and moisture to enter the boot. Replace if necessary as described in *Disassembly*.

2. Move each end of the front axle (B, **Figure 5**) in a circular motion and check the constant velocity joints for excessive wear or play.

Disassembly

Refer to **Figure 6**.

> *NOTE*
> *The outboard joint cannot be disassembled or repaired. If damaged or faulty, the drive axle assembly must be replaced.*

1. Open the clamps (A, **Figure 7**) on the inboard joint, then remove the clamps. Discard the clamps because they cannot be reused.

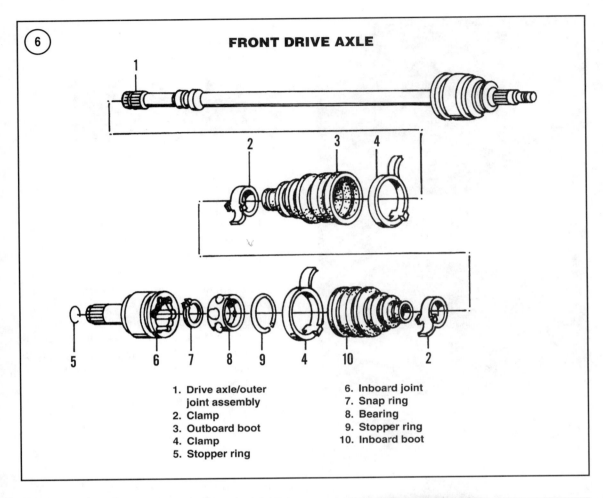

FRONT DRIVE AXLE

1. Drive axle/outer joint assembly
2. Clamp
3. Outboard boot
4. Clamp
5. Stopper ring
6. Inboard joint
7. Snap ring
8. Bearing
9. Stopper ring
10. Inboard boot

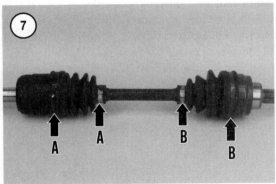

2. Carefully slide the boot (A, **Figure 8**) onto the front axle and off the inboard joint.

3. Wipe out all the grease from the inboard joint cavity (B, **Figure 8**).

4. Remove the stopper ring (**Figure 9**) from the inboard joint.

5. Remove the inboard joint (**Figure 10**).

6. Remove the circlip (**Figure 11**) and slide off the bearing assembly (**Figure 12**). Be careful not to drop any of the steel balls from the bearing cage.

7. Slide the inboard boot off the front axle and discard the clamp. It cannot be reused.

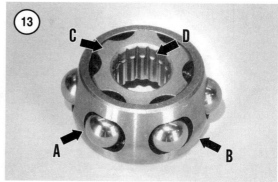

8. If the outboard boot requires replacement, perform the following:

    a. Open the clamps (B, **Figure 7**) on the outboard joint, then remove and discard the clamps.

    b. Slide the outboard boot off the drive axle and discard the clamp.

9. Inspect the drive axle as described in this procedure.

Inspection

    Refer to **Figure 6**.

CAUTION
Before cleaning the rubber boots, make sure the cleaning solvent does not damage rubber products.

1. Clean and dry the bearing assembly.

2. Inspect the steel balls (A, **Figure 13**), bearing cage (B) and bearing race (C) for excessive wear or damage.

3. Check the bearing race inner splines (D, **Figure 13**) for wear or damage.

4. If necessary, disassemble the bearing assembly for further inspection. Carefully remove the steel balls from the bearing cage and remove the bearing race from the bearing cage.

5. If any of the bearing components are damaged, replace the entire assembly. Individual replacement parts are not available separately.

6. Clean and dry the inboard joint.

7. Inspect the inboard joint ball guides (A, **Figure 14**) for excessive wear or damage.

8. Inspect the inboard joint stopper ring groove (B, **Figure 14**) for wear or damage.

9. Check the stopper ring groove (A, **Figure 3**) in the inboard joint shaft for cracks or other damage.

12

10. Inspect the axle and inboard joint splines (B, **Figure 3**) for excessive wear or damage.

11. Inspect the inboard joint (**Figure 15**) for cracks or damage.

12. Move the outboard joint axle through its range of motion and check for excessive play or noise.

13. Inspect the front drive axle for bending, wear or damage.

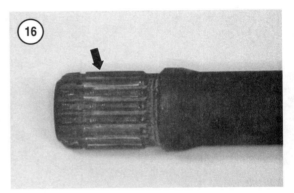

14. Inspect the inner end splines (**Figure 16**), the outer end splines (A, **Figure 17**) and the front hub cotter pin hole (B, **Figure 17**) for wear or damage.

15. Inspect the rubber boots for cracks, age deterioration or other damage.

16. Replace the front drive axle assembly if any components are excessively worn or damaged. Individual replacement parts for the front drive axle, other than the rubber boots and clamps, are not available.

Assembly

Refer to **Figure 6**.

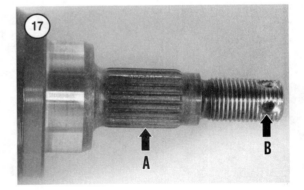

1. The rubber boots are not identical and must be installed on the correct joint. Honda replacement boots are marked with an identifying number (**Figure 18**) as follows:
    a. Inboard joint—68.
    b. Outboard joint—68L.

2. If the outboard boot was removed, install a new boot onto the front axle at this time.

NOTE
Install the new boot clamps with their tabs facing in the direction shown in **Figure 19**.

3. Install two new small boot clamps onto the front axle.

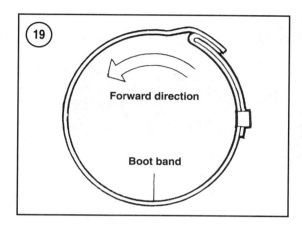

Forward direction

Boot band

Bearing case →

Wide inner
diameter →

Bearing case →

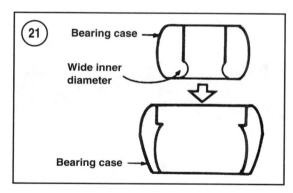

4. Install the inboard boot and move the small boot clamp onto the boot (**Figure 20**). Do not lock the clamp at this time.

5. If the bearing assembly was disassembled, assemble the bearing as follows:

   a. Position the bearing race with the wide inner diameter going on first and install the race (**Figure 21**) into the bearing case. Align the steel ball receptacles in both parts.

   b. Install the steel balls into their receptacles in the bearing case.

   c. Pack the bearing assembly with grease included in the boot replacement kit. Grease helps hold the steel balls in place.

6. Position the bearing assembly with the small end of the bearing going on first and install the bearing onto the drive axle (**Figure 12**).

7. Push the bearing assembly on until it stops, then install a new circlip (**Figure 22**) into the groove in the shaft. Make sure the circlip seats in the groove completely.

8. Apply a liberal amount of grease to the bearing assembly (**Figure 23**). Work the grease between the balls, race and case. Check for voids and fill with grease.

9. Lubricate the inboard joint inner surface with grease.

10. Install the inboard joint onto the bearing assembly (**Figure 24**) and install the stopper ring (**Figure 25**). Make sure the stopper ring seats in the groove completely.

11. After the stopper ring is in place, fill the inboard joint cavity behind the bearing assembly with grease (B, **Figure 8**).

12. Pack each boot with the following amounts of molybdenum disulfide grease:

   a. Inboard boot—55-75 g (1.9-2.6 oz.).

12

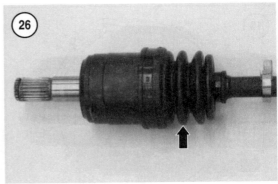

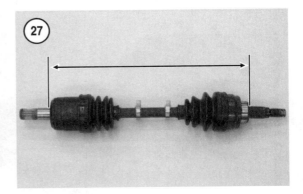

b. Outboard boot—50-70 g (1.8-2.5 oz.).

13. Move the inboard boot onto the inboard joint (**Figure 26**).

14. Move the inboard joint on the drive axle until the distance between the ends of the inboard and outboard joints are as specified in **Table 1** (**Figure 27**).

15. Move the small boot clamp onto each boot (**Figure 28**). Bend down the tab on the boot clamp and secure the tab with the locking clips and tap them with a plastic hammer. Make sure the tab is locked in place (**Figure 29**). Repeat for the opposite boot.

NOTE
Install the new boot clamps with their tabs facing in the direction shown in **Figure 19**.

16. Install the large boot clamps onto each boot. Make sure the boots are not twisted on the axle.

CAUTION
Make sure the inboard joint does not move while installing the boot clamps. The dimension achieved in Step 14 must be maintained at all times. This dimension is critical to

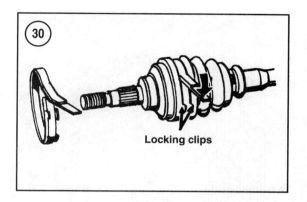

Locking clips

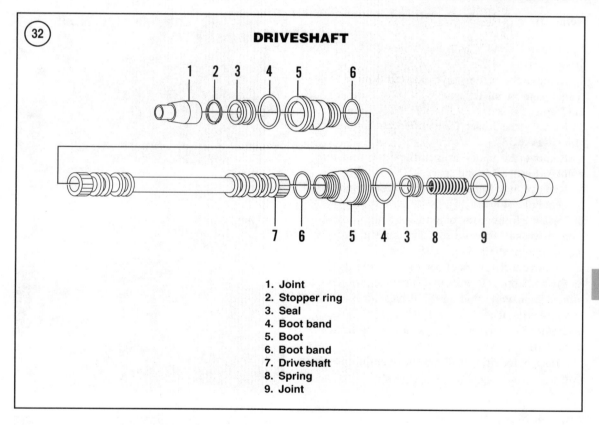

DRIVESHAFT

1. Joint
2. Stopper ring
3. Seal
4. Boot band
5. Boot
6. Boot band
7. Driveshaft
8. Spring
9. Joint

avoid stress on the rubber boots during ATV operation.

17. Refer to **Figure 30** and secure all large boot clamps. Bend down the tab (**Figure 31**) on the boot clamp and secure the tab with the locking clips and tap them with a plastic hammer. Make sure they are locked in place (**Figure 29**).

18. If removed, install a new stopper ring (A, **Figure 3**). Make sure the stopper ring is seated correctly in the drive axle groove.

19. Apply molybdenum disulfide grease to the drive axle splines.

DRIVESHAFT

The front driveshaft (**Figure 32**) can be removed without removing the front differential or front drive axles.

12

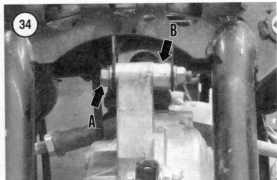

Removal

1. Support the ATV with the front wheels off the ground.

2. Remove the center mud guard and inner front fender panel on the left side of the ATV as described in Chapter Fifteen.

3. Remove the lower front differential mounting bolt (**Figure 33**).

4. Remove the upper front differential mounting bolt (A, **Figure 34**) and spacer (B).

5. Remove the front differential front mounting bracket bolts (**Figure 35**).

6. Push the front differential forward, then push the front driveshaft forward so it disconnects from the engine output shaft (**Figure 36**).

7. Remove the front boot band (A, **Figure 37**).

8. Push the boot (B, **Figure 37**) off the differential pinion joint while pulling the driveshaft rearward and removing it.

9. Remove the driveshaft joint and spring from the driveshaft.

10. Inspect the driveshaft as described in this section.

Inspection

1. Inspect the driveshaft for bending or other damage.

2. Examine the splines in each end for damage.

3. Examine the seals for excessive wear or damage. Install a new seal using the following procedure:

> *CAUTION*
> *The seal is a tight fit when passing over the shaft splines. Lubricate the splines and seal and use care not to cut the seal.*

a. Place a seal protector sleeve or plastic cone against the shaft end (A, **Figure 38**).

b. Place the lubricated seal on the cone (B, **Figure 38**). The open side must be toward the shaft as shown in **Figure 38**.

c. Push the seal onto the shaft, then work the seal into place on the seal seat as shown in **Figure 39**.

Installation

1. Lubricate the driveshaft splines and dust seals with molybdenum disulfide grease.

2. Push the front differential assembly forward in the frame.

3. Apply 5-8 g (0.18-0.28 oz.) of molybdenum disulfide grease onto the shaft splines at the differential end of the shaft.

4. Install the driveshaft into the differential pinion joint (**Figure 40**).

5. Insert a piece of wire between the driveshaft and boot to release air from the pinion joint. Leave the wire in place until Step 16.

6. Install the O-ring (**Figure 41**) onto the final driveshaft, if removed.

7. Apply 5-8 g (0.18-0.28 oz.) of molybdenum disulfide grease onto the rear driveshaft splines. Also apply grease to the O-ring (**Figure 41**).

8. Install the spring into the front shaft joint.

9. Install the spring and front shaft joint onto the driveshaft and under the boot.

10. Push the driveshaft forward and connect the driveshaft to the engine (**Figure 36**). If necessary, rotate the driveshaft to align the splines.

11. Move the front differential rearward and align the mounting holes with the frame.

NOTE
Do not tighten the differential housing mounting bolts until all of the fasteners have been installed.

12. Install the two bolts and the front mounting bracket (**Figure 35**).

13. Install the upper mounting bolt, nut and spacer. Install the spacer as shown at B, **Figure 34**.

14. Install the lower mounting bolt (**Figure 33**).

15. Tighten the differential mounting bolts to the following:

a. Tighten the front differential mounting bracket bolts to 22 N•m (16 ft.-lb.).

12

    b. Tighten the lower mounting bolt to 44 N•m (33 ft.-lb.).

    c. Tighten the upper mounting bolt to 44 N•m (33 ft.-lb.).

16. Remove the piece of wire installed in Step 5.

17. Install the inner front fender panel and center mudguard.

FRONT DIFFERENTIAL

The front differential gearcase can be removed with one front drive axle still attached to the steering knuckle. The front driveshaft may be removed before removing the differential or removed with the differential. If it is only necessary to remove the driveshaft, refer to *Driveshaft* in this chapter.

The front differential gearcase requires a number of special tools for disassembly, inspection and reassembly.

The face cams, differential housing and cover are available only as a unit assembly.

If the pinion gear, ring gear, gearcase, case cover, side bearings or pinion shaft bearing are replaced, perform the backlash and gear mesh pattern adjustments described in this section.

Removal

1. Remove the front wheels.

2. Remove the center mud guard and inner front fender panel on the left side of the ATV as described in Chapter Fifteen.

3. Remove one or both front drive axles as described in this chapter.

4. Disconnect the air vent hose on the top of the differential gearcase.

5. Remove the lower front differential mounting bolt (**Figure 33**).

6. Remove the upper front differential mounting bolt (A, **Figure 34**) and spacer (B).

7. Remove the front differential front mounting bracket bolts (**Figure 35**).

8. Push the front differential forward, then push the front driveshaft forward so it disconnects from the engine output shaft (**Figure 36**).

9. If desired, remove the front driveshaft as described in this chapter.

10. Remove the front differential gearcase from the frame.

11. Remove the front mounting bracket.

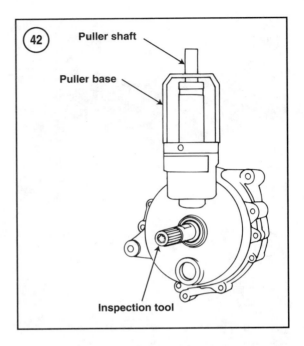

42

Puller shaft

Puller base

Inspection tool

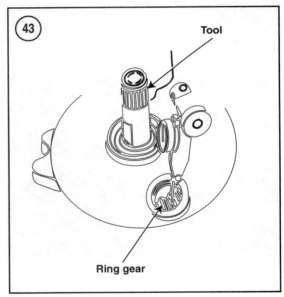

43

Tool

Ring gear

Special Tools

The following special tools are recommended when servicing the differential:

a. Pinion puller base (Honda part No. 07HMC-MM8011A).

b. Puller shaft (Honda part No. 07931-ME4010B).

c. Adapter (Honda part No. 07YMF-HN4010A).

d. Special nut (Honda part No. 07931-HB3020A).

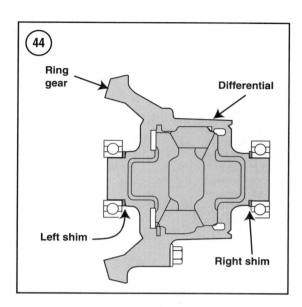

(44)

Ring gear

Differential

Left shim

Right shim

e. Differential inspection tool (Honda part No. 07KMK-HC5010A).

f. Locknut wrench (07916-MB00002).

Backlash Measurement/Adjustment

Perform gear backlash measurement before disassembly to determine gear wear and whether the internal shim thicknesses must be adjusted. Measuring gear backlash is also necessary after overhaul.

1. Install the pinion puller base, puller shaft, adapter and special nut as shown in **Figure 42** so any pinion end play is removed and the pinion cannot rotate.

2. Place the differential in a soft-jawed vise.

3. Insert the differential inspection tool into the right side of the differential so it engages the internal splines.

4. Remove the oil fill cap.

5. Position a dial indicator so the tip rests against a gear tooth (**Figure 43**).

6. To determine the gear backlash, gently rotate the differential inspection tool while reading the dial indicator. Refer to **Table 1** for the specified backlash.

7. Remove the dial indicator, then rotate the ring gear using the inspection tool and take two additional backlash readings 120° from the original measuring point. If the difference between any two readings exceed 0.2 mm (0.01 in.), note the following:

a. The differential assembly is not square in the case, which may be due to the incorrect seating of a bearing.

b. The housing may be deformed.

8. To correct the gear backlash, refer to **Figure 44** and note the following:

a. If gear backlash is less than the desired specification, reduce the thickness of the right shim and increase the thickness of the left shim.

b. If gear backlash is greater than the desired specification, reduce the thickness of the left shim and increase the thickness of the right shim.

NOTE
When adjusting shim thickness, adjust the sides equally. For instance, if the right shim is increased 0.10 mm (0.004 in.), decrease the left shim 0.10 mm (0.004 in.). Changing a shim thickness by 0.10 mm (0.004 in.) changes backlash 0.06 mm (0.002 in.).

Disassembly

Refer to **Figure 45**.

1. Remove the front mounting bracket from the gearcase.

2. Remove the cover retaining bolts in a crossing pattern (**Figure 46**).

3. Insert a prying tool in the gap between the gearcase and cover (**Figure 47**), and pry the cover off the gearcase.

4. Note the right-side shim on the differential housing (A, **Figure 48**). Remove the shim, label it and set it aside.

5. Remove the differential assembly (B, **Figure 48**).

6. Note the left-side shim on the differential housing (**Figure 49**). Remove the shim, label it and set it aside.

CAUTION
The pinion joint is retained by a wire ring on the pinion shaft that fits in a groove in the pinion joint.

7. Pull out the pinion joint (**Figure 50**).

8. Remove the O-ring (A, **Figure 51**).

12

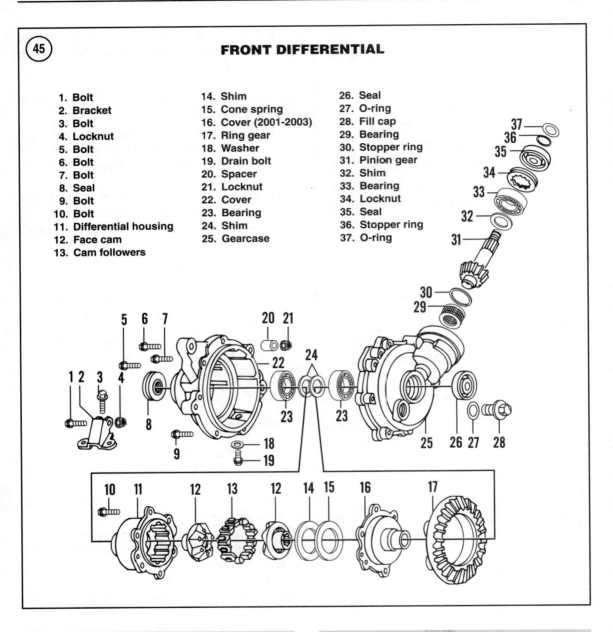

FRONT DIFFERENTIAL

1. Bolt
2. Bracket
3. Bolt
4. Locknut
5. Bolt
6. Bolt
7. Bolt
8. Seal
9. Bolt
10. Bolt
11. Differential housing
12. Face cam
13. Cam followers

14. Shim
15. Cone spring
16. Cover (2001-2003)
17. Ring gear
18. Washer
19. Drain bolt
20. Spacer
21. Locknut
22. Cover
23. Bearing
24. Shim
25. Gearcase

26. Seal
27. O-ring
28. Fill cap
29. Bearing
30. Stopper ring
31. Pinion gear
32. Shim
33. Bearing
34. Locknut
35. Seal
36. Stopper ring
37. O-ring

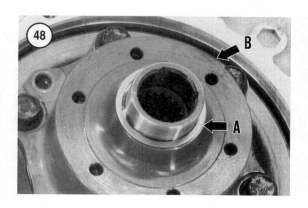

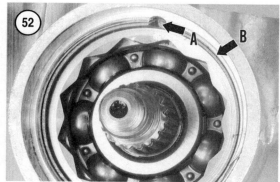

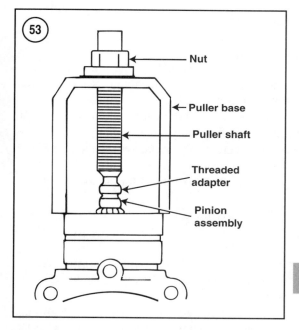

9. Using a suitable seal puller, remove the oil seal (B, **Figure 51**).

10. Rotate the pinion shaft and check for noisy or rough pinion bearings.

NOTE
Cover the internal parts when unstaking the locknut in Step 11 to prevent the entry of metal debris.

11. Using a grinder or metal removal tool, remove the staked portion of the locknut (A, **Figure 52**).

12. Using the locknut wrench (or equivalent), remove the locknut (B, **Figure 52**).

13. Assemble the tools identified in the *Special Tools* section as shown in **Figure 53** and remove the pinion and bearing assembly.

12

CHAPTER TWELVE

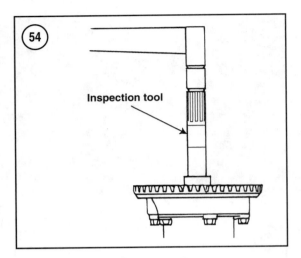

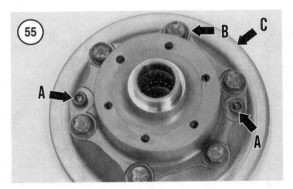

14. Before disassembling the differential unit, check the slip torque to determine its operating condition. Proceed as follows:

   a. Install the differential inspection tool into both face cams.

   b. Secure the flat surface of the tool in a vise.

   c. Rotate the tool with a torque wrench (**Figure 54**). Refer to **Table 1** for the specified torque reading.

   d. Disassemble, inspect and, if necessary, repair the differential unit if the torque reading is below specification.

15A. To separate the differential unit from the ring gear on 2001-2003 models, perform the following steps:

   a. Install two short 6-mm socket-head bolts into the differential housing (A, **Figure 55**) to hold the cap to the housing while removing the ring gear bolts.

   b. Remove the ring gear mounting bolts (B, **Figure 55**) and remove the ring gear (C).

   c. Remove the two temporary bolts and remove the differential cap (**Figure 56**).

NOTE
On 2004-on models the ring gear contains the left side of the differential unit. Prior models are equipped with a separate differential cap. Refer to **Figure 45**.

15B. On 2004-on models, remove the ring gear mounting bolts and separate the differential unit from the ring gear.

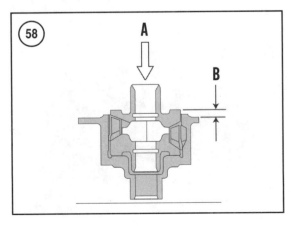

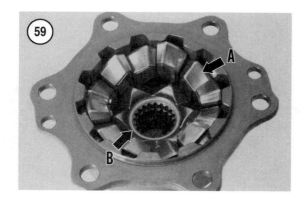

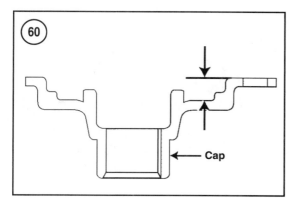

Cap

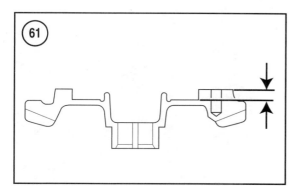

16. Remove the cone spring (A, **Figure 57**) and shim (B).

17. To check the differential unit for excessive wear, proceed as follows:

    a. Using a press or other means, apply 1.47 kN (330 lb.) to the face cam hub (A, **Figure 58**).

    b. Measure the distance from the face cam to the differential housing mating surface (B, **Figure 58**).

    c. If the distance is less than the specification in **Table 1**, the differential unit is excessively worn and should be replaced.

20. Remove the left face cam (C, **Figure 57**).

21. Remove the cam followers (A, **Figure 59**).

22. Remove the right face cam (B, **Figure 59**).

Inspection

1. Clean, then inspect all components for excessive wear and damage. Carefully remove gasket material from the mating surfaces on the differential cover and gearcase.

2. Measure the depth of the spring seating surface in the differential cap (**Figure 60**) or ring gear (**Figure 61**). Replace the cap if the depth exceeds the specification in **Table 1**.

3. Inspect the grooves and sliding surfaces in the differential housing (**Figure 62**).

4. Measure the height of the cone spring. Replace the spring if the height is less than the specification in **Table 1**.

> *NOTE*
> *If bearing replacement is required, install new oil seals after bearing installation.*

5. Remove the oil seals in the differential gearcase and cover using a suitable seal removal tool. Install a new oil seal so the flanged side is out (**Figure 63**).

6. Turn the bearings in the differential gearcase and cover with a finger. The bearings should turn freely and without any sign of roughness, catching or excessive noise. Replace the damaged bearings as described in Chapter One. The bearing must bottom in the gearcase or cover bore.

7. Examine the face cam sliding surface (A, **Figure 64**) and cam surfaces (B).

8. Examine the sliding surfaces of the cam followers (**Figure 65**). The cam followers must be replaced as a set.

12

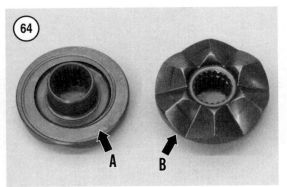

9. Inspect the pinion needle bearing (A, **Figure 66**) in the gearcase. If damaged, replace the bearing using the following procedure:

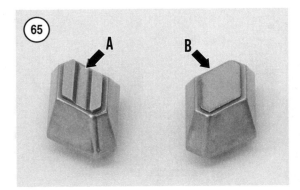

a. Using needlenose pliers, extract the wire retainer ring (B, **Figure 66**) through the access hole. Rotate the ring so the end is accessible, pry out the end and pull out the ring.

CAUTION
Do not use a flame to heat the gearcase. It can warp the gearcase.

b. Heat the gearcase in an oven to 80° C (176° F) and extract the bearing.

c. Install a new wire ring into the groove on the outside of the new bearing.

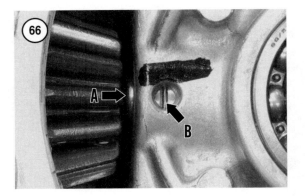

d. Install the bearing into the ring compressor tool.

e. Place the compressor tool with the bearing into a freezer for at least 30 minutes.

f. Heat the gearcase in an oven to 80° C (176° F).

g. Position the compressor in the gearcase and drive the bearing into the gearcase. Only one blow should be required. Multiple blows may dislodge the wire ring, which requires the installation of a new ring and bearing. Make sure the wire ring is properly positioned as viewed in the access hole (B, **Figure 66**).

10. Inspect the pinion gear and bearing. If the bearing must be replaced, use the following procedure:

a. Using a press or puller, remove the bearing from the pinion shaft.

b. If only the bearing is being replaced, use the original shim on the pinion shaft. If the differential cover or housing, ring and pinion gears or the side bearings are being replaced, install

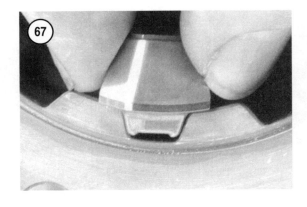

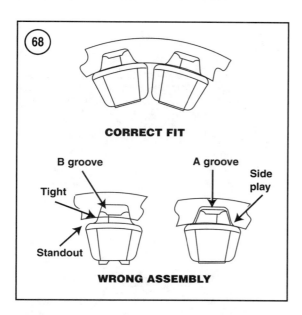

CORRECT FIT

B groove   A groove

Tight   Side play

Standout

WRONG ASSEMBLY

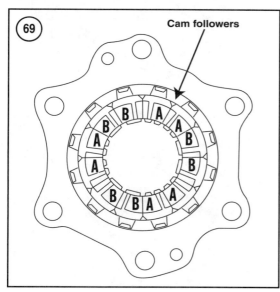

Cam followers

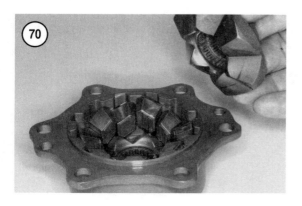

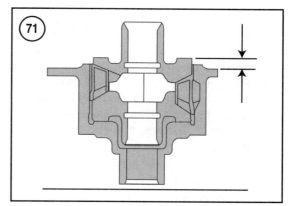

a 2.0 mm (0.79 in.) thick shim as a starting point for the gear position adjustments.

c. Press or drive the new bearing onto the pinion shaft so the marked side of the bearing is toward the threaded end of the shaft.

Assembly

1. Install the bearings and oil seals as described in *Inspection*.

NOTE
Lubricate all moving parts with SAE 80 hypoid gear oil.

2. Install the face cam into the differential housing.

3. Note there are two types of cam followers. Type A followers are ribbed while type B followers are flat. Refer to **Figure 65**. Each type of cam follower must fit into a corresponding groove in the differential housing **Figure 67**. The cam follower must engage the groove fully to its maximum depth without excessive side play. An A type follower in a B groove causes a tight fit and standout. A B type follower in an A groove has excessive side play. Refer to **Figure 68**.

4. Install the cam followers in pairs. Refer to the pattern in **Figure 69**.

5. Install the face cam onto the cam followers (**Figure 70**).

6. Determine the thickness of the differential unit shim (14, **Figure 45**) using the following procedure:

a. Measure the distance from the face cam to the differential housing mating surface (**Figure 71**).

b. Measure the depth of the spring seating surface in the differential cap (**Figure 60**) on
2001-2003 models or ring gear depth (**Figure
61**) on 2004-on models.

c. Subtract the face cam height (**Figure 71**)
from the cap depth (**Figure 60**) or ring gear
depth (**Figure 61**). From the result, subtract
1.7 mm. That result is the desired shim
thickness.

d. Select a shim closest in thickness to the calculated desired thickness.

7. Install the shim (A, **Figure 72**) and cone spring
(B). The cone side of the spring must be out.

8A. To install the differential unit onto the ring
gear on 2001-2003 models, perform the following
steps:

a. Install the cap. Secure the cap by installing
short 6 mm socket-head screws (A, **Figure
73**).

b. Install the differential unit onto the ring gear
(B, **Figure 73**). Tighten new bolts to 49 N•m
(36 ft.-lb.).

c. Remove the temporary socket-head bolts (A,
Figure 73).

8B. On 2004-on models, install the differential unit
onto the ring gear and install new ring gear mounting bolts. Tighten the bolts to 49 N•m (36 ft.-lb.).

9. Install the pinion gear and bearing into the
gearcase.

> *NOTE*
> *The torque wrench attachment point
> on the Honda tool specified in Step 10
> is offset. The actual torque specifica-
> tions is 98 N•m (72 ft.-lb.).*

10. Install the locknut (B, **Figure 74**). Using the
locknut wrench tighten the locknut to 89 N•m (66
ft.-lb.) as indicated on the torque wrench.

> *NOTE*
> *Do not stake the locknut if performing
> the gear mesh pattern check in Step
> 13.*

11. If the pinion, ring gear, bearings, gearcase or
cover have been replaced, check gear mesh pattern
using the following procedure:

a. Apply Prussian Blue or other gear marking
compound onto the ring gear teeth.

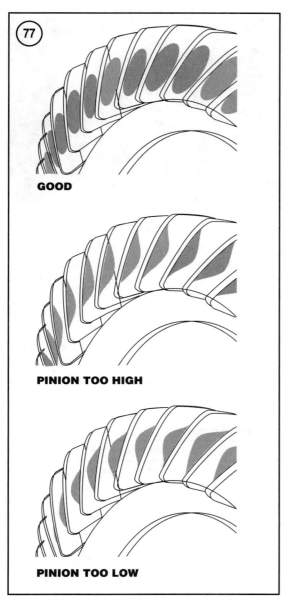

GOOD

PINION TOO HIGH

PINION TOO LOW

b. Install the side shims (24, **Figure 45**) onto the differential unit, then install the ring gear/differential unit assembly into the gearcase.

c. Install the cover onto the gearcase.

NOTE
While tightening the cover bolts in substep d rotate the pinion shaft.

d. Install the cover bolts. Install the two 10-mm bolts in the locations shown in **Figure 75**. Tighten the bolts evenly in a crossing pattern in several steps until the cover is seated on the gearcase. Tighten the 8-mm bolts to 25 N•m (19 ft.-lb.). Tighten the 10-mm bolts to 49 N•m (36 ft.-lb.).

e. Remove the oil fill cap.

f. Rotate the pinion shaft several rotations so a pattern is evident on the ring gear teeth. View the ring gear teeth through the gearcase oil fill hole (**Figure 76**).

g. Refer to the typical gear patterns in **Figure 77**. If the pinion is low, install a thinner shim (32, **Figure 45**). If the pinion is high, install a thicker shim (32, **Figure 45**). The pinion and bearing must be removed to replace the shim. Changing shim thickness 0.12 mm (0.005 in.) moves the contact pattern approximately 0.5-1.0 mm (0.02-0.04 in.).

h. If removed, reinstall the pinion gear and bearing as described in Step 10 and Step 11.

i. After obtaining a satisfactory gear contact pattern, be sure to check the gear backlash.

j. Remove the cover and differential unit and continue with the final assembly procedure.

12. Stake the pinion locknut (B, **Figure 74**) into the notch (A) in the gearcase.

13. Install the stopper ring (A, **Figure 78**) onto the pinion shaft.

14. Install the oil seal (B, **Figure 78**) so it is bottomed. Lubricate the oil seal lips with grease.

15. Apply grease to a new O-ring and install it onto the pinion shaft (C, **Figure 78**).

16. Lubricate the pinion shaft splines with molybdenum disulfide grease, then install the pinion joint (**Figure 79**). The joint groove must engage the stopper ring on the shaft. Pull lightly on the joint to ensure it is properly installed.

17. Install the side shims (24, **Figure 45**) onto the differential unit.

18. Install the ring gear/differential unit assembly into the gearcase.

19. Apply a liquid sealant such as Yamabond No. 4 to the mating surface of the differential cover, then install the cover onto the gearcase.

NOTE
While tightening the cover bolts in Step 20, rotate the pinion shaft.

20. Install the cover bolts. Install the two 10-mm bolts in the locations shown in **Figure 75**. Tighten the bolts evenly in a crossing pattern in several steps until the cover is seated on the gearcase. Tighten the 8-mm bolts to 25 N•m (19 ft.-lb.). Tighten the 10-mm bolts to 49 N•m (36 ft.-lb.).

21. Make sure the gears rotate freely without binding.

Installation

1. If removed, install the front mounting bracket on the gearcase, but do not tighten the bolt.

2. If a front axle remains installed, lubricate the axle splines with grease and insert the axle while installing the front differential.

3. Install the front differential and position it as far forward as possible.

4. Install the driveshaft as described in this chapter.

5. After tightening the upper and lower differential mounting bolts and the two front bracket bolts, tighten the front gearcase mounting bolt (**Figure 80**) to 22 N•m (16 ft.-lb.).

6. Install the front axle(s) as described in this chapter.

7. Connect the vent hose to the differential gearcase and secure it with the clamp.

8. Fill the front differential with the correct amount and type of oil (Chapter Three).

Table 1 FRONT DRIVE SPECIFICATIONS

	New	Service limit
Driveshaft spline grease		5-8 g (0.18-0.28 oz.)
Drive axle length between joints		
Left axle	353.3-373.3 mm (13.91-14.70 in.)	
Right axle	373.1-393.1 mm (14.69-15.48 in.)	
Drive boot grease		
Inboard		55-75 g (1.9-2.6 oz.)
Outboard		50-70 g (1.8-2.5 oz.)
	(continued)	

Table 1 FRONT DRIVE SPECIFICATIONS (continued)

	New	Service limit
Gear backlash	0.05-0.25 mm (0.002-0.010 In.)	0.4 mm (0.016 in.)
Differential slip torque	14-17 N•m (124-150 in.-lb.)	12 N•m (80 in.-lb.)
Face cam-to-housing distance		
2001-2003	6.3-6.7 mm (0.25-0.26 in.)	6.3 mm (0.25 in.)
2004	3.3-3.7 mm (0.13-0.15 in.)	3.3 mm (0.13 in.)
Differential housing cap depth (2001-2003)	9.55-9.65 mm (0.376-0.380 in.)	9.55 mm (0.376 in.)
Differential housing ring gear depth (2004)	6.55-6.65 mm (0.258-0.262 in.)	6.55 mm (0.258 in.)
Cone spring free height	2.8 mm (0.11 in.)	2.6 mm (0.10 mm)
Grease capacities		
Front axle		
Inboard boot		55-75 g (1.9-2.6 oz.)
Outboard boot		50-70 g (1.8-2.5 oz.)
Front driveshaft		
Front splines		5-8 g (0.18-0.28 oz.)
Rear splines		5-8 g (0.18-0.28 oz.)

Table 2 FRONT DRIVE TORQUE SPECIFICATIONS

	N•m	in.-lb.	ft.-lb.
Gearcase bolts			
8 mm	25	–	19
10 mm	49	–	36
Gearcase mounting bolts			
Front mounting bolt	22	–	16
Lower mounting bolt	44	–	33
Upper mounting bolt	44	–	33
Mounting bracket bolts	22	–	16
Pinion locknut*	89	–	66
Ring gear bolts	49	–	36

*Torque wrench reading using Honda tool.

12

REAR AXLE, SUSPENSION AND FINAL DRIVE

This chapter contains repair and replacement procedures for the rear wheels, rear axle, suspension and final drive unit.

Rear suspension specifications are listed in **Table 1** and torque specifications in **Table 2**. **Table 1** and **Table 2** are located at the end of this chapter.

CAUTION
Self-locking nuts are used to secure some of the rear suspension components. Honda recommends discarding all self-locking nuts once they have been removed. The self-locking portion of the nut is weakened once the nut has been removed and no longer properly locks onto the mating threads. Never reinstall a used nut once it has been removed.

REAR WHEELS

Refer to **Figure 1**.

Removal/Installation

NOTE
*The tire tread on the original equipment tires is directional and must be installed on the correct side of the ATV. The tire is marked with an arrow to indicate forward rotation (**Figure 2**).*

1. Park the ATV on level ground and set the parking brake. Block the front wheels so the ATV cannot roll in either direction.

2. Identify the rear tires with an L (left side) or R (right side) mark. Refer to these marks when installing the wheels.

3. Loosen the wheel nuts (**Figure 3**) securing the wheel to the hub/brake drum.

4. Raise the rear of the ATV so the rear wheels are off the ground. Support the ATV with safety stands or wooden blocks. Make sure they are properly placed before beginning work.

5. Remove the wheel nuts, then remove the rear wheel.

6. Clean the wheel nuts in solvent and dry thoroughly.

7. Inspect the wheel for cracks, bending or other damage. If necessary, replace the wheel as described in Chapter Ten.

8. Install the wheel onto the original side.

9. Install the wheel nuts with the curved end (**Figure 4**) facing toward the wheel. Tighten the nuts

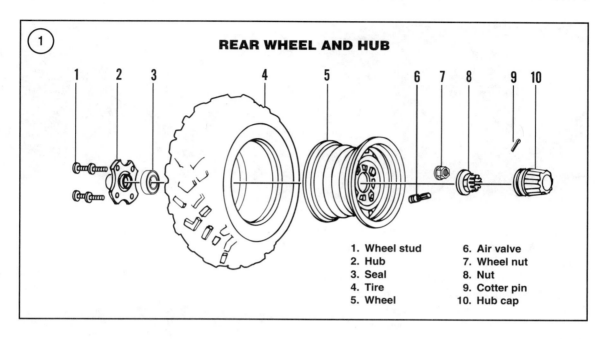

REAR WHEEL AND HUB

1. Wheel stud
2. Hub
3. Seal
4. Tire
5. Wheel
6. Air valve
7. Wheel nut
8. Nut
9. Cotter pin
10. Hub cap

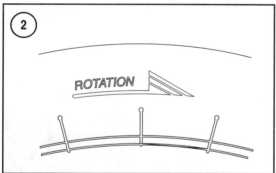

ROTATION

Curved side

11. After the wheel is installed completely, rotate it and then apply the rear brake several times to make sure the wheel rotates freely and the brake is operating correctly.

12. Lower the ATV so both rear wheels are on the ground.

SHOCK ABSORBERS

Removal/Installation

1. Support the ATV with the rear wheels off the ground.

2. If the left shock absorber is going to be removed, remove the muffler as described in Chapter Four.

finger-tight to center the wheel squarely against the brake drum or hub.

10. Tighten the wheel nuts (**Figure 3**) to 65 N•m (48 ft.-lb.).

13

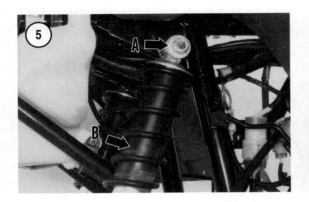

3. Remove the shock absorber upper mounting locknut (A, **Figure 5**) and washer. Discard the locknut.

4. Remove the shock absorber lower mounting bolt (**Figure 6**) and locknut. Discard the locknut.

5. Remove the shock absorber (**Figure 7**).

6. Inspect the shock absorber as described in this chapter.

7. Install the shock absorber by reversing the preceding removal steps, while noting the following:

   a. Install the lower shock absorber mounting bolt so it points inward.

   b. Install new locknuts.

   c. Tighten the upper shock absorber locknut to 40 N•m (30 ft.-lb.). Tighten the lower shock absorber bolt to 44 N•m (33 ft.-lb.).

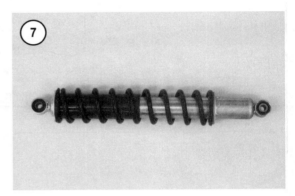

Inspection

1. Clean and dry the shock absorber (**Figure 7**).

2. Check the damper unit for leaks or other damage. Inspect the damper rod for bending.

3. Inspect the upper rubber bushing (**Figure 8**). Replace an excessively worn or damaged upper bushing.

4. Remove one of the dust seals (A, **Figure 9**) and inspect the bearing (B) and bushing (C) in the lower end of the shock absorber. Replace the bearing and bushing if corroded or damaged.

5. Inspect the spring for damage.

6. If the damper unit or spring is damaged, replace the entire shock absorber unit. Other than the end bushings, bearing and seals, individual components are not available.

REAR AXLE

Refer to **Figure 10**.

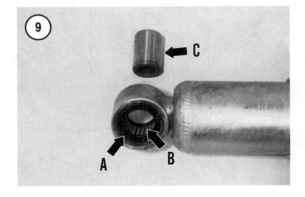

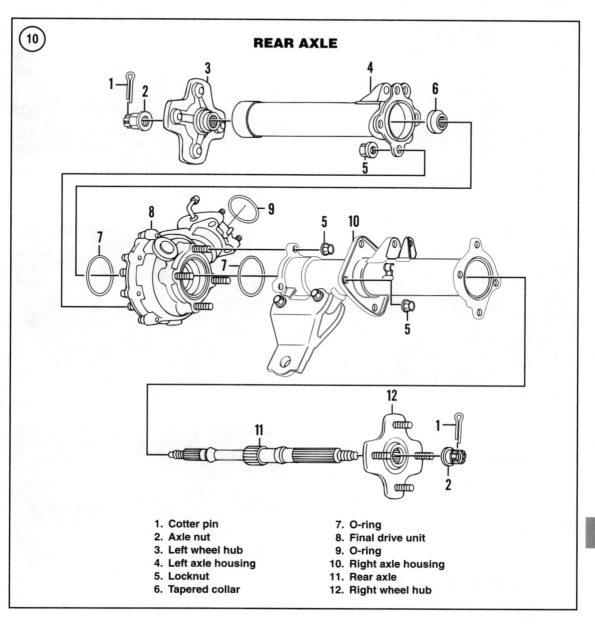

REAR AXLE

1. Cotter pin
2. Axle nut
3. Left wheel hub
4. Left axle housing
5. Locknut
6. Tapered collar
7. O-ring
8. Final drive unit
9. O-ring
10. Right axle housing
11. Rear axle
12. Right wheel hub

13

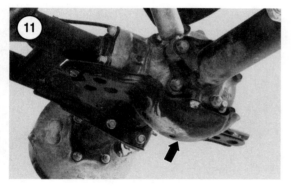

Removal

1. Remove both rear wheels as described in this chapter.

2. Remove the three retaining bolts, then remove the skid plate (**Figure 11**).

3. Remove the left rear axle nut cotter pin and discard it.

4. Remove the left rear axle nut (A, **Figure 12**) and rear hub (B).

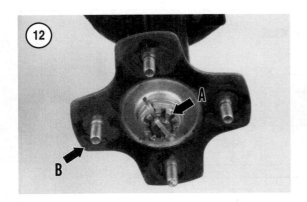

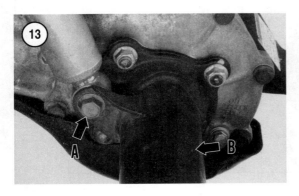

5. Remove the left shock absorber lower mounting bolt (A, **Figure 13**).

6. Remove the locknuts and the left rear axle housing (B, **Figure 13**). Discard the locknuts.

7. Remove the collar (**Figure 14**).

8. Remove the right rear axle nut cotter pin and discard it.

9. Remove the right rear axle nut (A, **Figure 15**) and rear hub (B).

10. Remove the brake drum cover, brake drum and rear brake panel assembly (Chapter Thirteen).

11. Remove the axle (**Figure 16**) from the right side. If necessary, drive out the axle with a rubber hammer.

12. Inspect the rear hubs and axle as described in this chapter.

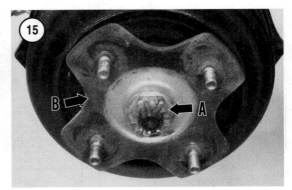

Wheel Hub Inspection

1. Inspect the hub inner splines (A, **Figure 17**) for wear or damage. Replace the hub if necessary.

2. Replace the dust seal (B, **Figure 17**) if worn or damaged.

3. Check the studs (C, **Figure 17**) for damaged threads. Replace damaged studs with a press.

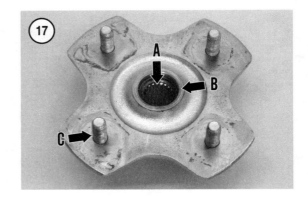

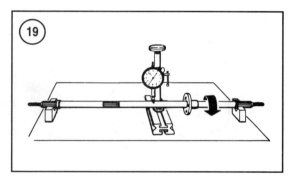

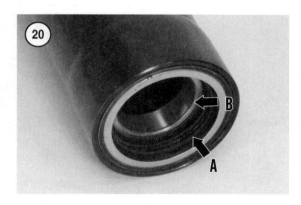

4. Inspect the bearing (A, **Figure 18**) and seal (B) contact surfaces on the wheel hub. Replace the wheel hub if excessively worn or damaged.

Rear Axle Inspection

1. Clean and dry the rear axle.

2. Inspect the axle splines for twisting or other damage.

3. Check the axle cotter pin holes. Replace the axle if either hole is cracked or damaged and cannot hold the cotter pin.

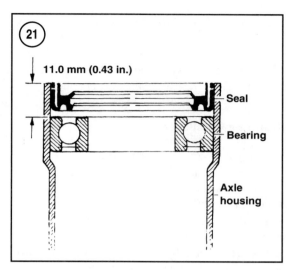

4. Place the rear axle on a set of V-blocks and measure runout with a dial indicator (**Figure 19**). Replace the rear axle if the runout exceeds the service limit in **Table 1**.

Left Final Drive Housing Axle Seal and Bearing Inspection and Replacement

1. Inspect the axle seal (A, **Figure 20**) for damage.

2. Check the bearing (B, **Figure 20**) by turning the inner race with a finger. The bearing should turn without roughness, catching, binding or excessive noise. If damaged, replace the bearing as described in this procedure.

3. Support the final drive housing and pry the axle seal out with a seal removal tool.

NOTE
If only replacing the seal, go to Step 8.

4. Remove the bearing by driving it out of the housing with a long drift or bearing driver.

5. Clean and dry the final drive housing.

6. Check the bearing bore for cracks or other damage.

7. Install the new bearing as follows:

   a. Install the bearing with the closed side facing out.

   b. Install the bearing into place with a bearing driver to the depth shown in **Figure 21**. Press on the bearing outer race only.

8. Install the new axle seal as follows:

13

a. Pack the oil seal lips with a waterproof grease.

b. Install the new oil seal into the housing in the direction shown in **Figure 21**. Install the new oil seal so it seats against the bearing.

Rear Axle Installation

1. Apply grease to the axle splines.

2. Install the rear axle (**Figure 16**) from the right side. At the same time, align the rear axle and final drive housing splines.

3. Install the rear brake panel, brake drum and brake drum cover (Chapter Thirteen).

4. Clean the rear hubs where they contact the brake drum (right side) or bearing (left axle housing).

5. Lubricate the axle shaft splines where the right axle hub operates.

6. Install the right rear hub (B, **Figure 15**) and axle nut (A). Tighten the axle nut hand-tight at this time.

7. Install the axle collar so the tapered side is in as shown in **Figure 14**.

8. Replace the final drive case O-ring (**Figure 22**) if damaged. Lubricate the O-ring with grease.

9. Install the left rear axle housing (B, **Figure 13**).

10. Install the left rear hub (B, **Figure 12**) onto the axle and into the axle housing to help center the rear axle. Install the left rear axle nut (A, **Figure 12**) and tighten hand-tight. Install new axle housing locknuts and tighten to 44 N•m (33 ft.-lb.).

11. Install the left shock absorber and the mounting bolt (A, **Figure 13**) and tighten to 44 N•m (33 ft.-lb.).

12. Tighten the left side axle nut (A, **Figure 12**) to 137 N•m (101 ft.-lb.).

13. Tighten the right side axle nut (A, **Figure 15**) to 137 N•m (101 ft.-lb.).

14. Secure each axle nut with a new cotter pin. Spread the cotter pin ends to lock it in place. Refer to **Figure 23**.

> *NOTE*
> *If the cotter pin hole(s) in the axle does not align with the castellations on the nut, tighten the nut further until hole alignment is correct. Never loosen the axle nut to achieve hole alignment.*

15. Install both rear wheels as described in this chapter.

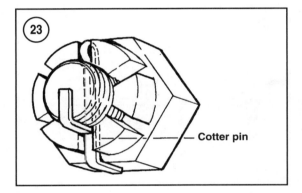

Cotter pin

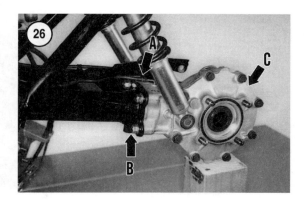

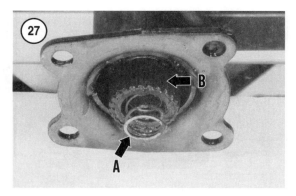

16. Install the skid plate. Tighten the mounting bolts to 32 N•m (24 ft.-lb.).

FINAL DRIVE UNIT

The final drive unit can be removed with or without the rear axle installed. If the final drive unit will be serviced, remove the axle while the final drive unit is mounted in the frame. If only servicing the swing arm, the final drive unit and rear axle can be removed as an assembly (**Figure 24**).

Removal

1. If necessary, remove the rear axle as described in this chapter.
2. Drain the final drive oil (Chapter Three).
3. Remove the three retaining bolts, then remove the skid plate (**Figure 11**).
4. Disconnect the vent hose from the clamp on the right axle housing.
5. Support the final drive unit with a jack or wooden blocks.
6. Remove the right shock absorber lower bolt (A, **Figure 25**).
7. Remove the right axle housing locknuts and bolts (B, **Figure 25**).
8. Remove the final drive unit locknuts (C, **Figure 25**), then remove the right axle housing (D).
9. Disconnect the breather tube (A, **Figure 26**) from the final drive unit fitting.
10. Remove the locknuts (B, **Figure 26**) and the final drive unit (C). Discard the locknuts.
11. Remove the spring (A, **Figure 27**) from the driveshaft.
12. Refer to the *Disassembly/Inspection/Assembly* procedure for further information.

Installation

1. Install the final drive unit O-ring (**Figure 28**), if removed. Lubricate the O-ring with grease.
2. Lubricate the spring with grease and install it into the end of the driveshaft (A, **Figure 27**).
3. Apply 5-8 g (0.18-0.28 oz.) of grease onto the driveshaft splines (B, **Figure 27**).
4. Install the final drive unit (C, **Figure 26**) onto the swing arm, being sure to engage it with the driveshaft and spring. Install new locknuts (B, **Figure 26**) finger-tight.
5. Reconnect the breather tube (A, **Figure 26**) onto the final drive unit.
6. Install the final drive unit O-ring (**Figure 29**), if removed. Lubricate the O-ring with grease.
7. Install the axle housing (D, **Figure 25**) onto the final drive unit (C) and swing arm (B) using new locknuts. Tighten the locknuts fingertight.
8. Tighten the right axle locknuts on the final drive unit (C, **Figure 25**) and swing arm (B) to 44 N•m (33 ft.-lb.).
9. Install the right shock absorber lower mounting bolt (A, **Figure 25**) and tighten to 44 N•m (33 ft.-lb.).

13

10. Attach the vent hose to the right axle housing hose clamp.

11. Install the skid plate. Tighten the mounting bolts to 32 N•m (24 ft.-lb.).

12. Install the rear axle as described in this chapter.

13. Refill the final drive unit with the recommended type and quantity of oil as described in Chapter Three.

Special Tools

The following special tools are recommended when servicing the final drive.

1. Pinion puller base (Honda part No. 07HMC-MM80011A).

2. Pinion holder (Honda part No. 07SMB-HM70200).

3. Puller shaft (Honda part No. 07931- ME4010B).

4. Special nut (Honda part No. 07931- HB3020A).

5. Locknut wrench (Honda part No. 07916-MB00002).

6. Pinion bearing ring compressor tool (Honda part No. 07YME-HN4010A).

Backlash Measurement/Adjustment

Perform gear backlash measurement before disassembly to determine gear wear and whether the internal shim thicknesses must be adjusted. Measuring gear backlash is also necessary after overhaul.

1. Install the pinion holder into the pinion joint and install the holder and drive unit into a soft-jaw vise as shown in **Figure 30** so any pinion end play is removed and the pinion cannot rotate.

2. Remove the oil fill cap.

3. Position a dial indicator so the tip rests against a gear tooth (**Figure 31**).

4. To determine the gear backlash, gently rotate the ring gear while reading the dial indicator. Refer to **Table 1** for the specified backlash.

5. Remove the dial indicator, then rotate the ring gear and take two additional backlash readings 120° from the original measuring point. If the difference between any two readings exceeds 0.2 mm (0.01 in.), note the following:

   a. The gear assembly is not square in the case, which may be due to the incorrect seating of a bearing.

   b. The housing may be deformed.

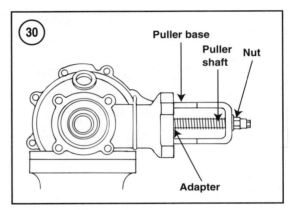

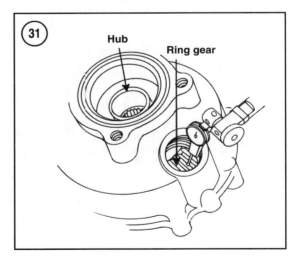

6. To correct the gear backlash, refer to **Figure 32** and note the following:

   a. If gear backlash is less than the desired specification, reduce the thickness of the left shim and increase the thickness of the right shim.

   b. If gear backlash is greater than the desired specification, reduce the thickness of the right

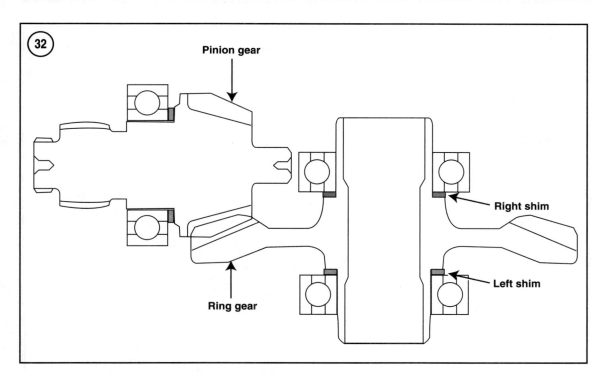

Figure 32

Pinion gear

Right shim

Left shim

Ring gear

shim and increase the thickness of the left shim.

NOTE
When adjusting shim thickness, adjust the sides equally. For instance, if the right shim is increased 0.10 mm (0.004 in.), decrease the left shim 0.10 mm (0.004 in.). Changing a shim thickness by 0.12 mm (0.005 in.) will change backlash 0.06 mm (0.002 in.).

Disassembly

Refer to **Figure 33**.

1. Remove the cover retaining bolts in a crossing pattern (A, **Figure 34**).

2. Insert a prying tool in the gaps between the gearcase and cover (B, **Figure 34**), and pry the cover off the gearcase.

3. Note the left-side shim on the ring gear (A, **Figure 35**). Remove the shim, label it and set it aside.

4. Remove the ring gear (B, **Figure 35**).

5. Note the right-side shim on the ring gear (**Figure 36**). Remove the shim, label it and set it aside.

6. Remove the pinion joint (**Figure 37**). Remove the O-ring on the pinion shaft (**Figure 38**).

7. Using a suitable seal puller, remove the oil seal (**Figure 39**).

8. Rotate the pinion shaft and check for noisy or rough pinion bearings.

NOTE
Cover the internal parts when unstaking the locknut in Step 9 to prevent the entry of metal debris.

9. Using a grinder or metal removal tool, remove the staked portion of the locknut (A, **Figure 40**).

10. Using the locknut wrench (or equivalent), remove the locknut (B, **Figure 40**).

11. Assemble the tools identified in the *Special Tools* section as shown in **Figure 41** and remove the pinion and bearing assembly.

Inspection

1. Clean, then inspect all components for excessive wear and damage. Carefully remove gasket material from the mating surfaces on the final drive cover and gearcase.

2. Remove the oil seals in the final drive gearcase and cover using a suitable seal removal tool. Install a new oil seal so the closed side is out (**Figure 42**).

13

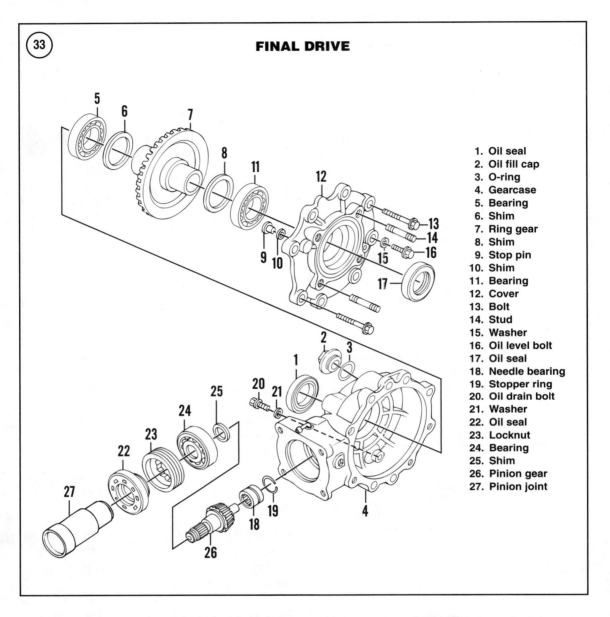

FINAL DRIVE

1. Oil seal
2. Oil fill cap
3. O-ring
4. Gearcase
5. Bearing
6. Shim
7. Ring gear
8. Shim
9. Stop pin
10. Shim
11. Bearing
12. Cover
13. Bolt
14. Stud
15. Washer
16. Oil level bolt
17. Oil seal
18. Needle bearing
19. Stopper ring
20. Oil drain bolt
21. Washer
22. Oil seal
23. Locknut
24. Bearing
25. Shim
26. Pinion gear
27. Pinion joint

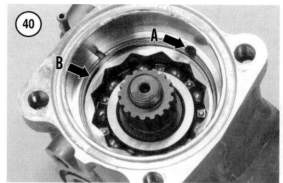

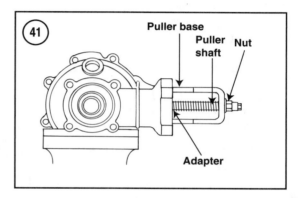

Puller base
Puller shaft
Nut
Adapter

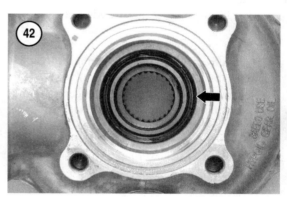

Oil seal

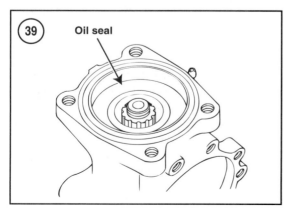

13

3. Turn the bearings (A, **Figure 43**) in the final drive gearcase and cover with a finger. The bearings should turn freely and without any sign of roughness, catching or excessive noise. Replace damaged bearings as described in Chapter One. The bearing must bottom in the gearcase or cover bore.

4. Inspect the ring gear and hub (**Figure 44**). Inspect the gear teeth, splines and seal running surfaces on the hub. Replace if excessively worn or damaged.

5. Inspect the pinion needle bearing (A, **Figure 45**) in the gearcase. If damaged, replace the bearing using the following procedure:

   a. Using needlenose pliers, extract the wire retainer ring (B, **Figure 45**) through the access hole. Rotate the ring so the end is accessible, pry out the end and pull out the ring.

CAUTION
Do not use a flame to heat the gearcase. It can warp the gearcase.

   b. Heat the gearcase in an oven to 80° C (176° F) and extract the bearing.

   c. Install a new wire ring into the groove on the outside of the new bearing.

   d. Install the bearing into the ring compressor tool.

   e. Place the compressor tool with the bearing into a freezer for at least 30 minutes.

   f. Heat the gearcase in an oven to 80° C (176° F).

   g. Position the compressor in the gearcase and drive the bearing into the gearcase. Only one blow should be required. Multiple blows may dislodge the wire ring, which requires the installation of a new ring and bearing. Make sure the wire ring is properly positioned as viewed in the access hole (B, **Figure 45**).

6. Inspect the pinion gear and bearing. If the bearing must be replaced, use the following procedure:

   a. Using a press or puller, remove the bearing from the pinion shaft.

   b. If only the bearing is being replaced, use the original shim on the pinion shaft. If the final drive cover or housing, ring and pinion gears or the side bearings are being replaced, install a 2.0 mm (0.079 in.) thick shim as a starting point for the gear position adjustments.

   c. Press or drive the new bearing onto the pinion shaft so the marked side of the bearing is toward the threaded end of the shaft.

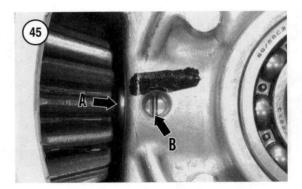

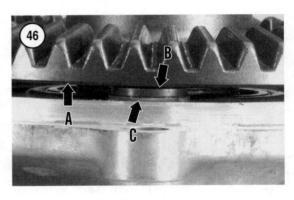

7. Check the ring gear side clearance using the following procedure:

   a. Install the ring gear and side shim into the cover.

   b. Using a feeler gauge, measure the clearance between the ring gear (A, **Figure 46**) and the stop pin (B). Refer to **Table 1** for the recommended clearance. The shim (C, **Figure 46**) under the stop pin is used to adjust the clearance.

   c. To adjust the clearance, heat the cover in an oven to 80° C (176° F). Remove the stop pin (B, **Figure 43**).

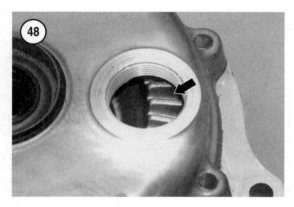

d. Install or remove shims as necessary to obtain the desired clearance.

e. Drive the stop pin into the cover and recheck the clearance.

Assembly

1. Install the bearings and oil seals as described in *Inspection*.

NOTE
Lubricate all moving parts with SAE 80 hypoid gear oil.

2. Install the pinion gear and bearing into the gearcase.

NOTE
The torque wrench attachment point on the Honda tool specified in Step 10 is offset. The actual nut tightening torque is 98 N•m (72 ft.-lb.).

3. Install the locknut (B, **Figure 40**). Using the locknut wrench (Honda part No. 07916-MB00002)

tighten the locknut to 89 N•m (66 ft.-lb.) as indicated on the torque wrench.

NOTE
Do not stake the locknut if performing the gear mesh pattern check in Step 3.

4. If the pinion, ring gear, bearings, gearcase or cover have been replaced, check gear mesh pattern using the following procedure:

a. Apply Prussian Blue or other gear marking compound onto the ring gear teeth.

b. Install the side shims (6 and 8, **Figure 33**) onto the ring gear, then install the ring gear into the gearcase.

c. Install the cover onto the gearcase.

NOTE
While tightening the cover bolts in substep d, rotate the pinion shaft.

d. Install the cover bolts. Install the two 10-mm bolts in the locations shown in **Figure 47**. Tighten the bolts evenly in a crossing pattern in several steps until the cover is seated on the gearcase. Tighten the 8-mm bolts to 25 N•m (19 ft.-lb.). Tighten the 10-mm bolts to 49 N•m (36 ft.-lb.).

e. Remove the oil fill cap.

f. Rotate the pinion shaft several rotations so a pattern is evident on the ring gear teeth. View the ring gear teeth through the gearcase oil fill hole (**Figure 48**).

g. Refer to the typical gear patterns in **Figure 49**. If the pinion is low, install a thinner shim (25, **Figure 33**). If the pinion is high, install a thicker shim. The pinion and bearing must be removed to replace the shim. Changing shim thickness 0.12 mm (0.005 in.) moves the contact pattern approximately 0.5-1.0 mm (0.02-0.04 in.).

h. If removed, reinstall the pinion gear and bearing as described in Step 1 and Step 12.

i. After obtaining a satisfactory gear contact pattern, be sure to check the gear backlash.

j. Remove the cover and continue with the final assembly procedure.

5. Stake the pinion locknut (A, **Figure 40**) into the notch in the gearcase.

6. Install the oil seal (**Figure 39**) so it is bottomed. Lubricate the oil seal lips with grease.

13

7. Install the side shims (6 and 8, **Figure 33**) onto the ring gear.

8. Install the ring gear into the gearcase.

9. Apply a liquid sealant, such as Yamabond No. 4, to the mating surface of the final drive cover, then install the cover onto the gearcase.

NOTE
While tightening the cover bolts in Step 10, rotate the pinion shaft.

10. Install the cover bolts. Install the two 10-mm bolts in the locations shown in **Figure 47**. Tighten the bolts evenly in a crossing pattern in several steps until the cover is seated on the gearcase. Tighten the 8-mm bolts to 25 N•m (19 ft.-lb.). Tighten the 10-mm bolts to 49 N•m (36 ft.-lb.).

11. Make sure the gears rotate freely without binding.

12. Apply grease to the O-ring and install it onto the pinion shaft (**Figure 38**).

13. If removed, install the circlip into the groove in the end of the pinion shaft (**Figure 50**).

14. Apply grease to the lips of the oil seal. Apply molybdenum disulfide grease to the pinion shaft splines, then install the pinion joint (**Figure 37**).

SWING ARM

All models are equipped with tapered roller bearings on both sides of the swing arm (**Figure 51**). Seals are installed on the outside of each bearing to prevent dirt and moisture from entering the bearings.

Special Tools

The Honda swing arm locknut wrench (part No. 07908-4690003 [A, **Figure 52**]) and a 17-mm hex socket (B) are required to remove and install the swing arm.

Removal

The swing arm can be removed with or without the final drive unit and rear axle installed in the swing arm. To service the swing arm, first remove the rear axle and the final drive unit as described in this chapter.

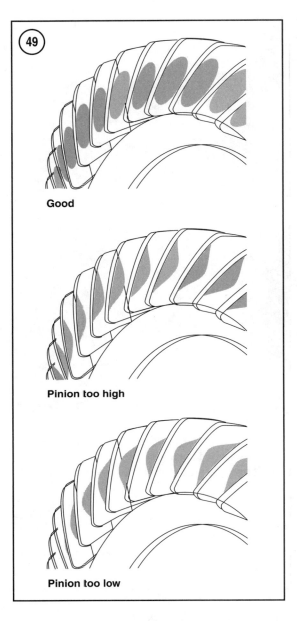

49

Good

Pinion too high

Pinion too low

50

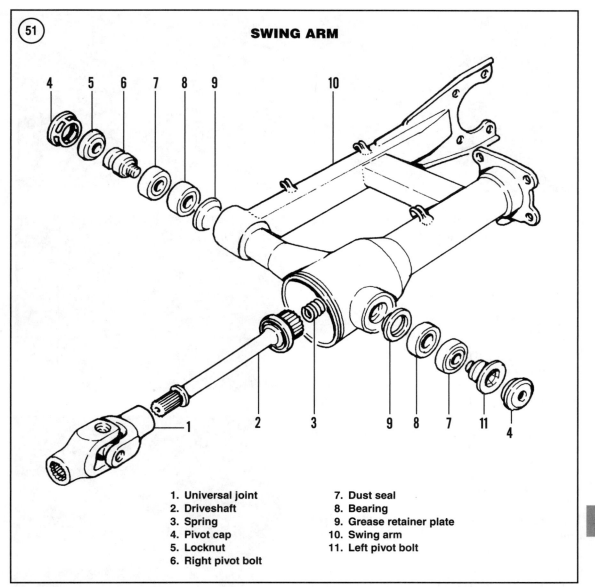

51 **SWING ARM**

1. Universal joint
2. Driveshaft
3. Spring
4. Pivot cap
5. Locknut
6. Right pivot bolt
7. Dust seal
8. Bearing
9. Grease retainer plate
10. Swing arm
11. Left pivot bolt

13

52

1. Remove the final drive unit as described in this chapter.

2. Grasp the rear end of the swing arm and try to move it from side to side in a horizontal arc. There should be no noticeable side play. If play is evident and the pivot bolts are tightened correctly, replace the swing arm bearings.

3. Loosen the swing arm boot clamp (A, **Figure 53**).

4. Remove the pivot cap (B, **Figure 53**) from each side of the swing arm.

5. Remove the breather tubes from the clamps on the swing arm.

6. Loosen and remove the right pivot locknut using the locknut wrench (**Figure 54**).

> *NOTE*
> *The bearings may fall out when removing the swing arm.*

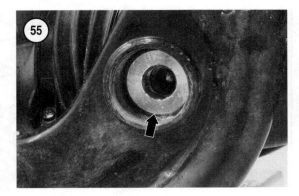

7. Remove the left pivot bolt using the 17-mm hex socket (**Figure 55**).

8. Remove the right pivot bolt (**Figure 56**) and rear swing arm (**Figure 57**).

9. If necessary, remove the universal joint and driveshaft if they did not come off with the swing arm.

10. If necessary, loosen the remaining clamp and remove the boot (C, **Figure 53**).

Swing Arm Inspection

1. Clean and dry the swing arm and the components.

2. Inspect the welded sections on the swing arm for cracks or other damage.

3. Remove the seal assembly (**Figure 58**). Inspect each bearing (A, **Figure 59**) for excessive wear, pitting or other damage. If necessary, replace the bearings as described in *Bearing Replacement* in this section.

4. Check that each grease retainer plate (B, **Figure 59**) fits tightly in the swing arm bore.

5. Inspect the pivot bolts (**Figure 60**) for excessive wear, thread damage or corrosion. Make sure the machined end on each pivot bolt is smooth. Replace if necessary.

6. Check the threaded holes in the frame (**Figure 61**) for corrosion or damage.

7. Replace the boot if damaged.

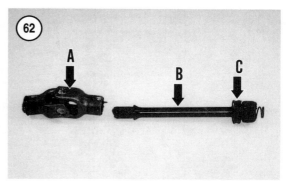

Driveshaft and Universal Joint Inspection

1. Check that the universal joint (A, **Figure 62**) pivots smoothly with no binding or roughness.

2. Inspect both universal joint spline ends for damage. If these splines are damaged, inspect the final drive case and engine output shaft splines for damage.

3. Check the driveshaft (B, **Figure 62**) for bending, spline damage or other damage.

4. Replace the dust seal (C, **Figure 62**) if leaking or damaged.

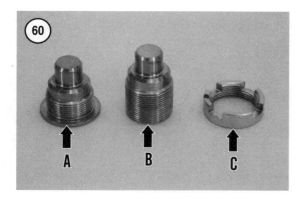

Bearing Replacement

Replace the left and right side bearings (**Figure 51**) at the same time. Note that the dust seal is attached to the roller bearing assembly and is not available separately. The following procedure describes removal of the inner grease retainer plate and the inner bearing race.

1. Support the swing arm in a vise with soft jaws.

NOTE
Removing the grease retainer should provide a sufficient gap behind the inner bearing race to insert the jaw flanges of a blind bearing puller.

2. Using a blunt tool that matches the indented diameter of the grease retainer (**Figure 63**), drive the grease retainer into the swing arm, then remove it.

3. Using a blind bearing puller (**Figure 64**) extract the inner bearing race.

4. Drive a new grease retainer into each side of the swing arm so the concave side is out.

5. Drive a new inner bearing race into each side of the swing arm. Make sure the race sits squarely in the swing arm bore.

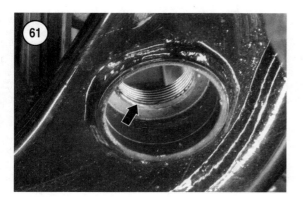

13

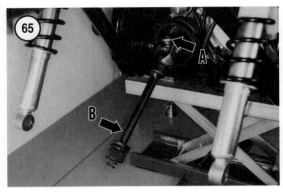

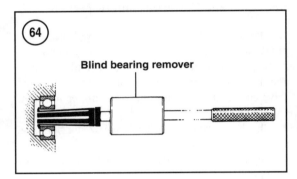

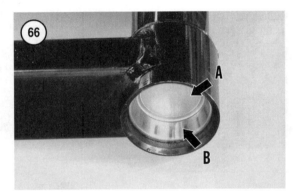

Blind bearing remover

Installation

1. If removed, install the boot (C, **Figure 53**) onto the engine with the tab marked HN0 facing up.
2. Lubricate the universal joint and driveshaft splines with molybdenum disulfide grease.
3. If removed, install the universal joint and drive-shaft as shown in **Figure 65**.

> *NOTE*
> *Refer to **Figure 66** to identify the pivot bolts when installing them in the following steps. Note that the left pivot bolt (A, **Figure 66**) is flanged.*

4. Install the swing arm (**Figure 57**) into the frame, while noting the following:
   a. Install the driveshaft through the swing arm.
   b. Install the right pivot bolt (**Figure 67**) and tighten fingertight.
   c. Install the left pivot bolt (**Figure 68**) and tighten fingertight.
   d. Move the swing arm up and down. Make sure it pivots smoothly with no binding or roughness.
5. Tighten the left pivot bolt (**Figure 68**) to 112 N•m (82 ft.-lb.).

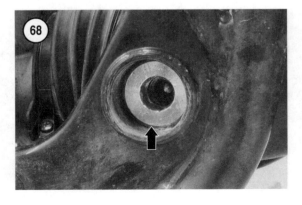

wrench, the torque value set on the torque wrench may not be the same amount of torque applied to the fastener. When using a horizontal adapter that lengthens the torque wrench, recalculate the torque reading. To do so, use the information supplied with the torque wrench or refer to **Torque Wrench** in Chapter One.

a. Hold the right pivot bolt with a 17-mm hex socket wrench (**Figure 71**).

b. Tighten the right pivot bolt locknut with the swing arm locknut wrench and a torque wrench (**Figure 71**) to 112 N•m (82 ft.-lb.).

10. Install the left and right side swing arm pivot caps (B, **Figure 53**).

11. Secure the breather tubes in the clamps on the swing arm.

12. Tighten the swing arm boot clamps (A, **Figure 53**).

13. Install the final drive unit as described in this chapter.

14. Install the rear axle as described in this chapter.

6. Tighten the right pivot bolt (**Figure 67**) to 10 N•m (88 in.-lb.).

7. Pivot the swing arm up and down several times to help seat the bearings.

8. Retighten the right pivot bolt (**Figure 67**) as specified in Step 6.

9. Install the right pivot bolt locknut (**Figure 69**) and tighten it with the swing arm locknut wrench (**Figure 70**) as follows:

NOTE
Because the swing arm locknut wrench can lengthen the torque

13

Table 1 REAR SUSPENSION AND FINAL DRIVE SPECIFICATIONS

Gear backlash	0.05-0.25 mm (0.002-0.010 in.)
Service limit	0.4 mm (0.016 in.)
Rear axle runout service limit	3.0 mm (0.12 in.)
Rear damper type	Double tube
Rear suspension type	Swing arm
Rear wheel travel	170 mm (6.69 in.)
Ring gear stop pin clearance	0.3-0.6 mm (0.01-0.02 in.)

Table 2 REAR DRIVE TORQUE SPECIFICATIONS

	N•m	in.-lb.	ft.-lb.
Axle housing mounting nut (both sides)	44	–	33
Gearcase bolts			
8 mm	25	–	19
10 mm	49	–	36
Gearcase mounting bolts			
Front mounting bolt	54	–	40
Side mounting bolt	54	–	40
Pinion locknut*	89	–	66
Rear wheel hub nut	137	–	101
Rear shock absorber nuts			
Upper	40	–	30
Lower	44	–	33
Skid plate mounting bolt	32	–	24
Swing arm			
Left pivot bolt	112	–	82
Right pivot bolt	10	88	–
Right pivot bolt locknut	112	–	82
Wheel nuts	65	–	48

*Torque wrench reading using Honda tool.

BRAKES

This chapter describes service procedures for the front and rear brake systems.

The front brakes are actuated by the hand lever on the right side of the handlebar. The rear brake is actuated by the brake pedal and left side brake lever. The left side brake lever is also equipped with a lock, which allows it to be used as a parking brake.

Brake specifications are listed in **Table 1** and **Table 2**. **Tables 1-3** are located at the end of this chapter.

BRAKE SERVICE

When working on hydraulic brake systems, the work area and tools must be clean. Place the parts on clean lint-free cloths and wipe all oil and other chemical residues off of the tools. Tiny particles of dirt in the master cylinder or wheel cylinders can damage the components. If there is any doubt whether the brake components can be serviced so they operate properly, take the job to a Honda dealership.

Note the following when servicing the front drum brake:

1. When adding brake fluid, use only a brake fluid clearly marked DOT 3 or DOT 4 and from a sealed container. Other types may vaporize and cause brake failure. Try to use the same brand name. Before intermixing brake fluid, make sure the two fluids are compatible. Brake fluid draws moisture, which greatly reduces the ability to perform correctly. It is a good idea to purchase brake fluid in small containers and discard any small left-over quantities properly. Do not store a container of brake fluid with less than 1/4 of the fluid remaining because this small amount draws moisture rapidly.

> *CAUTION*
> *Do not intermix silicone based (DOT 5) brake fluid because it can cause brake component damage leading to brake system failure.*

> *CAUTION*
> *Never reuse brake fluid, such as fluid expelled during brake bleeding. Contaminated brake fluid can cause brake failure. Dispose of used brake fluid according to local or regulations.*

2. Do not allow brake fluid to contact any plastic parts or painted surfaces because damage results.
3. Always keep the master cylinder reservoir and spare cans of brake fluid closed to prevent dust or moisture from entering. This would cause brake fluid contamination and brake problems.
4. Use only new DOT 3 or DOT 4 brake fluid to wash parts. Never clean any internal brake components with solvent or any other petroleum base

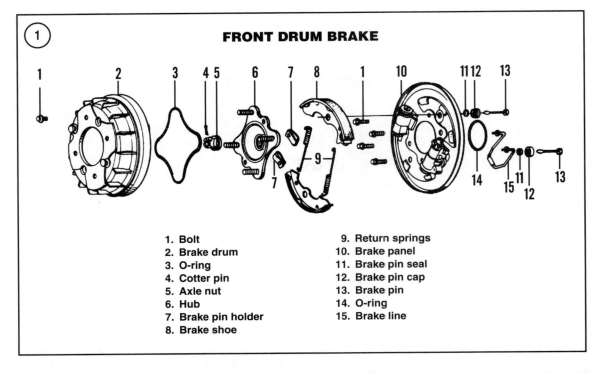

FRONT DRUM BRAKE

1. Bolt
2. Brake drum
3. O-ring
4. Cotter pin
5. Axle nut
6. Hub
7. Brake pin holder
8. Brake shoe
9. Return springs
10. Brake panel
11. Brake pin seal
12. Brake pin cap
13. Brake pin
14. O-ring
15. Brake line

cleaners because these cleaners cause the rubber components to swell, causing distorted, damaged parts.

5. Whenever any component has been removed from the brake system, the system is considered opened and must be bled to remove air bubbles. Also, if the brake feels spongy, this usually means air bubbles are in the system and it must be bled. Refer to *Brake Bleeding* in this chapter.

> *CAUTION*
> *Never reuse brake fluid. Contaminated brake fluid can cause brake failure. Dispose of brake fluid according to local regulations.*

> *WARNING*
> *When working on the brake system, never blow off brake components or use compressed air. Do not inhale any airborne brake dust because it may contain asbestos, which can cause lung injury and cancer. As an added precaution, wear an OSHA approved filtering face mask and thoroughly wash hands and forearms with warm water and soap after completing any brake work.*

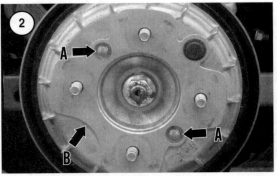

FRONT BRAKE DRUM

The front brake drum can be removed without having to remove the front hub.

Removal/Installation

Refer to **Figure 1**.

> *NOTE*
> *To remove the brake drum and front hub at the same time, refer to **Front Hub** in Chapter Eleven.*

1. Remove the front wheels (Chapter Ten).

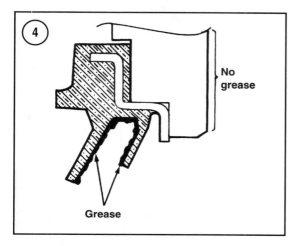

2. Remove the bolts (A, **Figure 2**) and the front brake drum (B).

3. Remove the O-ring (A, **Figure 3**), if necessary.

4. Inspect the brake drum and service the waterproof seal as described in this section.

5. Install the O-ring (A, **Figure 3**), if removed.

6. Lubricate the waterproof seal (B, **Figure 3**) with a multipurpose grease (NLGI No. 3) as shown in

Figure 4. If a new waterproof seal was installed, refer to the *Brake Drum Waterproof Seal Inspection and Replacement* for the correct amount of grease to apply to the seal.

> *WARNING*
> *Do not get grease on the inner surface of the brake drum where the brake shoe linings make contact because this contaminates the lining surfaces and reduces braking performance. If grease does get onto the brake drum, thoroughly clean off all grease residue with lacquer thinner.*

7. Install the brake drum (B, **Figure 2**) over the wheel hub and brake linings.

8. Install the brake drum mounting bolts (A, **Figure 2**) and tighten to 10 N•m (88 in.-lb.).

9. Install the front wheels (Chapter Eleven).

Brake Drum Inspection

1. Inspect the brake drum (**Figure 3**) for cracks, excessive wear or other damage.

2. Replace the O-ring (A, **Figure 3**) if excessively worn or damaged.

3. Inspect and service the waterproof seal (B, **Figure 3**) as described later in this section.

4. Check the brake drum contact surface for grease residue, scoring, cracks or other damage.

> *WARNING*
> *If oil or grease is on the drum surface, clean it off with a clean rag soaked in lacquer thinner. Do not use any solvent that may leave an oil residue. Keep the cleaning solution away from the waterproof seal.*

5. Measure the brake drum inside diameter (**Figure 5**) and compare to the service limit in **Table 1**. Measure at several points around the brake drum. Replace the brake drum if out of specification.

**Brake Drum Waterproof Seal
Inspection and Replacement**

The brake drum waterproof seal keeps water out of the brake drum. Inspect this seal and replace when necessary to prevent excessive brake drum and lining wear from water and other debris.

14

1. Remove the brake drum as described in this section.

2. Inspect the waterproof seal (B, **Figure 3**) for excessive wear, damage, hardness or deterioration.

3. Measure the waterproof seal lip length (**Figure 6**). Measure at several different points around the seal. Refer to **Table 1** for service specifications. Replace the seal if out of specification.

> *NOTE*
> *The following dimensions must be calculated because the inner portion of the waterproof seal cannot be seen when the seal is installed in the brake drum.*

4. Perform the following:
   a. Measure the brake drum and seal as shown in **Figure 7**.
   b. Calculate the clearance A and B between the brake drum and the seal. A = C-D and B = F - E.
   c. When the new waterproof seal is installed correctly, dimension A equals B.

5. Apply clean water to all surfaces of the new waterproof seal (**Figure 8**) and to the surface plate.

> *CAUTION*
> *The brake drum must be backed up with a round steel plate to prevent it from being warped or damaged. Place a steel plate about 140 mm (5.5 in.) in diameter and more than 10 mm (0.4 in.) thick on the brake drum during Step 6.*

> *CAUTION*
> *Do not exert too much pressure on the seal during installation or the seal lip may be damaged as shown in **Figure 9**.*

6. Place the new seal on a clean surface plate, then slowly and squarely press the brake drum (and steel backup plate) onto the new seal. Continue to press on the brake drum and frequently check the clearance between the seal and the drum. Refer to the dimensions calculated in Step 4. This dimension must be the same all around the perimeter of the brake drum. If the clearance is not equal, the seal either does not seal properly or wears prematurely.

7. After the seal has been installed correctly with the uniform clearance all around the perimeter, wipe all water from the seal with a lint-free cloth.

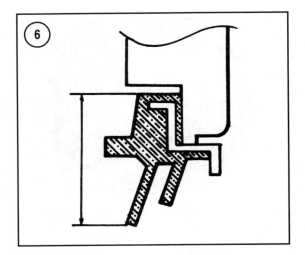

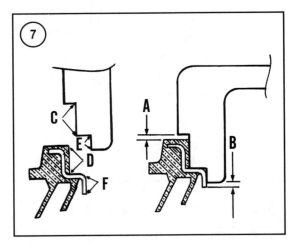

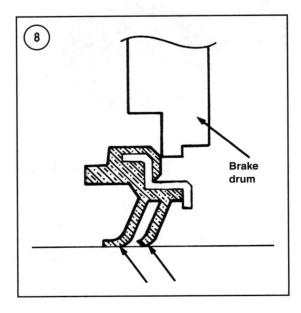

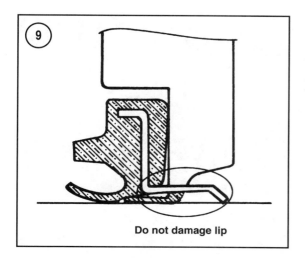

Do not damage lip

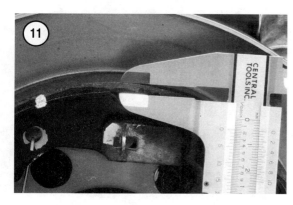

WARNING
Do not get grease on the inner surface of the brake drum where the brake shoe linings make contact because this contaminates the lining surfaces and reduces braking performance. If grease does get onto the brake drum, thoroughly clean off all grease residue with lacquer thinner.

8. Uniformly pack the sealing lip cavity (**Figure 10**) with multipurpose grease (NLGI No. 3) as shown in **Figure 4**. Apply 14-16 grams (0.5-0.6 oz.) of grease.

9. Install the brake drum as described in this chapter.

FRONT BRAKE SHOE REPLACEMENT

There is no recommended mileage interval for changing the front brake shoes. Lining wear depends on riding habits and conditions.

NOTE
Service one set of brake shoes at a time. Leave the other set intact as a reference for the proper location of the brake components.

Refer to **Figure 1**.

1. Remove the brake drum as described in this chapter.

2. Measure the brake shoe lining thickness with a vernier caliper (**Figure 11**) and compare to the specifications in **Table 1**. Replace the brake shoes if out of specification.

NOTE
If brake shoe replacement is necessary, continue with Step 3.

3. Remove the wheel hub as described in Chapter Eleven.

4. Rotate the brake pins 90° (**Figure 12**) and remove the brake pin holders (**Figure 13**).

NOTE
If the brake shoes are going to be reused, mark them so they can be reinstalled in their original positions.

14

5. Remove the brake shoes and springs (**Figure 14**).

6. If necessary, remove the brake pins (A, **Figure 15**), seals and caps.

7. Inspect the return springs for damaged or stretched coils. Replace both return springs at the same time.

8. Inspect the brake pins and pin holders and replace if excessively worn or damaged.

9. Inspect the wheel cylinders (B, **Figure 15**) for damaged boots or leaking brake fluid. If necessary, service the wheel cylinders as described in this chapter.

CAUTION
Silicone brake grease, used in the following steps, is not the same as a silicone sealant (RTV) used on engine gaskets. Make sure the lubricant is specified for brake use. For example, Permatex Ultra Disc Brake Caliper Lube (part No. 20356) is designed specifically for use on brake systems.

WARNING
Do not apply too much grease because it may fall onto the brake linings and cause brake slippage.

10. Apply a light coat of silicone brake grease to the brake shoe locating notches in the wheel cylinders and the brake shoe anchor (A, **Figure 16**).

11. Apply a light coat of silicone brake grease to the raised pads on the backside of the brake shoes metal plates where the brake shoes ride on the brake panel. Avoid getting any grease on the brake linings.

NOTE
Install the original brake shoes in their original mounting positions.

12. Install the new brake shoes and attach the springs as shown in **Figure 16**. Make sure to offset the spring coils as shown in B, **Figure 16**. Install the brake shoes with their flatter edges facing toward the wheel cylinders.

13. Install the upper brake shoe into the upper wheel cylinder notches (**Figure 17**).

14. Hold the upper brake shoe in place, then pull on the lower brake shoe and install it into the lower wheel cylinder notches (**Figure 17**). If a spring popped out of the shoe slot, reinstall it with a pair of locking pliers. Check that both spring ends are

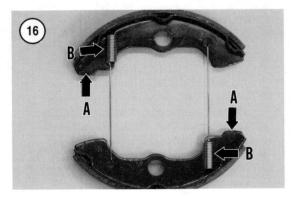

hooked securely into the brake shoe holes and slots (**Figure 17**).

15. Install the brake pins and holders as follows:
   a. Insert the pins, seals and cap into the brake panel.
   b. Insert a flat blade screwdriver behind the wheel cylinder to hold the pin in place.
   c. Install the holder (**Figure 13**) and secure it with a pair of pliers.
   d. While holding the pin in place with a screwdriver, compress the holder (**Figure 13**) with the pliers, then rotate the pin 90° (**Figure 12**) to lock the pin in place.
   e. Remove the pliers and screwdriver and repeat for the other retainer and pin assembly.
   f. Make sure both retainers and pins are properly locked in place. Refer to **Figure 18**.

16. Repeat the preceding steps to replace the brake shoes on the opposite side of the ATV.

17. Install the front brake drums as described in this chapter.

18. Adjust the brake shoes as described in Chapter Three.

FRONT BRAKE PANEL

Refer to **Figure 1**.

Warp Inspection

Before removing the brake panel, check it for warp as follows. A dial indicator and magnetic stand are required.

1. Remove the brake drum and brake shoes as described in this chapter.

2. Clean off any grease from the brake panel where the brake drum seal rides.

3. Install a metal plate (A, **Figure 19**) onto the wheel hub and secure it with a wheel nut. This plate provides a mounting location for the magnetic stand.

4. Attach a dial indicator and magnetic stand (B, **Figure 19**) to the metal plate and place the pointer in the area where the brake drum seal rides (**Figure 19**).

5. Slowly rotate the wheel hub and check for warpage. A variation of 0.4 mm (0.02 in.) or more indicates the brake panel is warped and must be replaced.

6. Remove the dial indicator and metal plate.

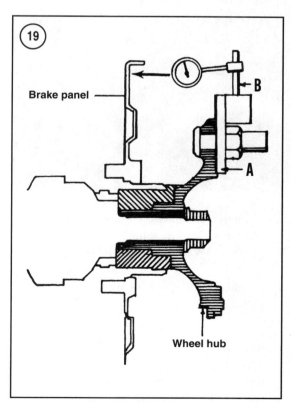

Brake panel

B

A

Wheel hub

14

Removal/Installation

1. Drain the brake fluid as described in this chapter.
2. Remove the brake shoes as described in this section.
3. Remove the brake hose banjo bolt and sealing washers (A, **Figure 20**) at the back of the brake panel. Place the loose end of the brake hose in a thick plastic bag or container to prevent the entry of dirt and foreign matter and to prevent brake fluid from leaking out onto the suspension and brake components. Tie the brake hose up out of the way.

> *CAUTION*
> *Wash brake fluid off any painted or plated surfaces immediately because it damages the finish. Use soapy water and rinse completely.*

4. Disconnect the vent hose (B, **Figure 20**) from the brake panel.
5. Remove the bolts (**Figure 21**) that hold the brake panel to the steering knuckle and remove the brake panel. Discard the bolts.
6. Remove the O-ring (**Figure 22**) from the steering knuckle.
7. Service the wheel cylinders as described in this chapter.
8. Perform the *Inspection* procedure in this section.
9. Install the brake panel by reversing these removal steps, plus the following:

   a. Install a new O-ring over the steering knuckle (**Figure 22**).

> *CAUTION*
> *Always install new brake panel mounting bolts. These bolts are treated with a special dry-coated material that is necessary for waterproofing.*

   b. Install the brake panel and new mounting bolts. Tighten the brake panel mounting bolts (**Figure 21**) to 29 N•m (22 ft.-lb.).
   c. Position the brake hose end between the stoppers on the backside of the brake panel. Refer to C, **Figure 20**, typical.
   d. Install a new sealing washer on each side of the brake hose. Tighten the banjo bolt to 34 N•m (25 ft.-lb.).

10. Repeat to service the other brake panel assembly.

11. Turn the handlebar from side to side while observing the movement of the brake and vent hoses. Make sure these parts are not kinked or pulled incorrectly.

12. Bleed the front brakes as described in this chapter.

Inspection

1. Remove all sealer residue from the brake panel and steering knuckle mounting surfaces.

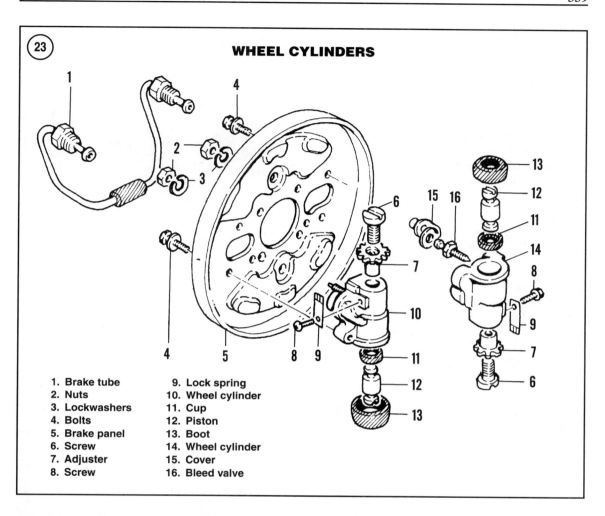

WHEEL CYLINDERS

1. Brake tube
2. Nuts
3. Lockwashers
4. Bolts
5. Brake panel
6. Screw
7. Adjuster
8. Screw
9. Lock spring
10. Wheel cylinder
11. Cup
12. Piston
13. Boot
14. Wheel cylinder
15. Cover
16. Bleed valve

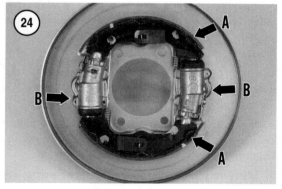

2. Wipe off all old grease from all of the brake panel parts.

3. Inspect the brake panel for damage.

4. Inspect the metal wheel cylinder brake tube. If necessary, replace as described in the *Wheel Cylinders* in this chapter.

WHEEL CYLINDERS

Refer to **Figure 23**.

Removal

1. Remove the brake panel from the steering knuckle as described in this chapter.

2. If not already removed, remove the brake shoes (A, **Figure 24**).

> *CAUTION*
> *Do not bend the brake tube when removing it in Step 3. Doing so can damage the brake tube and cause misalignment during installation.*

3. Loosen the brake tube fittings (A, **Figure 25**) and remove the brake tube (B). Store the brake tube

in a sealed plastic bag.

> *NOTE*
> *Identify each wheel cylinder so it can
> be installed in the original mounting
> position.*

4. Remove the wheel cylinder mounting nuts, bolts
and washers (C, **Figure 25**) and remove the wheel
cylinder. If the wheel cylinder is not going to be serviced, store it in a sealed plastic bag until installation.

5. Repeat Step 4 for the opposite wheel cylinder.

6. If necessary, service the wheel cylinders as described in this chapter.

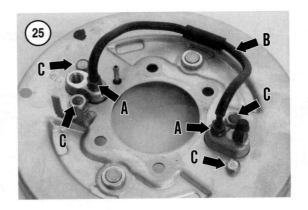

Disassembly

Refer to **Figure 23**.

1. Remove the screw, lockspring and adjuster from
the cylinder body.

2. Remove the bleed screw and cover.

3. Remove the boot from the groove in the piston
and cylinder.

4. Push the piston and piston cup out of the cylinder bore.

5. Remove the screw from the adjuster body.

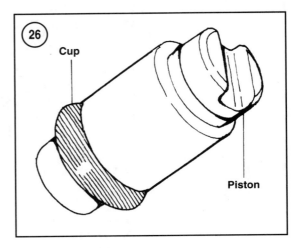

Inspection

Wheel cylinder

Refer to **Table 1** when inspecting and measuring
the wheel cylinder components in this section. Replace parts that are out of specification or show
damage.

> *NOTE*
> *It is a good idea to replace the boots
> and piston cups whenever the wheel
> cylinders are disassembled, even
> though they might not appear worn.*

1. Remove all sealer residue from the wheel cylinders where they mount on the brake panel.

2. Clean all the parts except the outer boot with
DOT 3 or DOT 4 brake fluid.

3. Clean the cylinder passages with compressed air.

4. Check the boot for damage.

5. Check the piston cup for excessive wear, cracks
or other damage.

6. Check the cylinder bore for deep pits, scratches
and other damage. Check especially the part of the
cylinder bore that contacts the piston cup. If the cylinder bore is excessively damaged, replace the
wheel cylinder assembly. The wheel cylinder housing is not available separately.

7. Check the piston for scratches, flat spots, cracks
or other damage. If the damage is excessive, replace
the piston.

8. Measure the wheel cylinder inside diameter and
compare to the service specification. If out of specification, replace the wheel cylinder assembly.

9. Measure the piston outside diameter and compare to the service specification. Replace the piston
if out of specification.

10. Inspect the lockspring for cracks, fatigue or
other damage.

11. Inspect the screw and adjuster body for corrosion. Check the adjuster body for excessively worn
or damaged adjuster arms.

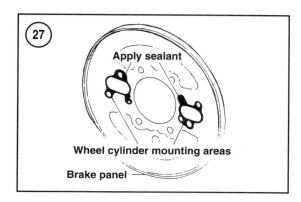

Apply sealant

Wheel cylinder mounting areas

Brake panel

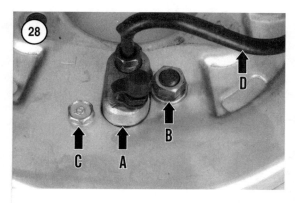

Brake panel

1. Remove all sealer residue from the brake panel where the wheel cylinders mount.
2. Check the brake panel for warpage, cracks or other damage. Replace if necessary.

Brake tube

1. Clean the brake tube with compressed air.
2. Inspect the brake tube for bending, cracks and corrosion. Check the two end nuts for damage.
3. Check the tube's flared ends for cracks or other damage. If these ends are damaged, do not repair them because this may distort or burr the ends and cause the tube to leak. If the tube is damaged in any way, replace it.
4. Store the brake tube in a sealed plastic bag until reassembly.

Assembly

Use new DOT 3 or DOT 4 brake fluid when brake fluid is called out in the following steps. Do not use DOT 5 (silicone based) brake fluid.

CAUTION
Do not allow grease or oil to contact the boots or piston cups when assembling the wheel cylinders. Grease or oil destroys the rubber parts.

1. When installing a new piston cup, perform the following:
   a. Soak the new piston cup in brake fluid for approximately 5-10 minutes.
   b. Lubricate the piston with brake fluid.
   c. Install the piston cup over the piston and seat it into the groove as shown in **Figure 26**.
2. Coat the piston cup, piston and cylinder bore with brake fluid.
3. Install the piston into the cylinder as shown in **Figure 23**. Make sure the piston cup does not turn inside out. The cup should be compressed when installed inside the cylinder.
4. Install a new boot over the piston. Make sure it is properly seated in the piston and cylinder body grooves.
5. Apply a light coat of silicone brake grease onto the screw threads, then install the screw into the adjuster body.
6. Apply silicone brake grease onto the adjuster threads and install the adjuster into the wheel cylinder.

Installation

1. Apply sealant onto the brake panel where the wheel cylinders mount. Refer to **Figure 27**.
2. Install the wheel cylinders as follows:
   a. Install the wheel cylinders (A, **Figure 28**) in their original mounting positions. Refer to **Figure 23**.
   b. Secure each wheel cylinder with the nut, lockwasher (B, **Figure 28**) and bolt (C).
   c. Tighten the wheel cylinder 8-mm nut (B, **Figure 28**) to 17 N•m (150 in.-lb.) and the 6-mm bolt (C) to 8 N•m (71 in.-lb.).
3. Repeat Step 2 to install the other wheel cylinder.
4. Install the brake tube (D, **Figure 28**) onto the wheel cylinders, then thread the nuts into the wheel cylinders and tighten to 16 N•m (142 in.-lb.).
5. Install the brake panel as described in this chapter.

14

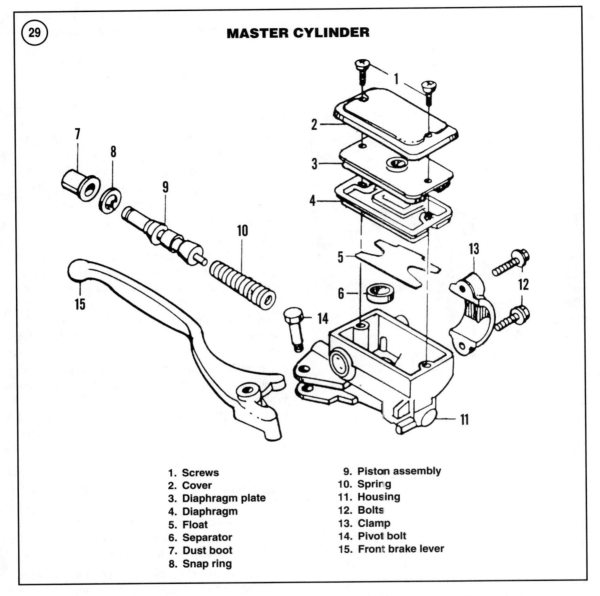

29. MASTER CYLINDER

1. Screws
2. Cover
3. Diaphragm plate
4. Diaphragm
5. Float
6. Separator
7. Dust boot
8. Snap ring
9. Piston assembly
10. Spring
11. Housing
12. Bolts
13. Clamp
14. Pivot bolt
15. Front brake lever

FRONT MASTER CYLINDER

Refer to **Figure 29**.

Removal/Installation

1. Park the ATV on level ground and set the parking brake.

2. Remove the dust boot (A, **Figure 30**) and disconnect the brake switch connectors (B).

3. Drain the brake fluid as described in this chapter.

4. Cover the area under the master cylinder to prevent brake fluid from damaging any component it might contact.

> *CAUTION*
> *If brake fluid should contact any surface, wash the area immediately with soapy water and rinse completely. Brake fluid damages plastic, painted and plated surfaces.*

5. Remove the banjo bolt (C, **Figure 30**) and the sealing washers securing the upper brake hose to

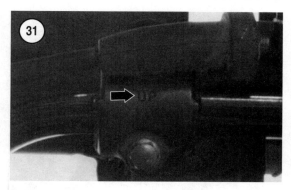

UP mark and arrow facing up (**Figure 31**). Tighten the upper master cylinder mounting bolt to 12 N•m (106 in.-lb.).

10. Turn the master cylinder to align the clamp surfaces with the punch mark on the handlebar (**Figure 32**), then tighten the lower master cylinder mounting bolt (**Figure 31**) to 12 N•m (106 in.-lb.).

11. Connect the brake hose onto the master cylinder using the banjo bolt and two new washers. Install a washer on each side of the hose fitting. Tighten the banjo bolt (C, **Figure 30**) to 34 N•m (25 ft.-lb.).

12. Refill the master cylinder with DOT 3 or DOT 4 brake fluid and bleed the brake as described in this chapter.

13. Connect the brake switch connectors (B, **Figure 30**) and install the dust boot (A).

> *WARNING*
> *Do not ride the ATV until the front brakes operate properly. Make sure the brake lever travel is not excessive and the lever does not feel spongy. If either condition occurs, repeat the bleeding operation.*

Disassembly

Refer to **Figure 29**.

1. Remove the master cylinder as described in this chapter.

2. Refer to **Figure 33** and remove the brake switch retaining screw and switch.

3. Refer to **Figure 29** and **Figure 33** and remove the nut, washer, sub-arm, spring, collar and washer.

4. Remove the pivot bolt and front brake lever.

5. Remove the screws, top cover, diaphragm plate, diaphragm and float.

6. Pour out any brake fluid and discard it properly. Never reuse brake fluid.

7. Remove the dust boot (**Figure 34**) from the end of the piston and piston bore.

> *WARNING*
> *If brake fluid leaks from the piston bore, the piston cups are worn or damaged. Replace the piston assembly.*

> *NOTE*
> *To hold the master cylinder when removing and installing the snap ring,*

the master cylinder. Place the loose end of the brake hose in a plastic bag to prevent the entry of dirt and to prevent residual brake fluid from leaking out onto the frame components. Tie the brake hose to the handlebar.

6. Unbolt and remove the master cylinder and the clamp (**Figure 31**) from the handlebar.

7. If necessary, service the master cylinder as described in this chapter.

8. Clean the handlebar, master cylinder and clamp mating surfaces.

9. Install the master cylinder, clamp and mounting bolts onto the handlebar. Install the clamp with the

14

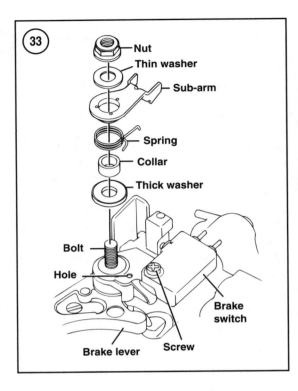

*thread a bolt with a nut into the master cylinder. Tighten the nut against the master cylinder to lock the bolt in place, then clamp the bolt and nut in a vise as shown in **Figure 35**.*

8. Compress the piston and remove the snap ring (**Figure 36**) from the bore groove.

9. Remove the piston and spring assembly (**Figure 37**).

10. Remove the oil seal from inside the reservoir.

Inspection

Refer to **Table 1** when inspecting and measuring the front master cylinder (**Figure 29**) components in this section. Replace parts that are out of specification or damaged.

1. Clean the diaphragm, reservoir housing (inside) and piston assembly with new brake fluid. Place the parts on a clean lint-free cloth.

NOTE
*Do not remove the secondary cup (C, **Figure 38**) from the piston when inspecting it in Step 2. If the secondary cup is damaged, replace the entire*

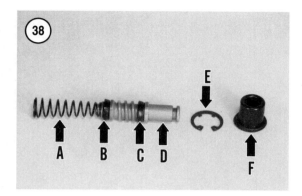

piston assembly. Leave the secondary cup in place for reference when installing the new cup onto the new piston.

2. Inspect the piston assembly (**Figure 38**) for:
   a. Broken, distorted or collapsed piston return spring (A, **Figure 38**).
   b. Worn, cracked, damaged or swollen primary (B, **Figure 38**) and secondary cup (C).
   c. Scratched, scored or damaged piston (D, **Figure 38**).
   d. If any of these parts are worn or damaged, replace the piston assembly. Individual parts are not available separately from the manufacturer.

3. Inspect the snap ring (E, **Figure 38**) for corrosion, rust, weakness or other damage. Replace if necessary.

4. Inspect the boot (F, **Figure 38**) and replace if damaged.

5. Measure the piston outside diameter (**Figure 39**) and replace if out of specification.

6. Inspect the cylinder bore (**Figure 40**) for scratches, pitting, excessive wear, corrosion or other damage. Do not hone the bore to remove nicks, scratches or other damage.

7. Measure the cylinder bore diameter (**Figure 41**). Replace the master cylinder assembly if the bore diameter is out of specification.

8. Check for plugged supply and relief ports in the master cylinder. Clean with compressed air.

> *CAUTION*
> *A plugged relief port causes the brake linings to drag on the drum.*

9. Check the entire master cylinder body for wear or damage.

10. Check the cover and diaphragm assembly for damage.

11. Inspect the banjo bolt threads in the master cylinder body bore. Repair minor damage with the correct size metric tap, or replace the master cylinder assembly.

12. Check the hand lever pivot holes and mounting lugs on the master cylinder body for elongation or cracks. If damaged, replace the master cylinder assembly.

13. Inspect the hand lever and pivot bolt and replace if damaged.

14

Assembly

1. Use new DOT 3 or DOT 4 brake fluid when brake fluid is called for in the following steps. Do not use DOT 5 (silicone based) brake fluid.

2A. When installing a new piston assembly, perform the following:
   a. Soak the new secondary cup in new brake fluid for at least 15 minutes to make it pliable.
   b. Lubricate the new piston with brake fluid.
   c. After soaking the secondary cup in brake fluid, install it over the piston as shown in C, **Figure 38**.
   d. Install the new primary cup onto the end of the new spring as shown in B, **Figure 38**.

2B. If reusing the original piston, lubricate the piston assembly with brake fluid.

> *CAUTION*
> *When installing the piston assembly into the master cylinder bore, do not allow the cups to turn inside out because this damages them and allows brake fluid to leak out of the bore.*

3. Install the spring and piston assembly into the master cylinder bore in the direction shown in **Figure 37**. Check that the cups did not turn inside out.

4. Push the piston in and hold it in place, then install the snap ring (**Figure 36**) into the cylinder bore groove. Install the snap ring with the flat edge facing out (away from the piston). Check that the snap ring is fully seated in the bore groove. Push and release the piston a few times. It should move smoothly and return under spring pressure.

5. Install the dust boot into the end of the cylinder bore. Seat the large boot end against the snap ring. Seat the small boot end into the groove in the end of the piston (**Figure 42**). Make sure it is correctly seated in the cylinder bore (**Figure 34**).

6. Refer to **Figure 29** and **Figure 33** and install the brake lever components and brake switch while noting the following:
   a. Install the brake lever and the pivot bolt. Tighten the pivot bolt to 1 N•m (8.8 in.-lb.). Operate the brake lever, making sure it moves smoothly.
   b. Install the straight spring end into the hole in the lever (**Figure 33**).
   c. Tighten the nut to 6 N•m (53 in.-lb.). Operate the brake lever and make sure it moves smoothly with no roughness or binding.

7. Temporarily install the master cylinder cover assembly.

8. Install the master cylinder as described in this chapter.

BRAKE FLUID DRAINING

The brake fluid should be drained before disconnecting any of the front brake hoses or lines. To drain the front brake system, obtain an empty bottle, a length of clear hose that fits tightly onto the wheel cylinder bleed valve and a wrench to open and close

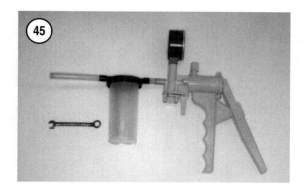

the bleed valve (**Figure 43** and **Figure 44**). A vacuum pump (**Figure 45**) can also be used to drain the brake system.

1. Turn the handlebar so the front master cylinder is level with the ground.

2. Remove the reservoir cover and diaphragm assembly.

3. Connect a hose to one of the wheel cylinder bleed valves. Insert the other end of the hose into a clean bottle. Refer to **Figure 44**.

4. Loosen the bleed valve and pump the brake lever to drain part of the brake system.

5. Close the bleed valve when fluid stops flowing through the valve.

6. Repeat Steps 4-6 for the other side. Because air has entered the brake lines, not all of the brake fluid drains out.

> *CAUTION*
> *Because some residual brake fluid remains in the lines, be careful when disconnecting and removing the brake hoses in Step 9.*

7. Reinstall the diaphragm assembly and reservoir cover.

8. Perform the required service to the front brake system as described in this chapter.

9. After servicing the brake system, bleed the front brakes as described in this chapter.

BRAKE BLEEDING

Bleed the front brakes when they feel spongy, after repairing a leak or replacing parts in the system or when replacing the brake fluid.

This section describes two methods for bleeding the brake system. The first requires a vacuum pump (**Figure 45**), and the second is with a container and a piece of clear tubing (**Figure 43**).

1. Remove the dust cap from the bleed valve on the wheel cylinder.

2A. If using a vacuum pump, assemble the pump by following the manufacturer's instructions. Connect the vacuum pump hose to the wheel cylinder bleed valve.

2B. If a vacuum pump is not being used, perform the following:

    a. Connect a piece of clear tubing onto the bleed valve (**Figure 44**).

    b. Insert the other end of the tube into a container partially filled with new brake fluid.

    c. Tie the tube in place so it cannot slip out of the container.

3. Clean the master cylinder cover of all dirt and foreign matter.

4. Turn the front wheels so the master cylinder is level with the ground.

5. Cover the area under the master cylinder with a heavy cloth to protect the parts from the accidental spilling of brake fluid.

> *CAUTION*
> *Wash spilled brake fluid from any plastic, painted or plated surface immediately because it damages the finish. Clean with soapy water and rinse completely.*

6. Unscrew and remove the master cylinder cover (**Figure 46**) and diaphragm assembly.

7. Fill the master cylinder with DOT 3 or DOT 4 brake fluid.

> *WARNING*
> *Use DOT 3 or DOT 4 brake fluid from a sealed container. Do not intermix different brands of fluid. Do not use a*

14

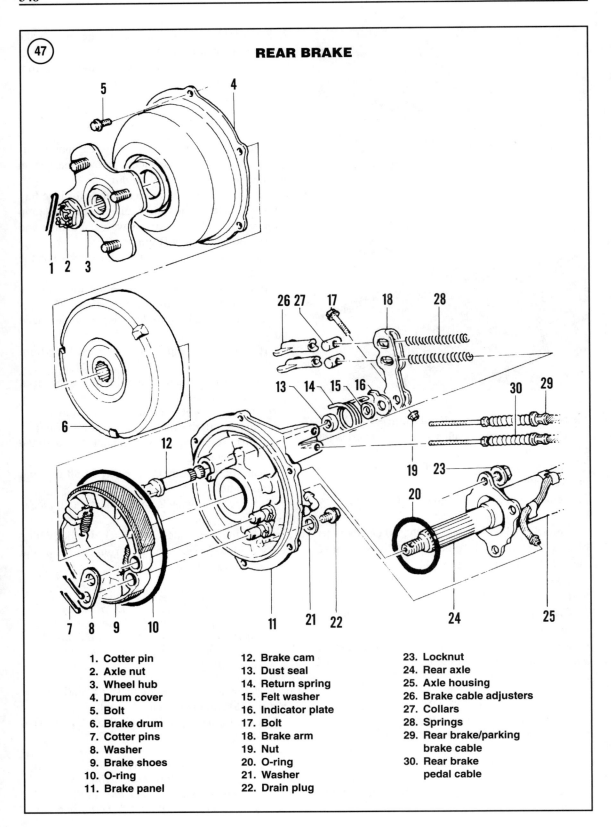

REAL BRAKE

1. Cotter pin
2. Axle nut
3. Wheel hub
4. Drum cover
5. Bolt
6. Brake drum
7. Cotter pins
8. Washer
9. Brake shoes
10. O-ring
11. Brake panel
12. Brake cam
13. Dust seal
14. Return spring
15. Felt washer
16. Indicator plate
17. Bolt
18. Brake arm
19. Nut
20. O-ring
21. Washer
22. Drain plug
23. Locknut
24. Rear axle
25. Axle housing
26. Brake cable adjusters
27. Collars
28. Springs
29. Rear brake/parking brake cable
30. Rear brake pedal cable

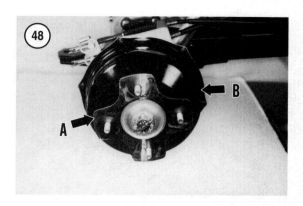

silicone base DOT 5 brake fluid because it can damage the brake components leading to brake system
failure.

NOTE
*When bleeding the front brake, fre-
quently check the fluid level in the
master cylinder. If the reservoir runs
dry, air enters the system. If this occurs, the entire procedure must be re-
peated.*

8A. When using a vacuum pump, perform the following:

   a. Operate the vacuum pump several times to
create a vacuum in the attached hose.

   b. Open the bleed valve 1/4 turn to allow extrac-
tion of air and fluid through the line. When
the flow of air and fluid starts to slow down,
close the bleed valve.

   c. Operate the brake lever several times and release it.

   d. Refill the master cylinder reservoir as necessary.

   e. Repeat for the opposite brake line.

   f. Repeat these steps until there is a solid feel
when operating the brake lever and there are
no bubbles being released from the system.

8B. If a vacuum pump is not being used, perform
the following:

   a. Operate the brake lever several times until resistance is felt, then hold it in the applied position. If the system was opened or drained
completely, there is no initial resistance at the
brake lever.

   b. Open the bleed valve 1/4 turn and allow the
lever to travel to the limit, then close the bleed
valve and release the brake lever.

   c. Operate the brake lever several times and release it.

   d. Refill the master cylinder reservoir as necessary.

   e. Repeat for the opposite brake line.

   f. Repeat these steps until there is a solid feel
when operating the brake lever and there are
no bubbles being released from the system.

NOTE
*If flushing the system, continue with
Step 8 until the fluid expelled from the
system is clean.*

9. Remove the vacuum pump or container and hose
from the system. Snap the bleed valve dust cap onto
the bleed valve.

10. If necessary, add fluid to correct the level in the
reservoir. It should be to the upper level line inside
the master cylinder reservoir.

11. Install the diaphragm and cover. Tighten the
screws securely.

12. Recheck the feel of the brake lever. It should be
firm and offer the same resistance each time it is operated. If the lever feels spongy, check all the hoses
for leaks, and bleed the system again.

REAR DRUM BRAKE

WARNING
*When working on the brake system,
never blow off brake components with
compressed air. Do not inhale any
airborne brake dust because it may
contain asbestos, which can cause
lung injury and cancer. As an added
precaution, wear an OSHA approved
filtering face mask and thoroughly
wash hands and forearms with warm
water and soap after completing any
brake work.*

Removal

  Refer to **Figure 47**.

1. Remove the right side rear wheel (Chapter Thirteen).

2. Remove the right rear hub (A, **Figure 48**) as described in Chapter Thirteen.

3. Remove the bolts and the brake drum cover (B,
Figure 48).

14

4. Remove the brake drum cover O-ring (**Figure 49**), if necessary.

5. Remove the brake drum (A, **Figure 50**). If the brake drum is tight, loosen the brake cable adjusters (B, **Figure 50**) to withdraw the brake shoes away from the brake drum. Remove the brake drum.

6. Clean and inspect the brake drum cover and brake drum as described in this section.

Inspection

When measuring the brake drum in this section, compare the actual measurement to the specification in **Table 1**. Replace the brake drum if out of specification or if it shows damage as described in this section.

1. Inspect the brake drum cover for cracks, warpage or other damage.

2. Inspect the brake drum cover dust seal (**Figure 51**) for excessive wear or damage. If necessary, replace the dust seal as follows:

    a. Support the brake drum cover and drive the dust seal out of the cover.

    b. Clean the dust seal mounting bore.

    c. Install a new dust seal by driving or pressing it into the brake drum cover. Apply pressure against the outer dust seal surface with a suitable bearing driver.

    d. Pack the dust seal lip with grease.

3. Check the brake drum surface (A, **Figure 52**) for oil or grease and clean with a rag soaked in lacquer thinner. Check the brake shoe linings for contamination.

> *WARNING*
> *Do not clean the brake drum with any type of solvent that may leave an oil residue.*

4. Clean the brake drum in a detergent solution, then dry thoroughly to prevent rust from forming on the drum surface.

5. Check the drum contact surface (A, **Figure 52**) for scoring or other damage.

6. Inspect the brake drum for cracks or damage.

7. Inspect the drum splines (B, **Figure 52**) for twisting or damage.

8. Measure the brake drum inside diameter (**Figure 53**) and compare to the service limit in **Table 2**.

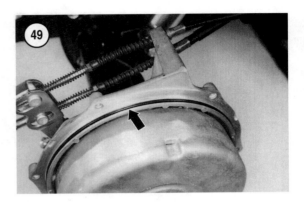

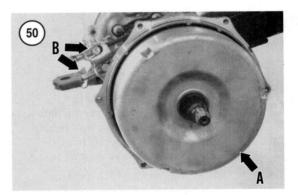

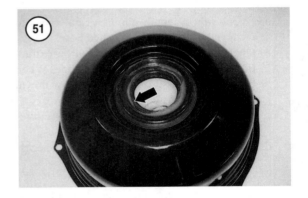

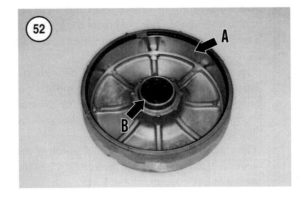

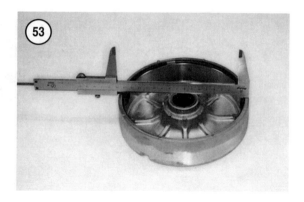

Installation

1. Apply grease to the brake drum cover dust seal lips (**Figure 51**).

2. Lubricate the brake drum splines (B, **Figure 52**) with grease.

3. Lightly lubricate the brake drum cover O-ring (**Figure 49**) with oil before installing it into the brake panel.

4. Slide the brake drum (A, **Figure 50**) over the rear axle and brake shoes.

5. Install the brake drum cover (B, **Figure 48**) and the mounting bolts. Tighten the brake drum cover mounting bolts securely.

6. Install the right rear hub (A, **Figure 48**) as described in Chapter Thirteen.

7. Install the right side rear wheel (Chapter Thirteen).

8. Adjust the rear brake as described in Chapter Three.

REAR BRAKE SHOE REPLACEMENT

Refer to **Figure 47**.

There is no recommended mileage interval for changing the rear brake shoes. Lining wear depends on riding habits and conditions.

1. Remove the rear brake drum as described in this chapter.

2. Check the rear brake shoe lining wear as described in Chapter Three. However, always measure the brake lining thickness with a vernier caliper (**Figure 54**) after removing the brake drum to check for any uneven wear (**Table 2**). Replace both brake shoes at the same time.

WARNING
To protect brake shoes suitable for re-installation from oil and grease, place a clean shop cloth on the linings during removal.

NOTE
If reusing the brake shoes, mark them so they can be installed in their original mounting positions.

3. Remove the cotter pins, washer (A, **Figure 55**) and brake shoes (B).

4. Disconnect the brake shoe springs and separate the brake shoes.

5. Inspect the springs and replace if there are any bent or unequally spaced coils. Always replace both springs at the same time.

6. Remove old grease from the camshaft and anchor pin surfaces.

7. Apply a light coat of high-temperature brake grease onto the camshaft and anchor pins. Avoid getting any grease on the brake panel where the brake linings can make contact.

8. Install the springs onto the brake shoes.

9. Install the brake shoes onto the brake cam and anchor pins.

14

10. Install the washer (**Figure 56**) with the chamfered side facing toward the brake shoes.

11. Install two new cotter pins (**Figure 56**) and bend their ends over to lock into place.

12. Install the rear brake drum as described in this chapter.

13. Adjust the rear brake (Chapter Three).

BRAKE PANEL

The brake panel (**Figure 47**) can be removed with the brake shoes attached. If also servicing the brake panel, remove the brake shoes before removing the brake panel.

Removal/Installation

1. Remove the rear brake drum as described in this chapter.

> *NOTE*
> *Leave the brake cables attached to the brake panel if brake panel service is not required.*

2. Unscrew the parking brake (A, **Figure 57**) and rear brake (B) adjusters from the end of the brake cables. Remove the collars and springs. Remove the brake cables from the brake panel.

3. Disconnect the vent hose from the brake panel fitting.

4. Remove the locknuts (A, **Figure 58**) and the brake panel (B). Discard the locknuts.

5. Inspect the brake panel assembly as described in this chapter.

6. Install the brake panel by reversing these removal steps, plus the following:
   a. Lubricate the dust seal lip (A, **Figure 59**) and O-ring (B) with grease.
   b. Secure the brake panel to the rear axle housing using new locknuts (A, **Figure 58**). Tighten the brake panel locknuts to 44 N•m (33 ft.-lb.).
   c. Adjust the rear brake as described in Chapter Three.

Brake Panel Inspection

1. Service and inspect the brake cam assembly as described in this section.

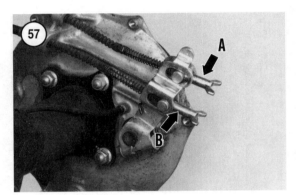

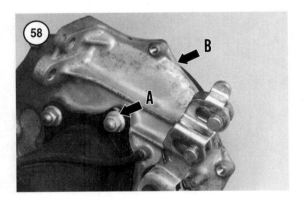

2. Inspect the dust seal (A, **Figure 59**) for excessive wear or damage. Replace the dust seal as described in *Rear Axle/Brake Panel Bearing Replacement* in this section.

3. Turn the inner race of the rear axle/brake panel bearings (B, **Figure 59**) with by hand. Both bearings must turn with no roughness or binding. Also check that the outer race of each bearing fits tightly in the brake panel. Replace both bearings as described in *Rear Axle/Brake Panel Bearing Replacement* in this section.

4. Inspect the O-ring (C, **Figure 59**) for excessive wear or damage. Replace the O-ring if necessary.

5. Check the brake panel for cracks or other damage.

Brake Cam Removal/Inspection/Installation

The brake cam can be removed with or without the brake panel mounted on the ATV. Refer to **Figure 47**.

1. If the brake panel is mounted on the ATV, disconnect the brake cables (**Figure 57**) from the brake arm.

2. Remove the brake shoes as described in this chapter.

3. Remove the brake arm nut and bolt (A, **Figure 60**).

4. If not already marked, make punch marks on the brake cam and brake arm (**Figure 61**) so they can be installed in the same position.

5. Remove the brake arm (B, **Figure 60**), return spring, indicator plate and brake cam.

6. Remove the felt washer and dust seal from the brake panel.

7. Inspect the brake cam for excessive wear or damage.

8. Replace the felt washer and dust seal if excessively worn or damaged.

9. Inspect the return spring for cracks and other damage.

10. Apply grease to the dust seal before installing.

11. Apply oil to the felt washer before installing it.

12. Install the dust seal and felt washer.

13. Lubricate the brake cam with grease and install it through the brake panel.

14. Install the return spring by hooking the end into the hole in the brake panel.

15. Install the indicator plate by aligning the wide tooth with the wide groove on the brake cam.

16. Install the brake arm (B, **Figure 60**) by aligning the punch mark with the punch mark on the brake cam (**Figure 61**). Hook the return spring onto the brake arm as shown in **Figure 60**.

17. Install the brake arm bolt and nut (A, **Figure 60**) and tighten to 20 N•m (177 in.-lb.). Move the brake arm by hand to make sure it moves smoothly. If there is any binding or roughness, remove and inspect the brake cam assembly.

18. Install the brake shoes as described in this chapter.

19. Reconnect the parking brake (A, **Figure 57**) and rear brake (B) cables at the brake arm.

20. Adjust the rear brake as described in Chapter Three.

Rear Axle/Brake Panel Bearing Replacement

The brake panel is equipped with a dust seal and two bearings (**Figure 62**). The bearings are identical (same part number).

14

1. Remove the brake shoes and brake panel as described in this chapter.

2. Remove the dust seal (A, **Figure 59**) with a wide blade screwdriver.

NOTE
If only replacing the dust seal, go to Step 8.

3. Remove the snap ring.

4. Support the brake panel in a press and press out both bearings. Discard both bearings.

5. Inspect the mounting bore for cracks, galling or other damage. Clean the mounting bore thoroughly.

6. Inspect the snap ring groove for cracks or other damage.

7. Install the new bearings as follows:
   a. Install both bearings with a bearing driver placed on the outer bearing race. Use a press or drive the bearings into the mounting bore. Check that each bearing turns smoothly after installing it.
   b. Install the outer bearing (2, **Figure 62**) so the sealed side faces toward the brake shoes. Install the outer bearing until it bottoms in the mounting bore.
   c. Install the inner bearing so the sealed side faces toward the snap ring and dust seal. Install the inner bearing until it bottoms against the outer bearing and the circlip groove is accessible.
   d. Install the snap ring into the mounting bore groove. Make sure the snap ring seats in the groove completely.

8. Install the new dust seal (5, **Figure 62**) as follows:
   a. Pack the new dust seal lip with grease.
   b. Align the dust seal with the mounting bore so the closed side (A, **Figure 59**) faces out.
   c. Tap the dust seal into place until it seats against the snap ring.

FRONT BRAKE HOSE REPLACEMENT

The upper brake hose can be replaced separately from the lower brake hoses. The lower brake hoses must be replaced as an assembly with the three-way joint (**Figure 63**).

1. Remove the front fender and inner front fenders as described in Chapter Fifteen.

2. Remove both front wheels (Chapter Eleven).

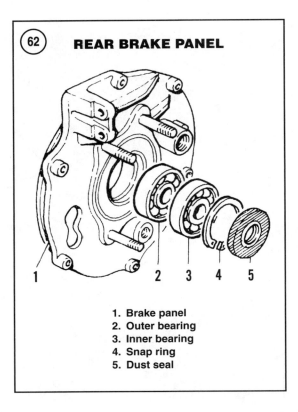

62 **REAR BRAKE PANEL**

1. Brake panel
2. Outer bearing
3. Inner bearing
4. Snap ring
5. Dust seal

3. Draw a diagram of the brake hose routing path from the master cylinder to the three-way joint and from the three-way joint to both brake calipers.

4. Drain the front brake fluid as described in this chapter. Because air has entered the brake lines, not all of the brake fluid drains out.

CAUTION
Because some residual brake fluid remains in the lines, be careful when disconnecting and removing the brake hoses in the following steps.

5. Remove any bolts and clamps securing the brake hoses to the frame or steering components.

6. Remove the banjo bolt and sealing washers (**Figure 64**) at the back of the wheel cylinder. Hold the open hose end in a container to catch any residual brake fluid. Repeat for the other side.

7. Remove the banjo bolt and sealing washers (A, **Figure 65**) securing the upper hose to the three-way fitting.

8. Remove the bolt (B, **Figure 65**) securing the three-way fitting to the frame.

9. Note the routing of the brake hose through the frame and the front suspension arms before re-

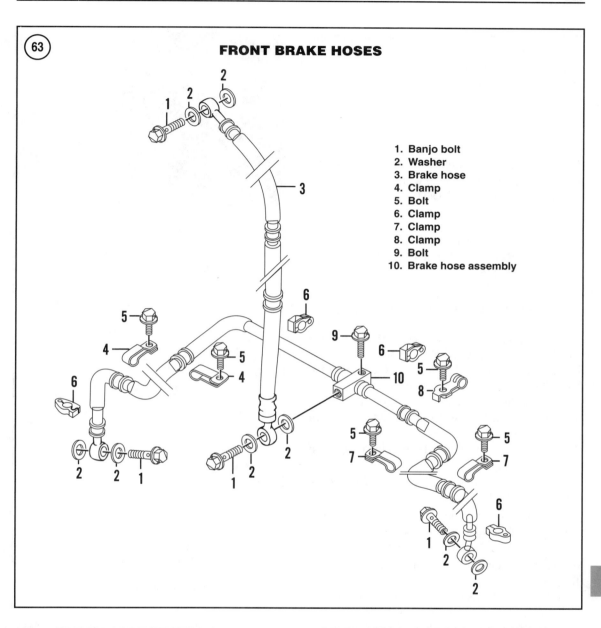

63

FRONT BRAKE HOSES

1. Banjo bolt
2. Washer
3. Brake hose
4. Clamp
5. Bolt
6. Clamp
7. Clamp
8. Clamp
9. Bolt
10. Brake hose assembly

14

64

65

moving the hose. Reinstall the hose through the same path to avoid damage to the hose during suspension arm movement when riding.

10. To remove the upper brake hose, remove the banjo bolt and sealing washers (**Figure 66**) from the master cylinder.

11. Install new brake hose(s) in the reverse order of removal. Install new sealing washers.

12. Tighten the banjo bolts to 34 N•m (25 ft.-lb.).

13. Refill the master cylinder with fresh brake fluid clearly marked DOT 3 or DOT 4. Bleed both front brakes as described in this chapter.

WARNING
Do not ride the ATV until the brakes
operate properly.

REAR BRAKE PEDAL AND CABLE

This section describes service to the rear brake pedal and cable (**Figure 67**). To service the rear brake lever/parking brake cable, refer to *Rear Brake Lever/Parking Brake Cable* in this chapter.

1. Loosen and remove the rear brake pedal cable adjusting nut (A, **Figure 68**), collar and spring from the brake arm.

2. Disconnect the brake cable from the bracket on the brake panel.

3. Disconnect the brake return spring (A, **Figure 69**) from the brake pedal assembly.

4. Remove the cotter pin, washer (B, **Figure 69**) and the brake pedal assembly (C).

5. Disconnect the brake cable from the brake pedal.

6. When replacing the rear brake pedal cable, perform the following:

   a. Remove the rear brake cable from the frame, noting any cable guides or brackets.

   b. Lubricate the new brake cable as described in Chapter Three.

   c. Route the new rear brake pedal cable along the frame and through any cable guides or brackets.

7. Remove all old grease from the brake pedal pivot shaft.

8. Check the brake pedal dust seals and replace if excessively worn or damaged.

9. Pack the dust seal lips with grease.

10. Apply grease to the brake pedal pivot shaft and brake cable end (brake pedal side).

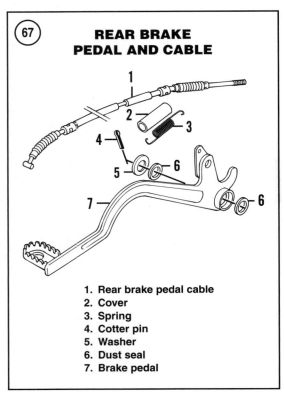

**REAR BRAKE
PEDAL AND CABLE**

1. Rear brake pedal cable
2. Cover
3. Spring
4. Cotter pin
5. Washer
6. Dust seal
7. Brake pedal

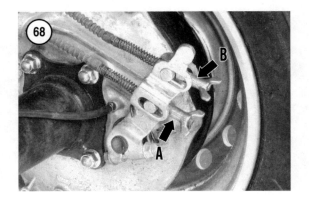

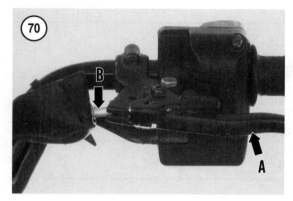

14. Reconnect the rear brake pedal to the brake panel. Install the spring, collar and adjusting nut (A, **Figure 68**).

15. Adjust the rear brake as described in Chapter Three.

> *WARNING*
> *Do not ride the ATV until the brakes operate properly.*

REAR BRAKE LEVER/PARKING BRAKE CABLE

The handlebar mounted rear brake lever (A, **Figure 70**) operates the rear brake and is also equipped with a lock, which allows it to be used as a parking brake.

1. Remove the front fender (Chapter Fifteen).

2. Loosen and remove the rear brake lever/parking brake cable adjusting nut (B, **Figure 68**), collar and spring at the brake arm.

3. Disconnect the brake cable from the bracket on the brake panel.

4. Disconnect the brake cable (B, **Figure 70**) from the brake lever.

5. Tie a long piece of heavy string to one end of the brake cable. When the brake cable is removed, the string follows the cable's original path, allowing correct installation of the new cable.

6. Remove any clamps or cable guides (**Figure 71**) securing the brake cable to the frame.

7. Remove the brake cable.

8. Lubricate the new brake cable as described in Chapter Three.

9. Cut the string and tie it to the end of the new brake cable. Pull the string and install the new brake cable along the original path.

10. Reconnect the brake cable to the brake lever (B, **Figure 70**).

11. Secure the brake cable with clamps or cable guides (**Figure 71**).

12. Reconnect the rear brake lever/parking brake cable to the brake panel. Install the spring, collar and adjusting nut (B, **Figure 68**).

13. Adjust the rear brake as described in Chapter Three.

> *WARNING*
> *Do not ride the ATV until the brakes operate correctly.*

11. Reconnect the brake cable to the brake pedal, then install the brake pedal (C, **Figure 69**) onto the pivot shaft.

12. Install the washer and secure with a new cotter pin (B, **Figure 69**). Bend the cotter pin ends over to lock it in place. Operate the brake pedal by hand. Make sure it moves without any binding or roughness.

13. Reconnect the brake return spring (A, **Figure 69**) to the brake pedal.

14

Table 1 FRONT BRAKE SERVICE SPECIFICATIONS

	New mm (in.)	Service limit mm (in.)
Brake drum inside diameter	160.0 (6.30)	161.0 (6.34)
Brake shoe lining thickness	4.0 (0.16)	2.0 (0.08)
Brake panel seal lip length	22 (0.9)	20 (0.8)
Brake panel warp limit	–	0.4 (0.02)
Master cylinder bore diameter	14.000-14.043 (0.5512-0.5529)	14.055 (0.5533)
Master cylinder piston outside diameter	13.957-13.984 (0.5495-0.5506)	13.945 (0.5490)
Wheel cylinder inside diameter	19.050-19.102 (0.7500-0.7520)	19.12 (0.753)
Wheel cylinder piston outside diameter	18.997-19.030 (0.7479-0.7492)	18.81 (0.741)
Waterproof seal lip length	22.0 (0.87)	20.0 (0.79)

Table 2 REAR BRAKE SERVICE SPECIFICATIONS

	New mm (in.)	Service limit mm (in.)
Brake drum inside diameter	180.0 (7.09)	181.0 (7.1)
Brake lining thickness	5.3 (0.209)	see text

Table 3 BRAKE TORQUE SPECIFICATIONS

	N•m	in.-lb.	ft.-lb.
Brake bleeder valve	6	53	–
Brake hose three-way joint nut	16	142	–
Brake hose banjo bolt	34	–	25
Front brake panel mounting bolts	29	–	22
Master cylinder brake lever			
Pivot bolt	1	8.8	–
Nut	6	53	–
Master cylinder mounting bolts	12	106	–
Master cylinder reservoir cap screw	2	18	–
Rear brake arm bolt and nut	20	–	15
Rear brake panel drain plug	12	106	–
Rear brake panel locknuts	44	–	33
Wheel cylinder			
Bolt	8	71	–
Nut	17	150	–
Brake line nuts	16	142	–

CHAPTER FIFTEEN

BODY

This chapter contains removal and installation procedures for the seat, body panels, tool box and handlebar cover.

Reinstall mounting hardware onto the removed part to prevent loss or misidentification. The part and the way it is attached to the frame may differ slightly from the one used in the service procedures in this chapter.

RETAINING CLIPS

The TRX500 uses a plastic retaining clip assembly to secure many body components to the frame or other parts. Refer to **Figure 1** for steps on how to remove and install the retaining clips.

RETAINING TABS

Some panels are equipped with directional tabs (**Figure 2**). The tab fits into a slot in the adjoining panel. Be sure to move the panel properly to disengage or engage the tab in the slot.

SEAT

Removal/Installation

1. Park the ATV on level ground and set the parking brake.
2. Pull the lever (A, **Figure 3**) to release the seat lock and remove the seat (B).
3. Slide the seat hook under the frame brace, then push the seat down until it locks in place.
4. Check that the seat is firmly locked in place.

WARNING
Do not ride the ATV unless the seat is secured in place.

RECOIL STARTER COVER

Removal/Installation

1. Pull out the upper end of the cover (**Figure 4**) to disengage the mounting studs from the frame grommets.

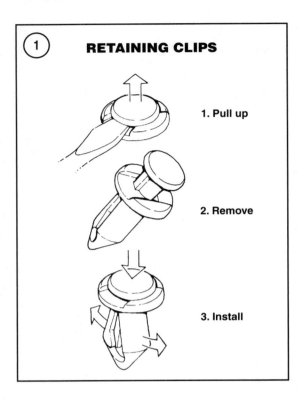

1. **RETAINING CLIPS**

1. Pull up

2. Remove

3. Install

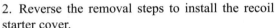

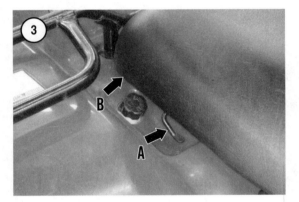

2. Reverse the removal steps to install the recoil starter cover.

RIGHT SIDE COVER

Removal/Installation

Refer to **Figure 5**.
1. Park the ATV on level ground and set the parking brake.
2. Remove the seat as described in this chapter.
3. Remove the retaining clips.
4. Push the side cover rearward to disengage the upper tabs, then remove the side cover.
5. Install the side cover by reversing the preceding removal steps. The upper corner of the side cover (A, **Figure 6**) must fit between the fuel tank cover and front fender.

LEFT SIDE COVER

Removal/Installation

Refer to **Figure 5**.
1. Park the ATV on level ground and set the parking brake.

2. Remove the seat as described in this chapter.

3. Remove the retaining screw (A, **Figure 7**).

4. Remove the retaining clips.

5. Push the side cover rearward to disengage the upper tabs, then remove the side cover.

6. Install the side cover by reversing the preceding removal steps. The upper corner of the side cover (B, **Figure 7**) must fit between the fuel tank cover and front fender.

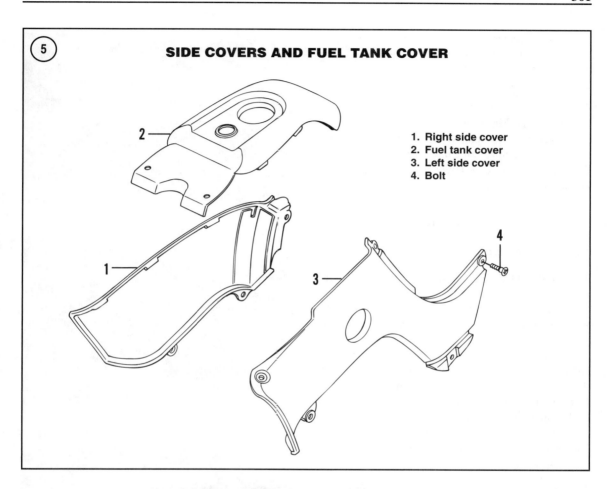

SIDE COVERS AND FUEL TANK COVER

1. Right side cover
2. Fuel tank cover
3. Left side cover
4. Bolt

15

FUEL TANK COVER

Removal/Installation

Refer to **Figure 5**.

1. Park the ATV on level ground and set the parking brake.

2. Remove the seat as described in this chapter.

WARNING
Fuel vapor is present when removing the fuel tank cap. Because gasoline is extremely flammable and explosive, perform this procedure away from all open flames (including pilot lights) and sparks. Do not smoke or allow someone who is smoking in the work area because an explosion and fire

may occur. Always work in a well-ventilated area. Wipe up any spills immediately.

3. Remove the fuel tank cap and breather hose.

4. Remove the four retaining clips securing the fuel tank cover (B, **Figure 6**).

5. Move the cover rearward to disengage the retaining tabs, then remove the cover.

6. Install the fuel tank cover by reversing the preceding removal steps.

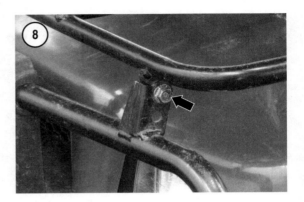

FRONT CARRIER

Removal/Installation

1. Park the ATV on level ground and set the parking brake.

2. Remove the bolts that secure the carrier to the front fender on each side (**Figure 8**). The collar may remain in the fender grommet.

3. Remove the rear retaining bolts on each side that secure the carrier to the frame brackets (**Figure 9**).

4. Remove the bolts securing the front carrier to the front bumper (**Figure 10**).

5. Remove the front carrier.

6. Install by reversing the preceding removal steps. Be sure the grommets and collars fit properly into the front fender.

FRONT BUMPER

Removal/Installation

1. Park the ATV on level ground and set the parking brake.

2. Remove the front carrier as described in this chapter.

3. Remove the headlight lower mounting bolts (**Figure 11**).

4. Remove the four bolts securing the front bumper to the frame.

CAUTION
Use care when removing or installing the front bumper to prevent damage to the fender or headlight assemblies.

5. Remove the front bumper.

6. Install by reversing the preceding removal steps. Tighten the bumper-to-frame bolts to 37 N•m (27 ft.-lb.).

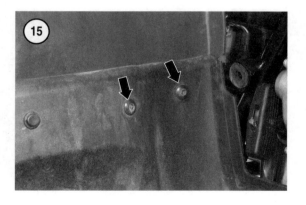

CENTER MUD GUARDS

Removal/Installation

1. On the right side, remove the recoil starter cover as described in this chapter.
2. On the right side, remove the two trim clips, then remove the lower cover (**Figure 12**) by moving it forward to disengage the retaining tabs.
3. Remove the footpeg (**Figure 13**).
4. On the right side, remove the socket bolts (**Figure 14**).
5. On the left side, remove the socket bolts (**Figure 15**).
6. Remove the retaining clips.
7. Remove the center mud guard.
8. Reverse the removal steps to install the center mud guard.

FRONT MUD GUARDS

Removal/Installation

1. On the right side, remove the recoil starter cover as described in this chapter.
2. On the right side, remove the two trim clips, then remove the lower cover (**Figure 12**) by moving it forward to disengage the retaining tabs.
3. Remove the retaining clips.
4. Remove the front mud guard.
5. Reverse the removal steps to install the front mud guard.

INNER FRONT FENDER

Removal/Installation

1. Remove the upper self-tapping screw bolts (A, **Figure 16**).
2. Remove the upper brace retaining bolt (B, **Figure 16**).
3. Remove the lower retaining bolt (A, **Figure 17**).
4. Remove the lower brace retaining bolt (B, **Figure 17**).
5. Remove the two retaining clips.
6. Detach the inner fender from the frame and remove it.
7. Reverse the removal steps to install the inner front fender.

15

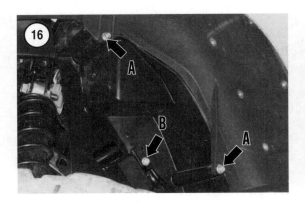

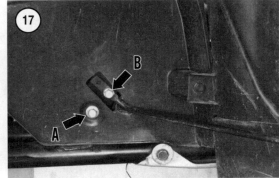

FRONT FENDER

Removal/Installation

1. Park the ATV on level ground and set the parking brake.

2. Remove the side covers and fuel tank cover assembly as described in this chapter.

3. Remove the front carrier and front bumper as described in this chapter.

4. Remove the gearshift knob retaining screws (A, **Figure 18**), then remove the knob (B).

5. Disconnect the headlight connector (**Figure 19**).

6. Remove the self-tapping screws under the fender on both sides (A, **Figure 16**).

7. Remove the retaining clips at the front of the mud guard on each side.

8. Remove the front fender while carefully spreading open the front fender around the fuel tank and steering shaft.

9. Reverse the removal steps to install the front fender.

HEADLIGHT GRILL

Removal/Installation

1. Remove the headlight housings as described in the *Headlight Lens* section in Chapter Nine.

2. Unbolt and remove the bumper cover (**Figure 20**).

3. Remove the mounting screws and retaining clips.

4. Remove the headlight grill.

5. Reverse the removal procedure to install the headlight grill.

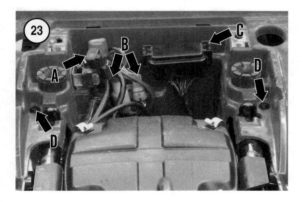

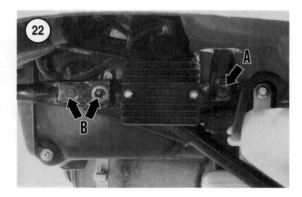

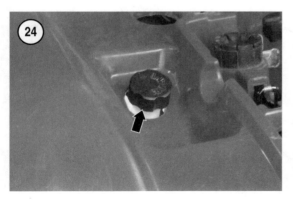

REAR CARRIER

Removal/Installation

1. Park the ATV on level ground and set the parking brake.

2. Remove the bolts that secure the carrier to the rear fender on each side (**Figure 21**). The collar may remain in the fender grommet.

3. Remove the bolt (A, **Figure 22**) securing the rear carrier on each side.

4. Remove the bolts (B, **Figure 22**) securing the rear carrier on each side.

5. Remove the rear carrier.

6. Install by reversing the preceding removal steps. Be sure the grommets and collars fit properly in the front fender.

REAR FENDER

Removal/Installation

1. Park the ATV on level ground and set the parking brake.

2. Remove the rear carrier as described in this chapter.

3. Remove the battery (Chapter Three).

4. Pull off the black rubber boot on the starter relay, then disconnect the starter motor lead from the starter relay terminal (A, **Figure 23**). With the starter relay in place, remove the mounting bracket screw and remove the relay and bracket.

5. Detach the electrical connectors (B, **Figure 23**) from the mounting bracket.

6. Detach the fuse box (C, **Figure 23**) from the mounting bracket.

7. Remove the coolant reserve tank cap (**Figure 24**).

8. Remove the clips (D, **Figure 23**).

9. Remove the air box retaining clips (**Figure 25**).

10. Remove the recoil starter cover as described in this chapter.

11. Remove the left side cover as described in this chapter.

12. Remove the fender retaining screw (**Figure 26**).

13. On the right side, remove the socket bolts (**Figure 27**) and the trim clips that secure the mud guard to the rear fender.

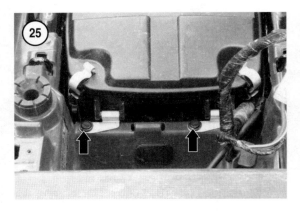

14. On the left side, remove the socket bolts (**Figure 28**) and the trim clips that secure the mud guard to the rear fender.

15. Disconnect the taillight connectors (**Figure 29**). The taillight connectors for the left side may be located under the fender (A, **Figure 30**) and near the ECM. Pull out the wire as needed until the connector is accessible.

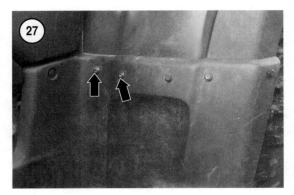

> *CAUTION*
> *If the muffler is hot, do not allow the rear fender to contact it.*

16. Remove the retaining clips.

17. Remove the rear fender while directing the electrical wires through the opening in the rear fender.

18. Reverse the removal procedure to install the rear fender. Be sure the air box mounting tabs (**Figure 25**) are not trapped under the fender during installation.

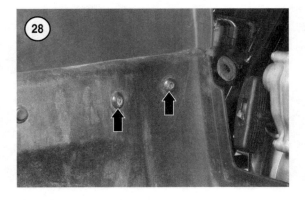

TOOL BOX

Removal/Installation

1. Remove the rear fender as described in this chapter.

2. Disconnect the ECM connectors (B, **Figure 30**), then move the ECM out of the way.

3. Remove the mounting screws on each side, then remove the tool box.

4. Reverse the removal procedure to install the rear fender.

HANDLEBAR COVER

Removal/Installation

1. Park the ATV on level ground and set the parking brake.

2. Remove the right inner fender as described in this chapter.

3. Disconnect the mode select switch connector (**Figure 31**).

4. Remove the left inner fender panel as described in this chapter.

5. Disconnect the white ignition switch connector (**Figure 32**).

6. Withdraw the fuel cap breather hose (A, **Figure 33**) from the handlebar cover.

7. Remove the handlebar cover cap (B, **Figure 33**).

8. Remove the handlebar cover mounting screws.

9. Release both ends of the handlebar cover from the handlebar, then remove the handlebar cover assembly.

10. Install by reversing the preceding removal steps. Check indicator light operation after starting the engine.

15

Table 1 BODY TORQUE SPECIFICATIONS

	N•m	in.-lb.	ft.-lb.
Front carrier 8 mm bolts	37	–	27
Front bumper 8 mm bolts	37	–	27
Rear carrier 8 mm bolts	37	–	27

INDEX

C

D

E

16

16

S

16

MAINTENANCE LOG

Date	Miles	Type of Service

WIRING
DIAGRAMS

2001-2004 TRX500FA

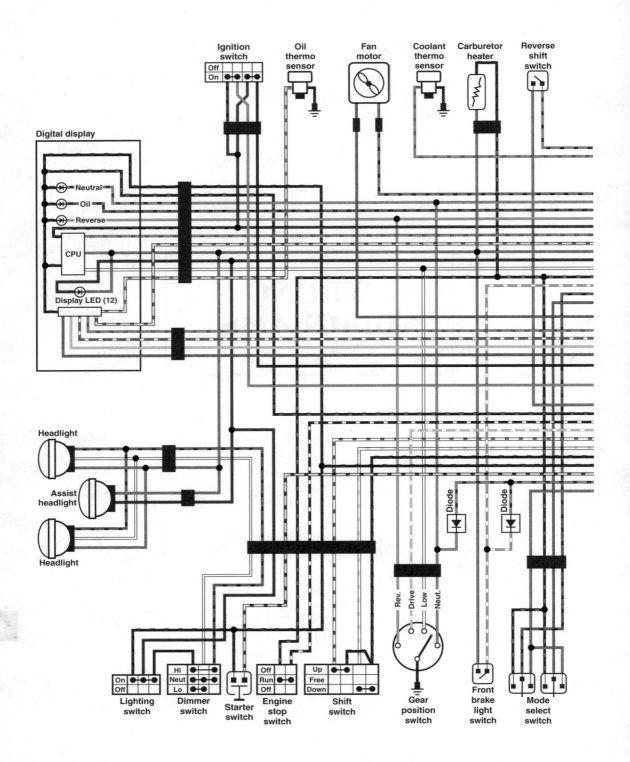

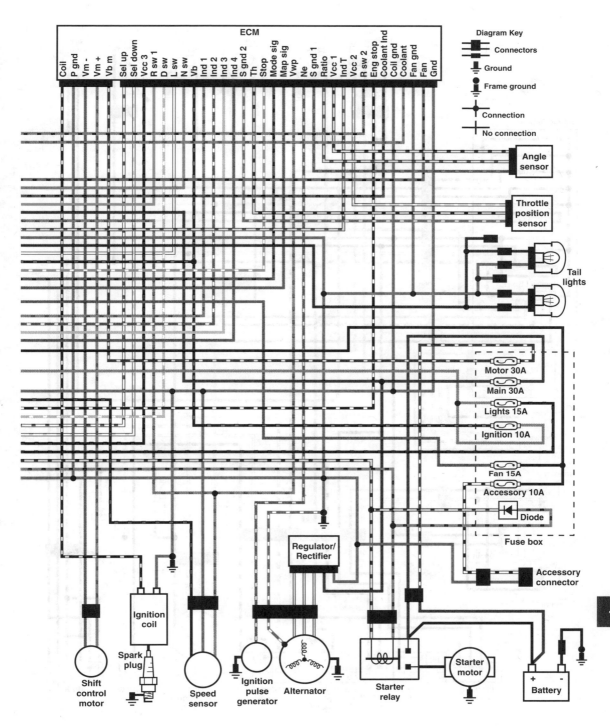

2004 TRX500FGA

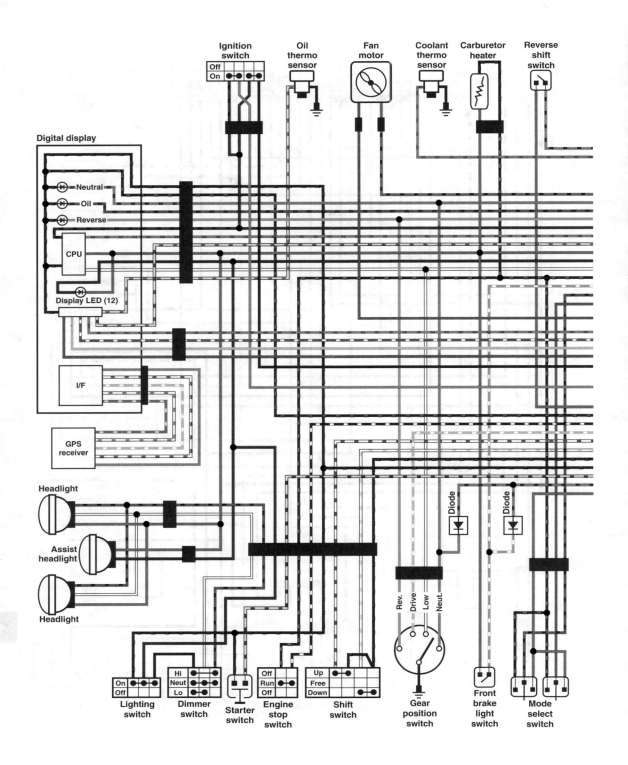

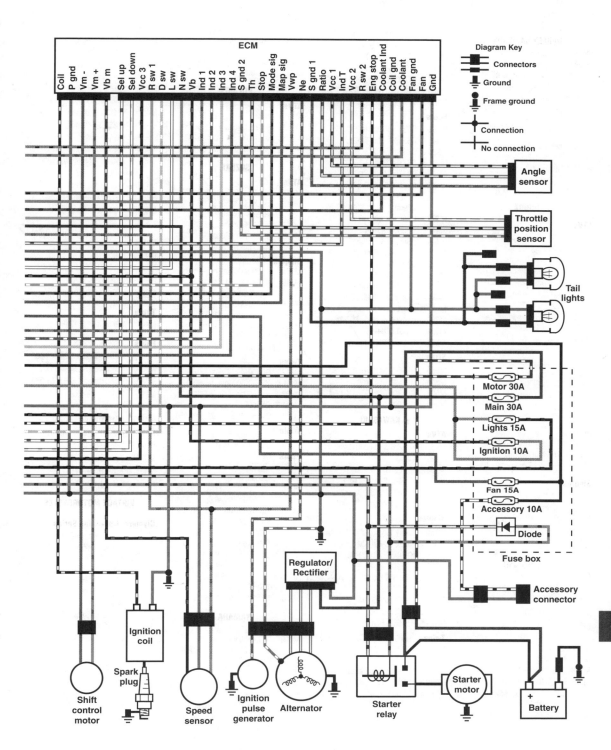

BMW

M308	500 & 600 CC Twins, 55-69
M309	F650, 1994-2000
M500-3	BMW K-Series, 85-97
M502-3	BMW R50/5-R100 GSPD, 70-96
M503-2	R850, R1100, R1150 and R1200C, 93-04

HARLEY-DAVIDSON

M419	Sportsters, 59-85
M428	Sportster Evolution, 86-90
M429-4	Sportster Evolution, 91-03
M418	Panheads, 48-65
M420	Shovelheads,66-84
M421-3	FLS/FXS Evolution,84-99
M423	FLS/FXS Twin Cam 88B, 2000-2003
M422	FLH/FLT/FXR Evolution, 84-94
M430-2	FLH/FLT Twin Cam 88, 1999-2003
M424-2	FXD Evolution, 91-98
M425-2	FXD Twin Cam, 99-03

HONDA

ATVs

M316	Odyssey FL250, 77-84
M311	ATC, TRX & Fourtrax 70-125, 70-87
M433	Fourtrax 90 ATV, 93-00
M326	ATC185 & 200, 80-86
M347	ATC200X & Fourtrax 200SX, 86-88
M455	ATC250 & Fourtrax 200/ 250, 84-87
M342	ATC250R, 81-84
M348	TRX250R/Fourtrax 250R & ATC250R, 85-89
M456-3	TRX250X 87-92; TRX300EX 93-04
M446	TRX250 Recon 97-02
M346-3	TRX300/Fourtrax 300 & TRX300FW/Fourtrax 4x4,88-00
M200	TRX350 Rancher, 00-03
M459-3	TRX400 Foreman 95-03
M454-2	TRX400EX 99-03
M205	TRX450 Foreman, 98-04

Singles

M310-13	50-110cc OHC Singles, 65-99
M319	XR50R-XR70R, 97-03
M315	100-350cc OHC, 69-82
M317	Elsinore, 125-250cc, 73-80
M442	CR60-125R Pro-Link, 81-88
M431-2	CR80R, 89-95, CR125R, 89-91
M435	CR80, 96-02
M457-2	CR125R & CR250R, 92-97
M464	CR125R, 1998-2002
M443	CR250R-500R Pro-Link, 81-87
M432-3	CR250R, 88-91 & CR500R, 88-01
M437	CR250R, 97-01
M312-13	XL/XR75-100, 75-03
M318-4	XL/XR/TLR 125-200, 79-03
M328-4	XL/XR250, 78-00; XL/XR350R 83-85; XR200R, 84-85; XR250L, 91-96
M320-2	XR400R, 96-04
M339-7	XL/XR 500-650, 79-03

Twins

M321	125-200cc, 65-78
M322	250-350cc, 64-74
M323	250-360cc Twins, 74-77
M324-5	Twinstar, Rebel 250 & Nighthawk 250, 78-03
M334	400-450cc, 78-87
M333	450 & 500cc, 65-76
M335	CX & GL500/650 Twins, 78-83
M344	VT500, 83-88
M313	VT700 & 750, 83-87
M314	VT750 Shadow, 98-03
M440	VT1100C Shadow , 85-96
M460-3	VT1100C Series, 95-04

Fours

M332	CB350-550cc, SOHC, 71-78
M345	CB550 & 650, 83-85
M336	CB650,79-82
M341	CB750 SOHC, 69-78
M337	CB750 DOHC, 79-82
M436	CB750 Nighthawk, 91-93 & 95-99
M325	CB900, 1000 & 1100, 80-83
M439	Hurricane 600, 87-90
M441-2	CBR600, 91-98
M445	CBR600F4, 99-03
M434	CBR900RR Fireblade, 93-98
M329	500cc V-Fours, 84-86
M438	Honda VFR800, 98-00
M349	700-1000 Interceptor, 83-85
M458-2	VFR700F-750F, 86-97
M327	700-1100cc V-Fours, 82-88
M340	GL1000 & 1100, 75-83
M504	GL1200, 84-87
M508	ST1100/PAN European, 90-02

Sixes

M505	GL1500 Gold Wing, 88-92
M506-2	GL1500 Gold Wing, 93-00
M507	GL1800 Gold Wing, 01-04
M462-2	GL1500C Valkyrie, 97-03

KAWASAKI

ATVs

M465-2	KLF220 & KLF250 Bayou, 88-03
M466-3	KLF300 Bayou, 86-04
M467	KLF400 Bayou, 93-99
M470	KEF300 Lakota, 95-99
M385	KSF250 Mojave, 87-00

Singles

M350-9	Rotary Valve 80-350cc, 66-01
M444-2	KX60, 83-02; KX80 83-90
M448	KX80/85/100, 89-03
M351	KDX200, 83-88
M447-2	KX125 & KX250, 82-91 KX500, 83-02
M472-2	KX125, 92-00
M473-2	KX250, 92-00
M474	KLR650, 87-03

Twins

M355	KZ400, KZ/Z440, EN450 & EN500, 74-95
M360-3	EX500, GPZ500S, Ninja R, 87-02
M356-3	Vulcan 700 & 750, 85-04
M354-2	Vulcan 800 & Vulcan 800 Classic, 95-04
M357-2	Vulcan 1500, 87-99
M471-2	Vulcan Classic 1500, 96-04

Fours

M449	KZ500/550 & ZX550, 79-85
M450	KZ, Z & ZX750, 80-85
M358	KZ650, 77-83
M359-3	900-1000cc Fours, 73-81
M451-3	1000 &1100cc Fours, 81-02
M452-3	ZX500 & 600 Ninja, 85-97
M453-3	Ninja ZX900-1100 84-01
M468	ZX6 Ninja, 90-97
M469	ZX7 Ninja, 91-98
M453-3	900-1100 Ninja, 84-01
M409	Concours, 86-04

POLARIS

ATVs

M496	Polaris ATV, 85-95
M362	Polaris Magnum ATV, 96-98
M363	Scrambler 500, 4X4 97-00
M365-2	Sportsman/Xplorer, 96-03

SUZUKI

ATVs

M381	ALT/LT 125 & 185, 83-87
M475	LT230 & LT250, 85-90
M380-2	LT250R Quad Racer, 85-92
M343	LTF500F Quadrunner, 98-00
M483-2	Suzuki King Quad/ Quad Runner 250, 87-98

Singles

M371	RM50-400 Twin Shock, 75-81
M369	125-400cc 64-81
M379	RM125-500 Single Shock, 81-88
M476	DR250-350, 90-94
M384-2	LS650 Savage, 86-03
M386	RM80-250, 89-95
M400	RM125, 96-00
M401	RM250, 96-02

Twins

M372	GS400-450 Twins, 77-87
M481-4	VS700-800 Intruder, 85-04
M482-2	VS1400 Intruder, 87-01
M484-3	GS500E Twins, 89-02
M361	SV650, 1999-2002

Triple

M368	380-750cc, 72-77

Fours

M373	GS550, 77-86
M364	GS650, 81-83
M370	GS750 Fours, 77-82
M376	GS850-1100 Shaft Drive, 79-84
M378	GS1100 Chain Drive, 80-81
M383-3	Katana 600, 88-96 GSX-R750-1100, 86-87
M331	GSX-R600, 97-00
M478-2	GSX-R750, 88-92 GSX750F Katana, 89-96
M485	GSX-R750, 96-99
M338	GSF600 Bandit, 95-00
M353	GSF1200 Bandit, 96-03

YAMAHA

ATVs

M499	YFM80 Badger, 85-01
M394	YTM/YFM200 & 225, 83-86
M488-4	Blaster, 88-02
M489-2	Timberwolf, 89-00
M487-5	Warrior, 87-04
M486-5	Banshee, 87-04
M490-2	YFM350 Moto-4 & Big Bear, 87-98
M493	YFM400FW Kodiak, 93-98
M280	Raptor 660R, 01-03

Singles

M492-2	PW50 & PW80, BW80 Big Wheel 80, 81-02
M410	80-175 Piston Port, 68-76
M415	250-400cc Piston Port, 68-76
M412	DT & MX 100-400, 77-83
M414	IT125-490, 76-86
M393	YZ50-80 Monoshock, 78-90
M413	YZ100-490 Monoshock, 76-84
M390	YZ125-250, 85-87 YZ490, 85-90
M391	YZ125-250, 88-93 WR250Z, 91-93
M497-2	YZ125, 94-01
M498	YZ250, 94-98 and WR250Z, 94-97
M406	YZ250F & WR250F, 01-03
M491-2	YZ400F, YZ426F, WR400F WR426F, 98-02
M417	XT125-250, 80-84
M480-3	XT/TT 350, 85-00
M405	XT500 & TT500, 76-81
M416	XT/TT 600, 83-89

Twins

M403	650cc, 70-82
M395-10	XV535-1100 Virago, 81-03
M495-3	V-Star 650, 98-04
M281	V-Star 1100, 99-04

Triple

M404	XS750 & 850, 77-81

Fours

M387	XJ550, XJ600 & FJ600, 81-92
M494	XJ600 Seca II, 92-98
M388	YX600 Radian & FZ600, 86-90
M396	FZR600, 89-93
M392	FZ700-750 & Fazer, 85-87
M411	XS1100 Fours, 78-81
M397	FJ1100 & 1200, 84-93
M375	V-Max, 85-03
M374	Royal Star, 96-03
M461	YZF-R6, 99-04
M398	YZF-R1, 98-03

VINTAGE MOTORCYCLES

Clymer® Collection Series

M330	Vintage British Street Bikes, BSA, 500–650cc Unit Twins; Norton, 750 & 850cc Commandos; Triumph, 500-750cc Twins
M300	Vintage Dirt Bikes, V. 1 Bultaco, 125-370cc Singles; Montesa, 123-360cc Singles; Ossa, 125-250cc Singles
M301	Vintage Dirt Bikes, V. 2 CZ, 125-400cc Singles; Husqvarna, 125-450cc Singles; Maico, 250-501cc Singles; Hodaka, 90-125cc Singles
M305	Vintage Japanese Street Bikes Honda, 250 & 305cc Twins; Kawasaki, 250-750cc Triples; Kawasaki, 900 & 1000cc Fours